COMPARATIVE EDUCATION

A Study of Educational Factors and Traditions

by

NICHOLAS HANS
Ph.D., D.Litt.

LONDON
ROUTLEDGE & KEGAN PAUL LIMITED

First published in 1949
Second edition 1950
Reprinted twice
Third edition (revised) 1958
Reprinted 1961, 1964, 1967, 1971

Published as a Routledge paperback 1967
by Routledge and Kegan Paul Limited
Broadway House, 68–74 Carter Lane, EC4V 5EL

Printed in Great Britain by
Hazell Watson & Viney Ltd
Aylesbury, Bucks

ISBN 0 7100 3266 8 (c)
ISBN 0 7100 4668 5 (p)

CONTENTS

v

PART III SECULAR FACTORS

PREFACE

The following book is based on the courses of lectures delivered in 1945–7 at King's College and the Institute of Education, University of London. It is a composite of two separate courses: for the Teachers' Diploma students and for the M.A. students. The first course included an abridged exposition of factors and traditions and the description of educational systems of America, France and Russia. The course for the M.A. students forms the first twelve chapters of the book. The chapter on England was added for foreign readers. Some of the material was written by the author before the war for various volumes of the *Year Book of Education*, published by Evans Brothers in association with the Institute of Education. The author is indebted to the publishers for the permission of incorporating some parts *in extenso* in Chapters VI, VII and VIII. The book is intended as a text-book for the present and future students of University Education Departments. Whilst it is sufficient for the examination requirements of the University of London for the Teachers' Diploma students, it forms but a part of a two years' course, which is delivered at the Institute of Education by Professor J. Lauwerys in conjunction with the author for the M.A. students. The latter are expected to extend the course by supplementary reading and special study of some particular country.

Although writing primarily for intending and actual teachers, the author had the general reading public in mind and treated the material accordingly. Educational reforms since the first World War are so intimately connected with politics, with problems of race, nationality, language and religious and social ideals, that they ceased to be of narrow professional significance and have become a matter of general interest as the main problem of democratic government. This book is an attempt to combine the two purposes: an academic text-book and a general introduction into Comparative Education as a study of contemporary solutions in various democratic countries. The present division of Europe into Western and Eastern halves may be better understood and surmounted if the origins and conditions of the actual divergence are studied on a historical background of educational

ix

traditions. The author, therefore, expresses the hope that besides his students, the book will find readers among the general public.

The author is greatly indebted to his colleague, P. P. Brown, of King's College, for reading through the manuscript and supplying many valuable suggestions.

The author must also gratefully remember the late Professor Karl Mannheim, who suggested the inclusion of this book in the International Library, of which he was the Editor.

N. HANS

King's College, London
  November 1947

NOTE. The present revised edition has substituted all out-dated figures in facts by the newest available information, especially in England, France and U.S.S.R. A Portuguese edition is being published in Brazil with two additional chapters on "Latin America" by the author and on "Comparative Education in Brazil" by Dr. A. Texeira.

N. H.

September 1958

CHAPTER I

DEFINITION AND SCOPE OF COMPARATIVE EDUCATION

It is only quite recently that Comparative Education has been admitted as a subject of academic studies. It is generally recognised now that intending teachers and educational administrators should have some knowledge of foreign educational systems and their comparative merits. In some Universities Comparative Education is even included in the requirements for Teacher's Diploma qualifications. However, there is no general agreement as to what Comparative Education comprises or exactly what methods should be used in its study. The first comprehensive scheme of comparative study of educational systems was devised by Marc-Antoine Jullien de Paris in 1817. In his *L'Esquisse et vues préliminaires d'un ouvrage sur l'Éducation Comparée*, Jullien quite clearly formulated the purposes and methods of comparative study of education. He envisaged an "analytical" study of education in all countries with a view to perfecting national systems with modifications and changes "which the circumstances and local conditions would demand." He said:

> Education, as other sciences, is based on facts and observations, which should be ranged in analytical tables, easily compared, in order to deduce principles and definite rules. Education should become a positive science instead of being ruled by narrow and limited opinions, by whims and arbitrary decisions of administrators, to be turned away from the direct line which it should follow, either by the prejudice of a blind routine or by the spirit of some system and innovation.

However, his detailed scheme of comparative enquiry remained unknown and was rediscovered only in the twentieth century.[1] Historically the beginnings of Comparative Education were not even comparative and were confined to description and information on education in foreign countries.

Reports on foreign schools and school methods abounded in the nineteenth century. Perhaps the first study of that kind was the two volumes of Professor John Griscom, of New York City, who after his return from Europe issued the results of his observa-

[1] See P. Rossello, *Marc-Antoine Jullien de Paris*, Geneva, 1943.

tions on educational institutions in Great Britain, France, Switzerland, Italy and Holland under the title of *A Year in Europe*, published in 1818–19. It had great influence on the development of American education. In 1831 Victor Cousin, Professor of Philosophy, by direction of the French Minister of Public Instruction visited Prussia and published his famous *Report on the State of Public Instruction in Prussia*. It was translated into English and influenced education not only in France, but in both England and America. But it was a straightforward description of the Prussian system and any conclusions on the comparative value of the system had to be made by the reader himself by comparing it with that of his own country. The pioneer of the American Common School revival, Horace Mann, after a six months' visit to Europe embodied his observations in his Seventh Report, 1843, and in it compared education in England, Scotland, Ireland, France, Germany and Holland, and incidentally put England at the foot of the list. This report, perhaps, was the first attempt at assessing educational values, but it was almost entirely devoted to comparison of school organisation and methods of instruction.

In this country the pioneer of Comparative Education was Matthew Arnold who, after visiting France and Germany in 1859 and 1865, made some caustic remarks on the differences in national character. More important were the *Special Reports on Educational Subjects* (1898–1911), published by the Board of Education and edited by Sir Michael Sadler. They followed the practice of giving detailed information on foreign systems established earlier by Henry Barnard in his thirty-one volumes of *The American Journal of Education*, 1856–81. On the same lines were the many valuable publications of the United States Bureau of Education from 1868 onwards. The twentieth century saw the culmination of these studies in P. Monroe's *Cyclopedia of Education* (five volumes, 1911–13), Foster Watson's *Encyclopedia and Dictionary of Education* (four volumes, 1921–2), Kandel's *Educational Yearbook of the International Institute*, 1925–44, the *Year Book of Education*, started by Lord Eustace Percy in 1932, and many other publications in English and foreign languages. However valuable was the information on foreign systems contained in these publications, the main purpose was the utilitarian use applied for the reform of education at home. The principles underlying the development of national systems were not yet included in the scope of these studies and only accidentally mentioned in some works.

The first approach to a comprehensive point of view was made by Sir Michael Sadler in his *How Far Can We Learn Anything of Practical Value from the Study of Foreign Systems of Education?* published in 1900. Sir Michael said:

> In studying foreign systems of education we should not forget that the things outside the schools matter even more than the things inside the schools, and govern and interpret the things inside. We cannot wander at pleasure among the educational systems of the world, like a child strolling through a garden, and pick off a flower from one bush and some leaves from another, and then expect that if we stick what we have gathered into the soil at home, we shall have a living plant. A national system of education is a living thing, the outcome of forgotten struggles and difficulties and of battles long ago. It has in it some of the secret workings of national life. It reflects, while seeking to remedy, the failings of national character. By instinct it often lays special emphasis on those parts of training which the national character particularly needs. Not less by instinct, it often shrinks from laying stress on points concerning which bitter dissensions have arisen in former periods of national history. But is it not likely that if we have endeavoured, in a sympathetic spirit, to understand the real working of a foreign system of education, we shall in turn find ourselves better able to enter into the spirit and tradition of our own national education, more sensitive to its unwritten ideals, quicker to catch the signs which mark its growing or fading influence, readier to mark the dangers which threaten it and the subtle workings of hurtful change? The practical value of studying in a right spirit and with scholarly accuracy the working of foreign systems of education is that it will result in our being better fitted to study and understand our own.

Most English-speaking writers on education are reluctant to take the last step and usually avoid any mentioning of "principles." The author remembers how Sir Michael half jokingly answered his plea for a definite philosophy of education. "The English recognise no philosophy of education," said Sir Michael, "the only philosophy they would accept is to have none." But Sir Michael himself had a philosophy of education and his studies served as an indispensable basis for the later development of Comparative Education.

The first attempt at dealing with Comparative Education from a philosophical point of view was made by a Russian philosopher and educationist, Sergius Hessen, who in 1928 published his "Kritische Vergleichung des Schulwesens der anderen Kulturstaaten" as a part of the German *Handbuch der Pädagogik*. Selecting four main problems of educational policy: compulsory education, the school and the State, the school and the Church and the school and economic life, Hessen analysed the underlying principles and then followed this up by giving a critical account of modern legislation in many countries on these questions. In his *Principles of Educational Policy*, published independently in 1929, the author used a similar method. In addition to the four problems dealt with by Hessen, the relations of the State and the Family, National Minorities, Universities, Finance and Political Education were also included. In the second edition, 1933, Vocational and Adult Education were added. In the preface it was stated that "the time has come when educational policy ought to be in conformity with some definite conceptions and should cease to be a temporary compromise between opposite tendencies." To find these principles the educational problems mentioned were analysed from a democratic point of view and the modern legislation of many countries supplied typical solutions. Neither Hessen nor the author, however, attempted in these works to connect in detail the national systems of education with their historical backgrounds. This was done by I. L. Kandel in 1933 in his *Studies in Comparative Education*, which became a recognised text-book in many Universities both in England and America. The aim and plan of his book were stated as follows:

The comparison of the educational systems of several countries lends itself to a variety of methods of treatment, depending somewhat on its purpose. One method of approach might be statistical . . . from this point of view there would be compared the total national expenditures for education, the cost, size and character o school buildings, *per capita* costs for different items of expenditure in educational systems, the enrolment, average attendance and retention of pupils through the different levels of educational ladder. By another method it might be possible to institute a comparison between education and national welfare and progress as expressed in statistics of illiteracy, the volume of trade and commerce, *per capita* wealth, or incidence of crime and poverty. These methods are attractive and may some day be useful; at the present stage it is impossible to institute comparisons of such a character until the raw material, the statistics, become more uniform and comparable. Still another method would be to undertake comparative studies of the quality of education in different countries; this, too, may be possible in time, but not before the instruments of measurement have been made more perfect and reliable than they are at present or when aims of education in different countries are more nearly alike, or finally, when tests have been developed which can measure more accurately the results of education rather than instruction in fundamentals of subject-matter. In the present volume [says Kandel] none of these methods has been followed. The task which has been undertaken is to discuss the meaning of general education, elementary and secondary, in the light of the forces—political, social and cultural—which determine the character of national systems of education. The problems and purposes of education have in general become somewhat similar in most countries; the solutions are influenced by differences of tradition and culture of each. The present volume seeks accordingly to serve as a contribution to the philosophy of education in the light both of theory and practice in six of the leading educational laboratories of the world—England, France, Germany, Italy, Russia and the United States.

Accordingly Kandel paid special attention to nationalism and national character as a historical background to actual conditions. He did not, however, analyse these factors in detail. But he quite clearly formulated the necessity of a historical approach and the study of determining factors.

The chief value of a comparative approach to educational problems [says he in his textbook] lies in an analysis of the causes which have produced them, in a comparison of the differences between the various systems and the reasons underlying them, and finally, in a study of the solutions attempted. In other words, the comparative approach demands first an appreciation of the intangible, impalpable spiritual and cultural forces which underlie an educational system; the factors and forces outside the school matter even more than what goes inside it.

In his monograph "Comparative Education," published in 1936 in the American *Review of Educational Research*, Kandel expressed the same idea still more succinctly: "The purpose of Comparative Education, as of comparative law, comparative literature or comparative anatomy, is to discover the differences in the forces and causes that produce differences in educational systems." And we should add here "to discover the underlying principles which govern the development of all national systems of education," which is certainly implied in Kandel's definition.

The present writer's contributions to the *Year Book of Education*: "Comparative Study of European Education" (1936), and "Comparative Study of Education in Latin America and Countries of Islam" (1937) emphasised still more the historical approach and dealt with education in each country as the result of cultural and national background. The next study, "Educational Traditions in the English-Speaking Countries" (1938), by its very title laid stress on a historical approach.

Among the German-speaking pioneers of Comparative Education we should mention Professor Friedrich Schneider, Director of the Institute of Comparative Education, Salzburg. Professor Schneider started his contributions to Comparative Education in Cologne in 1930 by editing the *International Review of Education* in four languages. Interrupted by the Nazi régime, he resumed the publication of the journal in Salzburg in 1947. In his latest book, *Triebkräfte der Pädagogik der Völker*, published in 1947 he systematically covers the whole ground of Comparative Education, adopting the historical approach to the educational problems of many countries. He has divided his material into the following factors which have influenced educational theory and practice: National character; Geographic space; Culture; Sciences; Philosophy; Economic life and Politics; Religion; History; Foreign influences; and the immanent development of Pedagogics. Based on a wealth of historical and factual material, Professor Schneider's work should be considered as one of the most important contributions to the study of Comparative Education.

It appears that Comparative Education has followed the way of earlier branches of comparative studies. The development of comparative law, comparative grammar, comparative religion and even of the scientific branches like comparative anatomy followed the same pattern. They all started by comparing the existing institutions, living languages or adult organisms. Gradually, however, these comparisons led the pioneers of these studies to look for common origins and the differentiation through historical development. It unavoidably resulted in an attempt to formulate some general principles underlying all variations. Montesquieu [1] was perhaps the first philosopher who established this pattern of comparative study. In his famous *L'Esprit des lois* (1747) he used both the historical approach and the formulation of principles in his classification of laws. The nineteenth century saw the rise of other comparative studies. Comparative Grammar was started in the eighteenth century by comparison of Sanskrit and Latin grammar. In the beginning of the nineteenth century the Dane Rask and the Germans Bopp and Grimm followed up the evolution of languages and formulated the first laws of their growth. Thus modern Comparative Philology was born. Comparative Religion had the same history. The modern classification of religions into tribal, national and universal employs both the evolutionary and philosophical methods. It is interesting to note that Comparative Anatomy, a scientific branch, has followed the

---

[1] Both Plato and Aristotle used comparative method, but their comparisons were limited to small Greek town-communities.

same way. The *Encyclopedia Britannica* says: "The study of comparative anatomy led to the development of the conceptions underlying the terms homology and analogy, and an attempt further to discriminate between these two caused comparative anatomists to begin the study of embryology in order to determine the homologies of structures from their mode of origin."

Comparative Education of the twentieth century has adopted the same method, and, as Professor J. Dover Wilson said in his preface to the present writer's book,

> there is no reason why Comparative Education should not prove as interesting and fruitful a study as Comparative Politics. The time will come when men realise that the structure of a nation's educational system is as characteristic and almost as important as the form of its constitution. And when it does, we shall have our educational Montesquieus analysing educational institutions and our Bryces classifying them.

We have not reached this stage yet, but a great deal of material has been collected and a start has been made in analysis and classification.

The task is tremendous and can be successfully completed only by team work of educationists of all countries and international educational agencies. The first step is to study each national system separately in its historical setting and its close connection with the development of national character and culture. For some European nations this work has been done by authors who combined the gifts of a historian and a philosopher. But in many cases, especially in non-European countries, the studies were disconnected and still await a comprehensive treatment. The history of education in England, for instance, in spite of many excellent volumes dealing with some periods or some aspects of education, has still many gaps to be filled and has not yet produced a single comprehensive work. The second step would be to collect data on existing systems of education in various countries. This task includes statistics on all aspects of educational administration, organisation and also tests of intelligence and achievements. The existing statistical information is still in a stage of raw material not yet ready for comparative treatment. The author attempted statistical comparisons in the *Year Book of Education* and has come to the conclusion that at present they have little value. Each country has its own terminology, based on national history, its own classification and its own method of collecting and compiling statistical tables. In some cases these statistics are only conjectures and serve the purposes of propaganda. Statistical comparisons are valid only when they deal with commensurable units and internationally equivalent terms. For instance the comparison of costs per pupil in different countries without going into lengthy explanations of economic structure, standards of living, rates of exchange, national traditions, as well as statistical methods, is not only valueless, but often misleading. Statistical comparisons of numbers of institutions and students, of hours devoted to each subject and of equipment are meaningless without their respective backgrounds. This is especially true of the institutions imparting secondary and higher education. Only the study of their historical development and their functional rôle in the social life of a particular nation can give a true insight into their values and thus lead to a valid comparison. To enable such statistical tables to be used by comparative education an international authority, like UNESCO, should establish a recognised dictionary of all educational terms in different languages and accepted equivalents of educational values.[1] The attempts made in this direction both by the *Year Book of Education* and the *Annuaire* of the Bureau International d'Éducation, Geneva, must be considered unsatisfactory, and the task is now inherited by UNESCO, which may succeed where previous efforts have failed.

The comparison of educational values by psychologists in applying various tests to pupils and students in different countries is still in its initial stage. This method may in future bring valuable results and lead to the establishment of internationally recognised quotients. At present this method can be used only within certain limitations as the standardised tests are fully applicable in the country for which they were devised. In the Soviet Union, for instance, the authorities discontinued the application of psychological tests devised in Russia to the pupils in the Central Asiatic Republics, as the Uzbeks, Tadzhiks and Turkmens were invariably below the Russian children in their I.Q., which did not correspond to real conditions in the majority of cases. Testing Indian or African children by European tests usually leads to quite wrong conclusions. It appears that at present at any rate neither the purely statistical nor the psychological method of approach can furnish Comparative Education with a firm foundation on which to build.

The question arises whether educational values can be compared at all. Our scepticism should not go so far. If educational

[1] This work is being undertaken by UNESCO.

values of different national systems often cannot be compared by mathematical methods, a valid comparison of their functional rôle in their respective situations may be successfully attempted and fruitfully achieved. That brings us back to the thesis that national systems of education as well as national constitutions or national literatures are the outward expression of national character and as such represent the nation in distinction from other nations. If we could separate and analyse the factors which historically were active in creating different nations we should go a long way towards a definition of the principles which underlie national systems of education. The English usage of the term "nation" is not a sure guide in this case. We speak for instance of the "British" and the "Irish"; both terms it appears may be applied to the Northern Irish, but not to the Southern Irish. We speak of Soviet "nation-wide" measures, implying by it that all the sixteen national Republics which constitute the U.S.S.R. are in fact a single nation. When we sometimes speak of the South Africans it appears again that we include in the term the white minority only, whether Boer or Briton, but not the native and coloured population, which forms the majority of permanent residents of the country. The English language in its common use of the term emphasises the citizenship rather than the "nationality."

In the "Educational Traditions" the author has enumerated five factors which make an ideal nation: (i) Unity of race, (ii) Unity of religion, (iii) Unity of language, (iv) Compact territory and (v) Political sovereignty. One of the factors may be lacking without seriously endangering the unity of national culture. Belgium, for instance, lacks linguistic unity, having two national languages, Flemish and French, and in spite of difficulties is nevertheless a nation. Holland is divided by religion, the Latin American Republics include in their population three distinct racial stocks, and Poland for a century was deprived of her political sovereignty, and yet all these countries are nations in the full sense of the word. In certain circumstances even two factors may be absent and if the divisions thus created do not coincide a nation may be formed. In Switzerland, for instance, the population is divided both by language and religion, but the lines of division cross and did not prevent the birth of the Swiss nations But in South Africa where racial, linguistic and religious divisions run parallel it is very doubtful if the Whites and the Blacks will ever form a single nation without fundamental changes in their present social segregation. Common citizenship by itself without cultural affinity and social intercourse between the two groups will hardly effect that result. Neither factor is potent enough if separated, only the combination of at least four of them can result in creating a cultural social unit called "a nation" clearly distinct from other "nations."

National character, therefore, is a complex result of racial intermixtures, linguistic adaptations, religious movements and historical and geographical situations in general. Because of this multiplicity of factors it could not be compared to a monolith, but rather resembles an old architectural structure with styles and additions of various centuries. National systems of education, even when they are intentionally set up by revolutionary governments to reform the inherited national character, are unavoidably influenced by these factors and are deeply rooted in the past. In its primitive tribal form education was a social adaptation of the individual to the tribal type with the single aim of preserving the racial, religious and linguistic features of the community. Tribal education was and still is essentially conservative and abhorred any deviation from rigidly established customs. The great historical migrations with resultant loss of tribal simplicity entirely changed the situation. Hybridisation of races and the rise of universal religious movements played havoc with original tribes and created the modern nations which could not follow the simple pattern of tribal education. Under the influence of universal ideals, both religious and social-political, the modern nations consciously endeavour to reform the past and create a better future through nationally controlled systems of education.

Thus education, from being a function of the national character, became itself a new factor in moulding it. This new tendency, however, is still too recent and too weak to override the heritage of the past, and even the most ruthless revolutionary movements had to adapt their new ideas to existing historical and geographical situations. As a result the modern national systems of education are projected both into the past and into the future. As their national past was formed by factors often common to many nations and as their ideals of the future are the outcome of universal movements, the problems of education in different countries are similar and the principles which guide their solutions may be compared and even identified. The analytical study of these factors from a historical perspective and the comparison of attempted solution of resultant problems are the main purpose of Comparative Education. The application of the findings of these studies is outside the scope of Comparative Education proper and belongs in its theory to the philosophy of education and in its practice to the administration and organisation of education. The contents of this book will, in consequence, be limited to the analysis of factors and their illustration from actual situations.

The growth of nations can be compared with the growth of an individual. The adult personality has matured under the constant influence of three groups of factors: (i) Endowment as the result of heredity, (ii) Environment, both physical and social, and (iii) Training, both in special educational institutions (schools, youth organisations, churches, etc.) and in actual productive work. The same can be said of the modern nations which have reached maturity in their development. Thus the first factor to be considered in this analysis is the influence of heredity or the racial factor. As a rule the members of the same nation are of the same racial origin, whether they represent a pure race or as the result of hybridisation. It presupposes the blood community between the co-nationals. The historical tradition of each nation invariably ascribes its origin to a common ancestry. Although wholesale tribal migrations and historical conquests have radically changed the original purity of racial groups, the idea of common ancestry still persists in national literature and art and thus continues to play an important rôle in the national consciousness. The study of racial differences whether real or imaginary and their influence on national systems of education is one of the main subjects of Comparative Education.

The second factor of great importance is the national language, accepted by all members as the natural medium of social intercourse and as an outward symbol of their nationality. Strictly speaking the language belongs to social environment and not to endowment, but its influence on the growing mind is so intricately interwoven with the ability to reason that it forms a bridge between heredity and environment. In the case of a nation language, as the repository of racial and national memory, should be considered as the most important influence in the formation of national character. The native tongue, or, as the Germans say, the *Muttersprache*, often decides the adherence of the individual to a particular nation irrespective of the place of his birth or citizenship. National systems of education by using national languages as the medium of instruction put into operation the most powerful tool in moulding the minds of the rising generation.

Bilingualism or the knowledge of foreign languages is on the other hand the surest method to wean the mind from national prejudices. Linguistic problems exist in most countries and their backgrounds and solutions are similar and can easily be compared. We shall devote a special chapter to language and its influence on educational systems.

Social and physical environments both in the case of an individual and of a nation are the third main group of influences which form the personality or the national character. Economic conditions and occupational activities create special attitudes and reactions in the individual and are studied by occupational psychology. A farmer, a factory worker, a clergyman or an officer, irrespective of their nationality or natural ability, are easily recognisable after a few minutes' conversation. The nations as a rule include all occupations and their members belong to all layers in the social structure of the community. But some nations are or were in the past predominantly agricultural, whilst others are industrial; the distribution of occupations changes as from country to country and this differentiation is reflected both in the national character and in the system of education. Industrial revolutions both in England and in Russia were closely followed by certain modifications of the national character and by radical changes in the systems of education. Geographical conditions play a similar rôle to that of social and economic environment in modifying the character. The insular or continental character of the country, mountains or great plains impart special features to the inhabitants and we distinguish the seafaring people from mountaineers; or we speak of an insular outlook. Educational systems have to adapt themselves to the configuration of the country and to the physical conditions of the climate. The administration and the organisation of education as well as its contents vary with the changes of physical environment. All these factors of heredity, language, social and physical environment can be grouped together as natural conditions existing before the real task of education starts and should be distinguished from the next group of factors, which can be called spiritual or the influences of conscious training.

In so far as the educational systems endeavour to adapt themselves to natural conditions they are limited by existing situations and more or less passively reflect the accidents of the historical past and geographical present. Under the influence of the next group of factors education assumes a guiding and active rôle and its purpose is to change and mould the inherited situation in accordance with some spiritual ideal. All great religious and political movements, all reformations and revolutions were inspired by some universal ideal which inevitably led to a change in the educational theory and practice. We should here distinguish the religious influences from the secular. While religious movements always laid more stress on the moral regeneration of the individual, often neglecting the deplorable economic conditions of the masses, the secular movements were more concerned with the amelioration of the social conditions of the masses, neglecting sometimes the moral aspirations of the individual. Both groups of spiritual factors have one feature in common—their universality. A religious or social-political movement may start within the narrow boundaries of a nationality or even within a section of a nation. But the broad human aspect of their ideals very soon divests them of their national or sectional roots and transforms them into universal doctrines acceptable to all branches of humanity irrespective of their origins or languages. Christianity was born in a Hebrew community on Palestinian soil, but has become a universal religion, incidentally repudiated by the very tribe which gave birth to it. Buddhism is of Indian origin, but has survived as a universal religion only outside India. Islam was started as a purely Arab way of life, but has crossed the tribal boundaries and has grown into a powerful influence in three continents. The same can be said of secular movements. Humanism based on the renaissance of Greco-Roman civilisation has spread as an ideal to races and peoples which have no connections with the classical world. Socialism born in the industrial West was first applied in practice in agricultural Eastern Europe and in its Marxian interpretation has become a most penetrating influence among coloured races, whose economic conditions are in no way comparable to those of the industrial West. Even nationalism, by its very definition limited to a particular nation, has assumed a universal character and displays the same features in various lands dissimilar in every respect.

By religious traditions humanity is divided into four main groups: (i) Christianity, concentrated in Europe and countries colonised by Europeans, (ii) Islam in the Middle East and the Indian Ocean, (iii) Hinduism in India and (iv) Oriental religions (Buddhism, Confucianism, Shintoism) in the Far East. Judaism is limited to a small dispersed community and influenced the religious traditions of other peoples only in so far as it was incorporated in Christianity and Islam. We distinguish here the important contributions of individual Jews to European culture from the influence of Judaism as religious tradition after the Jewish dispersal. The primitive tribal religions which still linger in some parts of the world have no chance of survival in competition with great universal religions or new secular movements. In an adequate treatment of Comparative Education all four main divisions should be included, but in this book intended for English-speaking students we have to limit the field of discussion. European nations and their former colonies are Christian by tradition and by the expressed beliefs of the overwhelming majority of their populations. Although Islam and Judaism have been associated with European civilisation for many centuries and still can count European adherents in millions, their influence on European systems of education has been limited and can be disregarded.

Christianity is the common foundation of all variations of European civilisation which gives to the Occident a certain unity of outlook and tradition. This unity is clearly seen by an outsider, by a Moslem or a Chinese, but for Christians it is often obscured by internal divisions and historical opposition, the result of religious wars, and half-forgotten dogmatic schisms. The division of the Roman Empire into the Latin West and the Greek East was the first cause of differentiation within the universal Christian Church. The new converts to Christianity, the Teutons and the Slavs, joined the Latin and the Greek varieties respectively and thus accentuated the traditional difference by tribal cleavage.[1] Geographical regions coinciding on a large scale with national-linguistic grouping and the new schism in Western Europe caused by the Reformation created three definite varieties of Christianity. Catholicism with the Latin liturgy became closely associated with those parts of Europe which were longest under Roman rule and were more or less permeated by Latin culture. Orthodoxy with a Greek or Slav liturgy was embraced by the Eastern part of Europe (Poland excepted) which for long was under Byzantine cultural influence. The Teutonic peoples around the North Sea seceded from the Roman Church and formed a third group of national Protestant Churches. Thus the

---

[1] The Czechs were originally converted from the East by a Slav missionary and always retained certain links with the Slav tradition. The Poles are the only Slav nation which definitely accepted the Latin form of Christianity.

division of Christianity was deepened by geographical regions and national-linguistic differences. This broad classification is only true as a rough generalisation; there are many exceptions in each grouping, but for our purposes of tracing the influence of religious traditions on education, it is very helpful. Each branch of Christianity has developed its own educational tradition and has thus profoundly influenced the national systems of education in the three different regions of Europe. In the general chapter on religious traditions we shall deal with Islam and Orthodoxy very briefly, but special attention will be given to Catholicism and Protestantism and three separate chapters will be devoted to them.

Catholicism is the general historical background of Western Europe and even the Protestant countries have inherited their educational systems from the medieval Catholic Church. Moreover, substantial Catholic minorities remained in all the English-speaking countries and formed separate school-systems which deviate from the general national pattern. Protestantism in Great Britain and her former colonies was not uniform as in Scandinavia and cannot be treated as one religious tradition. Anglicanism and Puritanism are two distinct currents of religious thought and often in marked opposition to each other. They should be discussed separately and to each a chapter is devoted. Of the two, Anglicanism is confined to the English-speaking countries only, whereas Puritanism in its Calvinist form affected many Continental countries and their colonies.

As has been mentioned, secular movements were not directed to the salvation of the individual in the religious-moral sense; they were prompted to protest and reform or even revolution by the deplorable conditions of the masses. Religious fanaticism, defective administration of justice, general ignorance and widespread superstition oppressed the minds of the masses in all countries in the Middle Ages and prevented the progress of science and general enlightenment. To liberate the common people from these shackles a movement of humanism was started by groups of scientists and philosophers in many European countries and their propagation of tolerance, justice and enlightenment marks the beginning of a new era in European history. Especially profound was the influence of humanism on the theory and practice of education.

Socialism, on the other hand, was mainly a protest against the economic exploitation of the masses by the ruling minority which became so pronounced under capitalism in the wake of the industrial revolution. Whilst humanism was primarily an educational movement, socialism is predominantly an economic doctrine, which influenced education indirectly, but nevertheless its influence was profound and radical. Most of the recent reforms in educational systems were inspired by these two secular movements.

The third secular movement of universal significance is nationalism. This movement is a natural expression of the national character and is quite legitimate if kept within bounds. The latest examples of extreme nationalism in all its naked brutality have little in common with the humanistic nationalism of Mazzini and Garibaldi, or the Czech national revival. Stripped of all elements of humanism the Nazi interpretation of nationalism perverted the cultural significance of the national character and used it for the outright exploitation and even extermination of other nations. The comparative study of nationalism both in its legitimate and its extreme form and of its influence on educational systems can elucidate many problems of education.

Thus we have arrived through our analysis at three definite groups of factors: Part I—Natural factors: (a) Race, (b) Language, (c) Environment. Part II—Religious factors: (a) Catholicism, (b) Anglicanism, (c) Puritanism. Part III—Secular factors: (a) Humanism, (b) Socialism, (c) Nationalism. To Part II we add an introductory chapter on religious influences in general and to Part III we shall add a concluding chapter on Democracy and Education. Each chapter will have short illustrations from actual situations in various countries. In Part IV we shall give examples of national systems of education as they exist today. We have selected for this purpose, besides England, three foreign countries which by their material resources and by the high level of their cultural achievements can be truly called together with Great Britain the Big Four: the United States of America, France and the Union of Soviet Socialist Republics.

PART I

NATURAL FACTORS

CHAPTER II

THE RACIAL FACTOR [1]

The term "race" is applied rather loosely both in everyday usage and in scientific books. In its broadest meaning it includes the whole human "race"; in its narrow sense it may be applied to a family, as in the expressions "the race of Abraham" or the "race of the Plantagenets." In its intermediate meanings it is often applied to a tribe, a nation or a group of nations, as in "the Arab race," "the German race" or "the Slavonic race." Strictly speaking none of these uses of the term is scientifically correct. Biologically "race" means an original ethnic group with permanent characteristic features which are transmitted from generation to generation. In this chapter we shall use it only in the sense of a distinct ethnic group which, whether it represents the original "race" or is the result of intermixtures of several original races, has acquired a certain permanency in its main characteristics. The greatest confusion in the minds of the general public has been created by the constant substitution of linguistic differences for ethnic characteristics. Language has nothing to do with "race" now, whatever their original connection may have been. Linguistic differences belong to philology, racial characteristics to biology. To speak, for instance, as the Nazis have done, of the "Aryan race" is not only unscientific but very misleading, for the term "Aryan" has a definite philological meaning and can be applied only to a group of languages and in no way to a group of peoples who speak these languages. The American Negroes, for instance, speak English, which is their native tongue, but they are certainly not of English descent, nor do they belong to any of the European "races." Any language may be imposed on a conquered population of quite different racial origin or, as has often happened, the warlike but more primitive conquerors may adopt the language of the more cultured victims of their aggression. In neither case do the languages spoken by their descendants belong to their racial heritage. From this it follows that modern "nations," distinguished by their national languages, may include

[1] A more detailed discussion of racial problems can be found in the *Year Book of Education*, 1949.

groups of various racial origin or that the same "race" may be represented in many nations, speaking different languages.

The hybridisation of originally distinct stocks has gone so far all over the world that to decide the "race" of any particular individual is sometimes quite impossible. It follows from the Mendelian laws of heredity, discovered by Gregor Mendel in 1866, that some characteristics may not be visible in the outer appearance of the individual, but may appear in his offspring. If the parents, or even more remote ancestors, belonged to two distinct racial groups, some features are "dominant," whilst others are "recessive." The offspring may resemble one race more than the other, but carry in his genetic cells the hereditary features of the other parent stock. In addition some characteristic features are segregated, or may appear independently of other features typical for any given race. Thus for instance eye-colour and hair-colour, which in original races were permanently connected, in a hybrid ethnic group may appear in all possible combinations. Let us take, for example, eye-colour and see how it is inherited according to the Mendelian law. It has been proved that a dark, whether black or brown, iris is "dominant," whilst a blue or green iris is "recessive." If one parent represents a pure stock with dark eyes and the other parent has blue eyes, all their children without exception will have dark eyes, but will carry the "blue" characteristic as a "recessive" part of their heredity. But should these hybrid offsprings intermarry among themselves their progeny will include individuals with blue eyes, and according to the law of probability with the frequency of one in four."

The following diagram illustrates this case:

D—represents dark-eyed parent; B—blue-eyed.

1. DD x BB—As D is dominant, the first generation DB will
      | all have dark eyes.
    all ↓ DB

2. D——D⎫ In the second generation there will be one DD,
      ╳   ⎬ two DB and one BB, or three dark-eyed and
    B——B⎭ one blue-eyed, of which only the first is of
pure racial type DD, two are hybrids DB, and the fourth is of pure racial type BB. The hybrid type, however, cannot be distinguished by appearance from the pure DD.

This means that if hybridisation has taken place on a large scale, the outward appearance of any individual cannot ensure the purity of his "race." Moreover the individual of mixed origin may combine the visible appearance of one race with the mental characteristics of another parent stock. That is what really happened in Europe and to a lesser extent in Asia and Africa. The racial mixture in America is comparatively recent and is still visible to any casual observer.

Modern anthropology distinguishes five main European stocks or "races" which gave rise to all existing European nations. We give here the usual names of the "races" with their three main characteristics. (i) Nordic—tall, fair, long-headed; (ii) Mediterranean—short, dark, long-headed; (iii) Alpine—short, brown, broad-headed; (iv) Baltic—medium, fair, broad-headed; (v) Dinaric—tall, dark, broad-headed. It is significant that the German text-books and the official Nazi classification of the German population recognised all five "races" as "Aryan" and thus officially exploded the popular Nazi identification of the Germans with the Nordic race. The Nordic myth was used by the Nazis solely for the sake of propaganda; for practical legislation they had to take into consideration the highly mixed origin of the German nation. The Germans are not an exception; all European nations are a mixture either of three or of all five races, usually described as European. As a matter of fact mixtures of these five races are also present in North Africa, the Middle East and as far afield as India. The only safe generalisation which can be made about the distribution of these races in Europe is based roughly on regions. In the North the Nordic race is represented in larger numbers than elsewhere, in the South the Mediterraneans predominate, the centre belt is mostly populated by the Alpine race, the North-east is the region of the Baltics and the South-east of the Dinaric group. But this distribution does not run parallel with any national boundaries, and even the Swedes, the purest racial group in Europe, include 5 per cent of dark-eyed people. The majority of Europeans are of mixed origin and typical representatives of each of the five races can be met with in any European country. It appears that in Europe, at any rate, there are no racial problems in a biological sense; all the differentiation of European nations is based, not on racial, but on linguistic, traditional and geographical grounds. The two groups, the Jews and the Gipsies, against which the Nazis enacted the famous Nuremberg racial laws, are not racial groups at all, but are as much racial mixtures as the Germans themselves, and, what is more, of the same racial stocks.

Racial problems, both political and educational, can be met with only in those countries which possessed a native coloured population which has been conquered and administered by Europeans. In some of these countries the Europeans form a small ruling group and make no attempt at turning them into "white man's" countries; in others they have settled in large communities and have gradually outnumbered the natives. To the first group belong the African colonies administered by Europeans, the most important of them under British and French rule. The Asiatic countries administered by Europeans are quite definitely on the way to independence and are now administered by the natives themselves. Their educational problems are linguistic rather than racial and do not belong to this chapter. To the second group belong most of the American Republics and the British Dominions. Some of the Latin American Republics where the original population even now greatly outnumbers the European colonists form the intermediate group. Racial problems as reflected in educational policy are quite different in these two main groups of countries.

In the colonies or countries with coloured populations the problem of European administration is to associate the natives with European civilisation and gradually raise them to a higher social level which eventually may lead to the creation of a new nation or their absorption in the controlling European nation, if all other circumstances are favourable. British India, Burma, Pakistan, Ceylon, Malay States, Dutch Indonesia, French Indo-China, became independent countries. Most of the Arab countries have attained full independence; others are still on the way, but fully conscious of their national identity. In all these countries the task of the European administration has either ended with the transfer of power to the natives or is limited to an advisory rôle. In Africa, on the contrary, the re-education of the natives is in its initial stage and the racial problem dominates both politics and economics.

The Black population of Africa has neither national traditions nor a national language. Whereas their Northern neighbours, the Moors and the Arabs, or even the Abyssinians, have national and religious traditions of their own and recognised languages with classical literatures, the Black Africans are still in the primitive tribal stage of evolution. Although they are very capable they have not yet evolved a culture or national traditions which could sustain competition with European civilisation. With the modern development of aviation no Black tribe even in the most remote corner of Africa can live in its previous state of isolation content with a primitive social and cultural organisation. Inevitably they are drawn into the vortex of world economics and politics and take an active part in the industrial and military activities of the Great Powers. Left to their own cultural resources these tribes would be doomed to the rôle of manual workers and would never be able to acquire social equality with the Europeans. Only with the assistance of the European administration can they ever hope to attain a status equal not only in law but in fact.

As the two typical variations of European policy in Africa we shall discuss the British and French aims and practice in their respective systems of education. Both Britain and France have officially recognised the necessity of the cultural elevation of the Africans, and their declarations of educational policy have clearly announced this aim. The British and French methods, however, are different if not exactly opposite. The British policy assumes the rôle of a guardian and strives to help the natives to build up a culture of their own from the elements available in their languages, tribal traditions and social customs. As the White Paper on Educational Policy in Tropical Africa, 1925, declared: "Education should be adapted to the mentality, aptitudes, occupations and traditions of the various peoples, conserving as far as possible all sound and healthy elements in the fabric of their social life; adapting them where necessary to changed circumstances and progressive ideas as an agent of natural growth and evolution." In conformity with these principles the British administration has built up a school system which includes primary, secondary and even higher institutions. In practice, however, the administration met with many difficulties. The first was the question of the medium of instruction. Obviously the declared policy demanded the use of mother tongues in the schools. In some territories the tribal groups are so small and so intermixed and their linguistic differentiation has gone so far that no tribal dialect could be used in the schools. To use English from the start would be contrary to the aim, and moreover the British policy quite definitely wants to avoid the creation of "Black Englishmen," who would be foreigners both in England and in Africa. Compelled by circumstances, the administration found a compromise in East Africa in adopting Swahili as the language of instruction. This is a kind of "Lingua Franca" on the East coast, but is not spoken by any tribe in their homes. Another difficulty was created by the recent war. Many thousands of Africans of various tribes took part in the world war as soldiers of the British Army or as workers in war industries. They have learned English and have acquired some technical skill and are reluctant to return to their tribal way of life. The tempo of industrial revolution in Africa appears to be overtaking the gradualness of the British educational policy and the problem has to be studied anew. The British Government is fully aware of this need and is taking steps to accelerate the process.

The French policy inspired by the ideals of the Revolution aimed from the very start at the association of the natives with French culture and at transforming them into Black Frenchmen. The Governor-General of French West Africa (Brévié) in 1930 made an official statement of French policy.[1] Its aim, he said, was:

> the recruitment of cadres of natives more and more content, more and more assured, and by a vigorous and progressive selection more and more advanced. It is the diffusion of the French language, by the contact established more intimately and more completely with French life and activities; it is the constitution of a native élite to the greatest possible extent, in whom the passionate striving towards a culture completely and jealously French could be strengthened.

The whole policy is very logical and based "on reason and imbued with a spirit of truth and good faith."[2] As the French Revolution declared the equality and brotherhood of all men as the principle of French policy, no difference of racial origin or colour should be taken into consideration. And as the French culture and language represent the highest attainment of European civilisation the black subjects of France should receive this gift in the fullest measure. It is a straightforward rational policy, founded on high humanist ideals, which is in no way vitiated by the later addition of military and economic motives. The French administration sincerely tried to implement it in practice, but met with many difficulties. At first the French aimed at establishing an exact copy of the French school system in Africa open to all the inhabitants without any restrictions. The cultural gulf between Africa and France and the linguistic difficulty compelled them, however, to create two parallel systems of schools—one for those, whether white or black, who speak French at home,

---

[1] See *Revue de l'Enseignement français hors de France*, January 1931.
[2] Statement of Governor Brévié in 1935.

and another for the rest. The first system is identical with the metropolitan system and is entirely French. The second takes local conditions into consideration and sometimes even employs local speech for the sake of expediency. But it is looked upon as a temporary measure, to be abandoned as soon as the diffusion of the French language and culture becomes more general. Gradually the French administrators have realised the immensity of the task of re-educating millions of primitive Negroes into cultured Frenchmen and have had to make concessions to hard facts without abandoning the original aim. As the Inspector-General of Education in West Africa, Albert Charton, said in 1935:

> The development of native society, according to the demands of time and circumstances, towards a practicable measure of French-inspired civilisation, will demand unremitting efforts, a constancy of purpose and a grasp of the realities of the situation, if we are to evolve a new social and psychological equilibrium.

Both policies, the British and the French, reflect the general political traditions of the two countries. The British policy is based on the principle of decentralisation and on building up of a Commonwealth of Nations, each of which should be free to develop its own culture and national character. As there is no intention of making Africans into Englishmen the question of "racial superiority" does not arise as the two communities are kept apart and the English administration is destined finally to be withdrawn and to make way for a native administration.[1] Quite different is the situation in the French territories. The French policy is based on the principle of centralisation and the absorption into France of all provinces and colonies which deviate from the centre in any way. In Europe Basques, Bretons, Flemings and even Alsatians developed into good Frenchmen under the combined influence of centralised administration and the attractive power of French culture, although the recent movements of regionalism challenge even this achievement. What happened in Europe was expected to happen in the overseas territories. However, the conditions are dissimilar. The non-French provinces in Europe are adjacent to the centre and share with it the heritage of Latin civilisation and of the medieval Catholic Church. The far-flung territories of the French Empire, populated by coloured races, have no community of heritage with the French nation; common culture has to be created on a soil permeated with different traditions and divergent interests.

[1] As happened in Ghana and Nigeria.

France, against her will, has had to withdraw from Syria and Lebanon, thus confessing the failure of her policy in the Middle East. France is gradually withdrawing from the East also, as the population of Indo-China quite definitely refused to become "yellow Frenchmen." The rising tide of Arab nationalism endangers the aims of French education in the North of Africa. Black Africa alone still remains under the undisputed leadership of the French educators; here alone the French policy may be crowned by final success. But this success will be entirely dependent on a satisfactory solution of the racial problem. The legal pronouncement of racial equality and brotherhood and the imposition of French culture and language on the Black Africans do not solve the racial problem, they only postulate it. The African population, in spite of aviation, is segregated from France by the Mediterranean Sea and the Sahara Desert, and, what is more important, by a distinct racial difference easily recognisable by the colour of its members. The welding of white and black Frenchmen into one nation is only possible through general social intercourse and free and frequent intermarriage. Although the French people have never officially exhibited the superior attitude of the white man, so typical among the Anglo-Saxons, it is doubtful whether any French village community would accept a black Frenchmen in its fold as an equal member. The few examples from Paris are no guide in this respect, as Paris is not France, and the few blacks who come to Paris are the result of special selection. The question will be decided not by the successful assimilation of a few thousand individuals, but by the assimilation of the African masses.

Perhaps some light on this problem may be shed by studying the conditions in Latin America, where the same problem of assimilating the native Indians and the imported Africans was attempted both by the French and the Spaniards. Of the twenty Latin American Republics we select three, Peru, Mexico, and Haiti, as the most interesting examples of racial problems in education. On the eve of the French Revolution the slave population of Haiti was a medley of various tribes of Africa, many slaves having been quite recently transported from their native forests to work on French plantations. There was no unity of native traditions, no single dialect common to all, so that the slaves had to speak French to understand each other. The French Revolution emancipated the slaves and the War of Independence won for them a national status recognised by all. Their first

President, A. Petion (1807–18), was a mulatto, educated in Paris, who was inspired by the ideas of the French Revolution. He established a constitution on the French model and initiated a school system borrowed wholesale from France. His declared aim was to shape his black co-citizens into Frenchmen. For more than a hundred years the Haitians followed this ideal, but whether they succeeded is doubtful. They speak a French *patois*, they are officially Roman Catholics, they have a constitution, a legal system, an educational organisation, including lycées and a university, they have a press, a theatre and clubs and cafés, they have churches, convents and religious Orders, all copied from French models and sounding very French. But with the exception of a small élite, who have completed their education in France, the population is still primitive and illiterate. In the remote parts of the island they still practise some of the cruel Voodoo rites of their African ancestors. From this example it seems probable that centuries may pass before the French policy succeeds in transforming the black population of Africa into real Frenchmen. During that time, however, the former British African Colonies may develop their own native self-government and become the centre of gravity for all the black tribes of Africa.

Another interesting example of the imposition of European civilisation on large native populations is provided by two Latin American Republics with Indian majorities—Peru and Mexico. Peru occupies the area which was the centre of the old Inca empire and is populated by five million Indians, who have preserved the traditions and the Quechua language of that interesting civilisation. For four centuries the Spanish-speaking minority imposed on them the language, religion and institutions of Spain. Even now the whole country is in the hands of the Spanish-speaking minority, the Creole aristocracy, who control the State, the Church and the schools. The official history of this Quechua country was made and is still being made by the Spanish Creoles, but the life of the bulk of the population has hardly been touched by all the revolutions and counter-revolutions of the South American pattern and the Quechua villages live essentially the same life as during the rule of the Incas, with the same form of village government, the same methods of agriculture and handicraft, the same songs and dances. Even the religion imposed by the conquerors with artillery and mass executions is still blended with old beliefs, and the villagers to this day paint the sign of the sun, the emblem of their old religion, side by side with the sign of the Cross on their huts.[1] There is no lack of signs of an Indian renaissance which might break the four centuries of Spanish dominion. The Indians have awakened from their long slumber, have allied themselves with the radical anti-clerical party and recently have initiated a Quechua press and Quechua village schools. The anti-clerical tendencies in Peru are as much the result of modern Socialism, inspired by Moscow, as of the resentment of the Indians against the religion of their conquerors. It appears to be only a question of time before the Indians reassert themselves and pick up the threads of their Inca traditions invigorated by modern Socialism. It is obvious that the Spaniards in Peru have failed to assimilate the Indian population; they have succeeded in building up a façade and an urban civilisation in a few centres without touching the masses. There are three main causes of this failure: first, the presence of an ancient civilisation and national language of Indian origin; second, the harsh methods of conversion used by the Spaniards after the conquest, and third, the total absence of an enlightened educational policy for the masses. To this must be added the economic division coinciding with the racial difference—the wealthy ruling Spanish oligarchy and the poor masses of Indian peasants. Although the Spaniards are not as race-conscious as some Northern European nations and accept mestizos in their social life, the prejudice against the pure natives, the "Indios bravos," is still strong, and keeps the two groups of the Peruvian population apart.

The second example of an Indian country conquered by the Spaniards is provided by Mexico. The population of Mexico consists of about two million "whites" of Spanish origin, about five million pure Indians and about ten million mestizos. The Indians are the descendants of the ancient Aztecs, who before the conquest possessed an advanced civilisation of native origin. The main difference between the Incan and Aztec empires was the absence of a national language in the latter. Whereas the Inca rulers succeeded in welding various Indian tribes into one nation with a recognised common language, Quechua, the Aztecs, in spite of their highly organised empire, failed to create a national language accepted by all Indians. Even now there is such a multiplicity of Nahuac and Mayan dialects [2] in Mexico, that often two neighbouring villages use varieties of native speech which are

[1] The Quechua still cleave to their old pagan religion, which survives curiously intermixed with a very strange Catholicism. This religion is kept secret and is only partially known. From a S.A. Report.

[2] There are forty-nine ethnic groups and thirteen general linguistic groups.

mutually unintelligible. Secondly, the presence of ten million mestizos, who all speak Spanish, has made the language of the conquerors the national language of Mexico, unchallenged even by the extreme Aztec nationalists. This circumstance, however, has not prevented the birth of an Indian renaissance. The consciousness of their Aztec ancestry and of their Indian cultural heritage has been present in the minds of Mexican patriots since the War of Independence. The national colours and the crest adopted by independent Mexico are those of the Aztec empire. The greatest Mexican statesman and reformer, Benito Juarez, was a Zapotecan Indian, fully conscious of his race; he clearly understood that Mexico's future was closely bound up with the regeneration of the Indian stock. After the revolutionary period of 1910–17, the new nationalism was tinged with Indian feelings. The Spanish culture was deprecated just because it was the culture of the conquerors who for centuries enslaved and exploited the natives, though the violent reaction against the Roman Catholic Church was as much the result of European anti-clericalism as of the enmity of the Indians towards Spanish tradition. Only Spaniards with anti-clerical and Socialist tendencies are welcomed as immigrants; the Spanish religious Orders and clergy are banned by a special law. The Indian renaissance which has been taking place during the last thirty years is especially marked in the field of education, and arts and crafts. The Mexican pioneer, Manuel Gamio, surveyed the ancient ruins of the Aztecs and the present economic conditions of Indian communities. Obviously under the influence of Soviet theory and practice, he arrived at the conclusion that the education of the Indians should be "integral." Integral education means the revival of old Indian craftsmanship and social life; it includes guidance in hygiene, in the making of a livelihood, in social relations, and in the integration of remote villages in the larger communities. Hundreds of rural schools were opened in Indian villages and a special Department of Native Culture was founded in 1921. The revival of native art penetrated the old schools, and new open-air schools were founded in which children exhibit a creative impulse which for centuries was expressed in native handicraft. The Indian renaissance in Mexico gives an example of the survival of racial characteristics notwithstanding the acceptance of a European language as a national medium.

These examples from Latin America show clearly that the transformation of coloured races into Europeans may succeed only in specially favourable circumstances and will take centuries of unremitting effort. They also prove that in those countries where the native masses have preserved their racial integrity and have not intermixed with Europeans on a large scale the problem of Europeanisation is almost insoluble and sooner or later may resolve itself in a total or partial renaissance of the original racial characteristics. Mexico shows partial success of Europeanisation because the majority of the population are mestizos and the gulf between the pure white and the pure native is bridged by gradual differences. Perhaps the failure of the Haitians to absorb not only its superficial trappings but the spirit of French culture is closely bound up with the total extermination of the whites and the mulattoes which followed the War of Independence and left the pure blacks in possession of the island. The difference between the coloured and white races is not necessarily connected with the so-called superior or inferior stocks. The Europeans are too ready to assess the level of culture by material standards and technical achievements. From this point of view the atomic bomb is the culmination of human evolution. Coloured races, although far behind the Europeans in technical inventions, have succeeded in building up independent civilisations of their own of a very high standard. No one disputes the high level of the ancient Chinese and East Indian civilisations. The American Indians possessed their own civilisation in the Inca and Aztec empires, before it was destroyed by the Spaniards. The innate ability of certain racial stocks cannot be measured merely by the state of their cultural achievements up to date. Their development may have been retarded by adverse conditions in their environment and tribal training. Granted a more favourable environment they may prove as able as the Europeans. The racial difference lies more in the sphere of the emotional-conative side of the mind than in the sphere of intelligence. The emotional-conative make-up of some coloured races diverges so much from the European that they cannot imbibe the spirit of European culture, not for lack of intelligence, but because it does not suit their racial character.

In this respect the example of the Maoris of New Zealand is very instructive. Even the first European discoverers were struck by their physical vigour, moral qualities and intelligence, although by ordinary standards they were just savage cannibals. Now anthropologists unanimously agree that Maoris are equal to Europeans in intelligence and qualities of character. Nevertheless the modern Maori, after having passed all the examinations in European schools, does not take to European ways, but returns to his native village to live the rest of his life as a Maori. Certainly he has ceased to be a cannibal, he is a member of some Christian denomination, he reads English newspapers and books and elects his member to the New Zealand parliament, but nevertheless his attitudes, his outlook and his social relations are Maori and not English. For how long he will be able to retain his racial individuality is difficult to predict, as even at present out of 100,000 Maoris in New Zealand probably only 50 per cent are of pure blood. The white New Zealanders have no racial prejudice or colour bar, and frequently intermarry with the Maoris. Their public school system is open to Maoris on equal terms with the European population, and more than half of the Maori children attend public schools, controlled by the District Boards. The rest attend the so-called Native Schools established by the Government specially for the Maoris and directly controlled by the Education Department. These schools were not intended to lead to the segregation of the races, as the Native Schools are also attended by white children, who amount to 10 per cent of all pupils in these schools. The primary purpose of Native Schools was to adapt their curriculum to the special needs of Maori village communities. The white administration did not believe in racial differences and was confident that the assimilation and total absorption of Maoris in the white population was a question of a few decades. Consequently the medium of instruction was English and the Maori language was strictly excluded. Although the curriculum took heed of local conditions, it was in fact only a slightly modified version of the general academic curriculum prevalent in the public primary schools. In spite of the language difficulties, the Maori children were on the whole as successful as the English-speaking New Zealanders; some of them passed to secondary schools and a few even to the Universities. But they remained Maoris and spoke Maori at home. Contrary to expectations even the half-caste Maoris did not lose their identity among the overwhelming majority of the white population. They clung to their tribal traditions, their old songs and dances and their hereditary chiefs. Their most outstanding leader, Sir Apirana Ngata, who for a time acted as Prime Minister of New Zealand, had to give way on ceremonial occasions to the hereditary chief of his tribe. He was most active as Native Minister of the Government in the economic and cultural renaissance of his race. He collected, annotated and published a large number of songs of various Maori tribes. He started the land resettlement schemes which provided a higher standard of life for thousands of Maoris. He was one of the group of young Maori students who in the nineties of the last century formed what was later known as the Young Maori Party, who set themselves the task of the cultural and economic regeneration of their people. The present renaissance of the Maori tribes is chiefly due to their labours and devotion. The Government helped in education and health services, but without the inspiration and zeal of the young Maori leaders their cause would have been lost. However valuable and equitable the educational facilities provided by the Government were, they were not exactly what the Maoris most needed. As Sir Apirana Ngata said to his young friends: "Never let us be false to our people. Whatever education may do for us, let it not put us out of touch with them, else our training will be a pitiful and lamentable failure." The schools for Maoris, which aimed at assimilation, had to be remodelled to suit the new spirit of racial preservation. In 1934 a new curriculum was introduced into Maori schools which aims at relating instruction to the practical and cultural needs of the race and at organically connecting the school with the Maori community. Although English is still the main concern of the schools, Maori traditions and Maori history are included as part of the curriculum. Special care was taken of the revival of native arts and crafts, particularly of the well-known Maori wood-carving. Even the question of the use and study of the Maori language is on the agenda for further reform.[1] Thus instead of aiming at the complete assimilation of Maoris to European ways of life, the present policy is to adapt them to changed conditions combining all the benefits of European democracy with their own cultural and social traditions. As the Reconstruction Committee of the New Zealand Educational Institute stated in 1944: "The aim should be to give to the Native School child an education which will be within the full spirit of the Maori Magna Carta, the Treaty of Waitangi, and which will enable him to take his place in the country as a full citizen with equal opportunities, equal advantages and equal rights to those enjoyed by his *pakeha* brother." [It should be mentioned here that by the Treaty of Waitangi, signed in 1840, the Maoris recognised the sovereignty

---

[1] The Maori language is one of the subjects which may be taken in Matriculation examinations.

of the British Crown and the British Government solemnly promised to respect their lands and their social traditions. Unfortunately it was not always faithfully observed by the white settlers, and led to a long racial war in the sixties of the last century.] From this description of the present situation it seems that the racial problem in education in New Zealand has finally found its satisfactory solution.

Now we pass to two countries where the racial problem is presented in its most acute form and up to the present has baffled the most well-meaning statesmen. These are the Union of South Africa and the United States of America. In each country the racial problem is closely bound up with the history of inter-racial relations during the last three hundred years. The entanglement of races in the Union of South Africa is the result of consecutive waves of immigration and settlement by different racial stocks. The original population was mainly Hottentot and Bushman people quite distinct from the Black Africans of Bantu stock. The invasion of the Bantu tribes, perhaps in the fifteenth century, entirely changed the situation. The original inhabitants were partly exterminated, partly subjugated and intermixed with the Bantu. Only a few groups in the south or in the desert preserved their racial purity. In the seventeenth century the first Europeans, the Dutch, settled at the Cape and gradually extended their settlement towards the interior. They encountered the peaceful Hottentot tribes, and miscegenation between the two races started very early. It produced a new group, the so-called "Coloured" people, to which a strain of Malay blood was added through the importation of Malay labour. Late in the nineteenth century a new immigration wave of East Indians still further increased the difficulties of the racial entanglement. As a result of subsequent waves of immigration the present population of South Africa is divided into four distinct groups: (i) Europeans, Boer and Briton—about two and a half million, (ii) Bantu, many distinct tribes—about eight million, (iii) Coloured people, a racial mixture—about 900,000, and (iv) Indians—about 300,000. With the exception of the Coloured people each racial group is quite distinct in colour, in social habits and in its legal status in the Union. The Coloured people present an intermediary group, the "whitest" members of which are indistinguishable from the Europeans and the darkest members lost in the mass of detribalised and urbanised Natives. They mix both with the whites and with the Natives, and thus apart from a natural increase within the group their numbers are growing through continuous mis-cegenation. No legislation or adverse public opinion can stop this process. The European community is acutely conscious of the situation and endeavours to preserve its racial identity by all possible means. Unfortunately education is also used as means to this end. As a leading educationalist of their country said of them, the South Africans are too humane to deny educational opportunities to the Natives, but they are too human to allow the Natives to use the fruits of their education. Accordingly the organisation of education is divided into four water-tight com-partments. The Europeans have a progressive school system, free and secular, with compulsory attendance for the ages seven to fifteen, whilst the other three groups have school systems inferior in all respects and no compulsory attendance.[1] Public expendi-ture on European schools is three times as much per scholar as in the non-European schools; the buildings, equipment, staffing in European schools in consequence are markedly superior to those in the Native schools. The results of this race discrimination in education are both quantitative and qualitative. Whereas all European children of school age (seven to fifteen) attend free public schools, only 25 per cent of Native children and 58 per cent of Coloured and Indian children of school age are receiving education in either public or private schools. Of the quality of education provided in State-aided schools for Natives, the *Report of the Interdepartmental Committee on Native Education* in 1936 pro-duced this evidence:

(i) The relatively short school life of the Native—estimated liber-ally at an average of less than three years. (ii) The necessarily small progress made during this short period—the majority of pupils not getting beyond Standard I. (iii) The high degree of "overageness" of Native pupils in comparison with European pupils in the same standards—they are from two to three years older on the average. (iv) The marked disparity between the designation of Native and European school standards (a difference in some cases as much as two standards) owing probably to the lesser effectiveness per unit of time of instruction given in Native schools than that in European. (v) The heavy elimination of Native pupils in the later primary and post-primary standards. If these facts are disregarded, one cannot expect the Native school to succeed fully in equipping the vast majority of natives for life—a life which for them is being rapidly disintegrated by economic and cultural contacts [concludes the Report. Or, quoting the Report again] The education of the white child prepares him for life in a dominant society and the education of the black child for a subordinate society.

[1] Compulsory attendance for the Coloured was enacted recently.

The situation in the schools for the Coloured and Indians is much better, but still markedly inferior to that of European schools.

Many white South Africans contend that the deplorable conditions of Native schools are the direct result of the "inferiority" of the black race and their innate inability to assimilate the high standards of European education. These assertions, so convenient to the white ruling minority, are still the subject of animated controversy among the psychologists and anthropologists. All the heavy artillery of scientific research was brought into action with a subconscious desire to justify the "superiority" of the white race. The results of many investigations, on the whole objectively conducted, are inconclusive; they have not proved the innate inferiority of the black race, but neither have they vindicated the claims of some Native leaders that the blacks can assimilate European culture on equal terms with the Europeans, granted similar environment and training. We can but briefly cover the ground, mentioning some of the recent works. M. Laurence Fick in his *The Educability of the South African Native* (1939), after applying intelligence tests to hundreds of white and native children, came to the following conclusions:

> Around the ages of thirteen and fourteen Native children are from four to five years inferior to European children in educability as gauged by the results of intelligence tests. . . . The inferiority of the Native in educability limits considerably the proportion of Natives who can benefit by education of the ordinary type beyond the rudimentary. [And lastly] The inferiority of the Natives occurring in certain tests in which learning or environment conditions are equalised for the Native and European groups does not appear to be of a temporary nature. [He also stated that the] Negroes of America are not comparable in educability with Natives of South Africa. The former owing to an admixture of European blood resemble the Coloureds of South Africa whose intelligence is far superior to that of the Natives of South Africa.

T. A. Jansen van Rensburg in *The Learning Ability of the South African Native* (1938) came to similar conclusions. After having devised special tests eliminating the influence of language, environment and training, he sums up: "It would seem from the foregoing investigation that the South African Native has not the learning ability to be able to compete on equal terms with the average European, except in tasks of an extremely simple nature." Although these authors, and others who worked on similar lines, took great care to eliminate the influence of language, environment and training, it is questionable if any tests can be devised completely independent of these factors. The early family training and the influence of the Bantu language, its structure and vocabulary, are very potent agencies in the formation of the minds of Native children and their elimination is hardly possible. Moreover the undoubted difference in emotional-conative characteristics of the two races may influence adversely the intelligence scores of the Native children when tested by Europeans in European surroundings. These investigations have only confirmed the school statistics and the results of the examinations, but they have not proved the *innate* inferiority of the native mind. S. Biesheuvel in his *African Intelligence* (1943) made a scrupulous investigation of the methods used by previous authors and of the results of their testing. He challenges the applicability of these methods to Native children and especially the conclusions drawn by them from the results. He suggests that Native intelligence may be different in quality from the European and that the present methods of equating the two types of mind are inadequate and favour the European child. The whole controversy is vitiated by wishful thinking and by social-political considerations. Whatever the results and conclusions of psychological tests the naked facts stare you in the face: there is race discrimination in education in South Africa, backed by legislation and almost unanimous public opinion of the white population. It does not at all mean that a just and democratic solution lies in mixing the children of all races in the same schools and trying to make the Natives into Europeans. In the present circumstances in South Africa it would be unjust both to white and black children, but the equalisation of opportunities for both races and the judicious adaptation of school curriculum and methods of instruction to the character and needs of the Native tribes is plainly demanded by the profession of a democratic creed, not to mention Christianity.

The Negro problem in the United States of America is of a quite different character and importance. Whilst in South Africa the white minority is in mortal fear of being swamped and submerged by the increasing majority of the blacks, in America the Negroes form only 10 per cent of the total population and can never dream of dominating American life and institutions. The Negro question is a very acute domestic problem in the States, but it is doubtful whether it is a racial problem. As a matter of fact the so-called "colour line" does not coincide with colour at all. There are "Negroes" as white as the average European and there are "whites" very dark in complexion. It appears that the dividing line is drawn on principles similar to the famous Nazi Nuremberg laws: those who had ancestors, even four generations back, who were slaves are *ipso facto* Negroes; those, even with an undoubted admixture of African blood, who can prove their European ancestry for several generations, were "white." The Americans, it appears, were quite sincerely deceived by the propaganda of the "Nordic myth" and based their immigration laws on the supposed superiority of the Nordic race. This super-stition—we cannot call it otherwise—persists in spite of several objective investigations which have proved that the majority of the "old Americans" were not Nordic at all. Extending this prejudice over the differences between the "whites" and the "non-whites," many Americans believe that any admixture of non-European blood influences adversely the intelligence and moral qualities of the offspring. In the past during the period of slavery the white planters were not so selective in their love affairs; many of them had illegitimate families from their slave concubines, and some of them cared for and educated their mulatto or quadroon offspring. In this way a large group of educated and rather wealthy "Negroes" came into being, which was later augmented by the offspring of the casual relations of soldiers, sailors and many others with "Negro" girls, especially during the Civil War. This group includes "Negroes" of all shades of colour, and the whitest of them "pass" into the white group by thousands. It has also been proved by scientific investi-gation that the Negro characteristics can be bred out after four generations of intermarriages with the whites. Many white Americans have "Negro" blood in their veins without knowing it. In these circumstances to speak about the American "Negro" as a race clearly distinct from the "white" Americans is rather ridiculous. Between the pure black and the pure white there are all shades of colour with imperceptible differences. As all people irrespective of colour are classified as "Negroes" if they cannot prove their pure European descent, the problem of America is not racial in a biological sense, but social. It is the stigma of slavery which is so important in American social relations, and not the colour, intelligence or character of an individual "Negro." The "Negroes" have no cultural, religious, linguistic or any other features which would distinguish them as a group from the rest of Americans; they are all Christians, all speak English or a variation of it, they are all loyal citizens of the United States and officially enjoy the same rights and carry the same burdens in peace and war. And yet in practice they are unequally treated both by public legislation and by public opinion. We must make one reservation in this respect: the legal inequality exists only in the seventeen Southern States, but social inequality is general throughout the States, although in the North in a much milder form.

The adverse opinion of the Negroes as an intellectually and morally inferior group was greatly strengthened by the results of the famous Yerkes intelligence testing of the Army drafts during the first world war. His results showed the "Negro" mean mental age as 10·4 years, whilst the "white" mental mean was 13·1 years, or almost three years' difference in mental ability. At first the adherents of the segregation of the two groups of Americans claimed the results as a scientific justification of their opinions. A more detailed examination of results by individual States, however, showed strange discrepancies: Negroes resident in the North had higher scores than the whites of the South. The scores of eight States were as follows:

MEDIAN SCORES

Southern Whites		Northern Negroes	
Mississippi	41·25	Pennsylvania	42·0
Kentucky	41·50	New York	45·0
Arkansas	41·55	Illinois	47·4
Georgia	42·12	Ohio	49·5

The adherents of racial difference promptly found an explanation of these higher scores: the Northern Negroes are a small selected group with a strong admixture of "white" blood. The Northern Negroes cannot be considered a small group, as more than 20 per cent of the total Negro population, or two and a half million of them, reside in the Northern States. During the decade 1920–30 about 600,000 Southern Negroes migrated to the North. The question whether these migrants were the intellectual élite of the Negroes was decided by a series of special investigations. The school careers of migrants were compared with those of Negroes who remained in the South. The results were not uniform; whereas in some Southern areas the migrants were above the average Negro scholars, in other areas they were decidedly below their schoolfellows who remained in the South. Moreover in New York the comparison of the school achievements with the length of stay in the North showed a very high correlation, which means that the change of environment and better social and educational conditions increased their scores. The present Negro population of New York cannot be distinguished from the rest by intelligence testings; they are equal to the whites. The same can be said about other Northern and Western cities. In Los Angeles, for instance, the average Negro I.Q. is higher than the average I.Q. of the whites. All these investigations point in one direction—the intellectual and social inferiority of the Southern Negro are the direct consequence of slavery reminiscences and unequal treatment in social relations and educational opportunities.

In 1860 perhaps only 5 per cent of the slave population could read and write. When they were emancipated there were no schools for the freedmen and no Negro intelligentsia which could lead them to a new life as equal citizens. All the pioneers of Negro education were the Northern white philanthropists. The well-known Negro institutions—Fisk, Atlanta, Howard and Hampton—were founded by Northern charity in the period 1865–80. The lead was given by General S. C. Armstrong who established the Hampton Institute in Virginia as an agricultural college. His pupil Booker T. Washington, the recognised Negro leader of his time, founded the Tuskegee Institute in Alabama. Guided by the experience of Hampton Institute, Booker Washington considered that the primary need of the emancipated slaves was agricultural and industrial education to raise their social and economic levels. His rival, another Negro leader, Du Bois, insisted, on the contrary, on the academic curriculum of the "white" schools, as he believed that only an identical content of education provided for both groups would equalise their social status. The subsequent development of Negro education has proved that both Negro leaders were right. The Southern Negro needs first of all agricultural and industrial training, because he is mainly occupied on the land and in the factory. On the other hand equality of opportunity in academic education is the only way of attaining social equality. The white administration of the Southern States solidly backed Booker Washington and contended that an academic education was unsuitable to the Negro mentality and contrary to his economic needs. In practice they were very reluctant to build up the Negro school system, as required by the Federal legislation, and the results of their policy are seen in the present situation in the seventeen Southern States. The segregation of the two groups in the educational system is most rigidly enforced, but the administration and supervision is entirely in the hands of the whites. The white directors and inspectors are not interested in the Negro schools, visit them only in exceptional cases, and do not take any steps to improve their conditions. The results of this deliberate policy of neglect are most deplorable. The majority of Negro schools are one-room wooden huts, often dilapidated and lacking the most elementary school equipment. The compulsory attendance is not enforced, the qualifications of the Negro teachers are not strictly supervised, and the salaries are far below the average for the white teachers. A few figures will show the existing inequalities. The attendance in Negro schools represents 84 per cent of the total Negro population of school age, as compared with 91 per cent for the whites in the seventeen Southern States. The average length of term is 167 days for the white schools and only 146 days for Negro schools. Three per cent of Negro pupils attend schools open for ninety days or less. Each Negro teacher has forty-three pupils on the average, whilst the white teacher has only thirty-four. The average salary of a Negro teacher is $450, the average for white teachers $907. The value of school property per pupil is $183 for white schools and only $36 for Negro schools. Though Negroes form 28 per cent of the population in the seventeen Southern States, they receive only 12 per cent of all public expenditure on education. In secondary education the inequality is still more pronounced. The enrolment in Negro High Schools was equivalent to 19 per cent of the Negro pupils of high-school age. In white High Schools it was 55 per cent.[1] We could multiply these comparisons for every aspect of the educational services, but the above statistics will suffice. No wonder that in the general atmosphere of social inferiority these Negro schools produced boys who in the Army drafts could not compete with the product of the white schools. As we have insisted all along, these conditions prevail only in the seventeen Southern States. In the North the Negroes have practically the entire educational system flung open to them without much discrimination. They are often taught in mixed schools and by white teachers; in some cases Negro teachers have white pupils. The District of Columbia presents a compromise between the Southern and Northern policies. It has two identical parallel school systems for the two groups. But the Negro schools are supervised and controlled by a Negro administration, which

[1] All figures for 1936.

forms a branch of the general service. The conditions of service, salaries, qualifications of the teachers, the buildings and the equipment of the two systems are identical. The Federal authorities and public opinion in the North and West are fully aware of the conditions in the South, and quite sincerely wish to extend the educational facilities for the Southern Negroes. Their humanitarian motives are strengthened by economic necessity, as hundreds of thousands of backward Southern Negroes migrate to the North and create new slums in their cities. The political influence of the solid South, however, especially in the Democratic Party, is very strong and compels the Federal authorities to move very cautiously in their reforms.[1]

These examples of racial or quasi-racial problems in education prove their complexity and the difficulty of finding a purely educational solution. The policies of the white rulers are more influenced by political, economic and social considerations than by the results of psychological investigations or the demands of educational principles.

[1] The Recent decision of the Federal Court against segregation of Negroes in Schools is still opposed in the South and has not finally solved the problem. However it had showed the way of inevitable change and actual equality of Negroes.

CHAPTER III

THE LINGUISTIC FACTOR

As we have mentioned, language is one of the symbols of a nation. It is probable that originally each racial stock evolved a different language which expressed the mental character of the tribe and reflected the features of their natural surroundings and activities. All human races possess this tool of expression which distinguishes them from the animals, but not all languages have developed in the same way and various groups of languages have marked differences in their structure, grammar and syntax. The primary causes of this differentiation can only be surmised by modern philologists and for our purposes are irrelevant. The fact remains that each tribe or group of tribes had an original language of its own which suited its environment and its stage of cultural development. Each succeeding generation grew to adulthood through the medium of that language and with it imbibed the tribal experience, tribal interpretation of the world and tribal superstitions and prejudices. Through the language they became members of their tribe and continued tribal traditions. As Fichte, the famous German philosopher, said in his "Speeches to the German Nation" (*Reden an die Deutsche Nation*, 1807): "Language forms men more than it is formed by them." It appears that language is more important in the building up of national character than any other factor. An individual of an alien race may in his early infancy be transplanted from his native soil and through the language of his foster-parents grow up as a member of the foster-nation, sharing their traditions and prejudices quite naturally. The situation would be quite different if a boy of six years old were to be transplanted in the same way. He would have his first impressions of the world and of himself interpreted in his native tongue and the language of his foster-parents would be foreign to him. The longer any child was under the influence of its native tongue the more difficult it would be to grow naturally into the modes of expression and the content of ideas of a foreign language. The names of concrete objects perceived through the senses would indeed present no difficulty; they would either be directly connected with the objects or translated from the mother tongue, the word "noir" or "nero" for instance being substituted for the word "black." There would be no change of meaning to cloud the child's understanding. It is in the world of ideas and relations that we encounter a great difficulty in grasping the precise significance of a foreign word, for in any original language the words denoting ideas and relations were gradually built up from a simile based upon some sense-impression and changed their meanings through a long process of linguistic adaptation. For a child speaking its native tongue it is not difficult to recover the connecting links between the original and the transferred significance of the word. For a child learning a foreign language the second, transferred meaning has to be learnt by heart just as the names of objects of sense-impressions have to be. The child thus loses the intermediate stage closely connecting the idea with sense-impressions and his knowledge of the meaning of the word is only verbal.

This may happen even within the sphere of a single language which through the ages has been subjected to strong foreign influences, as for instance the English language. The English have incorporated into their language thousands of foreign words which have lost their original significance and have become sounds denoting something accepted by common usage. With the words of kindred languages, like Anglo-Saxon or Danish, it is possible to recover the original meaning and thus to preserve the continuity of thought. With the Latin words it is very difficult, and can be achieved solely through the study of the classical Latin. With the borrowed Arabic words we have to rely entirely on the expert. Thus although the word "husband" has lost its original meaning in Anglo-Saxon of "husbanda"—master of the house, it can be easily recovered as the English word "housewife" provides a parallel. But the word "captain," derived from Latin *caput*, "head," has lost its origin, which can be retrieved only by the study of Latin. In the case of a word like "admiral," which is derived from Arabic *amir*, "prince," it is doubtful if any Englishman ever connects the word with its original meaning. Most people would link it with "admirable" or "admire" (Latin *admiror*) which have nothing in common with "admiral." With foreign words denoting ideas and relations it is still more difficult to recover their primary background, and for the majority of people who use them they have become mere sounds with a very vague significance.

If this has happened with the English, who speak their own living language, with an uninterrupted natural growth, more confusion results with people adopting a foreign language as a medium of instruction in the schools. Before entering school the pupils have acquired a proficiency in their mother tongue, have built up a vocabulary covering most of the objects of sense-impressions and their daily activities. At school they have to superimpose on this basis a language of ideas and abstract relations expressed entirely in a foreign medium. Their minds become split into two water-tight compartments—one for ordinary things and actions expressed in their mother tongue, and another for things connected with school subjects and the world of ideas expressed in a foreign language. As a result they are unable to speak of their home affairs in the school language and about learned subjects in their mother tongue. The so-called "Babu mind," so often ridiculed by some colonial administrators, is a direct result of this division of linguistic spheres and has nothing to do with the innate inferiority or superiority of the native mind. The same observations may be made in Europe on European children who were educated under similar conditions. Karl Vossler in his *The Spirit of Language in Civilisation* says:

> Many languages can be studied and acquired, but only that one can be immediately experienced which was used at the time at which one worked one's way from the state of an infant to that of a member of a language community. The concept of a national language as an experienced language, as opposed to a foreign language which has been learnt, rests on the natural fact that this ascent occurs only once in the lifetime of each person.

What happens with an individual may happen with a whole tribe or even a nation. History gives us examples when whole nations have adopted a foreign language as their medium of intercourse and thus made a break in their natural development. When a nation, possessing a culture and language of its own, is conquered by an alien nation three possible results may ensue. In the first case the conquerors may represent an inferior civilisation and a language less developed than the conquered. Settling among the native population the conquerors adopt their language and in a few generations are assimilated to the native stock, forming its ruling class. This happened, for instance, to the Northmen, who conquered Normandy in France and Sicily in Italy; they soon became Frenchmen and Italians respectively. It also happened to the Turkish tribe of the Bulgars, who conquered the Balkan Slavs and rapidly became Slavs themselves. In the second case the conquerors represent the same stage of cultural and linguistic evolution, and then a real fusion of the two languages results, as happened in England with the Norman-French and the Anglo-Saxon. In both cases there is no interruption of natural growth; the linguistic changes are accelerated by foreign influences but the native foundation remains intact.

In the third case the conquerors may represent a superior civilisation and speak a language far advanced in comparison with the native speech. If their numbers are considerable and they keep contact with their own country, the conquerors in this case will assimilate the native stock and impose their language upon them. Only in this last case is the natural growth of the mental structure of the conquered nation interrupted by a sudden jump over the intermediate stages of linguistic development. If the two nations are far apart in their cultures the new nation emerging from the mixture of the two may develop a split national consciousness similar to the "Babu mind" of an individual. In that case the superior culture of the conquerors and their "ideological" vocabulary will be adopted by the conquered without the immediate experience necessary for a complete integration of the new language with everyday life and sense-impressions. Fichte in his *Speeches* gave a correct analysis of the situation, but his application of this theory to the modern Latin nations of France, Italy and Spain appears to be exaggerated. It is a fact that the Romans conquered the Celtic populations of these countries and the natives adopted Latin as their national medium, abandoning their Celtic languages. But as both Latin and Celtic languages belong to the same linguistic family, and the cultural gulf between the Romans and the Celts was not very wide, it could be bridged by several centuries of common life without disrupting the mental integrity of the Celts.

The great stability and uniformity of the French language in distinction to the dialect fluidity of the German was mistaken by Fichte for a sign of decadence and inability for spontaneous growth. As a matter of fact it is the result of conscious efforts by the French Government to that end. Richelieu founded the Académie Française for that purpose, and the revolutionary National Assembly of 1790 continued his policy when they conceived a plan of eradicating all provincial differences and published an appeal to all old provinces "to banish all dialects, the last vestiges of feudalism and monuments of slavery." Since then the French Academy has stood on guard over the purity of the French language and given it a stability impossible in Germany, where every province is proud of its dialect and consciously displays its peculiarities. With the sole exception of the Bretons, who led a semi-isolated life on their peninsula, the French descendants of the original Celts have completely forgotten the language of their ancestors, and there is no possibility of a Celtic revival in France, except in Brittany. To stage a renaissance of native culture is possible only in those countries or provinces where the old speech still lingers in rural communities as a living language as in Brittany or in the *Gaeltacht* of Ireland. Another striking example is provided by the polyglot Jews, who preserved Hebrew in their religious ceremonies and thus were able to recover it as their national language in settlements in Palestine. The renaissance of the Slavonic languages in the nineteenth century falls into another category, as the Czechs, the Yugoslavs and the Ukrainians never ceased to use their national languages in their daily life. These revivals of national languages were closely connected with the nationalist movements of the nineteenth and twentieth centuries, and we shall return to this aspect of the linguistic factor in the chapter on Nationalism.

From this short introduction it is evident how closely the influence of language is connected with educational problems, and why it presents the main focus of all educational reforms and plans in many countries. But before we analyse the actual situation in various countries we should mention the main families of languages and the chief differences between them. Philologists distinguish agglutinative languages, flexional languages and isolating languages. In agglutinative languages two significant words are joined together in a new word, which combines the meaning of the two, whilst they retain their own. All kinds of affixes are used, but there is no internal change in the roots. The English word she-cat represents the principle. To this group belong Finnish, Estonian, and Hungarian, and all the Turkish languages.[1] In isolating languages also the roots are unchanged but they are not combined in new words. It is the order of the words that gives new shades of meaning. This group is represented by the Chinese language. The third group, the flexional languages, are the most numerous and most developed. To this group belong the two great linguistic families: the Indo-European (sometimes wrongly called Aryan [2]) and the Semitic languages.

---

[1] The Bantu and Sudanic languages of Africa are also agglutinative or isolating.

[2] "Aryan" can be used only in relation to Persian and Indian ancient and modern languages.

Flexional languages use not only all kinds of affixes (prefixes, suffixes and infixes), but also change the roots to differentiate the meaning of the word and to adapt it to the preceding or the following word. Some philologists consider that flexional languages are the most suitable for the expression of human thoughts, although we must not disregard the great achievements of an isolating language like the Chinese. The Indo-European languages include: Greek, Latin with all its modern derivatives, the Celtic languages, the Teutonic or Germanic languages, the Slavonic and Baltic languages, Sanskrit with all its modern Indian derivatives, Zend and Persian, and the Armenian and Albanian languages. The Semitic group of flexional languages is best represented by Hebrew and Arabic. Maltese also belongs to the Semitic group. These languages have a distinctive feature of their own. They use affixes like the Indo-European languages, but they do not change the consonants of the roots, confining the change to the vowels. From this short description it is evident that, whilst learning a foreign language of the same group is comparatively easy, to learn a language of another main type is very difficult, and to become truly bilingual requires long and laborious study.[1]

Thus the problem of bilingualism has quite different aspects in Europe, where the Europeans have to learn a kindred language, and in Asia or Africa, where the natives have to learn a language of another type. When a Turk, a Bantu or a Chinese studies a European language imperfectly he is apt to apply the structure of his language to the European vocabulary, and consequently dismisses the inflections and uses only the roots. The so-called "pidgin English," spoken in the Oriental ports, is a good example. It also explains the remarkable fact that "pidgin English" and "pidgin French" are so alike, because deprived of their inflexions and characteristic pronunciation the roots of these two European languages are very similar. Bearing in mind this difference we can approach the problem of bilingualism in various countries. In each country the necessity of speaking two languages was the result of historical causes, peculiar to each case. In some instances two or more linguistic groups through historical and geographical causes have formed one nation without either language assimilating the other, or the two languages fusing into a new one. In such a country, both languages acquire national status and the inhabitants are required both by the demands of daily life

[1] See four articles on language problems in the *Year Book of Education*, 1949.

and by State legislation to learn both. Such is the situation in Belgium, South Africa, and partly in Switzerland. In other countries minority groups, settled in compact communities, preserve their linguistic identity and have to learn the language of the majority, which is the recognised national language of the whole country. Such is the position of the Welsh-speaking population of Wales, and such was the situation in Ireland before its separation from Great Britain. The same is the position of the French Canadians in Canada. The third case is represented by large federations of many linguistic groups which use their languages in their autonomous areas, but recognise as federal one language which is introduced in all schools by law as the second compulsory language. Such was the old Austro-Hungarian Empire, and such is the present Union of Soviet Socialist Republics. In all these cases large sections of the population are bilingual, and their school-problems are different from those of unilingual countries. China presents an exceptional linguistic difficulty as she has a national written language which is pronounced in mutually incomprehensible ways in the North and the South. Norway has a difficulty of her own as she has two officially recognised national languages, which have branched off from the same origin but are spoken respectively in towns and in the rural districts. The linguistic problem of India is so complex and so controversial that it would require a separate book for adequate discussion. We shall now describe the situation in each country.

In Belgium two nationalities, the Flemings and the Walloons, the first speaking a language almost identical with Dutch and the second speaking a French dialect, were brought together in one State by a historical accident. After the Napoleonic wars Belgium was united with Holland as it had been united centuries before. Since the French Revolution the Belgians have been divided into secularist Liberals, mostly Walloons, and the Roman Catholic party, mostly Flemings. King William of the United Low Countries introduced a secular school system with the Dutch language as the medium of instruction. By doing this he alienated both Belgian groups. The Flemings accepted Dutch as a school-language, but strongly protested against secularism. The Walloons accepted secularism but violently objected to the abolition of French as the school medium. The two Belgian parties came together, revolted against Dutch rule in 1830 and declared Belgium an independent state. In order to agree among themselves the Catholic Flemings accepted French in the schools and the Liberal Walloons accepted the Catholic denominational character of instruction. This compromise could not last for long, and the Flemings demanded Flemish schools after a few decades of internal peace. The Walloons had to give way, and in 1883 Flemish was introduced into primary schools. The German occupation of 1914-18 forced the development. The Germans sided with the Flemings and introduced Flemish in the University of Ghent. When Belgium was liberated in 1918 it was impossible to return to the pre-war conditions, and Flemish was officially recognised as the second State language. The Belgian Government tried to introduce a bilingual system of education throughout the country, but met with strong opposition from both sides. The Flemings agreed to learn French, but only as a foreign language, while the Walloons flatly declined to learn Flemish at all. The final settlement was achieved on regional lines by the law of July 14th, 1932. The Walloon communities employ French in the schools and the Fleming communities Flemish. Only Brussels, the capital, and some border communities with mixed population have a bilingual school system. As a result most of the Flemings speak both languages fluently, whilst most of the Walloons have a very deficient knowledge of Flemish. Thus the bilingual system of education is only partially successful and depends entirely upon the future of Belgium as an independent state. If she survives this internal tension bilingualism will become the rule throughout the country, but if the Flemings join Holland and the Walloons France, then both groups will become unilingual again.

In the Union of South Africa the situation is not unlike that of Belgium. The white population consists also of two linguistic groups—the English-speaking and the Afrikaans-speaking. As in Belgium there are areas where one language predominates, English in Natal, Afrikaans in the Orange Free State, and as in Belgium there are great urban centres where the population is mixed and actually bilingual. As in Belgium the Flemings had to struggle for the recognition of their mother tongue as the second State language, so had the Boers to defend their speech against the domination of the English language. Even the attitude of both Flemings and Boers to the more advanced culture of Holland and High-Dutch with its great literature is similar. But the historical background is different, and it is this difference which imparted to Afrikaans nationalism a certain bitterness against the English absent in the Flemish movement in their relations to the French. When Great Britain annexed Cape

Colony in 1806 its white population, formed by Dutch, French and German Puritan colonists, had evolved its own language, Afrikaans, and possessed a Dutch public school system. The English administration very soon decided against the continuation of Dutch schools with the purpose of making the whole white population English-speaking. In 1822 a law was enacted forbidding the use of any language other than English in the schools of Cape Colony. In order to speed up the assimilation of the Boers Scottish Presbyterian ministers were appointed to all vacancies in the Dutch Reformed Church. The Boers were compelled to attend English schools, as there were no others, and to listen to Sunday sermons delivered in English by their Scottish ministers. But the policy did not bring the desired results; many Scottish ministers learned Afrikaans and started preaching in the language of the Boers. Moreover many Boers refrained from sending their children to English schools and taught them to read their Dutch Bibles at home. The enforcement of the English language was one of the contributory causes of the Great Trek in 1836, by which the Boers established two independent republics beyond the frontiers of Cape Colony. As the Boers had neither Afrikaans teachers nor Afrikaans textbooks, they imported Dutch teachers from Holland and established their new school systems in High-Dutch. Thus in both parts of South Africa the Afrikaans-speaking children were instructed through a foreign medium, although High-Dutch was more familiar to them since they read the Bible in that language. The situation was unsatisfactory, and in 1875 an Afrikaans Language Movement was started with a view to introducing it in the schools. But the Boers had to wait another forty years for the realisation of their aims. After the Boer War of 1899–1902 the British Government enforced an English school system throughout South Africa, but with the same results as a hundred years before. The Boers clung to their language and refused to be assimilated. The Act constituting the Union of South Africa of 1910 recognised the defeat of the old policy and formally declared the linguistic equality of High-Dutch with English. Afrikaans was recognised as the medium of instruction for Afrikaans-speaking children only in 1914. Thus the present bilingual school system came into being. When the Nationalist Party, led by General Hertzog, came into power in 1924, proficiency in both languages was made an official condition of any appointment in the civil service or in the school system. The practice of the four provinces varies. In Natal the percentage of Afrikaans-speaking children is very small and as a rule schools use English throughout, teaching Afrikaans as a second language. In the remaining three provinces, Cape, Transvaal and Orange Free State, the mixed character of the white community excluded the possibility of establishing territorially separated English and Afrikaans school systems. The solution, therefore, had to be based on the individual child rather than on some unit of local self-government. The principle of home speech was accepted as guidance, according to which each child receives instruction through the medium of its own language. But whereas in Natal Afrikaans is not compulsory for the English-speaking children, in the other provinces both languages are compulsory for all children, Briton or Boer. Thus some schools use English, some Afrikaans and some are bilingual. For the whole Union about 37 per cent of schools are English, about 53 per cent Afrikaans and only 10 per cent are bilingual. The results are similar to those in Belgium: all Boers learn to speak English fluently, but many Britons, especially in Natal, still know Afrikaans imperfectly. But the necessity of proficiency in both languages demanded by Union legislation, and the unrestricted social intercourse and frequent intermarriage, will soon lead to universal bilingualism in all provinces, as the possibility of secession of Natal from the Union becomes more impracticable with every year. Whether the two languages will ever merge into a new national language is questionable, as the intimate connection of South Africa with other members of the British Commonwealth of Nations demands an adequate knowledge of English.

Switzerland also belongs to the group of countries where more than one national language is officially recognised. Her geographical position in the centre where three great cultures meet on neutral ground promoted her policy of linguistic equality and tolerance. The magnificent background of Alpine mountains and valleys, shared by all linguistic groups in common, was the strongest tie of unity and national pride. In spite of being adjacent to great States speaking the same languages, the French-, German- and Italian-speaking Swiss are deeply attached to their little country and would resist to the last any attempt of their powerful neighbours to tear them asunder. In that respect they are much more solidly united into a nation than the Flemings and Walloons in Belgium, or Boer and Briton in South Africa. Quite a number of Flemings and Walloons look across the frontiers to Holland and France for inspiration, and the English-speaking South Africans even now speak of England as their "home." The Swiss, although acknowledging the language community with their great neighbours, never wish to identify themselves with them, and indignantly repudiate being called "Frenchmen," "Germans" or "Italians." They are Swiss, although there is no Swiss national language. (The so-called "Schwyzerdeutsch" is a German dialect.) In the field of education the Swiss Confederation is decentralised, and each of the twenty-five cantons has its own educational system. Accordingly the French cantons use French as their medium throughout, the German cantons German, and canton Ticino Italian. It is only recently that the language of the fourth linguistic group— Roumansch—was officially recognised as the fourth national language of Switzerland. As the Roumansch Swiss live in small enclaves surrounded by German-speaking Swiss, their children attend the German schools, although in the first years of the primary schools Roumansch is also used. With this exception the Swiss schools are unilingual and the widespread bilingualism is the result of economic and social intercourse rather than school instruction. Most of the educated Swiss speak at least two of their national languages, and the members of the Roumansch group very often speak all four with the addition of English, as their canton (Grisons) is a popular winter resort for English and American tourists. In all these countries, Belgium, South Africa and Switzerland, none of the linguistic groups can be properly called a "national minority," as each has absolute equality of status with the majority group and its language is used by the State side by side with the language of the majority. Different conditions prevail in Canada, Wales and Eire.

As is well known, Canada was originally settled by the French. When conquered by Britain in 1760 French Quebec had a population of 60,000, with an established system of government and legislation and a network of schools organised and administered by the Roman Catholic Church. The British régime did not alter the situation in Quebec and promised to respect the language and religion of the French population. After the secession of America thousands of "Loyalists" crossed the frontier into British Canada and settled in Upper Canada and the Maritime Provinces. The flow of emigrants from Great Britain strengthened the English-speaking population, which gradually outnumbered the French Canadians. It is remarkable that the latter without any influx of French emigrants managed to maintain their ground solely by natural increase. The original 60,000 which Britain inherited from France have increased to three and a half million in Canada plus about a million who crossed the frontier and settled in the U.S.A. They maintained their ground in cultural matters as well; they are all Catholics and speak French, although most of them can speak English also. This is largely due to the tolerant British policy and legal recognition of their linguistic and religious rights. The federation of Upper and Lower Canada in 1867 officially recognised French as the second national language of Canada for all Federal purposes, whilst Quebec recognised English as the second official language of the province. It must be added that the eight English-speaking provinces do not recognise French as the second language; the recognition is strictly limited to Federal purposes. Section 93 of the Federal Constitution protects the rights of Catholics to separate schools in the English-speaking provinces, which are Protestant, but does not mention the language of instruction. As a result eight provinces have English school systems, and when the French Canadians cross the borders of Quebec they can have their separate Catholic schools, but in English. Manitoba was the only English-speaking province which tried to introduce the principle of home speech as the school medium in her system. The French Canadians had French schools in Manitoba for a few years. This experiment was abandoned by the province in 1916, as all new immigrants, Poles, Ukrainians, Germans and others, started to create school systems in their own languages and the process of their assimilation was considerably delayed. Since 1916 English has been the only medium of instruction in all eight English-speaking provinces. Quebec alone has a French system, but had to concede the English-speaking minority the right to build up a separate school system of their own. At first the dividing line was strictly denominational—all Catholics attended French schools, all "Protestants" (including Jews, Orthodox and non-believers) attended English schools. Lately, however, the large number of English-speaking Catholics have been allowed to have Catholic schools in English. Thus the problem of bilingual instruction is actually absent even in Quebec, since the second language is taught as a foreign language. As a result most of the French Canadians speak English well because of economic and political necessity, but the English-speaking Canadians seldom speak French.

Although Eire is an independent country and the Irish people cannot be considered a national minority in any sense, the historical circumstances of her union with England and Scotland for centuries placed her in a position of a minority, and her linguistic problem belongs to this group. On the eve of the Reformation Ireland did not possess a national school system. The few schools which existed were small classes in some monasteries and convents which employed English in the study of Latin. The town population of the Pale and the aristocracy spoke English, the peasantry in the country continued to speak their native Gaelic tongue. By the Supremacy Act of 1537 the Catholic Church was deprived of its lands and property and the basis of the new school system was laid in the "Act for the English order, habit and language" of the same year. By it every Church of Ireland incumbent was obliged "to endeavour to learn, instruct and teach the English tongue to all and every being under his rule" with the definite purpose of making the Irish nation English-speaking. During the first period of the Reformation progress was slow, and many of the clergy of the Reformed Church were unable to officiate in English. Gradually, however, these parish schools and the later established diocesan and royal schools disseminated the knowledge of English beyond the boundaries of the towns into the rural districts. The opposition of the Irish population was concentrated on the religious issue, and even the Irish colleges abroad did not include the native Irish language in their curriculum. With their eyes entirely centred on the preservation of their faith the Irish did not notice the increasing growth of the English-speaking minority until the whole nation had become English-speaking. The native speech survived in small rural enclaves, was divided into three dialects, and lost its importance as a national language. Only a few of the illegal "hedge schools" in the eighteenth century still endeavoured to teach Irish to their pupils. After the emancipation of the Catholics in 1830 the religious Orders took the education of the whole nation under their control and established hundreds of schools. But all these Catholic schools used English as the medium of instruction. The Catholic Church of this period looked with disfavour on the possible revival of Irish. The first pioneers of the Gaelic renaissance were Protestants. At first the Gaelic League was confined to a few intellectual enthusiasts whose activities were hardly noticed by the mass of the people. But in 1893 the Gaelic League, under the leadership of Dr. Douglas

Hyde, came into the open and launched a campaign for the revival of Irish. Dr. Hyde was later elected the first President of the Irish Free State. The declared policy was to make the Gaelic speech and its expression in literature, music and design the leading instrument of thought and instruction in all schools. From 1908 to 1913 many bilingual schools were opened in the *Gaeltacht*, the Gaelic-speaking enclaves, and many schools in the towns introduced Irish as a subject. The British Government was on the whole tolerant towards the movement and in 1914 there were 215 bilingual schools, besides which 1,400 schools taught Irish as a subject. The new national party of Sinn Fein included the aims of the Gaelic League in their political programme, having accepted the idea of Fichte, that original culture can prosper only on the basis of a native language congenial to the psychology of the people. They won the overwhelming support of the population in Southern Ireland, and since the establishment of the Irish Free State in 1920 have endeavoured to implement their aims by legislation. The Catholic Church has changed its previous negative attitude and now wholeheartedly supports the Gaelic policy of Eire's Government. The compulsory teaching of Irish as a school subject is gradually giving place to teaching all subjects through Irish. Northern Ireland has not followed the policy of Eire and is determined to remain English-speaking. In these circumstances Eire is surrounded on three sides by English-speaking peoples—America, Great Britain and Northern Ireland—and can hardly dispense with the teaching of English. Irishmen because of their knowledge of English and their official connection with the British Commonwealth can move freely within the English-speaking world and can get employment outside the narrow borders of Eire. During the war hundreds of thousands of Southern Irish either joined the British Army or worked in war industries and on the land outside Eire. Because of these economic and social ties it is improbable that citizens of Eire will ever become unilingual Gaelic speakers. The most the Government of Eire can hope is to make the population bilingual. It appears that this limited aim is being successfully realised. Whether it will lead to a renaissance of original Irish culture distinct from that of the English-speaking countries is difficult to predict. Until now most Irish writers and most of the Irish press have used English as their medium and Irish plays are performed in English.

As a third case of a linguistic minority with a problem of

bilingualism we shall take Wales. Unlike their Gaelic cousins of Ireland and Scotland who, with few exceptions, became English-speaking, the Welsh population has preserved its language as a living medium throughout the centuries of English domination. A great rôle in this survival was played by annual festivals and competitions of bards known as *Eisteddfodau*. These are meetings of Welsh-speaking poets and singers from all parts of Wales where national prizes are awarded to the best examples of national Welsh literature and music. They are most popular gatherings to which many English visitors are attracted by the excellency of Welsh choir singing. While this institution is preserved there is no danger of the Welsh language becoming extinct. With the increasing English immigration, especially into the mining districts, the percentage of the Welsh-speaking population is diminishing, but the absolute number remains constant. In 1931 only 37 per cent of the total population of Wales could speak Welsh, while in 1901 it was 50 per cent. This relative fall is mostly due to English immigration, but there is no doubt that some part of the natural increase of the Welsh population has changed its speech for English. In these circumstances English is permanently the second or the first language of Wales and the school system has to be bilingual. The present practice follows the recommendations of the Departmental Committee on "Welsh in Education and Life" that as a rule the home speech should be followed in the school.

(1) In Infants' Schools, the language of the hearth, whether English or Welsh, be the medium of instruction, and no second language be introduced at this stage. (2) In schools for older scholars (a) where the population is predominantly Welsh-speaking, Welsh as a first language be used as the medium of instruction and English be taught as a second language. (b) where there is a fairly strong proportion of Welsh-speakers in a district the children be divided on the only natural basis, that of home language. (c) where English predominates English as a first language be used as the medium of instruction, and Welsh be taught as a second language.

This policy protects the Welsh-speakers from being swamped by English immigrants. As Wales has its own Education Department within the Ministry of Education and its own University, both of which promote Welsh culture and language, it appears that their future is assured. The demand by some extreme nationalists for home rule for Wales is impracticable, as the majority of voters are English-speaking.

It is interesting to observe the different approach to the problem of bilingualism in countries of Puritan and of Catholic traditions. South Africa and Wales, both predominantly Calvinist, approach it from the viewpoint of an individual child, for whom it is easier and more natural to learn through the medium of his home speech. Quebec and Eire approach the problem from the viewpoint of the community as a whole, often disregarding the home speech of an individual child. For Quebec the French language is important more as the means of preserving the Catholic tradition than as the natural speech of the children. They would sooner lose their Protestant compatriots as Frenchmen than allow French-speaking Protestant schools. In Ireland the popular decision to recover the national Gaelic language overrules the needs of most children for whom Irish is a foreign language. We shall return to this difference between religious traditions in separate chapters devoted to them.

The third case of a federation of many linguistic groups in one state is now represented only by the Union of Soviet Socialist Republics. Before 1918 Austria-Hungary was a typical case of such a federation, but after the first world war the Hapsburg Empire was broken up into its component parts, which now have become more or less unilingual. The U.S.S.R. is a multilingual federation in which as many as 180 languages and dialects are used in daily speech. The old Russian Empire was composed of many originally independent national units which were united under the sceptre of the Romanovs, partly voluntarily, partly by conquest. The Emperor of Russia was also officially King of Poland, Grand Duke of Finland, Grand Duke of Curland, King of Georgia, Khan of Tartary, etc., which clearly showed the composite character of the Empire. But although all the nations of the Empire were free to use their languages and even to establish private schools in their mother tongues, the whole public system of education maintained by central and local authorities was in Russian. Even the two lesser branches of the Russian nation, the Ukrainians and the White Russians, were not allowed to establish public schools using their own languages. Russian was the only official language throughout the Empire, with the sole exception of Finland. After the Revolution of 1905 the nationalities quite definitely demanded schools in their native tongues, but the Government refused to make a concession in this respect. The Revolution of 1917 led to the break-up of the old Empire. Poland, Finland, the Ukraine, Georgia, Armenia,

Lithuania, Estonia and Latvia seceded from Great Russia and declared themselves independent States. Gradually this centrifugal movement has spent itself and the necessity of consolidation has become apparent. But the fundamental principles of the new giant State had to be recast in a new mould. The Soviet Government recognised it from the very start. On November 3rd, 1917, the new Government issued a declaration of rights of nationalities, proclaiming the equality of all races, creeds and languages. The Third Congress of Soviets declared in January 1918 that "the Russian Soviet Republic is instituted on the basis of free union of free nations as a federation of Soviet national Republics." This declaration was accepted as the basic principle on which the later U.S.S.R. was built. One by one the independent Ukraine, Georgia, Armenia, Azerbaidzhan, Estonia, Latvia and Lithuania became the members of the U.S.S.R. and some other territories were given the full status of a Union Republic. At present the U.S.S.R. consists of sixteen national members of the federation: (1) Russia, (2) the Ukraine, (3) White Russia, (4) Georgia, (5) Armenia, (6) Azerbaidzhan, (7) Uzbekistan, (8) Turkmenistan, (9) Tadzhikistan, (10) Kazakhstan, (11) Kirghizstan, (12) Estonia, (13) Latvia, (14) Lithuania, (15) Finno-Karelia and (16) Moldavia. It is quite probable that in the near future the number of the federated Republics will be augmented by the adhesion of other Slav countries. In all the sixteen Union Republics the national language of the people is used as the official medium of instruction in all stages of education and as legal medium in all public institutions. But the Russian language, as the language of the Federation, is compulsory as a school subject throughout the Union. This federal structure of the Union has solved the linguistic problem of the sixteen largest national groups; for the smaller nationalities and tribes additional legislation was necessary. Accordingly smaller nationalities received the status of autonomous Republics within the territory of the sixteen members of the Union, and the dispersed small national and tribal groups were granted the right of using their mother tongue in their schools. The principle of equality of all linguistic groups within the Union, however, could not be realised at once. Many small tribes and national groups were at different stages of cultural evolution; some of them had no alphabet, no literary tradition and no intelligentsia. The transition to a national school system had to be gradual.

The Moscow Commissariat of Public Instruction issued the

guiding principles as early as April 27th, 1927. All tribal and national groups are divided into four categories. To the first belong those small and dispersed tribes which have no alphabet and no national culture. For them the Academy of Sciences appointed special Commissions to study their languages, to create an alphabet and a grammar and to write text-books. Until that task was completed these groups were taught through the medium of Russian. To the second category belong those small nationalities which also have no alphabet and no national culture, but which live together in compact communities and use their native language in their daily life. From the start these groups were taught in their mother tongues in the primary schools, but had to use Russian in secondary and higher institutions. The Academy of Sciences has completed its work for these nationalities, and as fast as the native teaching personnel has been trained the use of the native medium has been extended. The third category is formed by those larger nationalities or communities of foreign nations which have their own alphabet and intelligentsia. These groups have their own primary and secondary schools, including technical schools, but for higher academic education have to attend Russian or other Union Republican Universities. Special chairs of their languages are established in the adjacent Universities. The fourth and last group consists of those large nationalities which inhabit a compact territory and have their own culture and historical tradition. They have the whole educational system, including Universities, in their own language. The legislation and actual policy in building up national educational systems closely followed these principles. The results are highly instructive. Whereas in the old Russian Empire the non-Russian nationalities were mostly illiterate and had a very imperfect knowledge of the Russian language and literature, now the vast majority of non-Russian citizens of the U.S.S.R. have been educated in schools through the medium of their mother tongue and in addition can speak Russian and enjoy the great treasures of Russian literature.

Especially great change is noticeable in the predominantly Moslem Republics of Azerbaidzhan, Turkmenistan, Uzbekistan, Tadzhikistan, Kirghizstan and Kazakhstan, as well as in the Tatar Autonomous Republics within the R.S.F.S.R. (Russia proper). The Moslems of Russia, numbering about thirty million, used the Arabic script in their maktabs and medresses before the Revolution. This script was not well adapted to the

Turkish-Tatar languages, agglutinative in their structure and using vowels in a different way from Arabic. The Turkish-speaking Soviet leaders very soon discovered that the Arabic script was an obstacle to mass education. On their advice the Soviet Government initiated in 1922 a movement for the adoption of the modified Latin alphabet for all Turkish languages. In 1926 this step was decided on in Baku by the First Turko-Tatar Congress. Since then illiteracy among the Moslem population is gradually disappearing. The establishment of national universities, theatres and Press led to a remarkable renaissance of all vernaculars. All the classics of all the languages were dug out of the archives and republished in millions of copies. Russian classics were translated into most of the languages of the Union, and their combined influence produced a rich modern literature in many languages which either had been half-moribund for centuries or had never had any literature. Even foreign classics, Shakespeare for instance, have been translated into many languages and a visitor to Tashkent can attend a performance of *Hamlet* in Uzbek! Only one institution still uses Russian exclusively for all official purposes—the Red Army. On the parade ground and in battle all orders are issued in Russian irrespective of the national composition of the units. But in the barracks and in their free time both the officers and men use their own languages. It is remarkable that this linguistic revival, sponsored by the Government, did not affect the intense loyalty of all nationalities to the Federation as a whole. We shall discuss this result in a special chapter on education in the U.S.S.R.

India presents a problem very similar to that of the U.S.S.R. The Soviet Union is inhabited by three distinct races—white, brown and yellow, by adherents of four great religious traditions —Christian, Moslem, Judaistic and Buddhist, by nationalities speaking many languages belonging to distinct linguistic groups and socially and culturally in different stages of evolution. So is India; it is not a nation or a country in a European sense, it is a continent like the U.S.S.R., inhabited by different races, by Moslems, Hindus and Christians, not to mention other religious communities, by linguistic groups speaking languages as far apart as those of the U.S.S.R. But there is one fundamental difference: whereas in the U.S.S.R. the federal language, Russian, is the home speech of 57 per cent of the total population of the Union, in India the federal language—English—is spoken at home by an insignificant minority. If we add the Ukrainians and the White

Russians, whose languages are very akin to Russian, the percentage will be increased to 76. In these circumstances the Soviet solution of the linguistic problem was comparatively easy. In India on the contrary the English language can never become the language of the masses and can never be acquired by an average Indian with the same perfection as Russian is acquired by Georgians or Tatars, who hear it every day in the streets, in the Army and in Party gatherings. Whether the introduction of English as the medium of instruction by Macaulay in 1835 was a stroke of genius or the greatest mistake ever made by the British is still debatable, but it is clear from the documents that it was not meant as a permanent feature of the Indian educational system. If English has become a permanent feature for the last hundred years, the Indians are as much to blame for it as the British. They did not promote their mother tongues wholeheartedly, and on many occasions even protested against the introduction of vernaculars as the medium of instruction. Another great obstacle to the solution of the linguistic entanglement in India is the absence of a language which could replace English for Federal purposes. Since the separation of India and Pakistan, both Republics officially adopted national languages, Hindi for India and Urdu for Pakistan, whilst retaining English for legal purposes. It appears that any possible solution will have to follow the principles of Soviet legislation and practice. Each of the provinces will have to build up the whole school system in its own vernacular and for Federal purposes all provinces will have to choose some language by mutual agreement. We can only touch on the Indian problem in this book as an analogy to that of the U.S.S.R.

In conclusion we shall mention two linguistic problems which are unique in their character and are the result of exceptional circumstances. These are the problems of Norway and China. Strange to say, Norway has two national languages, which are both Norwegian. For four centuries Norway was united with Denmark and Danish was used in schools, in church and in law courts. It soon became the common speech of the urban population, although the Norwegian pronunciation was slightly different from the pure Danish. The rural districts were not affected by the diffusion of Danish in the towns and continued to speak native dialects derived from the old Norse, akin to the language of Iceland. After the separation of Norway from Denmark and its union with Sweden in 1814 the country speech or Landsmaal found literary expression in the works of Ivar Aasen and other poets and became a rival as the national language to the Riksmaal or urban Dano-Norwegian. The two languages are so similar that they are mutually comprehensible. The present legislation recognises both languages as national and the local authorities decide which of the two should be used in their schools. The general principle is to use as the medium of instruction the home speech of children. However, this bilingualism, it seems, is only a temporary problem. Both languages are converging to a common denominator which will become a universally accepted national language in the not far distant future.

China, on the other hand, presents a peculiar linguistic problem absent anywhere else. The Chinese language belongs to a monosyllabic isolating group and the number of monosyllables is naturally very limited; thus the Peking dialect has only about 400. To express all the shades of meaning to cover the needs of a developed civilisation the same syllable has to be used for many different purposes. For instance, the syllable "li" has about 120 meanings. In these circumstances a phonetic script would be highly ambiguous and if read aloud could be easily misunderstood. To eliminate such misunderstanding the Chinese invented a pictographic and ideographic script in which each meaning has a separate symbol.[1] The script was invented about four thousand years ago, and during this time the total number of symbols has grown to about 23,000, of which many had originally shared the same sound. These symbols with slight modifications have remained unchanged until now, whilst the spoken language has followed the laws of linguistic evolution and has split into many dialects. The most important are the Southern or Cantonese and the Northern or Pekingese dialects, which are both spoken by many millions of Chinese. They have diverged so far from the original roots that they are mutually incomprehensible and should be considered as two different languages. The original pronunciation of the written symbols is largely lost and the written language has parted company with everyday speech. Educated Chinese whether from Canton or Peking can read the ideographic script with ease, and can even correspond with each other, but they cannot converse or read their letters aloud, as they will not then understand each other. Even if both Chinese are members of the same community it is only the reader of the

---

[1] The original ideographs and pictographs have developed in course of time into "logographs," i.e. the symbols represent now "words," and not "ideas."

text who will know the meaning exactly; the listener has to guess which of the many meanings the particular sound represents in the context. The written language thus has become a silent medium and some of the symbols have no sound attached to them. Moreover to learn by heart 23,000 symbols is a prodigious feat of memory and requires laborious study for many years. It is evident that, if unreformed, the written language can never become the language of the masses—400 millions. After the Revolution of 1912 the University of Peking started a movement for the use of *Pai Hua*, the spoken Northern dialect, in the schools. In 1920 the Ministry of Education introduced it by order into all schools of China. Under the name *Kuo Yü* it was officially declared the national language of China. This order has not solved the problem, as the Kuo Yü is based on the Mandarin dialect spoken in Peking, and is incomprehensible in the South. The Mass Education Movement in China, started by James Yen, tried to simplify the written language by selecting one thousand symbols mostly used in Pai Hua. With this so-called "Foundation Character System" the Chinese teachers went to the masses and achieved notable success in combating illiteracy among the adults in the rural districts. However, all these reforms of the written language can hardly be considered as a final and satisfactory solution. The following difficulties still remain: (1) the literate Chinese farmer has to remember by heart one thousand characters, which can hardly promote universal literacy; (2) the Pai Hua reader cannot read the classical literature in the original, as the thousand selected symbols do not cover all the 23,000 meanings of the classical Chinese. In order to render them adequately Pai Hua has to use sometimes as many as twelve symbols to represent one classical symbol. It is therefore much clumsier and more unwieldy than the classical language. (3) Based on the Mandarin (Pekingese) dialect, Pai Hua still remains a foreign language to the Cantonese, and can be understood only by silent reading. What the final solution of all these difficulties will be a European can hardly predict. The introduction of a modified Latin script, following the example of the Turkish languages, is not exactly applicable to China. A phonetic script will inevitably split China into many independent linguistic groups, and with a monosyllabic language will be highly ambiguous unless some symbols differentiate the various meanings of the same sound. It appears that only a combination of a phonetic script with ideographic representation can solve the problem.

The examples of linguistic problems given in this chapter show clearly the importance of language in educational systems. Educators who boldly undertake to impose a foreign language as the medium of instruction run the risk of losing the fruits of all their efforts by producing a generation with a superficial verbal knowledge unconnected with its surroundings and previous experience. This danger is especially great when the mother tongue and the school language belong to different linguistic groups. From this point of view we express the doubt again whether the Negroes of Africa with their agglutinative and isolating languages can be transformed into French-speaking Europeans in any near future. Bilingualism as a mass phenomenon is possible only in countries where the two linguistic groups have a common cultural background and their languages belong to the same group. Otherwise it will be limited to a small selected group which by the very possession of two different cultural backgrounds will be divorced from the bulk of its own people.

CHAPTER IV

GEOGRAPHIC AND ECONOMIC FACTORS

Geography and economics are two other factors which confront the educational reformer with set conditions and limit by natural obstacles his zeal for innovation. It is quite probable, although the evidence we have covers too short a period to prove it, that the original differentiation of humanity into races was largely conditioned by climatic differences. Through long residence in the arctic regions the physiology of Eskimo tribes gradually adapted itself to the surroundings, as the colour, hair and other features of the Negro were an adaptation to a hot tropical climate. It is more difficult to explain the variations in cephalic index and height, as mass migrations of the prehistoric period led to the hybridisation of original races. During the brief period of recorded history the change of climate has not affected the outward features of the migrant groups. The Negroes of America after three hundred years in a different climate have remained black, and the Europeans who settled and lived in tropical zones for four centuries still remain "white." It is quite possible, however, that the system of inner secretion is influenced even by these short periods of residence in different climates. But whatever the influence of climate on the human stock may be, its influence on educational systems is obvious. The structure of the school system, the school buildings and equipment, the means and methods of transport of school-children, the age limits of compulsory attendance, are often determined by climate and the configuration of the country. On the other hand, the settlement of the Americas and the countries of the Southern Hemisphere by Europeans demanded the adaptation of home school systems to new geographical and climatic situations and thus inevitably led to divergence from the European models.

Economics, in its turn, determines to a great extent the content and methods of education. Even in the practice of primitive tribes the training of adolescents is differentiated in accordance with their main occupations. The tiller of the soil, the hunter, the fisherman, the warrior, were the chief products of tribal training, which required specially devised exercises and oral instruction for each separate occupation. In civilised countries the central and local authorities have to plan their systems of education in close relation with national and local economic conditions and needs. A highly industrialised country demands a different school system from a country which is mainly agricultural. Locally, a mining district has to develop a different bias from a coastal district. In the Middle Ages the differentiation of education was largely conditioned by occupational needs. The Latin grammar school prepared the clerics, the court and later the courtly academies trained the knights and secular rulers, the guilds had a system of their own for training craftsmen, and the peasantry was simply trained through sweat and toil to till the land. The idea of a general education unrelated to economic situations was introduced later, during the Renaissance. It was then that the Greek ideal, which was economically limited to the small ruling class, was extended by the Humanists to embrace the whole population. As a matter of fact the leading humanists demanded a differentiation of education in adaptation to occupations, and it was a distortion of their ideals which led to the monopoly of classical subjects in secondary education. The industrial revolution side by side with the political emancipation of the lower orders posed the problem of the co-ordination of economics and education with a new vigour. It could not be disregarded even by those traditionally inclined statesmen who were the products of a purely classical education. In some countries the influence of practical economics was further strengthened by the adoption of Marxian doctrine as the guiding principle of educational policy.

The influence of climate on school buildings and equipment is obvious. Open-air schools are impossible in Scandinavia with its severe winters and snow-storms, but they are the rule in tropical and sub-tropical countries. The type of architecture and the material of which the schools are built must suit the climate and the local supply of stone or wood. A most interesting example of climatic differentiation is provided by legislation on age-limits of compulsory attendance and the percentage of pre-school age children attending schools. Let us select four Northern countries: Denmark, Finland, Norway, and Sweden, and four Mediterranean European countries: France, Greece, Italy, and Spain, for comparison. It should be noted that all four Northern countries are Protestant and have an old tradition of progressive legislation in education, whilst of the four Mediterranean countries only one can be called progressive in education—France; the remaining

three, Greece, Italy, and Spain, should be classified as education-
ally backward countries.

The comparative (pre-war) figures are as follows:

Northern Countries			*Mediterranean Countries*		
	Age-limits of compulsory attendance	*Percentage of 3–7 ages in school*		*Age-limits of compulsory attendance*	*Percentage of 3–6 3–7 ages in school*
Denmark	7 –14	2	France	6–14	55 70
Finland	7 –14	3	Greece	6–12	8 30
Norway	7½–14	1	Italy	6–14	30 45
Sweden	7 –14	2	Spain	6–12	24 38

This remarkable difference has only one explanation: the
Northern countries start compulsory attendance one or two
years later because the severity of their climate makes it unsuitable for children under seven years of age to be out of doors
in the winter. That is why they have no infant departments
in their primary schools. The mildness of the Mediterranean
climate, on the contrary, allows even children of three to go to
school.

As a striking example of the dominating influence of geographical factors on the development of a modern nation we may
take Australia. This continent, almost equalling Europe in area,
contains the second-largest desert in the world. The whole area
is divided as follows: 21 per cent of the continent is suitable for
close settlement by Europeans, 42 per cent is arid, 34 per cent
suitable for pastoral purposes and 3 per cent for tropical agriculture. In these conditions the population is either congregated
in a few urban centres or widely scattered in the bush. The six
capitals of the six states: Sydney, Melbourne, Brisbane, Adelaide,
Perth and Hobart, contain 47 per cent of the total population of
Australia. The rural population on the other hand is sparsely
distributed throughout the country. Whereas in England the
density of the rural population is 120 per square mile, in Australia
it is only 1 per square mile. In these conditions Australia was
compelled by geography to develop two quite different systems
of education: one for the large towns, another for rural districts.
Sydney, Melbourne and other great cities have a city school

system very similar to the European or American city systems. Large schools, well equipped, with adequate qualified personnel and with sufficient differentiation of curriculum, are the rule. Secondary education, both of the traditional academic type and of technical and commercial types, is available for each able pupil of the primary school within easy reach by tram or train. The University can be attended without leaving the parental home. The conditions in the outlying rural districts are entirely different. The rural schools are small one-teacher institutions with ten to forty pupils. Secondary schools are all concentrated in urban communities. Only small intermediate schools for the ages twelve to fifteen are available in the country. In addition many farms are so far from the nearest rural school that daily attendance is impossible. Left to themselves these families would be quite unable to educate their children beyond reading and writing. As all six Australian states have accepted in their legislation the principle of equality of educational opportunity, the central government has had to take both the administrative and the financial responsibility into its hands. Thus the highly centralised systems of Australia, so contrary to the historical traditions of the English-speaking countries, are the direct result of geographical conditions. In the absence of local authorities the State was the only agency which could provide the means and organisation of correspondence tuition and travelling teachers. Thousands of isolated boys and girls receive their education through correspondence and occasional visits by travelling inspectors. Hundreds are trained in this way for the First and Second Class Primary Teachers' Certificates. Naturally technical and university education necessitates a transfer to a large city, but that is usual for many students even in England. With the development of motor transport and a substantial increase in rural population Australia will be able to adopt the principle of consolidation so successfully introduced in America and Canada, but at present her solution is the only way to implement the aims of modern democracy.

In the U.S.A. and in Canada the influence of geography was not so evident during the first three centuries of their history. Or to speak more precisely geography at first strengthened the historical traditions brought over from England by the early settlers. The Puritans had a very strong community organisation which was the result both of the old English form of local government and of their religious-political struggle against the encroachments of the central government. Having emigrated to a new country where they were surrounded by dense forests and hostile Indian tribes the early settlements clung to their little communities which decided on the spot all questions of religion, law and education. Thus the American, and later the Canadian system of small school districts was established and survives to this day. In the early conditions of settlement this system was well suited to the needs of sparsely populated rural regions of an expanding America, where the agricultural population had a fairly even distribution of wealth and was largely dependent on local taxation for school support. When the great migration started from the Atlantic coast towards the Pacific the people of New England and the Maritime Provinces transferred their traditional school districts to the great expanses of the Middle West and the Prairie Provinces. At first it resulted in the establishment of small primary schools adapted to the thoughts and wants of the country people of the frontier. With the shifting of the frontier towards the West in America and the North in Canada the life of the following generations became more civilised and the farming communities acquired a permanent character. The distribution of wealth became more unequal, and whereas larger and richer communities were able to build up an efficient system of primary and secondary schools, the outlying groups of farms had still to be content with a small inefficient one-teacher school without proper grading and without equipment. A general desire for wider courses of study than were available under the school district system became evident even in the middle of the nineteenth century. But local rivalries and the strong conservatism of farming communities were obstacles to a voluntary consolidation of schools. The district system continued to exist not only in the Middle West, but also on the Atlantic coast side by side with the most efficient city systems such as that of New York City. The generally accepted principle of equality of educational opportunities became a mockery which could no longer be tolerated in a modern democratic state. Historical tradition had to give way to geographical conditions and the new system of schools had to be organised by large areas under the direct supervision of states and provinces. As a special chapter will be devoted to the educational system of the U.S.A. we shall here limit our description of the change to Canada. The Canadian reform of their old-fashioned sectional school system is quite recent and is only now gathering momentum. The reorganisation of the Peace River District in British Columbia was started in 1933. Since then the demand for reform has become a national movement. The Peace River District is situated in the north-eastern part of British Columbia. Its area is approximately 7,000 square miles, of which only about 3,643 square miles are arable land. It is settled by 13,000 persons, among whom representatives of almost every nationality of three continents are to be found. In rural districts it is not uncommon to find sections entirely populated by one nationality such as Czechs, Germans, Swedes, Norwegians, Frenchmen, Americans or Scots. The diversity and sparseness of the population, coupled with the difficulty of building an adequate road system, presented obstacles which had to be surmounted before any reorganisation could be attempted. In July 1933 there were sixty-three school districts in operation. The schools were one-roomed log houses of the crudest possible structure with four bare walls and no ceiling. The majority of teachers were inexperienced young women, who came to this outlying part of the province in order to obtain a year's experience necessary for a post closer to the larger centres. There were few text-books and no library, no playground equipment and even no drinking water. Nevertheless the section communities clung to their schools and objected to their consolidation. The provincial authority had to step in and start the reorganisation by order of the Council of Public Instruction, which was carried out in October 1934. After two years the whole area was consolidated into one larger unit, which was called the Peace River Rural District, and was administered by an Inspector of Schools, who was also the Official Trustee. Some old schools were closed; eight new ones were built in areas where they were needed. Three high schools were established, one with technical courses, and free tuition provided for all scholars who wished to attend high schools. Equipment and libraries were provided and the teaching personnel was strengthened by adequately trained men teachers. With all these improvements there was a considerable saving to taxpayers through economy of organisation and equalisation of burdens among the sections. The success was so striking that it was followed up in other areas of British Columbia. Alberta passed a law in 1936 to allow the Minister of Education to create large school areas, and in 1937 Alberta already had consolidated 744 school districts into five divisions. The progress was accelerated during the following years. Other

Prairie Provinces followed suit and the movement spread to the Atlantic coast, the stronghold of the old tradition.

It should be noted that geographical and economic factors as a rule are closely connected, as the economy of a territory depends largely on its geography, but in the preceding examples geography played a dominant part in the organisation of school systems. In the following descriptions of the results of the industrial revolutions in England and Russia, on the contrary, the economic factor is predominant. The industrial revolution in England brought in its wake great social changes. The centres of population were shifted to the Midlands and the London area, the occupations of millions of people were altered, and life in spacious rural surroundings was exchanged for congested slums in new giant towns. The educational system of old England was quite unequal to all these changes both in the supply of schools and in their traditional curriculum. The adaptation to new conditions continued throughout the nineteenth century and all the educational reforms were largely prompted by the inadequacy of the old school system to meet the modern needs of an industrialised country. The adjustment was gradual and its progress was rather haphazard, as the British Government still believed in the policy of *laissez-faire* and was reluctant to introduce any regulation of the industrial change or any conscious planning from the centre. At first the educational system nearly broke down under the pressure of the economic and social transformation of the country, but gradually the new economic regions began to differentiate their school systems, adapting them to changed conditions. There was still little central planning in the distribution of schools of various types and the gradual regional adjustment was more the result of local initiative and local needs than of legislative measures of the central government. As mentioned, the industrial revolution continued throughout the nineteenth century, but we have no comparable statistics for the first half of the century and can make a statistical table only for the last ninety years. The table on page 70 represents the figures for fifteen English counties selected for their occupational characteristics. The first, the industrial group, is represented by five counties, Derbyshire, Durham, Nottinghamshire, Staffordshire and Yorkshire West Riding, where the population of fourteen years and over is mainly occupied in industry; the second—the agricultural group—is represented by Cambridgeshire, Herefordshire, Norfolk, Suffolk

THE RESULTS OF THE INDUSTRIAL REVOLUTION 1867–1954

Economic Areas by Counties	Percentage of population over 14 years occupied (1931)				1867		Changes during 1867–1954				1954 Number of pupils in Secondary Schools					Number of pupils per 10,000 population	
	Commercial Professional Clercial	Industry	Ariculture	No Occupation	Population	Secondary Schools	Population 1954	Per cent to 1867	No. of Grammar Technical and Comprehensive Schools	Per cent to 1867	Modern	Grammar	Technical	Comprehensive	Independent Grammar	Modern	All other Secondary
Industrial:																	
Derbyshire	32	52	7	9	341	11	840	246	44	400	25,943	10,577	153	1,358	1,725	309	164
Durham	34	54	3	9	502	8	1,470	293	43	538	35,047	13,998	1,013	463	1,687	239	117
Nottinghamshire	35	50	8	7	295	5	857	290	28	560	30,327	7,574	1,788	—	1,147	354	122
Staffordshire	37	51	5	7	736	23	1,637	222	44	191	42,278	11,407	1,680	—	1,345	258	88
Yorkshire, W.R.	39	49	4	8	1,674	62	3,581	214	120	190	78,764	42,828	6,003	2,040	3,075	220	152
Industrial area	36	51	5	8	3,548	109	8,385	236	279	256	212,359	86,384	10,637	3,861	8,979	253	142

Agricultural:																	
Cambridgeshire & Huntingdonshire	31	15	36	18	256	8	253	99	15	188	3,882	2,505	959	1,482	370	155	207
Herefordshire	26	19	41	14	126	6	127	101	9	150	1,359	1,978	—	—	168	105	166
Norfolk	34	24	30	12	435	15	550	126	19	127	11,303	5,837	363	525	586	206	134
Suffolk	32	23	30	15	340	20	453	133	22	110	12,563	4,584	—	—	1,300	279	131
Westmorland	28	30	30	12	63	9	99	157	11	122	703	1,693	—	207	229	70	193
Agricultural area	31	22	32	15	1,220	58	1,382	113	76	131	29,810	16,597	1,317	2,214	2,653	216	165
Metropolitan:																	
Essex	57	25	7	11	400	16	2,113	528	76	475	67,273	20,935	6,546	5,099	2,806	319	166
Kent	51	23	13	13	544	16	1,600	294	89	556	52,218	18,270	1,850	459	4,772	327	157
London	64	26	1	9	2,714	42	3,322	123	132	314	83,499	36,801	5,390	11,293	(4,000)	251	173
Middlesex	60	27	3	10	132	11	2,256	1,709	101	918	61,431	30,708	4,265	1,574	(5,000)	277	182
Surrey	54	24	8	14	265	8	1,635	639	93	1,162	41,849	18,920	1,914	—	8,730	255	180
Metropolitan area	62	25	3	10	4,046	93	10,926	270	491	527	306,270	125,634	19,965	18,425	25,308	283	173

From unpublished data of the Ministry of Education.   Population figures are in thousands.

and Westmorland, and the third group—metropolitan, mainly commercial—is represented by Essex, Kent, London, Middlesex and Surrey. The occupational differentiation is very marked and gives a character of its own to each group.

The movement of the population to the industrial and metropolitan areas started as early as the end of the eighteenth century, and in the middle of the nineteenth century greatly disturbed the fairly even distribution of secondary schools. The agricultural counties with their almost stationary populations had a sufficient supply of secondary schools and could keep pace with the slow natural increase, especially as a large part of the increase moved to other areas. The industrial and metropolitan areas, on the contrary, received such a rapid influx of population that they could not provide enough new secondary schools. As a result, in 1867, whilst the five agricultural counties had only 21,000 inhabitants per secondary school, the industrial counties had 33,000 and the metropolitan 43,000. During the following ninety years the industrial counties have more than doubled the number of secondary schools, but their population has increased by 236 per cent, and the ratio of population per secondary school has on the average remained the same. The metropolitan area has quadrupled the number of its secondary schools and has thus overtaken the rapid growth of the population. The five agricultural counties had but a 13 per cent increase, and with the addition of eighteen new secondary schools are in advance even of the metropolitan area, which has added 398 new schools during the same period. Thus a marked differentiation in the provision of secondary education has resulted in the three selected groups of counties through economic causes alone. If we compare the percentages of an age group entering all efficient secondary schools we notice that industrial counties (except Yorkshire W.R.) have the lowest figures and in fact Durham and Staffordshire have the lowest percentages in the whole of England. The agricultural and metropolitan areas have much higher percentages, and the highest figures for England are in Dorsetshire (25·1 per cent), an agricultural county, and in Hertfordshire (25·3) and Surrey (24·1), two metropolitan counties. We notice also a correlation between the percentages of the population having no occupation in the three selected areas and the percentages of an age group attending secondary schools. The agricultural and suburban areas have a high ratio of wealthy people, retired from work, who are able to send their children to private secondary schools, whilst the poorer industrial population is unable to do so. On the other hand general secondary education does not appeal so much to the parents of adolescents of industrial areas as to the children of the upper middle class, many of whom intend to continue their education in the Universities.

Another, and more important, result of the industrial revolution in England was the establishment of technical and vocational schools. But it took almost a century to convince the British Government of the necessity of technical education in an industrialised country. The first institutions imparting technical education to artisans and mechanics owed their existence to the initiative of working men themselves. These Mechanics' Institutes flourished in the first half of the nineteenth century, following on the foundation of the London Institute in 1825. State intervention began in 1840 with the establishment of the Art Department and in 1853 of the Science Department. In 1872 organised science schools came into being; only a few of them, however, later developed into full-time technical schools; the majority were transformed into ordinary secondary schools. The local authorities for technical education were created in 1889, so that the present system of technical schools is of quite recent origin. In 1867 there were few schools in the whole country, but in 1937 England possessed about 700 technical and vocational institutions. At last the needs of industry for technically trained personnel were recognised, but as there was no central planning the provision of schools is uneven and depends on local initiative. As would be expected, technical education is most developed in industrial areas and in London.[1] Here more boys and girls enter technical institutions, full-time and part-time, than the traditional secondary schools. In the agricultural and suburban areas, on the contrary, twice as many boys and girls enter secondary schools as the technical institutions. With the full operation of the 1944 Education Act this regional difference will become even more pronounced. The English example shows us that economic causes, without any central guidance and planning, have changed the whole structure of English education. It took more than a century to prevail against the conservative conception of post-primary education and the Government's policy of *laissez-faire*. In the next example of the industrial revolution in Russia we shall see how economic causes coupled with the conscious policy of the Marxist government have achieved similar results in the course of twenty

[1] Most of London vocational schools train for trade and commerce.

years, by introducing State monopoly both in economics and education.

The Russian school system, unlike the English, was created from the very beginning by the State and for State purposes. When Peter the Great founded the first secular schools, they were all technical schools with the definite aim of training the necessary personnel for promoting various industries within the Empire. This utilitarian aim was always prevalent in the development of Russian education. As early as 1773 the Higher Institute of Mining was founded in St. Petersburg and in 1815 Russia already had in addition a Military-Medical Academy, a Forestry Institute, an Institute of Ways and Communications and a Commercial Academy, all higher institutions which exist even now as the older technical schools of the U.S.S.R. The high standard of Russian technical schools was revealed to the Western world in the sixties of the nineteenth century in several international exhibitions. The Americans were so impressed by the methods of the Moscow Higher Technical School, founded in 1830, that the so-called "Russian system" was introduced in the eighties of the last century throughout America and has greatly influenced the development of American technical education. When the Soviet Government started a wholesale industrialisation of the country they had therefore a considerable highly trained cadre of engineers and technicians and about twenty Higher Technical Institutes with a long history behind them. Russian industry too was started by the initiative of the State, and all the first factories in St. Petersburg, Moscow and in the Ural region were State-owned, on State land, and employed labour specially conscripted by the State. But the industrialisation of Russia was impossible while serfdom remained the basis of the national economy. Only after the emancipation of the serfs in 1861 could industry be developed by private enterprise employing free labour. Gradually this process gathered momentum, and after the Revolution of 1905 Russia entered the period of industrial revolution. The first World War and the following Civil War interrupted the rapid growth of Russian industries for a decade. Only with the introduction of the famous Five Year Plan in 1928 was the rapid growth resumed. Side by side with the shifting of the centres of industrial population towards the east and the establishment of hundreds of new factories the Plan envisaged a fundamental reform of the whole educational system, paying special attention to the technical and vocational training of the new cadres. In the course of twenty years Russia was transformed from a predominantly agricultural country, with a rural population amounting to 80 per cent of the whole, into a giant industrial State with monopoly of control and singleness of purpose. The arguments for and against the State monopoly are beside the point here; what is important is the close connection between the economic structure of the country and the system of education. During the first ten years, 1918–28, progress was very slow as Russia had to rebuild and reconstruct her industries after the ravages of the World War and the subsequent Civil War. The population decreased considerably during these years, and the number of workers employed in industry fell also. Thus in 1913 the total number of workers in all industries on the territory of the present (1939) U.S.S.R. was 2,599,000; in 1923 it fell to 1,794,000 or by 31 per cent; then it began gradually to rise, and in 1928, the first year of the Five Year Plan, it just reached 3,096,000 or a little more than in 1913. With the introduction of the Plan the increase was very rapid: in 1933 there were 6,229,400 and in 1935, 7,404,000 workers in all industries. In 1947 the total number of workers in production reached 13,900,000, including the newly acquired territories.

The ratio of urban and rural population changed considerably, as the following table shows:

POPULATION OF U.S.S.R.

	Urban	Per cent	Rural	Per cent	Total
1913	24,686,600	17	114,626,100	83	139,321,700
1933	40,303,000	24	125,445,400	76	165,748,400
1939	55,909,900	33	113,609,100	67	169,519,000
1956	87,000,000	43	113,000,000	57	200,000,000
Increase	62,313,400	348	—1,626,100	0	60,678,300

During the period 1926–56 about 40 million peasants migrated to the towns and larger villages with 10 million population were transformed into urban districts. This shifting of the population towards the centres of industrial production was still more accelerated after the war and the percentage of the urban population rose to more than a third of the total. Many new centres of industrial production were founded on virgin soil, as for instance Magnitogorsk in the Urals, which did not exist in 1926, but in 1935 had a population of 210,600, which is now doubled. Another industrial centre, Stalinsk, had in 1926 only 3,900 inhabitants, 220,000 in 1935, and has also now doubled this number. Towns were founded even in the Arctic Zone like the famous Igarka. Another important feature of this industrial revolution was the more even distribution of production throughout the territory of the U.S.S.R. The Central Asiatic Republics, Transcaucasia and White Russia, which before the Revolution were almost devoid of any industrial development, have received their quota of industrial installations.

The following table shows the relative distribution of industrial workers in 1913 and 1935 (in thousands):

	1913		1935		
	Number of workers	Distribution per cent	Number of workers	Distribution per cent	Increase per cent
Leningrad area	273	11	788	11	190
Moscow area	888	34	1,174	16	32
Ural area	245	9	519	7	112
Ukraine area	292	11	1,399	19	380
The rest of U.S.S.R.	901	35	3,524	47	292
Total U.S.S.R.	2,599	100	7,404	100	185

This table shows that although industrialisation proceeded throughout the whole Union it was much slower in the three oldest centres, Leningrad, the Urals and Moscow, which were more or less saturated even during the old régime, and was most revolutionary in the south and east. The enormous increase in the industrial population, the change in its distribution within the Union and the change in technical methods of production have inevitably led to a transformation of the whole educational system. The new industries demanded hundreds of thousands of skilled technicians and tens of thousands of engineers for the training of whom the old system of technical education was entirely inadequate. There were three features of the new industrial development which necessitated a change in the technical school system. First of all the number of schools had to be trebled or quadrupled. Secondly, the distribution of schools had to be more even throughout the territory and not centralised in Leningrad and Moscow as before. And thirdly, entirely new institutions with new methods and curricula had to be created for the modern branches of chemical and metallurgical production. As both the industries and the schools were State-controlled it was easy from the administrative point of view to plan the development of technical education in accordance with local needs and with the territorial distribution of industries. The table on page 78 gives comparative figures for 1915 and 1933 of the territorial distribution of Higher Technical Institutes.

This table clearly indicates the great change in the system of higher education produced by the industrial revolution. In 1915 most of the higher institutions were concentrated in the two capitals, Leningrad and Moscow, as much as 70 per cent of all students of the whole country being in the two capitals. In 1956 only 27 per cent of all students were in Leningrad and Moscow. The second feature is the comparatively slow growth of cultural institutions. In Leningrad and Moscow the figures for 1933 are even lower than in 1915. The growth of cultural institutions was marked only in the non-Russian Republics, where the new national cultures had to be built up.

The third important feature of the change is the relative ratio of technical institutions. In 1915 technical students formed only 19 per cent of all students, in 1933 they were 49 per cent of all students. Similarly the agricultural students were only 1·6 per cent in 1915, but 13 per cent in 1933. The old system of higher education was mainly established in two cultural centres and 80 per cent of it was devoted to cultural needs. The new system is distributed more evenly throughout the country and 62 per cent of it is devoted to technical and agricultural needs. The same has happened in the field of secondary education. Just before the introduction of the Five Year Plan there were about 900,000 pupils in general secondary schools and about 400,000 in vocational and technical post-primary schools. In 1931 only 400,000 pupils remained in general secondary schools, while the number of pupils in technical and vocational schools rose to 1,100,000. These drastic measures were abandoned after the first emergency had passed and the new industrial cadres were trained. At present general secondary education has regained its importance and the numbers of pupils in general secondary schools are continually rising.

It is interesting to compare the industrial transformation in

NUMBER OF STUDENTS IN HIGHER INSTITUTIONS BY TERRITORIAL UNITS

Years	R.S.F.S.R.					Ukranian S.S.R	White Russian S.S.R	Three Trans-caucasian S.S.R	Three Central Asiatic S.S.R	Total U.S.S.R
	Leningrad area	Moscow area	Ural area	The rest of R.S.F.S.R.	Total					
Cultural Higher Institutes: Education, Medicine, Law and Art										
1915	32,821	31,672	—	7,026	71,519	20,586	200	300	—	92,605
1928	13,579	18,269	1,656	21,280	54,884	16,795	2,667	9,294	1,993	85,633
1933	21,770	31,012	4,363	53,214	109,359	40,946	5,011	11,336	6,901	173,553
Industrial Technical Higher Institutes										
1915	12,257	4,304	—	2,327	18,888	5,275	—	—	—	24,163
1928	12,024	13,625	967	7,831	34,447	7,035	—	4,438	869	46,789
1933	50,448	58,800	11,595	32,055	162,878	53,692	2,535	11,834	2,499	233,438
Agricultural Higher Institutes										
1915	3,322	3,224	—	447	6,993	839	—	—	—	7,832
1928	4,144	4,912	549	8,418	18,023	4,402	1,751	2,554	605	27,335
1933	4,500	7,379	1,482	24,551	37,912	11,550	2,104	6,854	3,804	62,224
Total Number of Students in all Higher Institutions										
1915	48,400	39,200	—	9,800	97,400	26,700	200	300	—	124,600
1928	29,847	36,806	3,172	37,529	107,354	28,232	4,418	16,286	3,467	159,757
1933	76,698	97,191	17,440	118,820	310,149	106,188	9,650	30,024	13,204	469,215

Increase during 1940-1956 in all Higher Institutions

Years	Leningrad	Moscow	Rest of R.S.F.S.R.	Ukranian S.S.R.	White Russian S.S.R.	Three Caucasian S.S.R.	Three Central Asiatic S.S.R.	Two New Central Asiatic S.S.R.	Four Western S.S.R.	Total U.S.S.R.
1940	85,100	141,900	251,100	196,800	21,500	54,200	24,400	13,500	23,200	701,700
1950	107,200	234,100	455,400	201,600	31,600	78,700	55,900	39,800	43,100	1,247,400
1956	155,300	363,300	657,500	325,900	50,500	93,100	92,100	62,800	67,500	1,867,900
Per cent of 1940	182	256	262	166	230	172	378	465	291	266

the two countries, England and Russia. Whereas in England the economic change was hardly a revolution, but might be more properly called an "industrial evolution" which took 150 years to achieve an adaptation of educational system to the economic structure, the change in Russia is in truth a most radical "industrial revolution." A hundred and fifty years of English economic and educational history were condensed into a period of less than twenty years and have produced the most radical and rapid change known in history. Even the famous transformation of Japan, which struck the imagination of the Western world, pales in comparison with this reconstruction of the U.S.S.R. Whereas in England the policy of *laissez-faire* permitted the educational system to lag behind the economic needs for more than a century, the Soviet centralisation and planning made the educational system one of the vital movers of the economic change. It is true that for a time the cultural needs of the country were partially sacrificed to rapidity of industrialisation and the Soviet Government was later compelled by events to pay more attention to cultural institutions and the general level of education of the millions of new technicians and engineers, but the purpose of the drastic change was achieved. The U.S.S.R. could enter the war of 1939–45 as a highly industrialised country capable of meeting the military and industrial machine of Nazi Germany on equal terms.

We pass now to the last aspect of economics in education to be discussed in this chapter. Educational finance is one of the most important factors in the development of national systems of schools. The percentage of national revenue spent on education, the division of burdens between the central and local authorities and the system of grants adopted by the Government are all reflected in the structure and quality of national systems. As was pointed out before the comparison of absolute figures of educational expenditure loses its significance because of variations in standards of living and the purchasing power of the currency. The relative importance of expenditure on education in the national budget, however, can be gauged and compared. The percentages should be calculated from the combined budgets of central and all local authorities and should represent the expenditure in a normal period. The war or reconstruction periods are unsuitable for comparison because of abnormally high expenditure on military or reconstructive tasks. Let us take the years 1929–30 as being just between the two wars when national budgets were more or less normal.

The percentages were as follows:

Denmark	11	Holland	21·3	Spain	3·7
Great Britain	9·8	Italy	6·2	Sweden	16
France	7·7	Norway	14·2	Switzerland	16
Germany	15	U.S.S.R.	10·9	U.S.A.	19

The difference between the progressive countries like the U.S.A., Holland, Switzerland and Sweden and a backward country like Spain is clearly shown by the relative national expenditure on education. In the case of Great Britain, France and the U.S.S.R., which spent large sums on the defence of their far-flung territories, the percentages are smaller than in the U.S.A. or even Germany, which had no standing armies or navies in 1930. Taking the two extreme cases, we have Holland with 21·3 per cent of her budget devoted to education and Spain with only 3·7 per cent. In consequence the Dutch educational system has a much broader financial basis than the Spanish and the Dutch schools are better in every respect. These figures only indirectly point out the value and diffusion of education in different countries and must be studied in relation to other items of expenditure and the specific needs of the country.

Another index of the financial support of education is given by the relative division of burdens between the central and local authorities in various countries. Complete centralisation of educational finance has never been introduced in any European country, as the local authorities and the parents have always contributed towards the costs in one way or another. The only example of centralised finance is provided by New Zealand, but taking into consideration the small population of the country, smaller than many European towns, it does not constitute a real divergence from the general principle. In the six Australian States educational finance is also centralised, but as the Federal government does not participate in the expenditure, the principle of centralisation is limited. In all the remaining countries local authorities carry part of the costs and the variation shows only the relative importance of local participation. In the U.S.A. and Canada the small local units carry the main burden, amounting up to 80 per cent of the total expenditure. In Latin countries, in France, Italy and Belgium, for instance, the local authorities contribute less than a third and the main burden is carried by the State. In the remaining countries the responsibility for the maintenance of the school system is more evenly divided between the two types of authorities. The average figures for the whole country, however, signify very little if the system of grants is not considered in detail. The central government may subsidise or even maintain only secondary and higher institutions, leaving the maintenance of primary schools to the local authorities, or it may subsidise all stages of the school system in accordance with some formula or principle. If the school administration is highly centralised, as in France, for instance, and all teachers are in fact civil servants, the local variation of equipment and quality of education is comparatively small and the educational opportunities are more or less evenly distributed throughout the country. But if the administration is decentralised, as in America and Canada, and the schools are maintained by small local units, then the quality of education imparted in wealthy urban centres and in poor rural communities is greatly differentiated and the principle of equality of educational opportunities is reversed. To judge the national educational system by average figures for the whole country, therefore, would be quite misleading in a country like the U.S.A. or Canada, whilst the average figures for France may be taken as representative of the whole country. The differences between the best and the worst schools in the U.S.A. are so enormous in every respect that they have attracted the attention of educational experts both in America and Europe and during the last forty years many schemes have been published advocating a better system of financial support.

In decentralised administration of education the grant system of the central authority should consider three factors of financial policy in order to realise an equality of opportunities. The first factor to be considered is the number of children in a given area, representing the "need" or the "necessity." The second factor is the expenditure of local communities, representing their "effort" and the third is the assessable value, representing their "ability." In addition the central authority has to establish by law certain minimum standards of expenditure per pupil and of teachers' salaries. All these conditions were not fulfilled in the American and Canadian systems of administration and finance with the well-known results of glaring inequality of educational opportunities. The grants from central sources were quite inadequate even to ensure the minimum requirements; they were allotted on the basis of the school census or the average attendance without considering the "ability" or the "effort" of local units of administration. It is quite unnecessary to go into intricate details of various American and Canadian systems of school support to understand the importance of the three factors mentioned. It is quite evident that the "need" of an area can neither be measured by the school enrolment nor by the average attendance, which reflect rather the efficiency of the compulsory attendance legislation than the educational needs of the population. The "effort" of the area again is measured by the rate in the £ and not by absolute figures of expenditure, and the "ability" by the assessable value per schoolchild and not by the absolute amount of wealth in the area. Thus a richer area may have comparatively more children than a poorer area and in consequence be lower in "ability" than the latter. On the other hand a poorer community even spending less than its richer neighbour may have a higher rate per pound and thus a higher "effort."

The interplay of the three factors in actual practice is clearly seen from the following tables representing a few selected English authorities, and giving the figures for elementary education for the years 1906 and 1936.

L.E.A. 1906	Product of 1d. rate per child in average attendance	Total expenditure from public funds: taxes and rates	Percentage of Board of Education grants	Rate in the £ to meet the expenditure	Total cost per child in average attendance		
	s. d.	£		d.	£	s.	d.
Counties:							
London	5 0	3,410,786	30·6	14·7	5	3	6
Middlesex	3 10	97,025	54·4	8·5	3	6	6
Kent	3 6	231,509	60·9	8·0	3	3	0
Yorkshire							
W.R.	2 8	514,785	54·3	11·0	3	0	11
Durham	2 2	261,949	58·3	10·6	2	12	3
County Boroughs:							
Bournem'th	6 8	18,843	66·3	2·9	2	15	9
Brighton	4 4	73,977	46·7	11·2	4	7	7
Manchester	3 4	368,806	49·8	13·1	3	16	0
Liverpool	3 0	488,030	47·5	15·4	4	6	5
West Brom.	1 6	36,855	66·4	15·0	3	14	2
Part III Authorities:							
Hove	9 4	15,725	35·0	6·7	4	11	5
Finchley	4 8	16,071	35·5	18·2	5	14	8
Luton	2 0	21,500	64·2	12·3	3	3	6
Jarrow	1 6	19,858	53·2	19·8	3	1	1
Felling	1 4	16,425	55·6	25·8	3	14	7

In this table the product of a 1d. rate per child represents the "ability" of the area, the rate in the £ its "effort." The grant formula used by the Board of Education in 1906 was mainly based on the number of schoolchildren, and thus failed to equalise the total costs per child and helped the richer areas more than the poorer. Thus Bournemouth and Hove are the highest in "ability," but their "effort" is the lowest in the table. Bournemouth managed to get two-thirds of its expenditure from the Board of Education, in spite of being one of the wealthiest areas and contributing the lowest rate in the £. On the other hand Felling, one of the poorest areas, received only 55·6 per cent from the Board and had to levy the highest rate in the £ to meet the expenditure.

In 1932 the grant formula was changed with a new grant for necessitous areas which considerably evened up the most glaring inequalities, but still failed to equalise the burdens and the costs per child.

We take the same authorities for 1937 and give figures under the same headings:

L.E.A. 1937	Product of 1d. rate per child in average attendance		Total expenditure from public funds: taxes and rates	Percentage of Board of Education grants	Rate in the £ to meet the expenditure	Total cost per child in average attendance		
	s.	d.	£		d.	£	s.	d.
London	11	0	9,402,079	36·6	24·4	21	3	2
Middlesex	8	4	867,955	38·9	22·4	15	4	8
Kent	5	1	1,062,411	47·2	31·1	14	18	5
Yorkshire W.R.	2	7	2,037,910	55·6	42·7	12	9	6
Durham	1	9	1,521,429	61·3	59·6	13	10	7
Bournemouth	15	10	109,647	18·4	12·8	12	7	7
Brighton	9	6	216,143	37·0	19·5	14	14	9
Manchester	5	6	1,485,748	47·7	31·5	16	12	9
Liverpool	3	11	1,683,845	51·5	33·9	13	14	4
West Brom.	2	3	146,641	58·0	46·0	12	5	4
Hove	22	6	49,764	8·5	12·2	15	0	8
Finchley	16	2	62,528	24·6	15·0	16	1	11
Luton	5	7	104,480	48·1	23·0	12	8	3
Jarrow	1	3	68,591	77·0	43·1	11	19	7
Felling	1	5	52,197	68·7	52·0	12	2	5

We see how the new formula changed the division of burdens

between the central and local authorities. The wealthiest of the boroughs—Hove—received only 8·5 per cent of its expenditure as a grant from the Board of Education, whilst the poorest borough—Jarrow—was reimbursed for 77 per cent of its expenditure on education. In spite of that Hove levied only 12·2d. in the £ and could spend £15 os. 8d. per child, whilst Jarrow had to levy 43·1d. in the £ and could spend only £11 19s. 7d. per child. This difference was the result of the wealth behind each child in Hove—22s. 6d., and the lack of financial resources in Jarrow—only 1s. 3d. behind each child. These tables are an enlightening example of the influence of the three factors on educational finance and of the necessity of an equalising formula for State grants. Up to the passing of the Education Act, 1944, the equalisation policy of the Board of Education was applied only in the field of so-called "elementary education"; in the field of secondary and higher education the Board reimbursed 50 per cent of the expenditure irrespective of the "ability" or "effort" of the local authority. By this policy and by aiding the direct grant schools the Board still more accentuated the different provision of secondary and higher education between richer and poorer areas. The Act of 1944, recognising this defect of the old policy, included all branches of the educational system within the working of the equalisation formula.

Although the influence of the financial policy and especially of various equalisation formulas is not noticeable at first sight in the quality of educational services, the financial factor is one of the most important economic influences. If geography and economics cannot influence the spiritual values of education and the definition of the aims and purposes of national culture, they provide that necessary background and basis without which the educational system hangs in the air and may train generations of young men and women who are unable to apply their theoretical knowledge to practical life. On the other hand undue emphasis on material conditions and concentration on training solely for the increase of industrial production may lead to the forfeiture of the cultural heritage and the loss of the historical individuality of a nation. The rapid, almost ruthless, industrialisation of Russia for a time endangered her cultural progress, and only because the Soviet Government saw the red light before it was too late and paid attention to cultural values as well after a period of neglect, was Russia saved from the deadening effect of a machine-like efficiency without any spiritual content.

PART II

RELIGIOUS FACTORS

CHAPTER V

RELIGIOUS TRADITIONS OF EUROPE

We have dealt with a group of natural factors, race, language, geography and economics, which to a great extent determine the work of an educator even before he starts educating. Now we have to discuss the spiritual factors which guide the educator in his activity and set before him a definite aim for the training of growing minds. The spiritual factors are not necessarily opposed to the material background—often they are complementary to it; and when both are working in harmony they produce a flourishing period of national culture. On the other hand a spiritual ideal conceived in the remote past and inherited without adaptation by following generations or transferred from a foreign country with a different tradition may become an obstacle to the natural growth of national culture and defer its progress. Among spiritual influences religion is the most powerful, because it appeals to the whole man and not only to his intellect. Religion penetrates the emotional depth of human nature, it conditions habitual reactions in daily life and it colours the reasoning ability of a creative mind. Thus the religious tradition, if it embraces the whole nation, becomes one of the characteristic national features, which is then perpetuated through education. Only a new religious ideal or a secular ideal which has elements of religion in it can break the established religious tradition and create a new atmosphere. The deepest cultural differences have been the result of religious schisms, reformation and revolutions which were mainly a protest against the established religion. The recognised division of humanity into East and West is neither racial nor linguistic, but is based chiefly on a difference in religious outlook and philosophy of life. Three main cultural features distinguish the European West from the Asiatic East: (a) the Greco-Roman (Hellenistic) heritage, (b) Christianity, and (c) the Renaissance and modern science. Japan has acquired the methods and application of modern science from the West, but nevertheless remains an Eastern country, as she does not share the two other fundamental features with Europe. The Middle

East shares with Europe the heritage of Hellenistic civilisation and the fruits of modern science; for a long period it shared even the influence of Christianity. But when it was conquered and dominated by Islam it parted ways with Europe and became a world of its own, creating a culture distinct from the European. In a sense Islamic countries present an intermediate stage between the East and West with more affinity to the latter. The real East begins in that area where Hinduism and Buddhism are dominant religious influences. Thus religious traditions were the chief factor dividing humanity into cultural groups. As we are mainly concerned with Europe and European colonies in other continents, we shall limit our discussion to those religious traditions which determined European civilisation.

Of the three great religions—Christianity, Islam and Judaism —which still count their adherents in Europe in millions, only the first became an integral part of European culture. Judaism during the three thousand years of its history has been the religion of a small community isolated from the surrounding population, and has influenced Europe only in so far as the teachings of the Old Testament were incorporated in Christianity. Islam, on the other hand, directly influenced Europe from the two Southern peninsulas, Spain and the Balkans, and has left traces of its impact on Europe in all fields of cultural activity. We shall, therefore, limit our description of religious traditions to Christianity with a short reference to Islam.

For a long period the jurisdiction of the Christian Church extended over the whole area within the frontiers of the Roman Empire, and it was, from the time of Constantine onward, a State-supported institution. As the Roman Empire was divided into the Western or Latin-speaking half and the Eastern or Greek-speaking half, so the Church quite naturally used the Latin and Greek languages in these respective territories. The philosophic tendency of the Greeks and the legal precision of the Romans imparted to the two branches of the universal Church characteristic distinctions which were evident even before the official schism. The fall of the Western Roman Empire and its division into many countries ruled by newly converted Teutonic kings made the only Western Patirarch—the Pope of Rome—the natural custodian of the Roman Imperial traditions and in a way the heir of the Roman Emperor. In the Eastern or Byzantine Empire the four Eastern Patriarchs were confronted with the continued centralisation of secular power in the person of the Emperor, and thus were not able to acquire the prestige and independence which were enjoyed by the Pope of Rome. The schism was a natural consequence of the existing differences and finally found its official recognition in dogma. The universal Christian Church branched off into the Roman Catholic and the Eastern Orthodox Churches, which developed the initial difference into opposition and even enmity. The Pope of Rome by historical events became the sole head of the Western Church and the recognised arbiter in the quarrels of the Teutonic kings. The Byzantine Emperor remained the supreme head of the Eastern Empire and the four Eastern Patriarchs were entirely dependent on his will. Whilst the Pope of Rome could excommunicate the recalcitrant king in the West, the Byzantine Emperor could dismiss the recalcitrant patriarch in the East. In both parts of the old Roman Empire the supreme power rested in the hands of one man. The Pope claimed secular suzerainty and in fact became Pope-Caesar. The Byzantine Emperor claimed spiritual sovereignty and became Caesar-Pope. Thus the rôle of the Church in the two halves of Europe was entirely different. In the West the Catholic Church was the cultural leader and initiator and founder of all educational institutions. In the East the Orthodox Church was a tool of the State in its cultural and educational policy. The political and religious division of the Roman Empire into Western and Eastern halves split the unity of European civilisation. After the schism the two sister civilisations, Roman and Byzantine, although derived from the same sources, went their ways separately. Europe was definitely divided and the schism made a deeper gulf than any racial, national or linguistic differences could ever make. For eight hundred years Eastern Europe was separated from the West, and only during the last two centuries have the twin civilisations again approached a certain semblance of unity.

Western Europe, however, was not so homogeneous as the Byzantine generalisation of all Westerners as "Franks" would suggest. Those Teutons who settled in the old Roman provinces and mixed with the Celto-Roman natives formed new Latin nations which accepted the Roman traditions as a guiding principle of their national life. The remaining Teutonic tribes were influenced only superficially by Rome and preserved to a great extent their native traditions and the communal form of self-government. Converted to the Latin form of Christianity and officially recognising the spiritual supremacy of the Pope of

Rome, they always resented his intervention in their secular affairs and his demand for financial support for his Italian curia. Yet the Reformation movement did not start among the Teutons. Peter Waldo, Fra Dolcino and Savonarola were all Italians, born and bred on Roman soil, but their revolt against Rome could not take deep root among the Latin nations. Only a few small Protestant communities surviving in Northern Italy remind us of the once powerful movements of the Waldenses and Albigenses, which shook the Roman Church to its foundations in the twelfth century. Connection with Rome and loyalty to Roman tradition was too strong among the Latin nations. But when the revolt spread to Teutonic lands it soon grew into a national movement, and one Teutonic nation after another seceded from Rome; and this caused a new schism in European civilisation. Perhaps the psychological and temperamental difference between the Teutonic tribes of the North and the Latinised population of the South also contributed to the religious schism. It may be that the Protestant varieties of Christianity, with their particularism and emphasis on individual judgment, are more congenial to the Nordic introvert type than the organisation and the external splendour of Catholicism, which so delights the extrovert Mediterranean type.

As a result of these two schisms Europe was divided into three cultural-regional groups: (a) Latin, Catholic nations bordering the Mediterranean, (b) Teutonic, Protestant nations around the North Sea, and (c) Eastern Europe, mainly Slavonic and Orthodox. This classification holds good only as a generalisation. There are many exceptions—Catholic Poland or Orthodox Rumania for example—but for the study of educational systems it is most helpful. The policy of the three varieties of Christianity towards science and education was different, and did not depend so much on religious dogmas as on the relations of the Church and State.

The medieval feudal society of Western Europe was not aware of national frontiers as they are now accepted. The whole territory of the old Roman Empire with the addition of the Teutonic lands had the same social structure, a universal language, the language of the Church, and one international system of education. In a way it realised the Platonic State on a grand scale and with inevitable modifications. The three medieval classes so well defined in German as the *Lehrstand* (learned class), *Wehrstand* (warrior class) and *Nährstand* (producing class) can be compared with the Platonic philosopher-administrators, military guardians and producing artisans and farmers. As in the Platonic State, so too in the Middle Ages each class had a special system of training for its functional rôle in society. The "clerics," who included the clergy, the teachers, the lawyers and the physicians, had a learned education based on Aristotle and Catholic theology and imparted entirely through the medium of Latin. The military class of knights and professional soldiers had a secular education mainly military and courtly in character, and the guilds of artisans had their own system of apprenticeship or learning by doing. The education of the "clerics" was controlled by the Church both in administration and in its contents. The teachers and the scholars were exempt from secular law courts and were under the jurisdiction of the canonical laws of the Church. All school subjects were taught from the point of view of Catholic dogma, and even philosophy was called *ancilla theologiae* (maid-servant of theology). Such a school system was quite unsuitable for mass education, nor did the Church intend it for the masses. It was destined for the intellectual élite, as was the educational system of the Platonic State. As in the latter it was open to the best minds of all classes irrespective of origin, and so in a sense was democratic. In medieval conditions when the Catholic dogma was accepted unreservedly by all and the supremacy of the Church was acknowledged by the most powerful secular sovereigns, ecclesiastical control of schools and dogmatic limitations of the contents of education were quite natural and most effective. Aristotle and the Catholic theology represented the sum total of contemporary knowledge and those few unorthodox minds who revolted against this spiritual monopoly were unable to offer anything which could rival the established philosophy of life. Plato was almost unknown, Aristotle was available only in fragments, modern science was not yet born, and the heretic could base his revolt on nothing more tangible than his emotional protest. In these circumstances the spiritual and educational monopoly of the Church was morally and legally justified as the only way of building up an educated society. The rediscovery of Aristotle and Plato and the renaissance of classical learning challenged the traditional philosophy based on dogma and gave an opportunity for a successful revolt against the supremacy of the Church of Rome. Catholicism had lost its universal character, which was earlier undermined by the schism of the Eastern Orthodox Church, and in fact became one of the many branches of the original universal Christian Church. As such it could not claim the same spiritual supremacy as the medieval Church, and perseverance in that claim led to many embittered struggles in the field of education in the post-Reformation period. We devote a special chapter to the Catholic tradition in modern times.

Medieval philosophy or scholasticism was not a single school of thought approved officially by the Church. Often theological and philosophical problems were interpreted by famous schoolmen in opposite ways. Although the Church was more inclined to accept the intellectualist philosophy of St. Thomas Aquinas, the philosophy of his opponents Duns Scotus and William of Occam was not condemned. These two British schoolmen in some points could be called the precursors of more modern views and especially of later English and Scottish empirical philosophy. In their emphasis on the will in opposition to the intellect they paved the way for later Protestant theology. The Reformers were as much the heirs of the medieval tradition as those who remained within the fold of the Roman Church. In the initial stages of the controversy it was a struggle between two points of view within the Church, and only when all hopes of reforming the Church from within had to be abandoned did a real parting of the ways take place. The main point at issue was defined by the German philosopher Schleiermacher as follows: "Whilst in Roman Catholicism the relation of the individual to Christ is dependent on his relation to the Church, in Protestantism the relation of the individual to the Church is dependent on his relation to Christ." This difference did not touch the fundamental dogma of the universal Church so much as the organisation and canon law of the Roman half of Christendom. The unity of the Church could have been preserved had the movement of Reformation not coincided with the revival of classical learning and the birth of national consciousness. Platonic philosophy and the beginning of modern science liberated minds from scholastic formalism and dogmatism, and the awakened national pride of the Teutonic nations imparted a national character to the revolt of individual reformers. In Catholic countries the Church remained the visible community of all its members, whereas in the seceding countries the Church was conceived as the invisible community of the faithful. The Catholic Church continued its existence as an abstract universal community; whilst Protestantism in its visible form became divided into many national and local

Churches. Protestantism is essentially a differentiating movement, and if it had not been checked by national consciousness tending towards unity it would have been split into innumerable sects. As it is, in America the number of Protestant religious bodies runs into hundreds. But in the main Protestantism can be divided into three great traditions: the Lutheran, the Calvinist, and the Anglican. As the Anglican and Calvinist traditions have greatly influenced the educational systems of all English-speaking countries we devote a separate chapter to each, and in this chapter we shall describe the Continental Protestant Churches which had little connection with Great Britain.

The Protestant Churches of Germany and Scandinavia owed their origin and inspiration primarily to one person, Martin Luther; but their school organisation and humanist tradition was the work of Philip Melanchthon, the "Praeceptor Germaniae." Catholic historians of the German Reformation often assert that it destroyed the medieval school system and that Luther's attitude towards academic education was negative. The explosive personality of Luther gave expression to many contradictory statements, but if he forcibly denounced the medieval educational tradition and severely condemned the admiration of heathen philosophers, he most vigorously promoted the education of the masses. He translated the Bible into German, and, recognising it as the source of truth, wanted to make it available to every German, so that each one should be able to find the true faith for himself. If the masses needed elementary education as the only way to salvation through the reading of the Bible, so did the Protestant clergy need the knowledge of Hebrew, Greek and Latin to be able to read the original sources. Thus Luther demanded academic education for the clergy and was himself a Professor of Wittenberg University. Admittedly his chief purpose in education was religious and theological, but he did not neglect the civic point of view and the needs of the State. For Luther the opposition of spiritual and worldly was united in the idea of Nature. Asceticism, which he had previously practised as an Augustinian friar, was supplanted by the natural increase of humanity through the family. "It is deeply rooted in nature to give birth to children," said he. For him the State and the Church, the family and the community were all natural and divine forms of life. Some of his utterances might lead to an identification of God and Nature. To the question, for instance, "Why are the Ten Commandments taught and accepted?" he replied, "Because natural laws are nowhere so well and so systematically expounded as in Moses." Or, "The Sabbath is a holiday not because it is a law of Moses, but because Nature teaches us that we have to rest in order to revive our strength." Having built up a national Church in close alliance with the secular power, Luther could not ignore the training of citizens, and for that utilitarian reason promoted vocational education which led to the foundation of new *Bürgerschulen*, later known as *Realschulen*. Thus natural science and practical studies were indispensable parts of Lutheran education. Philip Melanchthon, on the other hand, approached education from the humanist point of view. Nephew and pupil of Reuchlin, Melanchthon was steeped in humanism from his childhood. He became one of the leading classical scholars even before he joined Luther as a reformer. He sincerely believed that antiquity was the fountain-head of both secular and religious wisdom. And his life's purpose was to unite this wisdom with the reformed faith and make it available for the national regeneration of Germany. Invited by the Elector of Saxony to Wittenberg in 1518, he at once started the reform of Universities and grammar schools. He profoundly changed the curriculum and methods of academic education and brought them into close relation with the secular needs of the State. "The purpose of Providence that children should be brought up to be virtuous and religious is evident to all," said he in his address to the Nuremberg city council in 1526, "but the obligation is not limited to the children of this or that individual citizen; it extends to the entire youth of the State whose training demands corporate provision. For the ultimate end which confronts us is not private virtue alone but the interest of the public weal." Thus both Luther and Melanchthon worked for the dissemination of enlightenment among the whole population and influenced the Protestant rulers of Germany to introduce the first laws of compulsory attendance. Luther enforced the duty of visitations on the clergy, and Melanchthon says in his *Apology*: "With us the clergymen and sacristans are compelled to educate and examine the youth publicly." In his letter to the Elector John of Saxony in 1526 Luther stated: "Your Highness has the right to compel the communities to maintain schools." In 1530 Luther said in a sermon: "If the Government has the right to compel its subjects to carry guns and scale the walls during the war, it has still more right and even the duty to compel its subjects to send their children to school." As a result the

Schmalkalden Union of Protestant Princes in 1537 made it a duty of every Evangelical ruler to found schools. The Saxon *Generalartikel* of 1557, the Württemberg Church Ordinance of 1539 and the Brandenburg Visitation Ordinance of 1573 can be considered the first laws of compulsory attendance which had a practical application in life. Side by side with compulsory elementary education the foundation of new seats of academic learning grew apace. In the period 1518–1600 Protestant Germany founded about two hundred new gymnasia and reformed about one hundred old grammar schools. Seven old Universities were reformed and three new ones founded (Marburg, Königsberg and Jena).

The education of girls was also promoted and in all Protestant towns special schools for girls were established. The Church Ordinances of Hesse, Lippe, Lower Saxony and Strasbourg even required the establishment of schools for girls in rural communities. Thus in direct connection with the Reformation Protestant Germany, after the end of the sixteenth century, became the leading European country in educational theory and practice. Through the close alliance of the Lutheran Church with the secular power and the introduction of compulsory education much earlier than in the rest of Europe Germany maintained that position until the end of the nineteenth century. It was challenged by other European countries only in the twentieth century when compulsory education became a universal principle.

In Scandinavia, after a short and decisive struggle, the Lutheran Reformation was accepted in all three kingdoms and became one of the most important factors of their national life. As in Germany, it led to universal elementary education. The Danish Church Ordinance enacted for Denmark in 1537 and for Norway in 1539 says:

> The children must everywhere be so instructed that the children of the peasants as well as others must obtain knowledge of that which not alone peasants, but even the nobles and kings, have hitherto not known. . . . The Clerk of the parish shall instruct the young peasant folk one period per week in such place and at such time as the pastor may decide. All country clerks shall themselves learn what is included in such learning for the children, and if they cannot do so, they are unfit for the office.

According to the Danish and Norwegian law of two centuries later (Frederick VI, 1739) every parish had to erect a schoolhouse and name a teacher. For scattered parishes travelling schools had to be organised. The local pastor and his dean were to examine and appoint the candidates presented. Attendance was compulsory for the ages seven to ten. Both the Church and the secular authority could be invoked to enforce attendance at parish schools. Owing to the opposition of the peasantry this part of the law of 1739 was not enforced and the responsibility of organising and erecting schools was relegated to local communities. A local board was established representing the clergy, secular authorities and four men from each parish. The Board marked out the plan of school organisation, but the peasants had the right of veto, of which they often took advantage. In the nineteenth century both in Denmark and in Norway the Lutheran Church gradually lost its administrative powers and the whole school system was taken over by the State and local authorities.

In Sweden the Lutheran Church became the champion of national independence, while the Catholic party advocated union with Poland under the Catholic branch of the Vasa dynasty. The early school laws as in other Lutheran countries were enacted as parts of Church law in 1571 and later in 1686. All the school edicts were made and approved by the clergy, who insisted on literacy as a condition for marriage and participation in Holy Communion. Gustavus Adolphus, the famous champion of the Reformation, issued the first secular laws in 1619 enjoining the towns to establish children's schools (*Barnarskolor*), and especially arithmetic schools. In his Resolutions of 1620 Gustavus Adolphus outlined a system of education which included gymnasia in larger towns, "trivial" schools in smaller towns and "little trivial" schools in rural communities. By his law of 1625 on the "Discipline of Youth" he imposed fines on negligent parents whose boys over seven years old did not learn to read, write and cipher. The fine was ten *daler* per month, and if money was not forthcoming the guilty parent had to "smart with his body." The school-ladder of Gustavus Adolphus was realised in 1649 by his daughter Christina under the personal influence of Comenius. The Lutheran Church of Sweden continued to administer schools throughout the nineteenth century. By the law of 1842, the parish vestries were made responsible for the maintenance and administration of primary schools. The parish pastor was *ex officio* the chairman of the School Board. In towns, the School Boards were elected partly by the Church and partly by the town councils. All School Boards for primary education were supervised and controlled by the Chapter (*Dom kapitel*), a diocesan Church council consisting of the bishop and the dean of the cathedral as president and vice-president and four or more lectors of State secondary schools as members. Only in the twentieth century has the Church gradually lost its administrative functions in education. In 1904 secondary schools were exempted from Church supervision and in 1932 the whole school system was secularised. Thus the Lutheran Church in Sweden was the guiding authority up to the third decade of the twentieth century, and even now in rural parish councils Lutheran pastors play the leading part. In Sweden, as in other Scandinavian countries, the Church since the Reformation has been as national as the secular government, and there was never any shadow of opposition. The secularisation laws were merely the more modern expression of the actual situation. In Germany, on the other hand, the Churches, both Catholic and Protestant, have entirely lost their powers, and during the Nazi régime their moral influence on the education of German youth was negligible.

After the war the whole system was secularised in the Russian zone of Germany, whilst in the three Western Zones the pre-Nazi division into denominational, Catholic and Protestant, and undenominational schools was restored.

After the schism the Eastern Orthodox Church was dominated for five hundred years by the Byzantine Emperors and had to adjust its policy to the secular interests of the State. The Patriarchs were enthroned and deposed at will by the Emperors every time they dared oppose the State. With the fall of Constantinople in 1453 the Eastern Patriarchs became subjects of the Turkish Sultan and their dependence on the secular power was even more evident. On the whole the Sultans did not interfere in the administration of the Eastern Church and the Patriarch of Constantinople in fact enjoyed more authority over the enslaved Christian nations than under the Emperors. The whole Christian population irrespective of nationality was organised as the "Roman nation" (*Rum milleti*) and was placed under the jurisdiction of the Patriarch of Constantinople, who resided in the Phanar on the banks of the Golden Horn. The Greek officials appointed from the Phanar were called "Phanariotes." The whole situation in the Balkans under the Turk was highly paradoxical. The great majority of the "Roman nation" were Slavs —Serbs, Macedonians and Bulgars; Vlachs and Moldavians (Rumanians); and Albanians, who did not speak Greek and were independent in their national kingdoms before the Turkish conquest. In their countries the Orthodox Church became a cultural influence only with the invention of the Slavonic alphabet and the introduction of a Slavonic Liturgy. This greatest cultural event in the history of the Slavs happened as early as the middle of the ninth century, when the two Slav apostles from Macedonia, Cyril and Methodius, converted the Southern Slavs and the Czechs to Christianity and invented the Slavonic alphabet. The Czechs were later converted to the Latin form of Christianity, and the Southern Slavs, both Serbs and Bulgars, lost their independence in the fourteenth century and were forced to adopt the Greek liturgy. Only in the nineteenth century were the modern Serbian, Bulgarian and Rumanian national Churches of the Orthodox Communion re-established. After the conquest by the order of the Sultan the Slavs and Vlachs became subjects of the Greek Patriarch in Constantinople and were denied the recognition of their nationality. The Patriarch appointed Greeks exclusively to their national sees, prohibited the use of the Slavonic liturgy and enforced the Greek language in all Slavonic and Rumanian territory. Usually the Sultan appointed the Greek bishop who paid him the largest sum of money as a "gift" to be Patriarch, so the Patriarch, to reimburse himself, appointed as bishops those Greeks who would pay him substantial "gifts." The bishops appointed to Slav sees in their turn made every effort to reimburse themselves from the alien population. In the last resort the Slav and Rumanian peasantry had to foot the whole bill. The resulting hatred of the Greeks was not even surpassed by the Slav hatred of the Turks. The peasants often boycotted the Churches where the Greek liturgy was used and there were cases when Greek bishops officiated in Slav cathedrals under the protection of Turkish bayonets and in the total absence of a Slav Christian congregation. Thus a kind of unholy alliance was established between the Phanar and the Sublime Porte. In their favour to the Phanar the Sultans went so far as to appoint Phanariote Greeks as vassal princes of Wallachia and Moldavia, and many Phanariote families grew fat by exploiting the Rumanian peasantry. In these circumstances the Eastern Church could not play any cultural rôle in the Balkans. On the contrary the Phanar was the greatest obstacle to the establishment of Slavonic or Rumanian schools or any cultural movements of a national character. When the time for liberation came the initiative was taken by the Slav peasantry themselves, and the struggle was directed simultaneously against Turkish secular rule and Greek spiritual oppression. Invariably the Slavs seceded from the Eastern Church and re-established their old auto-cephalous churches which had been suppressed by the Phanar. Invariably they reintroduced the Slavonic liturgy and the Cyrillic alphabet. Only after the liberation were the reborn Slav Orthodox Churches able to play their natural part in the cultural life of the nation. But as they had been re-established by successful revolts of national secular movements they could only approve the educational measures of the secular Government and reinforce them by their influence. Thus whether under the Byzantine Emperors or Turkish Sultans the Eastern Orthodox Church has been a tool of the secular Government and did not initiate any school system of its own. Its only claim to European gratitude was the preservation of the ancient Greek learning which was transferred to the West by Greek refugees after the fall of Constantinople. The greatest contribution to the Renaissance in Italy was made by Bessarion, the Metropolitan of Nicaea. Having settled in Rome he became the patron of all Greek refugees, and with their help introduced the study of Plato and other Greek classics to the Western world.

We see a certain similarity between the Protestant countries and the Orthodox countries of the Balkans. In both cases the national Churches were established in close alliance with the secular power and as a result of national revolts against foreign domination—that of Rome in the West, of Constantinople in the East. But whereas in the West the Protestant Churches inherited the great school system of the medieval Church which enabled them from the very start to lead in the cultural progress of their nations, in the Balkans the new national Churches had to start from scratch, while the secular Governments had already established the first foundations of national school systems.

The Russian Orthodox Church has a history of its own, which is the history of its cultural isolation. Russia accepted Christianity from Constantinople in the tenth century and soon after the schism definitely joined the Eastern Orthodox part of the Christian Church. The Slavonic liturgy and the Slavonic alphabet very soon became the official symbols of the Church and of the national tradition. In the thirteenth century Russia was separated from the rest of Europe by the Mongol invasion and for the next four centuries lived in complete isolation. After the fall of Constantinople the Russian Church became quite independent of the Eastern Patriarchs, and in 1589 the Metropolitan of Moscow was raised to the status of fifth Patriarch. The Russian Tsars, claiming the heritage of the Byzantine Emperors, were the actual rulers and heads of the Russian Church, and the Moscow Patriarchs seldom dared to oppose them, since opposition invariably led to imprisonment or even death. Peter the Great cut short even the semblance of independence by abolishing the Patriarchate in 1721 and establishing the Holy Synod, which in fact was nothing more than a Government department. In such conditions the Russian Church could hardly initiate an independent educational system as the Church in the Roman West had done. Only in that part of Russia which was under the rule of Catholic Poland was the Russian Church able to assume the rôle of a spiritual leader. Here, pressed by a foreign secular power and by organised Jesuit *propagatio fidei*, the Russian Church rose to the occasion. When the Western Russian bishops accepted the union with Rome the lower clergy and the laity rose in national revolt and compelled the Polish kings to recognise the continued existence of the Russian Orthodox Church. The leading rôle was played by religious brotherhoods, which organised a system of parochial and secondary schools which was crowned by the Kiev Academy, founded by the Metropolitan Peter Mogila in 1627. These schools educated not only the future clerics, but nobles, Cossacks and simple citizens, and thus preserved the Orthodox faith and Russian nationality from Roman Catholic and Polish domination. The Moscow branch of the Russian Church was stimulated by this example only after the reunion of the Ukraine with Muscovite Russia. The first Academy in Moscow was opened in 1687 and was staffed by Kiev graduates. The few Church schools which grew out of this beginning were reorganised by Peter the Great and placed under the direct control of the secular Government. From that time the Church schools were maintained by the Government and were used by reactionary Tsars as tools for enforcing their policy of Autocracy, Orthodoxy and Nationality. They became the mainstay of reaction and produced a strong anti-clerical movement in all sections of the Russian people. The Church schools were highly unpopular and disappeared almost overnight after the Revolution of 1917. Since then the Church has not interfered in the educational policy of the State and is concerned exclusively with the training of the clergy. In 1944 the Soviet Government allowed the newly established Patriarch of Moscow to open a

Theological Academy in Moscow, which is under the control of a Government Ministry of Orthodox Affairs.

This short description of the three main Christian traditions in Europe explains clearly the difference between the Catholic, Protestant and Orthodox countries and the influence of religion in their educational systems. Although in Latin Catholic countries the anti-clerical movement has won an official victory and has introduced a public secular school system, the Catholic Church never surrendered its right to educate and has maintained its influence by building up a parallel private school system. In Protestant countries the national character of the local Churches and their long alliance with the secular power led to a compromise by which the public school system has retained religion as an integral part of the school curriculum. In the Eastern part of Europe, where the Orthodox Church had no educational tradition of its own and was always subservient to the secular Government, the secularisation of education is the most radical and final solution, unchallenged even by the official representatives of the Church. After the War of 1939–45 the policy of the Soviet Union was followed by all the Slavonic States and Rumania, which completely secularised their school systems and disestablished their Orthodox Churches.

Of the 300 million Moslems in the world about 30 million are in the U.S.S.R., about 20 million under France in Africa and about three million in the Balkans. With the exception of Egypt the remaining Moslems are all in Asia. The presence of these millions of Moslems in Russia, Yugoslavia, Bulgaria and Albania makes Islam one of Europe's religious traditions. However, medieval Europe was most profoundly influenced by Islam through the Moorish kingdoms of Spain and Sicily. The Turkish Empire included for many centuries Greece, Yugoslavia, Bulgaria, Rumania, half of Hungary and the southern part of Russia, and was in fact a European State. But whereas the influence of the Spanish variation of Islam was most stimulating in the development of European science and education, the influence of the Turkish variety was only negative and held up the cultural development of Eastern Europe for five centuries. As already mentioned, Islam occupies an intermediate position between Christianity and Oriental religions. In culture the frontier between East and West does not coincide with the Bosphorus dividing Europe from Asia. Hellenistic civilisation was common for a thousand years both to Europe and to the Near East.

Christianity was the dominant religion for seven centuries in the countries which are now the centres of Islamic culture. The original Islam of Muhammad was a synthesis of Judaistic and Christian beliefs with the social customs of Arab nomads. Islamic mysticism and philosophy are comprehensible only when viewed in the light of Christianity and Greek philosophy. In its historical-political connections Islam was also closely related to Europe. In Islam, as in Christianity, there were two chief currents of religious thought. One, the orthodox, was mostly represented by Arabs; the other, the liberal, by Moslems— descendants of old cultural nations such as Hellenised Syrians or Persians. The orthodox tradition expressed the fanatical outlook of Semitic Arabs and their aristocratic contempt for all non-Arabs. Arabic as the form of expression, and the Koran as a source of knowledge, were the only recognised bases of culture. Although the Koran was more than a religious book and included a system of law, it was too narrow a foundation for an important contribution to the advancement of knowledge. Whenever the orthodox party was in power, learning was neglected and free intercourse with non-Moslems was almost non-existent. The orthodox schools limited their curriculum to Arabic grammar and learning by heart the Koran and the Tradition (*Hadith*). With the expansion of the Arabian-Moslem Empire beyond Arabia proper, the conquerors inevitably came into closer contact with ancient Greek and Persian civilisations and had to make concessions to the native populations which professed Christianity. Conversion to Islam was very gradual and continued for centuries before the Near East became overwhelmingly Moslem. There were three chief causes which prevented a wholesale conversion. First, Christianity and Judaism were recognised by Muhammad himself as two preliminary stages of Islam, which partially contained the true religion. The Jews and the Christians are the "People of the Book," and in the two parts of the Bible they possess the revelation of the true God. The heathen, on the contrary, are idolaters and worshippers of false gods. The attitude of Moslems towards the two kinds of non-believers is defined in the Koran as follows: "Fight those who do not believe in God and in the day of judgment . . . those who have received the Book until they pay you a poll-tax and be subject to you." Accordingly the first were converted to Islam at the point of the sword or were killed. The second were left unmolested provided they submitted and paid a poll-tax. The second reason against a wholesale conversion was that Moslems did not pay poll-tax and there was an economic necessity for a growing Empire to preserve large non-Moslem communities as taxpayers. Thirdly, in the beginning Islam was identified with Arab nationality, and non-Arabs could become Moslems by being adopted by some Bedouin tribe. Thus Moslems tolerated the Jews and the Christians and often had Christian wives, who were allowed to profess their faith freely. With the transference of the capital from Medina to Damascus the liberal tendencies prevailed. The Omayyad dynasty, as usurpers, were not recognised as Caliphs by orthodox Arabs, and in consequence had to rely more on the Syrians for support. The Syrians, being newly converted ex-Christians, had lived for centuries within the sphere of Hellenistic Christian civilisation. Inevitably their outlook was more liberal than that of the desert Arabs, and the heritage of Hellenistic culture was gradually incorporated in Islam. A new change took place in A.D. 750, when the new dynasty of Abbasides transferred the capital to Baghdad. The refugee Omayyads established their rule in Spain, where they initiated the most liberal and tolerant régime known in Spanish history. The Abbasides under the Persian influence very soon lost their fanaticism and promoted education and learning in the Baghdad Caliphate. Christian schools existed in all the countries conquered by the Arabs, not only in Alexandria and the late Byzantine provinces, but even in Persia. The Nestorians founded many famous centres of learning, as, for instance, the College of Nisibis, and were invited to come, by Persian Shahs and Baghdad Caliphs, as teachers. The famous medical school of Junde-Shapir had Nestorian lecturers, and most of the physicians of the Abbaside period graduated from there. During the Omayyad period the Christian theologian John of Damascus was a trusted adviser of the Caliph. In Baghdad the famous Caliphs Al Mansur, Harun al Rashid and Al Mamun, surrounded themselves with Christian and Persian philosophers, physicians and scholars. Al Mamun (A.D. 813) founded the Dar al Hicma in Baghdad (House of Wisdom), which can be considered the first Moslem university. He employed Christian scholars for translating Syriac and Greek manuscripts and thus started the rediscovery of Greek philosophy which ended in the Renaissance in Europe. Philosophy, mathematics and medicine flourished in all the great cities of the Caliphate. Especially was this the case in Spain, where under the tolerant Moslem kings Jewish, Moslem and

Christian scholars vied with each other in the promotion of learning. Avicenna (Ibn Sina) of Bokhara in the tenth century and Averroes (Ibn Roshd) of Cordova in the twelfth century were scholars and philosophers who influenced the subsequent development of European science and philosophy. This early Renaissance in Islamic countries was suddenly set back with the sack of Baghdad by the Turks in 1258. As so often happens, the new converts to Islam, the Mongolian Turks, became more fanatical and orthodox than the older Moslems. Islam regularly changed its dominant features with the change of its adherents. The primitive Islam of the desert Arabs was transformed by the cultured Syrians and Persians and Moslems of Spain into a more liberal and tolerant religion. When the banner of Islam was taken over by the newly converted Turks, it again assumed features more suitable to its bearers. This change in the main representatives of Islam led to a cultural cleavage between Christian Europe and Islamic countries which previously did not exist. During the early Renaissance, the Christian and Moslem scholars not only influenced each other through their works and correspondence, but often had personal contact and friendly relations. Since the fourteenth century, however, Europe and the Near East, including the Balkans, have been separated and the unity of a common Hellenistic civilisation has been broken. In Spain different causes led to similar results. Catholic princes started the reconquest of Spain and in the bitter struggle developed a narrow and fanatical brand of Christianity which put a full stop to the earlier tolerance and promotion of learning under the Moslems. The remnants of the Moors, thrown back to Africa and isolated, returned to the primitive and fanatical Islam of their ancestors. After the fall of Constantinople Europe took the path of Renaissance, Reformation and Revolution, while Islam stagnated in newly found orthodoxy. The conquest of the south-eastern part of Europe by the Turks resulted in the same stagnation among millions of Christians who were deprived of their own cultural influences but were not given anything to replace them. The Turkish Empire had a system of primary Koran schools or *maktabs* and secondary schools or *medresses*, modelled on Persian and Arabic schools. But the barren scholastic methods of learning by heart the Arabic text of the Koran could hardly promote enlightenment among the few boys who attended these schools. Moreover Arabic was a foreign language both to the Turks and to the converted Balkan Slavs and Albanians.

The Moslem masses were quite illiterate and fanatical in spite of being the ruling class in the Empire. The Christians having lost their own tradition and being kept in subjugation by the Turks developed into a similar illiterate and fanatical mass of people, whose only guiding principle of life was an intense hatred of the oppressors. As we have mentioned, the Eastern Orthodox Church by insisting on the Greek language added a new obstacle to the educational progress of the enslaved Slavs and Rumanians. Both the Moslem and the Christian peasantry of Slav and Albanian origin were completely neglected by their rulers in every respect, and only after the liberation of the Balkan nations from the Turks and the Greeks could they start any movement of enlightenment among the masses.

In conclusion we may compare the results of religious influences on the diffusion of education in different parts of Europe. We notice at once that the Protestant countries lead in all aspects of education. They were the first to introduce compulsory attendance and to make primary education universal; they were the first to provide secondary education for a large section of the population, and they were the first to introduce equal educational opportunities for both sexes. In those countries where Catholicism was dominant universal primary education was introduced much later, and in Portugal and Spain even now does not embrace the total population of school age. Secondary education for girls is less developed than in Protestant countries, and there is a marked difference in methods, curricula and facilities as between the sexes. The countries of Orthodox tradition lagged behind Western Europe for centuries and only lately by the efforts of secular governments have they made marked progress. The Moslem population of Europe is the most backward of all groups. Even the ruthless drive and straightforward policy of equalisation adopted by the Soviet Government has not yet eliminated the difference created by centuries of neglect. In the U.S.S.R., if the population is grouped by religious traditions, the Protestants (Estonians, Germans, Latvians) take the first place in educational development, the Orthodox (Russians, Ukrainians, Georgians) the second place, the Catholics (Lithuanians) the third, and the Moslems are still far behind the first three groups. It will take another two or three decades before the equalisation of educational opportunities closes this gap. Another striking example is provided by Yugoslavia. This country includes areas which for centuries were dominated by different religious traditions.

Slovenia on the Italian-Austrian border was part of Austria up to 1918, is entirely Catholic, and in its educational history followed that of Austria which combined the Catholic tradition with the German legislation on compulsory attendance. Croatia next to it is predominantly Catholic, but includes an Orthodox population (24 per cent) as well. Croatia, before 1918, was included in Hungary where compulsory attendance was not strictly enforced. Voevodina is another ex-Hungarian province, but is populated by Orthodox and Catholic Serbs. Serbia proper is Orthodox and was liberated from the Turks more than a century ago. Macedonia is mostly Moslem and was liberated in 1912. Bosnia and Herzegovina are Moslem and Orthodox and were administered by Austria-Hungary until 1918. Montenegro was an independent country never conquered by Turkey, but was entirely isolated. If we compare the incidence of illiteracy in all these parts of Yugoslavia just before World War II we find: Slovenia 9 per cent; Voevodina 23 per cent; Croatia 32 per cent; Serbia 65 per cent; Montenegro 67 per cent; Bosnia and Herzegovina 80 per cent; and Macedonia 84 per cent. The influence of the Protestant tradition may be gauged from the figures of Voevodina, the only province which had a Protestant minority of 10 per cent; their presence accounts for the higher literacy in Voevodina as compared with Croatia. These differences in cultural background and general literacy are the greatest obstacles to the unification of Yugoslavia into a single nation. The new constitution of the Yugoslav Republic has recognised this by creating a federation of six self-governing Republics according to traditional linguistic and religious divisions. Albania is another example where three religions met and for centuries influenced different sections of the population. The majority of the Albanians are Moslem, the minority Orthodox and Catholic. The Catholic section is the most advanced and provides most of the Albanian intelligentsia, the Orthodox section lags far behind the Catholics, and the Moslems until recently were quite illiterate. Just before the war only 35 per cent of all children of all sections of school age attended primary schools. Albania is the most backward country in Europe.'

We add here a table showing the number of adolescents

Predominantly Protestant countries		Predominantly Catholic countries		Predominantly Orthodox or Moslem countries	
Denmark	44	France	18	Albania	4
Germany	44	Italy	25	Bulgaria	18

Sweden	37	Belguim	10	Greece	25
Switzerland	42	Poland	17	Rumania	12
England	47	Portugal	14[1]	Turkey	19
Scotland	43	Spain	12	Yugoslavia	40

receiving post-primary education, both secondary and vocational, for every hundred pupils in elementary schools (for 1950–51).

Of course these figures only partially reflect the influence of religious traditions, and there are many cross-currents which confuse the clear-cut differences, but the better provision of education in Protestant countries is quite evident.

The U.S.S.R., since the introduction of Universal seven-years schools in rural areas and ten-years schools in towns, has the highest figure of 65 pupils in secondary grades for each 100 pupils in primary grades.

[1] In Portugal 80 per cent of school-age children are in primary schools, in Spain only 47.

CHAPTER VI

THE CATHOLIC TRADITION [1]

After the Renaissance and Reformation the position of the Catholic Church in Europe varied from country to country. In Spain, Portugal and Italy the Church was not challenged by reforming movements, retained its traditional hold on the population, and only in the eighteenth and nineteenth centuries had to withstand a furious attack from the secularist intelligentsia. In France, Southern Germany and Poland the Catholic party led several religious wars against the strong Protestant party and regained its official supremacy only after an embittered struggle. The North of Europe and Britain, with the exception of Southern Ireland, were irretrievably lost. The policy of the Church had to be differentiated according to the situation. In the South of Europe Catholicism assumed the most orthodox and rigid aspect with an enforced monopoly and persecution of heretical individuals. In France, Southern Germany and Poland the Church in close alliance with the secular power made every effort to maintain the adherence of the masses by alternate policies of conciliation and persecution. In Protestant countries the Catholic Church appeared as the champion of freedom of conscience and legal recognition of minorities. The Protestant movement, both in the seceding countries and in France and Southern Germany, made a rapid advance in the organisation of a reformed system of education, and the old medieval school system of the Catholic Church was entirely inadequate to maintain its ground against the encroachments of the new rivals. A new organisation was necessary to save France, Southern Germany and Poland from going over to the camp of the Reformation. In 1540 the Spaniard Ignatius Loyola founded the Society of Jesus and thus provided the Church with means and weapons to start an offensive against the growing menace. Loyola's Society was not an order of monks devoted to contemplation, but a fighting Catholic organisation, on a military model, with a General at its head and highly centralised control. Its double purpose was to conquer new countries for Catholicism through missionary activities, and to

---

[1] Most of the contents of Chapters VI, VII and VIII were published in the *Year Book of Education*, 1936, 1937 and 1938. See page 5 and Bibliography.

preserve or win back the old countries through the control of education. Supported by the Pope of Rome and the Catholic sovereigns, the Jesuits succeeded in building up the greatest international system of secondary and higher educational institutions known in history. In their *Constitutions* of 1559 a whole book was devoted to education, and their *Ratio Studiorum* of 1599 served for three centuries as a code for hundreds of Jesuit Colleges. Both the Church and the Catholic kings entrusted them with the education of the upper classes. Old Universities were handed over to them and hundreds of new colleges were founded by municipalities and princes to be controlled by the Society. A well-organised and uniformly directed international system of colleges came into being during the first century after the foundation of the Society. The Jesuits were the spearhead of the militant Catholic Church, and their educational aims and policy were entirely subordinated to the ends of the spiritual supremacy of Rome. They were not concerned with the elevation of the masses, because the ignorant and superstitious peasants were easily controlled by the clergy and kept under the authority of the Church. Even the *Constitutions* said: "None of those who are employed in domestic service by the Society ought to learn to read or write . . . for it suffices for them to serve with all simplicity and humility our Master, Jesus Christ." The danger came from the middle and upper classes which, in view of their superior education and greater independence, could be led astray by reforming preachers and anti-clerical propaganda. The aim of the Jesuit system was to educate the élite, to win all the leading minds irrespective of origin, and thus to secure the domination of the Catholic Church. The Society never established elementary schools for the masses in Europe and concentrated its efforts on secondary and higher education. There was only one exception to this policy; in the Jesuit republic of Paraguay, in order to Christianise savage Indian tribes, the Society did establish a system of elementary education. The masters of Jesuit Colleges belonged to many nationalities, but only the language of the Church—Latin—was used as a medium of instruction and of daily intercourse. National history, national languages and literature were not taught at all. The competition of humanist reformed gymnasia compelled the Jesuits to accept the Latin of the Renaissance and the new methods of teaching Latin and Greek, but they took care to incorporate the external form only without the substance. As the General of the Society, Beckx, declared in

1854: "The colleges will remain what they are by nature, a gymnastic for the intellect, which consists far less in the assimilation of real matter, in the acquisition of different knowledge, than in a culture of pure form." By these methods of formal training, by their special disciplinary measures and by the complete detachment of pupils from their families, the Jesuits succeeded in training a new generation of devout and subservient members of the Church ready to side with Rome against the interests of their country or nationality. Thus they stemmed the expansion of the Reformation in France, Germany and Poland, and triumphed over more liberal tendencies in the Catholic Church herself. In Poland they even succeeded in converting the Russian Orthodox gentry to Catholicism and Polish nationality, thus creating the cause of the embittered religious and national wars between the Western Russians and the Poles. It is an irony of history that after the suppression of the Society at the end of the eighteenth century in all Catholic countries it found an asylum in Orthodox Russia under the special protection of Tsar Alexander I. The Society continued its official existence in White Russia simply because the Tsar forbade the publication of the Papal Bull of Dissolution in Russia. Restored in 1814, the Society could not regain its previous monopoly of Catholic education, and had to modify its rigidity to suit the post-revolutionary period.

The Jesuits were the most typical representatives of the Catholic tradition in education, but the Church harboured within its fold other tendencies as well. Certainly these tendencies could not find expression in Spain, Portugal or Italy, which were under the complete monopoly of the Society of Jesus. But in France for a period the Huguenots enjoyed legal freedom of worship and education and a certain tolerance of unorthodox opinions was permitted. By an oversight of the Church the Jansenist doctrine of grace, determinist and akin to Calvinism, was openly accepted by many leading Catholics and even religious Orders. Opposed to the Jesuits both in their doctrine of grace and in their general attitude towards children, the Jansenists in their educational theory and practice represented more liberal views. There were two French societies influenced by Jansenism. The Sodality of l'Oratoire or the Oratorians was founded by Cardinal Pierre de Bérulle in 1611. It was a voluntary association without monastic vows, devoting itself to education. From the start the Oratorians opposed the Jesuit system and tradition. They accepted French as the medium of instruction and, for the first time, introduced

History and Science as separate subjects. They were vigorously denounced by the Jesuits, who accused them of disseminating a spirit of "independence and liberty" and of republicanism. The Oratorians were the only Catholic community which later accepted the French Revolution and were not dissolved by the first revolutionary Government. The Society of Port Royal founded its first schools in 1643 and introduced new methods of teaching, which it shared with the Oratorians. Both these societies were French institutions in contradistinction to the international Society of Jesus. They defended the independence of the Gallican Church and as Jansenists even refuted the infallibility of the Pope. A bitter polemic ensued between Jesuits and Jansenists in which neither side spared its opponents. The *Lettres Provinciales* of Pascal did immense injury to the Society of Jesus and opened the way for a secular attack. After twenty years of struggle the Jesuits triumphed. The doctrine of Jansen was officially declared a heresy, the members of Port Royal were arrested and put into prison and their schools were closed. This persecution resulted in the Jansenists seceding from the Catholic Church and joining the Protestants. The school system of the Oratorians, on the other hand, survived the struggle and later influenced the reform of Catholic education in France. On one point, however, the Jansenists agreed with the Jesuits; they were against the education of the masses and concentrated their efforts on the education of an élite. Whilst the monopoly of the Catholic faith was not in danger there was no need to educate the masses.

The Church began to pay attention to elementary education among the peasantry only when the monopoly was endangered either by the Protestants or secularists. The first attempt at founding a Catholic system of primary schools was also made in France, but against the opposition of the Church. In 1684 J. B. de La Salle, a Catholic priest, founded the Institute of Christian Brothers (Frères des écoles chrétiennes). This was a community of lay brothers devoted to the idea of the moral regeneration of poor children through religious education. Looked upon by the Church with suspicion as innovators, the Brethren met obstacles everywhere. La Salle himself said that "he was persecuted by the men from whom he expected help." In spite of difficulties he persevered, and at the time of his death in 1719 the Christian Brothers had already a large number of primary schools. Only after his death did the Christian Brothers receive the pontifical sanction, in 1724, and the protection of the French king. La Salle was an innovator in other respects as well. In 1685 he opened at Reims the first Catholic Seminary for schoolmasters for the training of teachers in rural districts. He also organised a school near Rouen, whose "purpose was to prepare the student for commercial, industrial and administrative occupations." In spite of the rigidity of their school regulations and a severe moral discipline unsuitable to children, the Christian Brothers partially redeemed the neglect of primary education by the Catholic Church. The Brothers were dissolved by the French Revolution but were reconstituted in 1797. The law of 1802 practically left them in control of the French elementary school system. They were again dissolved in 1905 by the secularisation laws, but were allowed to open their schools later. The example of La Salle was followed only in Ireland, where the Irish Christian Brothers were the pioneers of Catholic elementary education in the nineteenth century. In Spain, Portugal and Italy primary education was neglected by the Church until very recently, when secular Governments introduced compulsory attendance.

In the Iberian peninsula Roman Catholicism even now is not only a form of religious belief, but an integral part of the national character. The long and bitter struggle with the Moors made Catholicism a lasting feature. The Society of Jesus was born in Spain and was the most important factor in the development of Spanish culture. Within a century of its foundation the Jesuits controlled all the Spanish Universities and had founded about a hundred new colleges. For three centuries the Spanish ruling class was brought up and educated by Jesuits. The religious fanaticism and intolerance of the Spaniards found its expression in the Inquisition, which never had actual power in France or Central Europe, and could burn heretics at will only in the three Southern Latin countries. The influence of this institution on the progress of European science is well known. It is sufficient to remember that the famous philosopher Giordano Bruno, for preaching pantheism and opposing the philosophy of Aristotle at Paris, was burnt at Rome in 1600; that Vanini for his philosophical opinions was condemned at Toulouse in 1619 to have his tongue cut out and afterwards to be hanged and burnt; that Galileo was compelled to go to Rome in 1633 solemnly to abjure his theory of the movement of the earth, and that Descartes' works were included on the Index and he himself "had always feared to be remarked by the Church" (Bossuet) and lived in Holland to be safely out of reach. Whilst in Italy the political

division of the country into many rival principalities and republics
provided a certain opportunity of escaping the clutches of the
Inquisition, in Spain the all-pervading autocracy of the Catholic
king made it supreme. In such conditions no such innovators as
the Jansenists or even La Salle could flourish on Spanish soil,
and the Jesuits could enjoy their monopoly in education without
fear of rivals. The first signs of opposition to their domination
came from the Bourbon kings, who inherited from Louis XIV
his ideas on a centralised State. In 1767 the Jesuits were banished
from Spain and their institutions were handed over to the
diocesan bishops for the formation of Catholic seminaries. The
Jesuits came back in 1814, were banished in 1820 and returned
in 1823. They were expelled again in 1836 and came back in the
fifties. In 1857 a Concordat with Rome was signed, according
to which "Public instruction in the Universities, Colleges,
Seminaries, public and private schools of every description must
be at all points in harmony with the teaching of the Catholic
Church." The last time the Jesuits were expelled was by the
Republican secularist Government in 1931, but with the victory
of Franco they were installed once more to control Spanish
education. The Catholic Church and the Jesuits openly sided
with the Franco régime. Spain is the only country in Europe
where the Catholic Church is in open alliance with a fascist
régime. Educational progress cannot take place in such conditions, and Spain is destined to remain a backward country
until the next change of régime. The history of Portugal is
similar, with constant changes of Catholic and secularist Governments, but in comparison with Spain the mutual persecutions
were more moderate and did not result in a fanatical hatred of
each other by the two parties to the conflict.

The Spanish interpretation of Catholicism was transplanted
by the "conquistadores" into America, and moulded the life and
development of Latin America on Spanish lines. As in Europe
the Spanish settlers were dominated in their cultural traditions
and their educational systems by the Catholic Church. As in
Europe the Catholic tradition was implanted under the leadership of the Society of Jesus. Although other religious Orders had
a number of schools under their control, the most important
seats of learning were in Jesuit hands. The University of Mexico,
founded in 1553; the University of San Marcos at Lima, founded
in 1571; the College of Cordoba, founded in 1611; the later
Universities of Santiago de Chile and of Chuquisaca in Bolivia

were all Jesuit institutions. The College of Cordoba was declared the *Colegio maximo* for all Spanish colonies in America. In 1613 it was reformed into the College of San Francisco Xaver and served as a model for all the higher institutions of South America. The Universities were properly constituted as institutions of higher learning only in 1644, when their Statutes were drafted by the Jesuit Andrea de Roda. In America the Jesuits had to change their policy as the situation was different. The Spanish "conquistadores" were fierce adventurers greedy for gold, and had little respect for culture; they looked upon the Indian population as a source of speedy enrichment and slaughtered them by thousands at the slightest provocation. Following on their heels came the Inquisition, which started a wholesale conversion of millions of natives, burning any Indian who after being converted relapsed to his old religion. The Society of Jesus in their missionary activities aimed at a sincere conversion and enlightenment of savage tribes and thus became the champions of the Indians, defending them against cruel governors and the fanatical policy of the Inquisition. Here in America the Jesuits met with a heathen population, and their task consisted not solely in educating an élite, as in Europe, but in christianising the Indians. In the Jesuit Republic in Paraguay the Society established a system of elementary schools and novitiates in which the whole population was instructed in the Catholic faith and in elementary knowledge. In their policy towards the Indians, the Jesuits proved to be humane and successful teachers, and it is largely due to their labours that some of the Indian tribes were christianised and brought into contact with Latin culture. Without the enlightened activity of the Society of Jesus and some other representatives of the Church during the colonial period, the conquest of America by the Spaniards would present an unrelieved picture of barbarism and cruelty. However, the Society could play its cultural rôle only so long as the Catholic religion had an undisputed monopoly of cultural life. As soon as other cultural traditions penetrated into Spanish colonies the Society inevitably became the upholder of the established order and the ally of all reactionary movements. Their monopoly was ended in Brazil in 1759 and in Spanish America in 1767. They were restored in 1814 and the familiar pattern of Spanish civil wars was repeated throughout the nineteenth century in all the newly established Republics. The Jesuits everywhere definitely associated themselves with the party of reaction and often were the source of an embittered civil strife which in Latin America was conducted by both sides with primitive savagery. The Catholic Church in Latin America developed into a political organisation which unscrupulously used all means to further her ends. On the whole the secularists had the upper hand in this struggle although the Church and the Jesuits had their periods of triumph. In Ecuador, for instance, a concordat with Rome was concluded in 1862, according to which all schools, whether private or public, had to teach "entirely in agreement with the doctrine of the Catholic Church." The control of the whole system was entrusted to the Society of Jesus. Protestants and other sectarians were deprived of their civic rights by the constitution of 1869 and in 1873 the whole republic was consecrated to the Sacred Heart of Jesus by a special law. The new constitution of 1897 abolished these provisions of monopoly. Another instance of alliance of the Church with reaction happened in Argentina in 1829, when Rosas became dictator for twenty-three years. Rosas in many ways was the precursor of Mussolini and Hitler. He established a personal rule based on the monopoly of his own party, he used the same methods of terrorism and imprisonment of his opponents, and even invented a special brand of nationalism, strange in Latin American conditions. He had one advantage over his two imitators of the twentieth century: he *was* blue-eyed and red-haired. He invited the Jesuits in 1836 to take control of secondary and higher education. However in 1841 he quarrelled with the Society on personal grounds, the Society being too independent for his liking, and he expelled the Jesuits once more. In all Spanish-speaking countries the policy of the Catholic Church showed the worst features of intolerance and fanaticism. Enforcing monopoly of thought by terroristic methods the Catholic party engendered a violent anti-clerical movement in which emotion and fanaticism played the same rôle. Mutual hatred led to many bloody civil wars in which the Church invariably backed the reactionary dictators and thus still more intensified the hatred of the Church in the opposite camp. In the total absence of Protestant bodies who could exert a moderating influence it is quite impossible for the two extremes to come to a compromise, and as the general trend is towards secularisation it seems that only a final victory of the secularists will enable Spain to follow Mexico on the way to constructive educational reform.

We have seen that in France Catholicism never attained such an exclusive monopoly of thought as in Spain, and although France also had her religious wars and the struggle of clerical and secularist parties, it never assumed such an irreconcilable character as in Spain. The two parties in spite of continuous opposition very often placed the interests of France above their sectional advantages and never pursued a policy of mutual extermination. The same happened in Italy, Belgium and Southern Germany. The secular State having won the legal supremacy in education permitted the Church a limited sphere of influence and the Church after some hesitation accepted that position. Quite different was the situation in Protestant countries. According to the principle *cujus regio, ejus religio*, the Protestant countries prohibited Catholic schools, and the policy of the Catholic Church in these circumstances was directed towards the defence of freedom of thought and instruction. In the Scandinavian North the Catholics were represented by individuals and thus the question never arose, but in Holland and in the English-speaking countries Catholics represent a strong compact minority and the problem of Catholic education was and still is one of the thorniest questions of educational politics.

In Holland after the Calvinist Reformation Catholic schools were prohibited by law and could only exist illegally. Education was controlled by the Dutch Reformed Church. The French Revolution spread to Holland and put an end to denominational control. A monopoly of the secular State was instituted in all branches of education. For a while the Catholic minority remained silent, gathering strength for an organised protest. In 1822 the situation became more favourable and the Catholics started a campaign for freedom of instruction, carefully avoiding a narrow denominational issue. At first the Calvinists held themselves aloof, not desiring to help the Catholics against their own Government. After twenty years of defending the freedom of thought the Catholics succeeded in conquering Calvinist prejudices and the latter joined hands with them in a common demand for denominational schools. To such a powerful alliance the State had to make concessions, and freedom of instruction was officially declared in 1848. Having founded many denominational schools both Churches now demanded public grants. The Churches won the elections of 1888 and were able to introduce a new article into the constitution empowering the State to grant subsidies to denominational schools under certain conditions. Still the equality of status was not attained. The State secular schools were maintained by local authorities with State grants. The denominational schools received only State grants, the communes and the provinces giving no support. Now the Churches demanded an absolute equality of financial support. It was evident that there would be no peace unless the last concessions were made. The necessary revision of the constitution was enacted in 1917, and since then this compromise seems to have satisfied the contending parties. It must be borne in mind that Dutch Catholics are broad-minded and liberal and as intensely patriotic as their Calvinist neighbours, which circumstance greatly enhanced their reconciliation. The situation in the English-speaking countries was slightly different.

Whereas in Holland the Catholic population is congregated in the southern part of the country where it even forms a majority and where it has been permanently settled since the Middle Ages, the Catholics of Great Britain, America and the Dominions are dispersed minority groups, very often a result of the migration of Irish Catholics. It is only in Quebec and Southern Ireland that the majority of the native population remained true to the old faith and could claim Catholicism as their national tradition. The policy of persecution after the Reformation isolated the Catholic groups from the rest of the population. Two centuries of cultural separation made an interchange of ideas and practice difficult. As a result, in all English-speaking countries the Catholics have established a separate school system existing side by side with the national systems, without contributing much to the general development of educational traditions. Although all Catholic schools resemble each other to a great extent, their legal status and influence are different in each country.

In England in 1558 all the clerics, including University dons, who refused to accept the separation from Rome were deprived of their livings and University posts, and it soon became evident that there was no hope for a second revival of Catholicism. The exiled University dons and priests went to Catholic countries and started English colleges abroad. In England the continuity of Catholic education was interrupted and no schools existed from the time of Elizabeth to that of James II. During the short reign of James II a few Catholic schools were established, but were closed after his deposition. The only school which could claim continuity from that period was the school at Twyford, near Winchester. Another school was founded in 1762 by

Bishop Challoner at Sedgley Park. With these exceptions, the Catholic gentry of the eighteenth century was educated abroad in the famous colleges of Douai, St. Omer or Bornhem. Living abroad among French-speaking people and meeting Catholics of all nations made the Catholic gentlemen and priests less insular than their Protestant contemporaries, and perhaps less narrow-minded in some respects. On the other hand, exclusion from the public services and the Universities made them half foreigners in their own country. A sudden change in the fate of Catholic education in England was brought about by the French Revolution. In 1793 all the English colleges in France and Belgium were closed down and their property confiscated. The English Catholics became refugees for a second time, but now they fled towards their native shores. Prejudice against Catholics in England was gradually disappearing. Although the disabling Acts were not entirely abolished, some measure of relief was passed by the Government in 1778. Side by side with the legal amelioration of their civic status went the change of attitude of Catholics themselves. From being rebels and Jacobites for a century they became loyal citizens of their country. The so-called Cisalpine spirit became predominant among the Catholic gentry. Granted the basis of Catholic dogma, the Cisalpines concentrated their attention on their civic obligations. In theory they accepted the dogmatic teaching of the Holy See, yet they resented any interference from the Pope and hierarchy in civic affairs. The Cisalpine Club represented the Catholic laity during the struggle for emancipation. They accepted the Government proposal of veto against the advice of Bishop Milner, which almost ended in their excommunication. Thus the English Catholics became nationally conscious. In these circumstances the English Colleges were repatriated without hindrance. Douai College moved to Ushaw, and the Jesuits of St. Omer to Stony-hurst. The Benedictine College of St. Gregory gave rise to Downside School, and that of Dieuleward continued its existence at Ampleforth. The Cisalpine parents of scholars from exiled colleges founded their own college at Oscott in 1794. Thus at the end of the century the Catholics in England possessed half a dozen Colleges with an established tradition which could rival the great public schools of the Anglicans. A new period of Catholic education was connected with three independent events: Catholic emancipation in 1829, the Irish famine of 1845 and the subsequent emigration to England, and the conversion of Newman and his followers in 1845 and later. Catholic emancipation gave a new impetus to the development of secondary schools, especially convent schools for girls. Foreign Orders, mostly from France, established branches in England together with their convent schools and thus introduced Continental ideas and methods. The conversion of many High Church Anglicans of the Oxford Movement gave rise to a new situation. Cardinal Manning, himself a convert, says in his letter to Talbot, also a convert and Secretary to the Holy See:

> changed conditions require new kinds of work. The contact with English society requires a new race of men as teachers, directors and companions. The work of the Church in relation to the Government in all public services, civil and military, at home and in the colonies, needs a class of men of whom we possess very few. The Catholic laity is beginning to be dissatisfied with the standard of education both in themselves and in their priests. The close contact with the educated classes of English society forces this on them. A large number of our laity, chiefly converts, are highly educated, and our priests are, except individuals, not a match for them.

The converts led by Newman brought with them the English tradition of great public schools and Oxford, and demanded Catholic schools modelled on them. In 1848 the convert Cornelia Connelly founded the first purely English Society of the Holy Child Jesus and established her first convent school at St. Leonards. She combined the Catholic and English traditions and thus brought a new element to Catholic education. The open-air spirit of freedom, born of trust and self-government, was a welcome addition to the previous seclusion and monastic discipline of Convent schools. Newman, in answer to the explicit desires of many converts, founded in 1860 his Oratory School at Birmingham on the model of Eton. Among the masters was Thomas Arnold who, although converted to Catholicism, was steeped in English tradition. These new schools influenced the older Catholic schools of Continental origin, and gradually Catholic secondary education became more English in its atmosphere. The previous impenetrable barrier between Protestant and Catholic schools was removed, but a certain consciousness of a different tradition is jealously preserved and accentuated. As the President of Catholic Colleges said in 1936:

> Our boys ... must feel not merely equality, but a sense of difference, a sense of the superiority of their Catholic culture, a conviction that they hold a key position containing the adequate and ultimate

solution of all problems. They must be wary of the corroding acid of a neo-pagan contact, and, without being prigs or recluses, look upon themselves as a race apart.

In the field of elementary education the position of Catholics was entirely changed by the Irish immigration in the wake of famine. Before the coming of the Irish peasants and labourers the English Catholics were chiefly squires and their dependants, and the merchants of the City. The Irish famine drove the starving population towards the English industrial centres. Within a few years thousands of Irish Catholics settled in Lancashire and elsewhere, thus changing the character of the Catholic community. The few existing elementary schools could not accommodate the newcomers, and new Catholic schools were necessary. In 1847 the Catholic Poor School Committee was founded and in 1849 received the Government grant on equal terms with the National and British and Foreign Societies for the maintenance of their schools. Since then the Catholic schools have been included in the national system of education with the same rights as other denominational schools. A new difficulty arose when the reorganisation of elementary schools along the lines of the Hadow Report was accepted as national policy. The Catholic elementary schools refused to take part in the general reorganisation and remained a separate system. Their attitude may be summarised by the declaration of Manchester Catholics that (a) they would not abandon the old traditional parochial system, (b) in no circumstances would any children be transferred from Catholic schools to Council schools, (c) as they must maintain the parochial system they did not propose to send schemes for the grouping of Catholic schools. With few exceptions this attitude is shared by other local Catholic bodies, and thus presents an obstacle for a true national system of education. It appears that in spite of the financial concessions of the 1944 Act the Catholic school system has decided to be separate and thus perpetuate the dual character of English education. On the other hand, English traditions have modified the original rigidity of Catholic school methods and softened down the extreme tendencies of Ultramontanism. Newman has become an English classic and Lord Acton an exponent of the English historical tradition at Cambridge.

In Ireland the Reformation was not successful and very few native Irishmen joined the new Church of Ireland. The colonisation of Ulster, and the Plantation under Cromwell, introduced many English and Scottish settlers, mostly Presbyterians. Thus the Irish population was and still is divided into three distinct groups: the majority, comprising almost all the native Irish and some descendants of the Anglo-Norman gentry, remained Catholics; the urban population of the Pale, together with the aristocracy, joined the established Church of Ireland; the colonists of Ulster are predominantly Presbyterian. During the immediate post-Reformation period Catholic schools existed only on sufferance. In the seventeenth century several Jesuit schools were established, but after a short existence were suppressed one by one. The Irish Catholics followed the example of the English Oxford exiles and founded colleges on the Continent. All the Irish clergy and many members of the gentry were educated abroad. To stop this practice the English Government enacted penal laws prohibiting any Catholic schools in Ireland and the sending of boys to Irish colleges on the Continent. During the period of penal laws the only opportunity for education was afforded to Catholics by the so-called Hedge Schools. These were small illegal schools constantly persecuted by informers and the police. They had no proper buildings, no school apparatus and no regular attendance. The teachers were lay Catholics, who had somehow managed to get some education either at Protestant schools, or abroad. Usually they taught the three R's, to which the Catholic catechism was added in the majority of schools. In some cases Irish and classical languages were also taught. They were Catholic rather in their negative attitude to Protestants than in a dogmatic sense, and the Catholic hierarchy looked upon them with disfavour. The enactment of the Relief Acts at the end of the eighteenth century permitted Catholic teachers to establish schools under certain conditions and resulted in a revival of Catholic education. Catholic Poor School Committees were formed which founded schools. Four Catholic Diocesan Colleges were opened, and the Government even endowed a Catholic College at Maynooth in 1795 with the chief purpose of preventing the training of the Irish clergy on the Continent. The foundation of the Irish teaching Orders, especially of the Christian Brothers in 1808, still more furthered the development of Catholic schools. After the restoration of the Society of Jesus in 1814 the Jesuits founded three colleges for boys. But all these foundations were inadequate for a population of about eight million. The emancipation of Catholics in 1829 compelled the Government to take the initiative in establishing a national

system. Being Protestant the Government was reluctant to found
a Catholic denominational system and in their National schools
they adopted the principle of neutrality towards religion. At
first the Catholic hierarchy, led by Archbishop Murray, accepted
the undenominational national system with united secular and
divided religious instruction. Soon, however, the hierarchy
changed its attitude. The Bishop of Tuam, McHale, was the first
to denounce the national system and to prohibit the co-operation
of the clergy of his diocese with the National Board. The new
Archbishop Cullen was an extreme ultramontane and sum-
moned a synod in 1850, which officially declared a boycott of
national schools by Catholics. The laity, however, continued to
send their children to national schools, but the uncompromising
attitude of the hierarchy engendered a spirit of denominational
strife and retarded the natural growth of the national schools.
The educational ideas of the Catholic hierarchy of that period
were expressed by Cullen as follows: "Too high an education
will make the poor oftentimes discontented, and will unsuit them
for following the plough or for using the spade, or for hammering
the iron, or for building walls." He would limit the education
of the poor to the three R's and the catechism. When the Government established the University with three constituent Colleges
as an undenominational institution, Cullen and his synod denounced them as "Godless" and urged all Catholic students to
boycott them. Cullen, however, understood that a purely negative policy would not keep the Irish students away from the new
University and started a campaign for founding a strictly Catholic
University. Collections were made in all Churches and Dr.
(later Cardinal) Newman was invited from England as the first
Rector of the new University. In 1854 the Catholic University
came into being and Newman zealously began to organise it.
He invited well-known English converts, among them Thomas
Arnold, as professors. His idea was to combine the best traditions
of Oxford with the religious atmosphere of Catholicism and to
make the new University a cultural centre for all English-speaking
Catholics. His vision was unacceptable both to the Irish hierarchy and to the English laity. The English gentry would not
send their sons to Ireland, preferring Oxford, which had just
opened its doors to Catholic students. The Irish hierarchy was
not interested in Newman's imperial dreams, and did not approve
of a wholesale transportation of Oxford converts. Newman,
finding himself restricted in his plans, was compelled to resign

and returned to England disillusioned in 1858. The Catholic University was handed over to the Society of Jesus, which has controlled it ever since. Under Jesuit guidance University College, Dublin, became the leading institution of the new nationalist Ireland and took an active part in the promulgation of the new constitution of Eire, which is an interesting attempt at combining the Catholic dogma with the ideals of democracy. In spite of its bitter opposition to England and Protestantism, Irish Catholicism was greatly influenced by English traditions and has incorporated many features of the English public schools in its system.

In the British Dominions we find the same opposition of the Catholic hierarchy to the establishment of a national educational system as we do in Great Britain. We described the situation in Quebec, Canada, where the Catholic hierarchy is in full control of the provincial school system and prevents any possibility of a common school for all denominations. In English-speaking Ontario the question of separate Catholic schools has been in the forefront of political agitation for decades. When the two provinces of Upper (Ontario) and Lower (Quebec) Canada were united under one Government in 1840, it became evident that the public school system could only be established on the basis of a compromise between the Catholics and Protestants. As the English-speaking Protestants of Quebec demanded separate schools, it was only just to concede the same rights to the Catholic minority of Ontario. Therefore the law of 1841 introduced uniform legislation for both provinces. At first the Catholic hierarchy worked in full agreement with the Government of Ontario. The ultramontane party, however, was not satisfied with certain limitations concerning separate schools and demanded complete equality of financial and legal provision as between the common public schools and the separate schools of the Catholic minority. When the French noble, Count de Charbonnel, became Bishop of Toronto in 1848, the ultramontane party found in him a champion of their ideals. He based his demands on the claim of the Catholic Church to be divinely appointed to the mission of teaching the world. He wrote to the Chief Superintendent of Ontario, Dr. Ryerson, in 1852:

> In default of these conditions it is forbidden to our faithful to send their children to public schools, on pain of the refusal of the Sacraments: because the soul and heaven are above everything . . . it is their right, so sacred and inalienable, that every wise and

paternal Government has made laws respecting instruction only in harmony with the teaching Church—the Bishops united to their supreme and universal Head, and this right is so inviolable, that of late, as well as in former times, in France, in Belgium, in Prussia, in Austria and in Ireland, the Bishops, with the Pope, have done everything to overthrow or modify every school or university system opposed to the mission given by Jesus Christ to His Sacred College: "Go ye, therefore, and teach all nations."

In 1856 Charbonnel went even further in his Lenten Pastoral:

Catholic electors in this country who do not use their electoral power in behalf of separate schools are guilty of mortal sin. Likewise parents who do not make the sacrifices necessary to secure such schools, or send their children to mixed schools. Moreover, the confessor who would give absolution to such parents, electors or legislators as support mixed schools to the prejudice of separate schools would be guilty of mortal sin.

This was intervention in a political issue with a vengeance. The Government tried to uphold the right of individual Catholic parents to decide for themselves to which schools they should send their children, and the controversy raged for years. Bishop Charbonnel retired to France in 1860 and the agitation gradually died down. The new Federal Constitution of 1867 confirmed the rights of the Catholic separate school system, but refused to compel the Provinces to extend their grants to secondary and higher Catholic institutions. This solution stabilised the interdenominational relations for a time. With the new policy of consolidation and equalisation of financial support the separate Catholic schools will inevitably prove to be an obstacle to its realisation.

In Australia we see the repetition of the same struggle for the control of education. In 1848 the Government of New South Wales established a dual system under two Boards, denominational and national. This arrangement proved to be unsatisfactory and there was a demand for a comprehensive national system. When a Bill was introduced in 1862 the Catholic bishops opposed it vigorously and issued a statement that: "We signalise as objectionable especially the non-recognition of the control over education which the Catholic Church holds to have been conferred on Bishops by Our Lord and Saviour Jesus Christ, when He said to His Apostles, 'Go, teach all nations.' No system of education can be accepted which does not recognise the guardianship of the bishops over the education of Catholic children, and to the security of such guardianship are essential the ownership of the schools and the control over the teaching by the power of appointing and dismissing teachers." The Bill was not passed owing to Catholic opposition. The new Education Act of 1866 introduced the separation of secular and religious instruction in all public schools and aroused strong protest. The Catholic bishops issued new decrees in 1869. "We condemn that education of Catholic youth, which is separated from the Catholic faith, and from the power of the Church, and therefore we shall take care to remove Catholic children from those schools which are called mixed schools." In 1873 Archbishop Vaughan issued his Pastoral letter, which indirectly led to the final separation of Church and State. His attack on public schools as "godless" and "leading to immorality and national dishonour" was greatly resented by the majority of Australians. In his letter Vaughan said: "Let all Catholic parents know that they cannot without serious guilt place their children in proximate danger of perversion. Let them bear in mind that to do so is to set at defiance the teachings of the Catholic Church, and that . . . no confessor can absolve such parents as are willing to expose their children's souls to the blighting influence of an alien creed or a secularist system." After the final secularisation of education in 1880 the Catholics withdrew their children from public schools and have built up an entirely independent and separate school system in New South Wales. In Victoria, separated from New South Wales in 1851, the same controversy led to the appointment of a Royal Commission in 1867, which reported that: "the question of the obligation or expediency of communicating religious instruction in the public schools, and the claims of the clergy of the different sects to direct or supervise such instruction, have contributed in this colony, as in other countries, more than all other causes combined to disturb opinion and to raise practical obstruction in the way of public instruction." In New Zealand the struggle was not quite so bitter and was confined to Auckland, but the outcome was the same, i.e. complete secularisation of education and a separate private school system for the Catholics.

In the U.S.A. the situation was much more complicated. Even one of the original English colonies—Maryland—was founded by Catholics, and the first Maryland law stated that: "The Holy Church shall have and enjoy all her rights, liberties and franchises wholly and without blemish." But during the Civil War in England the Puritans of Maryland overthrew the Catholic Government and proscribed Catholicism. Thus Catholic schools did not take root on the Atlantic border, but when new territories were added after the Declaration of Independence the policy of proscription could not be continued. It was against the principles of the American Constitution, and the new territories were settled by Catholics and had a school system of their own before they were joined to the U.S.A. The Spanish Catholic schools of Florida and New Mexico were completely destroyed by Indian revolts at the end of the eighteenth century, but the French schools of Louisiana passed to the U.S.A. with the territory intact. These Catholic schools received great reinforcement after the French Revolution, when many priests and religious Orders emigrated to America. Especially influential was the Sulpician Father Richard, who established a complete Catholic school system at Detroit from 1798 to 1832. It included high schools and teachers' training colleges, and in 1817 Richard helped to found the "Catholepistemiad or University of Michigania." With the help of European Catholic Orders the school system grew to such dimensions in the thirties that it attracted public attention. The question of State and communal grants to Catholic schools had to be decided. Denominational schools of Protestant churches had enjoyed public support since the planting of colonies. It was quite natural that the Catholics should demand the same privileges. In 1840 Bishop Hughes petitioned the State of New York for State grants to Catholic schools. Although Catholics agreed to accept all regulations and State inspection, both petitions were refused. The Catholics were compelled to build up their own separate school system as they could not send their children to Protestant or secular public schools. In the middle of the last century the Catholic population of America was almost doubled by the immigration of Irish and German Catholics. Later the immigrants from Italy, Poland, Austria-Hungary and Lithuania added to the Catholic population people of different origin and with traditions quite foreign to the common ideals of the English-speaking nations. The teaching Orders of American, of English, Irish, French and German derivation were unable to cope with the magnitude of the problem. Many new Orders from all European countries were invited to help in the task. But the lack of parish schools, and the necessity for substantial financial sacrifices on the part of the poor immigrants to maintain Catholic schools, compelled many Catholic parents to send their children to public non-sectarian schools. No less than one-third of the Catholic children attended public schools. The hierarchy prompted from Rome redoubled its efforts to organise a complete school system capable of embracing the whole Catholic child population. The first Plenary Council of Baltimore in 1852 unified the systems of various dioceses and exhorted the bishops to establish schools in all parishes, and to provide money from the revenues of the churches for the support of teachers. The next council at Cincinnati, in 1855, adopted the following decree: "We admonish pastors of souls again and again to strive by all means in their power to prevent boys and girls entrusted to them from frequenting those schools which they cannot attend without great danger to their faith and morals." The Second Council of Cincinnati of 1857 decreed: "It is the judgment of the Fathers that all pastors of souls are bound, under pain of mortal sin, to provide a Catholic school in every parish." These decrees were later affirmed, in 1875, by the Congregation of Propaganda at Rome. The Roman instruction concluded as follows: "Parents who neglect to give this necessary Christian training and instruction to their children or who permit them to go to schools in which the ruin of their souls is inevitable, or, finally, who send them to the public school without sufficient cause and without taking the necessary precautions to render the danger of perversion remote—that such parents, if obstinate, cannot be absolved." The question was not definitely settled by the instruction of the Roman Curia. There were many Catholics who recognised the right of the State to control the education of its citizens, and wished to arrive at an agreement with the State. In 1891 the Professor of Moral Theology at the newly founded Catholic University at Washington, Thomas Bouquillon, published a pamphlet: *Education, to Whom Does it Belong?* He admitted that the State, beside a vague general right to educate, possessed also "the special and proper right" to educate the rising generation. It had also the right to compel attendance at school, to prescribe a minimum of education and to inspect private institutions. The Jesuits attacked Bouquillon's views and denied the right of the State to enact compulsory legislation in education. Cardinal Satolli was sent from Rome and assembled half the American bishops at New York in 1892. They arrived at a compromise allowing parents to send their children to public schools in the absence of Catholic schools. This decision was not accepted by the ultramontane party, and they appealed to Rome. The Pope confirmed the total prohibition and thus definitely ended the attempts at a compromise. Public non-sectarian schools were incompatible with the ideas of Catholic education, and henceforward all Catholic schools had to form a separate and independent system. The American hierarchy succeeded in building up a well-organised system with high schools, training and general colleges and separate Catholic Universities.

Thus in all the English-speaking countries as well as in Holland the Catholic minority chose to separate themselves from the rest of the population by building up an independent school system. In America, Australia and New Zealand Catholic schools receive no public support, but in Great Britain and Holland they are maintained by central and local authorities and are subject to inspection. That this intransigent attitude is not necessary in the atmosphere of tolerance prevailing in these countries, is shown by the example of the Maritime Provinces of Canada where the majority of Catholic children attend public undenominational schools and have special time allotted to their religious instruction. As a matter of fact the severe condemnation of the "mixed" schools was not a universal policy of the Catholic Church. In Germany the so-called *Simultanschulen* with divided religious instruction were the rule in many "lands," as well as in Austria-Hungary, and the Catholic hierarchy tolerated this state of affairs, because the secular Governments were firm in refusing their demands for an exclusive Catholic system. In all countries, however, the Catholics, if in a minority, tried to build up a "nation" within a nation with their own legislation and administration in school matters. Two main causes contributed to this separation. The first was the change of policy of the Catholic Church, closely connected with the rise of the ultramontane party and the personality of Pope Pius IX. The second was the introduction of compulsory attendance and the growing intervention of the State. We have noticed that in all Protestant countries since the emancipation of the Catholics and up to the fifties of the last century there was on the whole a peaceful collaboration between the civic authorities and the Roman Church. The Cisalpines in England, the old Catholics of Scotland, the early Irish hierarchy trained in Continental Universities, the early Canadian and American bishops as well as the Catholics of Australia were all ready to accept the assistance of the State on the condition of mixed education and the separation of dogmatic instruction from the rest of the curriculum. The Irish National system, similar to the German *Simultanschulen,* was not only approved by the hierarchy of Ireland, but was considered a model compromise both in America and Australia. The election of Cardinal Mastai as Pope Pius IX in 1846 changed the situation. The new Pope was considered a liberal and was even reputed to be a freemason. His election inspired the Italian patriot Gioberti with the hope of unifying Italy under his liberal rule. But the Roman revolution and his exile from Rome embittered the new Pope, and Pius IX soon disappointed the Italian liberals by unexpectedly becoming the leader of the ultramontane party. In 1864, he issued his famous Encyclical of December 8th with the appended Syllabus, in which he not only condemned secular education divorced from the Catholic religion, but equally definitely condemned any intervention of the State and the system of "mixed" education. In 1869, he convened the Vatican Council, which resulted in the pronouncement of the dogma of Infallibility. The way to a compromise with secular Governments was closed, and in all countries we notice an immediate stiffening of attitude on the part of the Catholic hierarchy; Manning in England, Cullen in Ireland, Charbonnel in Canada and Vaughan in Australia were among the prominent representatives of this generation of Catholic bishops. The second cause was contributed by State legislation in the second half of the nineteenth century. After the French Revolution the monopolistic control of education by the Church could hardly survive as a principle even in Catholic countries. The necessity for universal education if citizens were to participate in a more democratic government was at last officially recognised and all European countries started to introduce compulsory legislation. In Protestant and in some Catholic countries a truly national system of education, by force of circumstances, could only be undenominational. There were religious minorities everywhere, and there was a growing section of secularists hostile to any dogmatic instruction. Whereas the Protestants of all creeds were able to accept "undenominational Christianity" as the basis of a compromise, for the devout Catholics it amounted to a negation of the claims of their Church and an open revolt against the pronounced decrees of the Pope. The attitude of some Protestant and secularist bodies was openly hostile, and this still more alienated the majority of Catholics. In these circumstances it is not astonishing that all the efforts of moderate Catholic elements were futile. During the twentieth century the influence of the ultramontane party was on the wane and the attitude of the Church became more moderate and conciliatory towards the secular Governments. The rise of the dictators, on the other hand, tempted the Church to use them in an endeavour to stem the growing influence of Marxist materialism. Franco in Spain, Petain in France, Mussolini in Italy, Dollfuss in Austria, Tiso in Slovakia and Pilsudski in Poland all profited by this policy of the Church for their own ends, and it was owing to the Christian Democratic movement that Catholicism was not utterly compromised by such an alliance. Even in Germany the Church was ready to conclude a concordat with Catholic Hitler and Jesuit-trained Goebbels, but the openly pagan philosophy of Rosenberg made such a compromise impossible, and the Church was driven into opposition to the Nazi régime. In the Third Reich the German Catholics looked upon England as a country of tolerance and fair justice towards their Church, and listened with envy to the privileges of Catholic schools within the national system. In France, Italy and Belgium the Christian Democrats even entered into a coalition with the Socialists and Communists in a common effort to save their countries from the débâcle wrought by totalitarian dictators. This conciliatory attitude may lead to a final solution of the religious difficulty in education.

CHAPTER VII

THE ANGLICAN TRADITION

Whereas the Catholic, the Puritan and the secular traditions were not limited to the English-speaking countries, but were disseminated throughout the world, the Anglican or Episcopalian tradition was the result of the peculiar circumstances of the English Reformation and thus may be considered as the English tradition *par excellence*. If the typical feature of the English-speaking nations of moral responsibility found its best expression in the Puritans, and their love of freedom and fair play in the secular tradition, their aristocratic pride of race and insular tendency towards splendid isolation were represented by the Anglican tradition. Whereas the Catholics, even after the secession of the Protestants, never forgot the universal character of their Church, the Anglican Church, though inheriting the claim to monopoly, never seriously attempted to spread its jurisdiction beyond the national frontiers. At first the Church of England was confined to the realm of England, but when Scotland became part of the United Kingdom and overseas territories were colonised by Britons, the Church attempted to establish its monopoly in those countries as well. This policy was pursued in a half-hearted way, it lacked the militant drive of the Catholic Church, and after a few unsuccessful attempts was abandoned in favour of a policy of tolerance. The universal basis and logical structure of the medieval Catholic Church did not on the whole appeal to the individualistic and empirical minds of the English. The centralised hierarchy dominated by a foreign Pope was contrary to the old democratic traditions of self-governing communities and the insular pride of a seafaring people. The Lollard and Wycliffite movements were the first signs of the coming Reformation and subsequent severance from the Latin World. Henry VIII by his legislation split the popular movement and saved some semblance of continuity with the medieval Catholic Church. Without his intervention it is probable that the Reformation in England would have followed the example of Wittenberg and Geneva. At first the Church of England retained its Catholic character and resembled the Gallican Church of France more than the Churches of Luther and Calvin. Under the pressure of popular demand, Cranmer tried to give to the new Church a definitely Protestant stamp. The reaction which followed frustrated his attempt and later Queen Elizabeth firmly established the Church of England in its intermediate position. The resultant continuous struggle on two fronts impeded the growth of uniformity within the Church itself. At some periods in its struggle with Roman traditions the Church accepted the help of Protestant Dissenters; at other periods, whilst fighting the Puritans, the Church was lenient to Catholic tendencies.

In the Middle Ages, the only existing clerical schools selected their pupils rather in accordance with their abilities than with their birth. The system of grammar schools was intended to educate the intellectual élite necessary for the professions which used Latin. The elementary schools for the population at large were scarce and the lower classes were illiterate. Thus the pre-Reformation system was not democratic in our sense, but the large number of grammar schools, many of which were free, afforded ample opportunity for the middle classes to enter learned professions. The Church of England inherited the system and the school traditions of the medieval church. During the Reformation period many of the endowed grammar schools were closed as ecclesiastical institutions and often the endowments were despoiled by members of the aristocracy. Neither the ruling class nor the newly established Church was eager to spread the light of knowledge among the lower classes. The Commissioners of 1541 were of the opinion that the sons of husbandmen were not called to learning as their labour was needed in the fields and that "all sorts of men may not go to school." Cranmer, possibly influenced by the Lutherans, represented a more enlightened attitude and replied: "If a gentleman's son be apt to learning, let him be admitted, if not apt, let the poor man's child that is apt, enter his room." The question was only raised in respect of grammar schools, and there was no intention of promoting universal literacy. On the contrary, Bible reading was forbidden to the labouring classes during the reign of Henry VIII. The Catholic reaction and the growth of Puritanism compelled the Church to concentrate its attention on religious conformity rather than the spread of learning. The Canons of 1604 established a monopoly of the Church in education. Neither public nor private teaching was permitted unless the teacher were approved by the Church as a man of learning and of sound doctrine. The Acts of Edward VI and Elizabeth ordering the clergy to teach their parishioners to read and write were practically ignored everywhere. After the brief interval of the Commonwealth, the monopoly of the Church was restored by the Uniformity Act of 1662. The Five Mile Act of 1665 definitely forbade Dissenters to teach in any school. The Revolution of 1688, successful only through the help of Protestant Dissenters, brought some alleviation. The Acts of Toleration of 1689 and 1711 relieved Dissenters in the field of elementary education, but secondary and higher education legally remained the monopoly of the Church for another century. We must add that toleration did not embrace Catholics, Quakers or Unitarians. By legal recognition of Dissent the Church of England definitely lost its hold on the middle classes and became the Church of the aristocracy and of the poorer classes. Thus an unbridged gulf grew up between the upper and the lower groups within the Church. This fact explains why the leaders of the Church were unable to conceive a national system of education. For them the education of the two classes had to be separate and of different content; for the ruling classes, grammar schools and Universities, and for the "deserving" poor, charity schools of very elementary standard.

The actual practice of the eighteenth century, however, was much more democratic than the official theory of the High Church party. The old grammar schools, including the great public schools and the two medieval Universities, continued their life under the new Church authorities with little change. Out of two hundred grammar schools inherited from the past, about a third were closed or despoiled, but the rest were refounded under the auspices of the Church. To the three old colleges of Eton, Winchester and Westminster, the new foundations of Harrow, the Merchant Taylors', Rugby, St. Paul's, Shrewsbury, were added in the sixteenth century and Charterhouse in the seventeenth, and these nine schools later became the famous great public schools. Both the grammar schools and the great nine were originally intended mainly for "poor boys," but whilst the majority of grammar schools continued to cater for boys of all classes, the great nine gradually became the preserve of the aristocracy and the gentry. Eton and Westminster especially were almost exclusively patronised by the titled aristocracy, the squirearchy and the upper ranks of the clergy. The provincial grammar schools on the contrary continued to accept the sons of farmers, craftsmen, merchants and the local clergy. Side by side

with the endowed grammar schools, private classical schools
flourished and were as a rule maintained by local rectors and
vicars of the Church of England. If the higher hierarchy of
the Church belonged by birth to the ruling class, the majority
of parish priests were of humble origin, who very often received
their classical training in these private schools. The two Universities gradually lost their former character of open institutions
for all able boys and became exclusive and expensive colleges
for the rich. However, there was a way for a poor boy to receive
academic training. He could enter the Universities as a "servitor"
or a "sizar" and by serving his aristocratic colleagues pay his
way through the University. Their social status was inferior and
they did not take part in college life, but they attended the
lectures and passed the examinations, which many of their temporary masters failed to do. Most of the University distinctions
were awarded to these "servitors" of humble origin. But they
formed the minority of students and could not arrest the general
decline of the two Universities. As institutions of learning both
Oxford and Cambridge lagged behind the Dissenting academies
and independent learned societies and individuals. The religious
tests and the strict orthodoxy of their lectures excluded all pioneering spirits from their precincts. As a contrast to the school system
mainly destined for the members of the ruling class, the Society
for Promoting Christian Knowledge, founded in 1698, represented the Church policy towards the poor. Its charity schools
had the double aim of training the children of the poor in the
habits of labour and industry and in proper humility towards the
ruling class. In the second half of the century new motives were
added to this class policy of the Church. The movement of
enlightenment and the propagation of Deism began to reach the
working men of large cities. Deistic clubs and societies abounded
and the Church was losing its hold on the population. The
subsequent revolutions in America and France aroused fear lest
seditious doctrines and political revolution should be disseminated
in England. Two quotations will suffice to illustrate this attitude
of suspicion of mass enlightenment. An Anglican writer said in
1797 in the *Gentleman's Magazine*:

> Industry is the duty to impress on the lower classes. A little
> learning makes a man ambitious to rise, if he cannot by fair means
> then he uses foul. His ignorance is a balm that soothes his mind into
> stupidity and repose, and excludes every emotion of discontent,
> pride and ambition. A man of no literature will seldom attempt to

foment insurrections or form an idle scheme for the reformation of the State.

The Bishop of London in his charge of 1803 affirmed that

men of considerable ability say that it is safest for both the Government and the religion of the country to let the lower classes remain in that state of ignorance in which nature has originally placed them.

These views were prevalent among the High Church party, but they were shared by many Evangelicals, who by political affiliation and family traditions were Tories. Historically the Evangelical party traces its origin to Cranmer and to the early Puritans within the Church. But a real impetus to their activities was given by the religious revival started by John Wesley. At first Wesley and the Evangelicals worked together as one group within the Church of England. By consecrating ministers for America himself, Wesley separated his community from the Church and formed a new movement, Methodism. The Evangelicals wanted to preserve the national character of the Establishment and remained within the fold of the Church. By their missionary and educational activities the Evangelicals were brought into closer contact with the industrial population and gradually changed their outlook. Their Puritan sense of moral responsibility could not for long maintain an aristocratic contempt for the poorer classes. When the Sunday Schools were started by Evangelicals in 1770 their aim was as limited as that of the charity schools founded a century earlier by the High Church party. Hannah More narrowed down her curriculum to the Bible and Catechism and "such coarse work as may fit children for servants. I allow no writing for the poor." Even the champion of the slaves, W. Wilberforce, an active supporter of popular education, told the poor in his *Practical View of Christianity* that "their more lowly path has been allotted to them by the hand of God; that it is their part faithfully to discharge its duties and contentedly to bear its inconveniences." He approved of various schemes for educational reform, but did not press them lest he should embarrass the repressive measures of the Government against the spreading of revolutionary ideas. In spite of their fear of a political revolution the Evangelicals quite sincerely recognised their obligation to elevate the masses. The Society for Bettering the Conditions of the Poor, founded by them in 1796, quite definitely advocated the establishment of a national system of education which would comprehend all classes as well as both Churchmen and Dissenters. Its secretary, Sir Thomas Barnard, says in his *Digest of the Reports*:

> In the ornamental branches of the fine arts—in painting, sculpture and music, in literary attainments and in professional science, education must be as various as the condition, situation and talent of man. But in the acquisition of the alphabetic and numerical language, the poor have as good a right to the instruction which illumines and directs their path through life as the greatest and most elevated of their fellow subjects.

The schools founded by the Society were very advanced compared with the previous charity schools. However, neither these schools nor the Sunday School movement could really satisfy the need and the demand for education among the poorer classes. The ideas of the French Revolution did reach the masses and they clamoured for popular education.

The Benthamites joined hands with the Quaker Lancaster and started the British and Foreign School Society, which established many schools with undenominational religious instruction. The Church was compelled to take action. Dr. A. Bell, the inventor of the Madras system, for years propagated his method in Church circles. He was hailed as the champion of the Church tradition in his tragi-comic contest with Lancaster. The latter was denounced as a revolutionary and an infidel. Especially vitriolic was Mrs. Trimmer, one of the pioneers of Sunday Schools. In answer to her pamphlet on Lancaster, Dr. Bell suggested in 1805 a "scheme of education patronised by the Church and State, originating in the Government and superintended by a member of the Establishment." The Government, however, did not move in spite of the battle-cry "The Church and religion in danger." The Church was left to its own resources. Francis Place, in one of his manuscripts, thus describes the motives of the new movement: "When the Church did begin to move its unwieldy mass, its first efforts were made in the hope of destroying Lancaster and his schools by setting up and keeping up the howl of Infidelity, not by establishing schools themselves. Could they have destroyed Lancaster and his schools, there would have been none of those schools miscalled National." However true this indictment may be, the National Society was certainly started with the object of combating Lancastrian schools. The aims of the new Society were narrow and strictly denominational. Dr. A. Bell, in an unguarded moment, frankly admitted in 1805: "It is not proposed that the children of the poor be educated in an expensive manner, or even taught to write and cipher. . . . There is a risk of elevating, by an indiscriminate education, the minds of those doomed to the drudgery of daily labour above their conditions, and thereby render them discontent and unhappy in their lot." Southey wrote that "the children must be instructed according to the established religion—fed with the milk of sound doctrine." The position of the High Church party was best expressed by Archdeacon Denison: "The Church can never have the 'comprehensive' school, in which the State employs the term. It may indeed 'comprehend' others than Church children in its schools for missionary purposes; but this exclusively upon its own terms only." As late as 1839, it was stated in *Blackwood's Magazine* that "ignorance is the parent of contentment," and that "the only education which could be fitly and safely given to the poor was a religious education, which renders them patient, humble and moral, and relieves the hardship of their present lot by the prospect of bright eternity." Nevertheless, there was an influential minority, besides the Evangelicals, who sincerely wanted a truly "comprehensive" system. Men like Dr. Whately, later Archbishop of Dublin, Dean Hook, Bishop Stanley and Dr. Arnold of Rugby were as progressive as their adherence to an established Church permitted. Arnold went so far as to advocate a "comprehensive" national Church, which would include all Protestant Dissenters with the sole exception of Quakers and Unitarians. The High Church party, however, monopolised the Church school system and would not hear of any compromise. When in 1811 the National Society came into being Dissenters were admitted to Church schools on condition of conformity and church attendance. Within twenty years, in all schools of the National Society, including Sunday Schools, the number of pupils rose to 900,000. Whatever the motives, whatever the limitations, the voluntary efforts of the Church could not have achieved such results without wide support from the country, and the term "National" was therefore not entirely a misnomer. But if the Church system satisfied the majority of the nation, it was still unacceptable to an influential minority, and thus could not grow into a truly national system for all classes and all creeds. In 1833, the Government began its annual grants towards education, to be divided between the two societies, Lancastrian and National. The control of the schools was left entirely in their hands and the Church did not protest against this "intervention" of the

State. But when the Committee of the Privy Council was created in 1839 to regulate the administration of the grants, the Church became alarmed. Bishop Blomfield denounced it as a step advised by secularists with the object of destroying the Church. When the first secretary of the Committee, Kay Shuttleworth, proposed a State Training College, the opposition of the Church was so great that the scheme was abandoned and the system of training the teachers was built up on denominational lines. The next struggle was over the right of inspection. The Church succeeded again, and the Government agreed to appoint inspectors only with the approval of the Church, who had to report annually to the Archbishop of Canterbury. Thus the foundation of the dual system was laid and the "religious difficulty" was legalised as a permanent feature of the school system. F. Adams, in his book *The Elementary School Contest*, thus characterises the Church policy:

> From the beginning of the struggle to its close the Church, while doing its utmost to extend education of its own kind, by its own methods, and for its own purposes, has been the grand and chief obstruction to any national system. The National Society prescribed the tests and methods, laid down terms of union and from the sanctuary at Westminster claimed the right to dictate the terms upon which the education of the people should be permitted to proceed.

Nevertheless, times were changing, and a new generation of Churchmen was growing up.

The Chartist Movement and the social disorders connected with it aroused the Church from its lethargy. The Evangelicals found an outstanding leader in the Earl of Shaftesbury, who in 1843 started the "Ragged Schools" for destitute children in London, neglected by all other educational bodies. More influential was the movement of "Christian Socialism" started in 1848 by F. D. Maurice and Charles Kingsley both Anglican clergymen. They combined a warm humane impulse with the ideas of University leadership and the national character of the Church. Being both a clergyman and a University professor, Maurice was not a democrat; he felt social injustice deeply, and sincerely wanted to find a Christian solution for social problems. His desire to educate the working class led to the foundation of the Working Men's College in London in 1854. The education offered was to be humane rather than technical because the workman was "a person, not a thing, a citizen and not a slave or even a wage-earning animal." The influence of his institution led later to the University Extension and Settlement movements. His chief idea was "the union of labour and learning." Maurice's lectures at King's and Queen's Colleges were denounced by orthodox clergy as "modified Pantheism" and he was deprived of his chair of History at King's. The majority of clergymen were not infected by his enthusiasm for the poorer classes, and even looked upon him as a dangerous agitator. Every concession from the Church party in favour of a national system of education, controlled by the State, was gained after an embittered struggle. In 1870 the opposition of the Church frustrated the Government's plan for a State system of education by compelling the recognition of the denominational principle. As a matter of fact Catholics profited more from this recognition than the Church of England, because the Anglican schools were gradually absorbed in the local authorities' system, while the Catholics remained outside. The "religious difficulty" impeded the natural growth of the national system up to the enactment of the 1944 Act. For the time being the solution is accepted by all parties, with the exception of the Roman Catholics, as satisfactory.

Much more lasting and valuable was the contribution of the Church in the field of secondary education. If the official Church system of Grammar Schools and the nine great public schools could be described in Professor R. L. Archer's words: "Their low moral tone, their narrow classical curriculum, their poor intellectual results, their roughness and bullying, their bad feeding and housing," the Anglican clergy throughout the country established hundreds of private secondary schools which were free of all these defects. In these private schools of the eighteenth century, kept by local parish priests, the moral atmosphere was truly Christian, the training imparted of high standard and general conditions resembled family life more than military barracks. Some of these schools produced outstanding pioneers of modern methods and ideas and this prepared the way for the subsequent reform of the grammar schools. As an example of such schools we would mention Cheam School, which has existed uninterruptedly from 1647 to the present day. Its great headmaster William Gilpin in the second half of the eighteenth century introduced into the school all those features which later made Rugby under Arnold so famous. In the nineteenth century another headmaster of Cheam, Dr. Charles Mayo, was a pioneer in introducing Pestalozzian methods into this country. If in the eighteenth century the great public schools mismanaged the education of the élite entrusted to them by the nation, the private Anglican schools of the eighteenth century deserve better fame than total neglect in all histories of education. The great public schools badly needed a reform. Their moral instruction could hardly be called religious if it led to the immorality prevalent in those schools in the eighteenth century. Although Dr. Arnold of Rugby could not be called an original reformer, bearing in mind William Gilpin's example, he was a leader who succeeded in building up on the defective ground of the grammar schools the best and most lasting features of the Anglican tradition. He was not an orthodox member of the High Church party. For him, the Church of England would only become truly national by the inclusion of all Protestant Dissenters. Common Christianity he valued more than the Church hierarchy. Without being a Puritan, he had the Puritan's sense of moral responsibility, and tried to introduce into his school that moral attitude which was lacking. Assailed by orthodox clergymen on the grounds that "his education was not based on religion," Arnold answered that it was "itself religious." He was the first headmaster of Rugby to be appointed chaplain, and used his chapel successfully for imparting that common Christianity in which he believed. His reform of school organisation based on self-government and games became the model for all public schools, and later influenced even the State system of elementary education. The reformed public schools became once more popular, and the number of pupils increased enormously. New Anglican public schools were added, such as Cheltenham, Haileybury, King's, Lancing, Marlborough, Oundle, Radley, Rossall, Wellington, Weymouth and others. For the middle classes cheaper schools on the same lines were founded by Woodard, who was so old-fashioned that at Lancing he built two halls, for the upper and middle classes respectively, as he did not believe in mixing socially members of different classes. The last great Anglican reformer of secondary education was Thring of Uppingham. Strangely enough he combined the modernisation of the curriculum in the grammar schools with the most reactionary views on popular education and bitterly opposed the introduction of free compulsory education.

In the field of higher education the Church was as slow to provide the initiative as in elementary education. The two ancient Universities were controlled by the Church and could accommodate all the Anglican students from the public schools. No new Universities were considered necessary. The foundation of an undenominational University College in London showed the Church that her inertia would be used by secularists for establishing modern Universities divorced from Anglican theology. To counteract the new danger the Church decided on the foundation of new Universities on a strictly Anglican basis. As one of the founders of King's College, Dr. George D'Oyly, pointed out to Sir Robert Peel, theology was so intimately bound up with other subjects that none of them could be satisfactorily taught except in connection with theology. Two new University institutions were founded, King's College in 1829 and Durham University in 1831. But that was the last effort of the Church to stem the tide. All the provincial Universities were founded as undenominational institutions and the Anglican foundations soon lost their exclusive character and became national institutions open to all.

In other English-speaking countries Churches of the Anglican communion could never attain such a dominant position as in England and their influence on the formation of a national tradition in education was noticeable only in the field of secondary education. In Scotland the Presbyterian Church moulded the national school system on the lines drawn by John Knox, which from the very start avoided that class division which was prevalent in England. The training of the élite was performed by Scottish parish schools as well as by burgh schools, and Scottish Universities gave equal opportunities to boys from both groups. The revival of the public schools in England and their success in training the ruling class found followers among the Scottish Episcopalians. The first Episcopalian school on English public school lines was founded by an Englishman, Dr. Langhorne of Loretto, in 1827. Trinity College, Glenalmond, was founded in 1841. These two Episcopalian colleges influenced some Presbyterian foundations like Edinburgh Academy, Merchiston Castle and Fettes College. Having joined the English Headmasters' Conference these Scottish schools accepted the Anglican tradition of training the élite and as a rule preferred Oxford and Cambridge to their own Universities. The great majority of the Scottish secondary schools continued to develop their democratic tradition and thus the English influence in Scotland was limited to a small group. In Wales the Anglican influence resulted in the foundation of two public schools, Llandovery College and Christ College, Brecon.

In Ireland the Church of Ireland of the Anglican communion played rather a negative rôle and was rather an obstacle to than a promoter of popular education. By the Supremacy Act of 1537 the lands of great abbeys and religious houses were vested in the Crown, and the Catholic Church was deprived of its wealth in favour of the Episcopalian Church of Ireland. Whereas in England the reformed Church inherited from the past a system of grammar schools and two Universities, in Ireland the new Church had to build up the whole school system from scratch. At the same time the Government ordered the founding of parish schools in every parish, but that legislation was not enforced and remained a dead letter. In many districts the Anglican clergy were not able to fulfil their statutory obligations because the Catholic population refused to send their children to these parish schools. In 1570 Elizabeth tried to create a secondary school system under the auspices of the Church of Ireland. "It may be enacted, that there shall be from henceforth a free school within every diocese of this realm of Ireland, and that the schoolmaster shall be an Englishman, or of the English birth of this realm, and that the lords Archbishops and Bishops shall have the nomination, institution and appointment of the schoolmasters within their several dioceses." The clergy, as in the case of the parish schools, were not very eager to shoulder this new obligation and only a few dioceses worked the Act. The enforcement of the Act was enjoined several times, but in spite of that many dioceses never had such schools. The Commissioners of 1808 stated that in thirteen out of a total of thirty-four dioceses no school existed at any time, and that in 1808 there were only thirteen effective diocesan schools in the whole of Ireland. Very few Catholics attended these schools, and in practice they were used by the Anglican clergy for the education of their sons. The conversion of the Catholics was not promoted by the parish and diocesan schools, and a new Act of James I in 1608 definitely aimed at speeding up the diffusion of Protestantism by establishing new Royal Schools. They were destined "to recall the province of Ulster from superstition, rebellion . . . to the true religion of Christ and to obedience." They had to educate the youth of Ireland "in literature and knowledge of true religion; to the end that they may learn their duty towards God and true obedience to us." The patronage of all royal schools was vested in the Crown, but in Armagh and Dungannon the masters were usually appointed by the Anglican Archbishop of Armagh.

These schools, like the previous foundations, completely failed in their purpose. Catholics very seldom attended them and they soon became the preserve of the Church of Ireland. All these schools were initiated by the Government and the Church of Ireland played rather a passive rôle. But in 1731 the Anglican Primate Boulter conceived an idea of converting the Catholics by means of special schools, established for that purpose. In 1730 he wrote to the Bishop of London: "The Papists here are so numerous that it highly concerns us in point of interest, as well as out of concern for the salvation of these poor creatures, who are our fellow subjects, to try all possible means to bring them and theirs over to the true religion, and one of the most likely methods we can think of is, if possible, instructing the young generation." The Royal Charter of 1733 for establishing Protestant schools says: "If some effectual method be not made use of to instruct these great number of people in the principles of true religion and loyalty, there is little prospect but that superstition and idolatry and disaffection to us and our Royal posterity will from generation to generation, be propagated amongst them. Amongst the ways proper to be taken for converting and civilising of the said deluded persons . . . has always been thought to be erecting and establishing of a sufficient number of English Protestant schools." The original scheme contemplated day schools only. Very soon it was found that the conversion of Catholic children living with their parents was almost impossible. It was decided, therefore, to take them from their parents and transplant them to boarding schools in remote localities. No Catholic priest or any relatives of that persuasion were allowed to converse with the children, except in the presence of the master. When it was found that few Catholic parents could be induced to part with their children, nurseries were opened in 1757 to serve as feeders for the schools. In spite of all these measures the schools could not be filled with Catholic children and the Church of Ireland had to register another failure in her missionary attempts. After 1825 these schools were changed into denominational schools for members of the Church of Ireland only. Intended originally for "poor Papists," the schools became fee-paying boarding institutions for the Anglican clergy and gentry. In the nineteenth century, with the emancipation of the Catholics, the previous monopoly of the Church disappeared and its policy in education required a new attitude. The minority of Churchmen, led by Archbishop Whately, recognised the changed situation and sincerely collaborated with the National Board in trying to establish an undenominational system free of any suspicion of proselytism. In a private letter, however, Dr. Whately expressed the hope that the National system would "gradually undermine the vast fabric of Popery in Ireland." The majority of Churchmen could not reconcile themselves with the new situation and still maintained that the Established Church was the national Church of Ireland and that it was its duty to convert Catholics through education and legislation. They bitterly opposed the National system, and in 1839 founded the Church Education Society for establishing denominational schools on a voluntary basis. In 1845 the Bishops petitioned the Government and claimed State grants for their schools. As they would not abandon the policy of proselytism, the petition was rejected. With the disestablishment of the Church in 1869 all pretence of monopoly had to be abandoned, and the Church of Ireland reconciled itself to the position of a minority community.

In the field of higher education the Church of Ireland also assisted in the political purposes of the Government. The reasons for the foundation of Trinity College, Dublin, were more political than educational. The letter of Elizabeth, establishing the College, says in the preamble: "Whereby knowledge and civility might be increased by the instruction of our people there, whereof many have usually heretofore used to travel into France, Italy and Spain to get learning in such foreign universities, whereby they have been infected with popery and other ill qualities, etc." At first the new College accepted Catholic students, no religious tests being instituted, and many Catholics contributed liberally to the original endowment. With the accession of James I the political aim of conversion was insisted upon and for the early Puritan provosts and fellows were gradually substituted more orthodox followers of the ecclesiastical policy of proselytism. The educational disabilities of the Catholics were removed only in 1793 and since then many Catholic leaders of Ireland have graduated from Trinity. In 1873 Trinity College became officially an undenominational institution open to all creeds on equal terms. The Church of Ireland could never claim the status of a national Church, like her sister Church of England, as the majority of the population remained Catholic, and thus had no historical right to impose a monopoly or to use the national income for sectional interests. Certainly the Church was not a free agent but a tool of the Government, the idea of the integration of State and Church being prevalent at that time among all creeds and parties. The whole policy of the combined Church and State, both in its conception and its execution, was contrary to the interests of the country and, instead of promoting the cause of education, obstructed it. The openly proselytising policy of the Church led only to an embittered feud between the creeds and achieved an opposite result to what it aimed at. If Irish education, nevertheless, has been influenced by the English tradition and the English school system, it was due to Newman and other converts rather than the Church.

The educational history of English-speaking Canada begins with the removal of 70,000 United Empire Loyalists in 1783 from the newly born U.S.A. to the Maritime Provinces and Upper Canada. The emigrants were mostly Episcopalians and included clergymen and many graduates of American colleges. Although the Church of England never had a legal monopoly of education in Canada, its position gave it many privileges which other Churches did not possess. The growing immigration of Dissenters in the nineteenth century, coupled with the secession of the Methodists, very soon put the Episcopalians in a minority. But this minority formed the ruling class, which tried to dominate the dissenting majority both in politics and religion. The policy of the Church of England only reflected this general tendency. When Upper Canada was constituted a separate province in 1791 Governor Simcoe wanted to establish grammar schools and an Anglican University on the English model. In his letter to Bishop Mountain in 1795 he said: "By giving means of proper education . . . we may bring within the pale [of the Church] a very great body of sectaries, who . . . offer themselves to its protection and re-union. The Episcopal clergy in England, from pious motives as well as policy, are materially interested that the Church should increase in this province. . . . Its preservation depends upon a university being erected therein." The conversion of the Dissenters and the spread of loyalty to the King were the chief aims of the proposed University. In 1799 Dr. Strachan of Aberdeen was invited to organise the schools and the University, for which purpose 550,000 acres of Crown lands were set apart. In 1803 Strachan joined the Episcopalian Church and was ordained by Bishop Mountain. He founded the first two grammar schools in Upper Canada, which were followed by the foundation of six more district grammar schools, all in fact controlled by the Church. In 1812 Strachan was appointed Rector of York (Toronto), where he came into close contact with the ruling group of Episcopalian loyalists known as the "Family Compact." He became their leader in religious and educational matters. They were not averse to education as such, but their zeal took the form of promoting higher education for the upper class. In 1829, a Board of Education was established with Strachan as its president. He devoted all his energy to the foundation of the University with classical district schools as feeders, but made no provision for elementary schools. Strachan went to England and in 1827 obtained a Charter for the University of King's College in Upper Canada. His ideas and reasons were clearly expressed in his appeal on behalf of the University: "It is indeed quite evident that the consequences of a university . . . possessing in itself sufficient recommendations to attract to it the sons of the most opulent families, would soon be visible in the greater intelligence and more confirmed principles of loyalty of those who would be called to various public duties required in the country, i.e. the governing class." His other reason was that Canadians often completed their education in the States across the border and imbibed disloyal notions, both in politics and religion. According to the charter, the new University was to be distinctly a Church of England institution. The Anglican Bishop was to be its visitor; the Archdeacon of York (Strachan) was to be *ex officio* its president and all the members of its council were to be members of the Church of England and subscribe to the Thirty-nine Articles. Strachan quite frankly stated that the University was to be "a missionary College of the Church of England," and that by its teaching "the greater portion of Canada might through the Divine blessing be brought up in the communion of the Church of England." This open aim of proselytism aroused bitter opposition from all the other denominations, which formed the majority of the population. The charter was challenged not only in Canada, but also in the House of Commons. The Government stayed the proceedings under the charter and asked for its surrender. Strachan and the College Council refused to comply. The Canadian House of Assembly had a dissenting majority, whilst the Legislative Council was in the hands of the "Family Compact," led by Strachan. After a prolonged struggle a compromise was finally reached in 1836, by which the official control of the Church was abolished, but in practice Strachan and his party remained entrenched in the College Council. King's College was duly opened in 1842, but its existence as a Church institution was very short, as it was completely secularised in 1850 by the Canadian Government. Strachan went to England again and obtained a Royal Charter for the University of Trinity College in 1850. It was a purely Anglican institution but on a voluntary basis. Strachan collected £100,000 in England and Canada and the new Anglican University was opened in 1850, as a complete replica of Oxford with residential staff and students. The dons had to subscribe to the articles and remain celibate. These features were preserved even when Trinity College became affiliated to the "godless" University of Toronto in 1903. In the field of elementary education the Church always sided with the Catholics in the demand for separate denominational schools, and for long obstructed the building up of the national common school system. Only in the second half of the nineteenth century did the Anglicans under the influence of two leading superintendents, Dr. Ryerson and G. Hodgins, finally agree to an undenominational public school system. In the Maritime Provinces a similar struggle took place with the same results. When the new Prairie Provinces were added the question was definitely settled in favour of an undenominational public system. In 1876 the last link with the Church of England and the see of Canterbury was broken and the Canadian Episcopalian Church became independent with its own Primate. Canada became quite democratic in its social structure, but the Anglican tradition is still strong in those independent boarding schools which follow the model of English public schools and claim to train the social élite.

In Australia the colony of New South Wales was founded in 1788 and the Church of England was recognised as the Established Church of the colony without any special act. In 1790 King George III issued an act making provision "for the Church by allotting in each township 400 acres for the maintenance of a minister and half that quantity for the maintenance of a schoolmaster." In 1809, the Governor, Lachlan Macquarie, began to assist schools of other denominations as well. The Church protested, considering that the land grants were intended for the schools of the Church only. After an investigation by a Royal Commission the Government agreed with the Church's contention and in 1825 George IV issued "Letters Patent for erecting a Corporation for the management of the Church and school lands in the Colony of New South Wales." It placed the management of those lands under the control of the Church. The schools

were made subject to the order, superintendence and control of
the Anglican clergy. The Bishop was made *ex officio* the visitor.
The influential minority of Dissenters strongly opposed this
monopoly of the Church, and the Home Government revoked
the Charter in 1833. The property of the Corporation reverted
to the Crown, and the control of the schools was taken over by
the Colonial Government. Whilst the Church was in power two
grammar schools were founded under the name of King's Schools,
one in Sydney, the other at Parramatta. The first was soon
closed, but Parramatta King's School developed into a typical
Anglican public school. It was a boarding institution, available
only to the "wealthier part of the community," as the Governor,
Sir Richard Bourke, complained. Because of this character of
the school and its denominational control, the Government
withdrew its grant in 1838. Since then the Parramatta School
has become a voluntary institution of the Church. In 1836 Sir
Richard Bourke, the Governor, started a campaign for the introduction of a national undenominational school system. The
opposition of all the Churches led by Bishop Broughton and the
Anglican clergy frustrated his plan. He succeeded only in passing
the Act of 1836 by which all Christian Churches were to receive
State support on equal grounds. The struggle for an undenominational public school system continued for fifty years and finally
in 1883 all State grants to denominational schools were withdrawn and the Church had to build up a voluntary system. The
Anglicans henceforth directed their efforts to the support of
denominational boarding schools on the English model and
theological seminaries. In other States of Australia similar
developments took place and the Anglicans everywhere concentrated on secondary education and theological training. They
have succeeded in transplanting the English public school system
to the antipodes. Australia is a democracy in every sense, but
there are six great public schools and many smaller grammar
schools, independent and denominational, which train the social
élite on English lines. If the number of outstanding Australians,
trained in these schools, were compared with the rest, we should
find that these "aristocratic" schools play a rôle similar to their
prototypes in England.

In New Zealand only Canterbury was settled by Anglicans
under the auspices of the Church. The promoters of the settlement had a comprehensive scheme of Church schools headed by
a college. For this purpose, both religious and educational, one-

third of the proceeds of the sale of Canterbury lands was to be reserved. The first "college and grammar school" was founded in 1851 in Lyttleton, and transferred to Christchurch in 1852. It was endowed by the Provincial Council out of the fund. The purpose was clearly expressed in the act of incorporation: "We do hereby found the said College to the honour and glory of the eternal and ever blessed Trinity for the propagation of the most holy Christian Religion as it is now professed and taught by the Church of England, and for the promotion of sound piety and useful learning." It was a boarding institution on English lines with a preparatory school. The common school system was established on denominational principles under the control and supervision of the respective Churches. Bishop Harper, besides being the head of Christ's College, became virtually a Director of Education. However, there was discontent with the denominational system and in 1864 the Provincial Council took over the schools in spite of the protest of the Diocesan Synod. Complete secularisation followed in 1871 and Christchurch College and the Anglican grammar schools became voluntary institutions. In South Africa the Church could never play a dominant rôle, but was active in founding grammar schools and colleges on traditional Anglican lines.

The American colonies were not homogeneous from the religious point of view. State reasons prompted the Home Government to relax the strict monopoly of the Church in America, and even to allow in some colonies the establishment of Dissenting Churches. Thus the school policy of the Church of England could only be manifested in those colonies where the Church was established with the foundation of the colony, or was later imposed by force. The Church was established in Virginia and in both Carolinas from the Plantation. Virginia was a typical reproduction of the English society and legislation of that period. The monopoly of the Church was introduced in 1606 and the Dissenters were persecuted and expelled. The ruling class was similar in composition and way of living to the English upper class. The educational policy did not differ very much from that of the Mother Country. Two different school systems were founded under the control of the Church for the two classes of white population. For the planters and associated groups of the clergy, merchants and professional men, grammar schools and the College of William and Mary were founded. For the poor whites, many of whom were transplanted orphans and indentured labourers, charity schools were established. The first grammar schools of Virginia were founded, as in England, by gentlemen for the children of poor freeholders and their management was usually left to the vestry of the local parishes. As in England, the intended "free schools for poor pupils" very soon became fee-paying schools for the well-to-do planters. This class character of the few endowed schools developed only in the eighteenth century, as in the seventeenth century the planters educated their sons at home under the guidance of clergymen, and then usually sent them to England. The College of William and Mary was founded in 1693. The charter granted land endowments, and the right to collect taxes and receive profits arising from the office of Surveyor-General. The aims of the new college were expressed as follows: "To the end that the Church of Virginia may be furnished with a seminary of ministers of the Gospel, and that youth be piously educated in good letters and manners, and that Christian faith may be propagated among the Western Indians, to the Glory of Almighty God." According to the charter, J. Blair, the Church Commissioner, was appointed the first President, and the Bishop of London the first Chancellor. The College included a grammar school, a school of philosophy and a school of divinity. Although the College was administered by the Church, the early students included Dissenters, which proves that the Church monopoly was not strictly enforced. After the American Revolution, under the influence of Jefferson, the College lost its official connection with the Church, and was completely secularised after the Civil War. The attitude of the colonial Church and the Anglican governors towards the education of the lower classes can be seen from the famous report of Governor Berkely in 1671: "But I thank God there are no free schools nor printing; and I hope we shall not have these hundred years: for learning has brought disobedience and heresy and sects into the world and printing has divulged them and libels against the best government. God keep us from both." On the whole, Virginia in the colonial period was as prejudiced against popular education as England, and did not attempt to found a public school system. In the Carolinas and Georgia Churchmen were outnumbered by Dissenters and the monopoly of the Church had to be enforced. The first grammar schools and colleges were all under Church control. The Queen's College in North Carolina, in 1771, and the College of Charleston, South Carolina, in 1785, were both founded as Anglican institutions under the supervision of the Church. After the Declaration of Independence, one by one the colleges were secularised. The famous King's College of New York, founded in 1754 by King George III, was also a Church institution. The Royal Charter provided that the President must be a Churchman and that a collection of Church prayers should be read in the College. In 1784 the College was refounded as Columbia University and lost its official connection with the Church. In Maryland after the Revolution of 1688 the new Protestant masters passed in 1694 "An Act for encouragement of learning and the advancement of the natives of this province." The encouragement of learning meant grammar schools for the upper class and the advancement of the religious conversion of the natives, but elementary schools for the lower classes of whites were not mentioned. A letter to the Bishop of London said: "We are confident you will favour our pious design in this province, wherein in instructing our youth in orthodox religion, preserving them from the infection of heterodox tenets and fitting them for the service of the Church and the State . . . are our cheerful end and aim." In 1785 King William's School was merged into St. John College and gradually lost its denominational character. The activities of the Church in America, as we have seen, were concentrated on the education of the upper class and missionary work. Whilst the efforts of Anglican missionaries were directed towards the conversion of Indians and Negroes, the Dissenters could not protest. But when in 1701 the "Society for the Propagation of the Gospel in Foreign Parts" was founded with the intent of converting the Dissenters themselves, they opposed vigorously. The Society indeed succeeded in converting hundreds of Presbyterians and Quakers, but these facts themselves engendered a denominational animosity which became an obstacle to any educational progress. With the American Revolution and the disestablishment of the Church the work of the Society lost all its importance. The majority of the clergy and many of the Episcopalian laity were staunch loyalists and often fought on the side of the English. The Declaration of Independence and the defeat of the English army led to a mass emigration of loyalists to Canada and England. In Virginia, for instance, of 95 parishes with 164 churches and 91 clergymen before the Revolution, only 36 parishes with 36 clergymen remained after the end of the war. The Church could not remain any longer a branch of the Church of England, and had to be reorganised as an independent Episcopalian

Church of America. All the colleges and grammar schools founded by the Church and maintained from public grants were taken over by the States and became undenominational public institutions. The Church founded new schools and colleges on a voluntary basis and preserved the Anglican tradition intact. If the "public school boys" are unknown in America because the term is a misnomer in American conditions, the graduates of independent boarding schools enjoy social privileges which the Americans are reluctant to recognise.

The theory of the integration of Church and State was inherited by the Church of England from the Middle Ages and was shared by both Catholics and Calvinists alike. The policy of monopoly in education was not a peculiar feature of the Church, it was the common policy of all parties of that period. In those parts of the Empire where other churches were previously established, the Church did not attempt to monopolise education. Witness Catholic Quebec, Puritan New England and the Dutch Reformed Cape Colony. Ireland alone is a striking example of an extreme application of the general theory contrary to the wishes and beliefs of the population. And only in Ireland did the intolerance of the Church lead to the most deplorable results. Aristocratic in its origin, and intimately connected with the ruling class, the Church inevitably developed an aristocratic policy in education and tended to neglect the masses. The education of the élite was always the main aim of the Church, and in this respect one cannot say that it failed. The great public schools of England and similar Church institutions in all parts of the English-speaking world have successfully trained generations of statesmen and leaders in all fields of public and professional activity. The English public school tradition is an original and important contribution to the theory and practice of education, and has influenced not only the public systems of all the English-speaking nations, but the systems of many foreign countries as well. The proverbial "old school tie," however ridiculed, is the symbol of a historical tradition, which can be incorporated into a modern democratic school system with a few adaptations to changed conditions.

CHAPTER VIII

THE PURITAN TRADITION

Puritanism is not necessarily connected with any specific religious creed, but is rather the attitude of mind towards problems of life based on the moral responsibility of the individual. There were not only Puritans within the Church of England, but it is conceivable to speak of some Roman Catholics as Puritans. In the historical development of post-Reformation Europe and America, however, Puritanism was usually a common feature of those religious communities which were connected with Calvinism or derived their origin from a Calvinist stem. In our sketch of the Puritan tradition in education we have to limit ourselves to the original Church of Calvin and its Continental branches, the French Huguenots and the Dutch Reformed Church, and in the English-speaking countries to the original Dissenters—the Presbyterians, the Congregationalists and the Baptists and the two smaller bodies of Quakers and Unitarians which have developed from them. In spite of their different local colour and divergent policies in education, and at times an embittered struggle and mutual persecution, all these Protestant Churches have a common outlook and a Puritan tradition which sharply distinguishes them from both the Roman Catholics and the Anglicans. It is more difficult to point out the dividing line between the Calvinists and the Lutherans, as their attitude towards education was almost identical, but whereas in Lutheran countries the supremacy of the State has always been tacitly recognised, in Calvinist communities the supremacy of the Church was openly postulated in their claims for theocracy. In contrast to the educational conservatism of Catholics and Anglicans, the Puritans were innovators and reformers, and in this respect in more recent times were often allied with the secular traditions in education. In those countries where Calvinism was accepted as the form of religious revival it played a similar rôle to Lutheranism in Germany and Scandinavia.

In Switzerland, Holland, Scotland and America, Calvinism led to the reform of methods of instruction and to universal elementary education. Indirectly, Calvinism also led to a development of democratic ideas of self-government. The most powerful and valuable contribution of Calvin to democracy was not in his theology, but in the organisation of his Church. For there the consistories, provincial assemblies and national synods were excellent training ground for self-government. Although orthodox Calvinism was extremely intolerant and, whenever in power, vied with Roman Catholics in the persecution of heretics, it included the germ of a more liberal outlook. It is not a mere coincidence that Calvinist communities gave birth to many pioneers of modern liberalism and tolerance. Thus we have to distinguish two currents in Calvinist thought, the orthodox, intolerant and domineering, and the liberal and conciliating. The two pioneers of Calvinist education, Cordier and Sebastian Chateillon (Castellio), were both of the second group. Mathurin Cordier started his career as a Catholic priest and teacher at Paris University. Here Calvin attended his lectures and Cordier was converted to Calvin's interpretation of Christianity. Being a scholar and humanist of outstanding ability, Cordier did not share Calvin's fanatical zeal for orthodoxy and was tolerant and conciliating towards Catholics. When André Gouvéa, the principal of the Catholic "Collège de Guyenne" at Bordeaux, invited him as his assistant in 1534, Cordier accepted the post and helped Gouvéa to shape the new college on humanistic and tolerant principles. Both Catholics and Huguenots attended this school without coming to blows. Two years later his former pupil Calvin invited him to Geneva to help to found the great Calvinist "Collège de la Rive," which soon became the educational and theological centre for all exiled Calvinists, including English and Scottish scholars of the Reformed faith. Here Cordier spent the rest of his life until 1564, when he died, devoting all his energy to reforming and organising schools. He did not interfere in Calvin's political government and thus was able to instil the Calvinist educational traditions with liberal ideas. He reformed the system of monitors or prefects, used before him as a kind of school police. He says in his *Colloquia*:

> The master, unable to supervise everything in detail, calls to his aid the eldest scholars who stand in the position of elder brothers to the rest. They are invested with their responsibility for one month, after consultation between the master and the boys themselves. It is an election as in the sight of God: the monitors are installed with prayer. They gather in the master's study when they are instructed in their solemn functions, and the name of the Saviour is invoked to inspire them with a due sense of their duty. They must show no favour nor antipathy, they must not take

vengeance nor lose self-control; they must fear no threats but fear the Lord only.

We here observe that solemn sense of moral responsibility which became the lasting feature of Calvinism. For Cordier learning and piety were closely interwoven as *pietas literata* or *eloquens et sapiens pietas*. Besides Latin and Religion, Greek, Mathematics, Logic and Natural Philosophy were taught in his college. His Latin text-books were used in all countries both in Catholic and Protestant schools and were still in use in England as late as the middle of the nineteenth century. Sebastian Chateillon, the other pioneer of Calvinist education, was of a different temper. He is famous as the first translator of the Bible into French. Invited by Calvin to reform the Genevan schools, he advocated a policy of tolerance and vigorously opposed the burning of the Spanish scholar Servet as a heretic. In consequence he quarrelled with Calvin and had to leave Geneva. He was appointed a professor at Basle University and had many adherents among Calvinists. His influence and Zwingli's humanism moderated the original orthodoxy of Calvinism in Switzerland, and in this milder form it became the basis of the Swiss democratic system of education. In France, as we have seen, both faiths could work together at Bordeaux and in other places and a policy of tolerance prevailed for a time. But by 1535 the Catholic Church had persuaded Francis I that Calvinism was inimical to the stability of the State, and tolerance was gradually withdrawn. Calvin, Cordier, Chateillon and many other Frenchmen had to go into exile at Geneva. The period of the Huguenot wars ensued which tended to increase fanaticism on both sides. But even during this period the Huguenot leaders did not forget the cause of education. In 1560 the States-General of Orleans, led by the Protestant nobility, sent a memorial to the French King: "May it please the King to levy a contribution upon the Church revenues for the reasonable support of teachers and men of learning in every city and village, for the instruction of the needy youth of the country; and let all parents be required, under penalty of fine, to send their children to school, and let them be constrained to observe this law by the lords and the ordinary magistrates." They also demanded that public lectures be given on the Holy Scriptures in French. These Protestant principles were unacceptable to the Catholic majority of France and the country remained illiterate. In 1598 the famous Edict of Nantes of Henri IV pronounced the equality of creeds in education: "There should be no difference or distinction concerning the members of the Reformed Religion to be educated in schools, colleges or universities." If the French Catholics refused to establish a national system of education for all classes, the Huguenots were free now to establish schools for their own community. Many Calvinist schools and academies were founded, the best-known at Nîmes, Montauban and Saumur. In the atmosphere of tolerance the professors of the Academies were much more liberal than Calvin. The rigid antagonism between Calvin and Luther was no longer maintained and the Academy of Nîmes looked for points of agreement with other bodies which had broken away from Rome. The teachers of the Saumur Academy were definitely inclined to the Arminian, liberal interpretation of Calvinism, which was gaining ground in Holland. Within the Huguenot community there was a measure of equality to be found nowhere else in the social life of contemporary France. Some of the Huguenot writers might be considered as precursors of Locke. François Hotman, the author of *Franco-Gallia*, La Boétie, the author of *A Discourse on Voluntary Slavery*, and the unknown author of the *Defence against Tyrants*, expounded liberal ideas which undoubtedly influenced the constitutional theory of England in the seventeenth century. After the Revocation of the Edict of Nantes by Louis XIV and the subsequent persecution the Huguenot educational system was suppressed and the Huguenots started their mass exodus from France. Their influence, however, left visible traces on the cultural development of France and in all countries which accepted Huguenot exiles they played an important cultural rôle.

In Holland, on the contrary, Calvinism took deep root and, combined with secular power, moulded the subsequent development of the educational system. In the Northern Netherlands from the early times Calvinism was divided into two schools. The strict Calvinists, known as "Precisians," were intolerant and persecuted both Roman Catholics and Protestant Dissenters. The liberal Calvinists, or "Evangelicals," advocated tolerance. In 1602 Jacob Harmensz, known as Arminius, was appointed to the chair of theology at Leyden, and became the leader of the Liberal party, which was known as the Arminians. His colleague at the University, Franciscus Gomarus, was the leader of the strict Calvinists. The struggle between the two parties took a political turn. The Arminians were republicans and adherents of provincial autonomy and of a policy of tolerance, whilst the Gomarists advocated centralisation and more powers to the Stadtholders combined with the monopoly of strict Calvinism. The States-General took the part of the Gomarists and forced Prince Maurice, the Stadtholder, to arrest Oldenbarenveldt, De Groot (Hugo Grotius) and Hoogerbeerts, the leaders of the Arminians. Oldenbarenveldt was condemned and executed, but Hugo Grotius managed to escape to France, where in his writings he laid the foundation of modern international law, and the policy of tolerance. It is an irony of fate that at the time when the Netherlands were an asylum for all pioneers of science and religious freedom, their greatest son had to live in Catholic France. William the Silent and most of his descendants, however, followed the liberal tradition of the Arminians and promoted education and tolerance. The first Dutch University was founded at Leyden in 1579; others followed, at Franeker (1584), Groningen (1614), Amsterdam (1632), Utrecht (1636), and Harderwijk (1646). For a time the Netherlands became the centre of learned men who flocked to her Universities from all Protestant countries. Descartes, a Catholic, and Spinoza, a Jew, expounded their philosophical systems and founded their schools in the Netherlands. The Uniformity Act of 1662 in England closed the doors of Oxford and Cambridge to English Puritans, and hundreds of English students went to Holland to receive theological training in Calvinist Universities. Leyden became almost an English University, as the Puritan students were followed by many Anglicans, attracted by the famous schools of Medicine and Law at that University. During a hundred and fifty years several thousands of English and Scottish students were educated in Holland. In the field of elementary education for the masses the Synod of Dort decreed in 1618 that "schools must be instituted in country places, towns and cities. Religious instruction must be given. The Christian magistracy should see to it that well-qualified persons teach with suitable compensation. The children of the poor should be instructed free. In all schools only orthodox Christians may teach. . . . The duty of the ministers with an elder is to visit all schools, private as well as public." By this law a Calvinist monopoly in education was established and the Roman Catholics, who formed a strong minority in Holland, were deprived of any schools of their own denomination. That was a general policy in all Protestant countries at that period after the terrible religious wars which devastated half Europe, and left indelible traces on the Dutch mentality. The

Catholics, as we have seen, received just treatment only in the nineteenth century.

In the English-speaking countries we observe the same two currents of Calvinist tradition. Whilst the orthodox Calvinists followed the same policy of monopoly and persecution, the liberal wing of the Puritans were pioneers of tolerance and scientific research and produced almost all the forerunners of universal education. Sometimes it is even difficult to decide whether men like Sir William Petty, J. Priestley, J. Lancaster, G. Birbeck or even Horace Mann of Massachusetts should be described as representatives of the Puritan or the secular tradition. The division of the Reformation movement in England into two definite groups had already begun in the time of Henry VIII. During the reign of Edward VI, John Knox preached at court and was at variance with Cranmer and the official Church party. But he and the first Presbyterian congregations were still within the fold of the Church, being content to endeavour to reform it from within. The Catholic reaction under Mary drove many English Protestants abroad, where some of them quite definitely joined the Calvinists or were influenced by German Baptists. Thus when Elizabeth restored the Anglican Church and insisted on conformity, a powerful group of Puritans was unable to join the national Church. Dissenting congregations came into being, and a Presbytery was inaugurated at Wandsworth. The Dissenters were divided from the start. The Presbyterians chiefly opposed everything in the Elizabethan Prayer Book that savoured of the "childish and superstitious toys" of Popery. They agreed with the principle of national establishment, and at first did not even oppose Episcopacy as contrary to Christian tradition. Perhaps John Knox might have been an Archbishop of Canterbury had he not published in exile a venomous attack on the *Monstrous Regiment of Women* and thus irreconcilably antagonised Elizabeth. Only later did differences in dogma become more pronounced. Influenced by the organisation of the Genevan Church, the Presbyterians favoured a more democratic national Church than the King and the bishops could accept. Gradually the religious cleavage developed into political opposition. When King James I at the conference at Hampton Court angrily exclaimed that "Presbytery as well agreed with Monarchy as God with Devil!" and repeated loudly: "No bishop, no king," the Presbyterians had to draw their conclusions. The Church became identified with the King and the Presbyterians sided decidedly with Parliament. But both parties agreed on the necessity for uniformity, and both were against the policy of toleration. Indeed, the Presbyterians even outstripped the Anglicans in their intolerant attitude towards the minor sects.

Side by side with the main stream of Calvinist opinion a group of Calvinists developed different ideas, influenced by the German Baptists. This German sect in its extreme form preached anarchism and a total denial of the authority of the State. In education their leader, H. Denck, was an outstanding reformer and a pioneer of tolerance in Germany and Switzerland. The Baptists were fiercely denounced by Luther and ruthlessly persecuted. The English Baptists were a milder copy of the German original. They went a step further than the Presbyterians and denied even a democratic centralisation of the Church. The Baptists and the Brownists, known as Separatists or Independents, relied entirely upon a spiritual idea of a Church and affirmed the private nature of communion with God. Beyond the voluntary organisation of a congregation they would not go, and, therefore, vehemently opposed any interference by the State in religious matters. Only during the Civil War, when the persecutions and intolerance of the Presbyterians goaded them into revolt, did they play false to their principles and abuse their military power. Some groups of Baptists and other sectaries were organised by George Fox, and became known as Friends or Quakers. They were the only sincere adherents of religious tolerance at that period. They extended toleration even to Papists and Jews. From their point of view, all organised religion, theology or ritual were mere inventions of man. To them, the only true Church is the mystical union of believers. Divine knowledge is not withheld from any, whether Papist or Protestant, Jew or heathen. Such views were heretical in the eyes of all, and Quakers were cruelly persecuted by Anglicans and Puritans alike. This difference in religious ideas influenced the attitude of the Dissenters towards education. The Presbyterians of the seventeenth century always had the example of Scotland in their minds, and strove to establish a national system of education under the control of presbyteries. They accepted the principle of universal compulsory education so long as they controlled it. It was certainly an advance on the Anglican policy, which demanded conformity without universal education. The Independents, including Baptists and Quakers, on the other hand, were jealous of their denominational self-government, and would not brook any central supervision of education. There was another difference: the Presbyterians retained the rite of ordination, and considered a sound theological knowledge based on a liberal education necessary for their ministers. The Independents, later known as Congregationalists, used the ordination rite occasionally and agreed with the Presbyterians on the necessity for a sound education for the ministry. The Baptists and the Quakers distrusted theological learning and believed in the Inner Light, which could qualify a person for the ministry who might be entirely lacking in a knowledge of ancient languages and of theology. Hence their different attitude towards university studies.

Being in a minority, the Puritans were not able to direct the national policy in education. The only chance of doing so was given them during the period of the Commonwealth when, at first, the Presbyterian Church was officially established by Parliament, and later, when the Independents had the upper hand during the Protectorate of Cromwell. The Presbyterians endeavoured to establish a national system of education based on the principles of monopoly. In 1641, the House of Commons resolved to abolish all deans, chapters, canons and other institutions of the Church, and that "all lands taken by this Bill from deans and chapters shall be employed for the advancement of learning and piety." Very little came of it, as the Civil War absorbed the major part of the fund. That the desire was genuine is witnessed by Comenius, who in his letter from England to his friends at Leszno (October, 1641) says: "They are eagerly debating on the reform of schools in the whole kingdom, namely that all young people should be instructed, none neglected." The central supervision of schools was entrusted to a Committee in 1643, which "shall have power to enquire after malignant schoolmasters." The purpose was more political and religious than educational and some schoolmasters were removed for their Anglican sympathies. Later, under Cromwell, Commissioners were appointed "to eject scandalous, ignorant and inefficient ministers and schoolmasters," who had a purely educational supervision. When Commissioners ejected R. Mossom solely for his Anglican tendencies, the Protector ordered his immediate reinstatement. During the whole period of the Commonwealth, the Government granted subsidies to many schools and schoolmasters. The most important example was the Act of 1649, by which the first-fruits and tenths created by Henry VIII were vested in trustees "to pay yearly all such salaries, stipends, allowances and provisions, as have been appointed for preaching the Gospel, preaching ministers or schoolmasters in England and Wales." If the revenue from these sources for educational purposes did not reach £20,000 per annum, the Treasury should make up this deficiency. £2,000 of this sum was allotted to the Universities. How many schools were actually established during the Commonwealth period is difficult to say. In 1818–37, according to the Charity Commission, thirty-three grammar schools and forty non-classical schools still existed, which were founded in 1651–60. In the Universities the Puritans tried to instil a new spirit of scientific research, and it was in the Oxford of the Commonwealth that the new science was born, where the new men of Puritan tendencies, such as Ward, Wallis, Wilkins, Goddard, Rook and Sir William Petty, were appointed. Among the new appointments at Cambridge were Whichote and Cudworth, the prominent Cambridge Platonists. Cromwell even founded a new University at Durham, but the Restoration put an end to this foundation.

The Restoration led to a reaction, the promises of the King were broken and the Uniformity Act of 1662 was passed. The Presbyterians against their wishes were grouped together with Independents and other Dissenters. Deprived of the supervision of the General Assembly, they gradually lost their cohesion, and circumstances compelled them to approach the Congregational model. About 150 of the ejected schoolmasters opened private schools; many of them were private tutors in rich Dissenting families, but some of them had large schools, for example Samuel Shaw, who had 160 boys in a free school at Ashby-de-la-Zouch in 1668. Another ejected minister, Adam Martindale, continued to teach at Manchester Grammar School, where he taught mathematics, including logarithms, which was an unusual feature at that time. The Five Mile Act of 1665 forbade Dissenters to teach in any school, yet in practice they were allowed to teach if appointed by the founder of the school. In 1672, Thomas Gouge, an ejected minister, started schools in Wales, and the Bishop did not disturb him. The Presbyterians, the Quakers and other Dissenters even endowed their own schools before the Toleration Act of 1689. The Quakers, for instance, had at least fifteen schools in 1671, in which boys and girls were instructed "in whatsoever things were civil and useful in creation." Higher education, too, was not neglected by the Puritans during this period of persecution. Many fellows, lecturers and heads of

Oxford and Cambridge Colleges, having been ejected from their posts, started academies of higher learning in all branches of University study. During the sixties eight academies came into being, followed by six more in the seventies, and another six in the eighties of the seventeenth century. With the passing of the Toleration Act in 1689, the Puritan Dissenters could openly endow their institutions and were not compelled to change the place every year. The Presbyterians and Independents came together and as "United Brethren" established a common fund for higher learning, which later was separated into two funds. With the aid of these funds new academies were endowed and many students maintained, and some were sent to Scotland and Holland to continue their studies. Hundreds of students were maintained in this manner. In the eighteenth century new public funds were established which were augmented by private funds created by Puritan benefactors such as Lady Hewley and Dr. Williams.

The academies, even of the early period, were not narrow sectarian institutions. Students were accepted without any tests and many Churchmen attended them in preference to Oxford and Cambridge. They taught theology as a matter of course, but also trained students for the legal and medical professions. The methods were more up-to-date and scientific apparatus was extensively used. The liberal ideas of ejected Oxford men had a considerable influence. Charles Morton, the founder of Newington Green Academy in 1667, and later Vice-President of Harvard, Massachusetts, wrote that he was "willing to have knowledge increased and not confined to the clergy or learned professions, but extended or diffused as much as might be to the people in general." The narrow policy "might well enough comport with popish designs to keep people in the dark." Frankland's methods and breadth of view at Rathmel Academy were also well known. In the eighteenth century the position of the Dissenters was much more assured. The Hanoverian kings could not dispense with their support in view of the Jacobite risings and the kings used to grant subsidies to the Dissenters out of their own purse. In 1727, the Presbyterians, Independents and Baptists united under the name of the "Protestant Dissenting Ministers of the Three Denominations" and received a right of petition in order to protect and defend their constitutional rights. In this freer atmosphere the Dissenters could openly endow non-classical schools and academies, but not grammar schools. An interesting experiment in introducing new methods was made by the Society of Friends. One of the Friends, John Bellers, submitted to the House of Commons a scheme for a co-operative community, which he called the "College of Industry" and which included a plan of agricultural and industrial education. The Friends' Yearly Meeting accepted his scheme in 1697. A school was founded on this plan at Clerkenwell in 1702. It was a scheme of labour education, combining productive manual work with school instruction. The experiment, it seems, proved unsatisfactory and in 1790 it was abandoned, and from then on the school was run on ordinary lines. The boarding school at Ackworth, founded through the efforts of Dr. Fothergill, was also based on the principle of "labour and learning properly intermixed." In general the Friends were suspicious of classical schools and insisted on "real" subjects.

The development of Dissenting academies entered its third stage from the middle of the eighteenth century. The academies ceased to be private institutions and were maintained and fully controlled by public dissenting bodies. The most famous of the academies of that period was the Warrington Academy founded in 1757. The plan at the Academy and its aim was "to unite in the best manner the advantages of the public and more private methods of education" and to provide "for the extensive learning of our youth and the security of their morals." Students would gain "some knowledge of the more useful branches of literature," leading "to an early acquaintance with the true principles of religion and liberty." For the future ministers, too, "it will be an invaluable advantage to have them educated where they may freely follow the dictates of their own judgments in their enquiries after truth, without any undue bias imposed on their understanding." The new attitude towards dogmatic indoctrination was evident in the lectures of Dr. Taylor, who usually began his course on theology thus: "That you keep your mind always open to evidence. That you labour to banish from your breasts all prejudice, prepossession and party zeal. That you study to live in peace and love with all your fellow Christians; and that you steadily assert for yourselves, and freely allow for others, the inalienable rights of judgment and conscience." Still more explicit was another famous tutor of the Academy, Dr. Joseph Priestley. He claimed complete freedom for all "whether Christians, Papists, Protestants, Dissenters, Heretics or Deists, the same liberty of thinking, debating and publishing." "Can we think," said he, "that wisdom will die with us? No: our creeds, could we be so inconsistent with ourselves as to draw up any, would, I make no doubt, be rejected with equal disdain by our posterity." He introduced two new subjects into the curriculum—Civil History and Civil Policy. In his *Essay on a Course of Liberal Education for Civil and Active Life* (1765) Priestley advocated "observation and experience as the only safe guides." Science was also taught at Warrington Academy, and many students were prepared for the medical profession. The Academy was closed in 1786, after having been a successful rival of the two old Universities for twenty-nine years. This change towards dogmatic instruction was not sudden, but grew gradually during the period of persecution. Even during the Commonwealth many Puritans, including Cromwell, were against any monopoly in religion. The Restoration by persecuting them compelled even the Presbyterians to champion freedom of conscience for all. Generations of Puritans were often educated in Holland and Scotland where they came under the liberalising influence of such famous scientists as Boerhaave at Leyden, or philosophers as Hutcheson at Glasgow. The works of Locke, Shaftesbury and Newton were available in the English academies and were popular among the students. To what results in some cases these influences led can be inferred from the case of John Toland. As an exhibitioner from the Presbyterian Fund, Toland studied at Utrecht, and in the end refused connection with any form of organised Christianity and became the leader of the English Deists. The influence of Dutch Arminians led the English Presbyterians away from rigid Calvinism and they more and more tended towards Arianism. Priestley relates that whilst he was a student at Daventry Academy "it was in a state peculiarly favourable to the serious pursuit of truth, as the students were about equally divided upon every question of much importance, such as Liberty and Necessity and all the articles of theological orthodoxy and heresy, in consequence of which all these topics were the subject of continued discussion. Our tutors were also of different opinions, one taking the orthodox side of every question and the other that of heresy." Thus gradually the Presbyterian divines through the stages of Arminianism and Arianism arrived at a completely heterodox interpretation of Christianity akin to that adopted by the Unitarians. Not all of them took the last step—the famous Dr. Richard Price remained an Arian and disagreed with Priestley, who became the leader of the Unitarians. The process of emancipation from the rigid dogma of Calvinism was greatly furthered by the intimate association of Puritan leaders with the secularists—the Deists and Freemasons. Toland became a Deist, Price, Priestley, Kippis and Rees were members of clubs and societies started by Freemasons. The Dissenting College at Hackney, where Price, Priestley, Kippis and Rees lectured, became a hotbed of radical opinions both in religion and politics, and even went so far as to hold a dinner party to honour the famous, or in orthodox opinion infamous, Thomas Paine. The Puritan academies were thus the pioneers of religious and political freedom and as such were far in advance of the orthodox sterility of Oxford and Cambridge. In science the works of Price and Priestley introduced new methods and new subjects and made the Academies the precursors of modern Universities, whereas Oxford and Cambridge were still steeped in the medieval classical atmosphere. In the nineteenth century the abolition of tests and the foundation of the secular University of London deprived the Academies of their previous importance as places of scientific learning, and they became purely theological institutions for dissenting ministers. The majority of Academies did not survive the change, but about a dozen still exist as separate denominational colleges. The Warrington Academy having undergone many transformations has found its final place at Oxford as a Unitarian College. Thus the tradition of Puritan Academies is not extinct, but is still a living force in English education. In the field of elementary education the Puritans joined forces with the secularists and demanded an undenominational national school system, which was realised through their support.

In Scotland, as in England, the beginning of the Reformation was a mixture of political and religious motives. The Scottish nobility sided with the reformers for selfish reasons and were interested in Church organisation in so far as the general upheaval helped them to despoil the riches of the old Church. The question of the final adoption of Presbytery or Episcopacy was decided only after a century of strife. But from the beginning strict Calvinism, imbibed by Knox at Geneva, gave a strong Puritan tendency to the Scottish movement. When the Reformation was adopted by Parliament in 1560, Knox was the acknowledged leader, and his ideas moulded the policy of the new Church. Both the democratic organisation of the Church and the theocratic claim to monopoly were transplanted wholesale from

Geneva. The policy of intolerance and persecution was likewise accepted, but was not followed in practice with the same vigour. Heavy penalties, with death on a third conviction, were enacted against any person celebrating Mass or even being present. It seems, however, that nobody was executed under this Act, although some heretics, for example John Cunningham, a teacher, were burned for witchcraft in 1591. In education the Reformed Church claimed the sole right of administration and control from the start. All the institutions inherited from the Middle Ages were taken over. Besides the three Universities the Reformed Church received some grammar schools and the basic outline of the parish school system. Education was entirely disorganised by war with England and civil strife and the Privy Council appointed a Commission in 1560 "to draw up the policy and discipline of the Kirk," including education. The selected divines, known as the Six Johns, Knox, Douglas, Rowe, Spottiswood, Willock and Winram, produced the famous *Book of Discipline*, of which Knox seems to have been the chief author. The chapter entitled "Of Schools and Universities" is devoted to education. It envisaged a complete system of education far in advance of the period. Education was to be universal and compulsory, irrespective of social position. "It must be carefully provided that no father, of whatever estate or condition he be, use his children after his own phantasy, especially in their youth, all must be compelled to bring up their children in learning and virtue." Every parish had to have an elementary school, and in towns, teachers should be appointed "as are able to teach Grammar and Latin tongue." Special examiners should select pupils from elementary schools for continued education in the grammar schools. Again, at the end of the grammar school course, future University students should be selected after an examination. The examiners should be

> the ministers and elders with the most learned men in every town. . . . In every course the children must either proceed to further knowledge, or else they must be sent to some handicraft, or to some other profitable exercise. . . . Provision must be made for those that are poor, and are not able by themselves, nor by their friends, to be sustained at letters, especially such as come from landward. . . . The children of the poor must be supported and sustained at the charge of the Church, until trial be taken whether the spirit of docility be found in them or not. If they be found apt to letters and learning, they may not, neither the sons of the rich nor the sons of the poor, be permitted to reject learning. They must be

charged to continue their study, so that the Commonwealth may have some comfort by them.

Bursaries should be established at the Universities, seventy-two at St. Andrews and forty-eight each in Glasgow and Aberdeen. The Universities should have eight-year courses, of which three years should be devoted to the arts and five to the professional studies of medicine, law or divinity. The admittance to the arts course was to be on presenting a certificate as to "learning, docility, age and parentage" from the master of the school and parish minister. The financing of the whole system was to be based on the patrimony of the old Church. The administration and control of all institutions was to be entrusted to the Church. The system thus comprised: (i) Rural elementary schools in every parish (two years); (ii) Grammar schools in towns (four years— ages eight to twelve); (iii) Ten colleges in larger towns (seats of Protestant bishops) (four years—ages twelve to sixteen) and (iv) Three Universities (Arts sixteen to nineteen, professional faculties five years, nineteen to twenty-four). Religion and dogmatic instruction in the tenets of the Reformed Church were compulsory and formed the most important parts of the curriculum at all stages. This ambitious scheme could be realised only if the patrimony of the Church remained intact. However, the aristocracy would not part with the spoliated estates and opposed the plan, so that Parliament did not pass the measure. Thus the scheme was never put into practice, but the grandeur of the whole conception undoubtedly moulded the subsequent history of Scottish education.

The Church repeatedly requested Regent Murray and Queen Mary to stop the spoliation of Church lands and to apply the revenue to schools, but to no avail. The Church found a new champion in Andrew Melville. By his *Second Book of Discipline* he gave to the Church a definite Presbyterian character and exalted the Church above all secular power with such force as to rival the ultramontane conception of the Roman Curia. The spiritual monopoly of the Church was recognised by Parliament in 1592, but the Church lost most of its lands, and the educational provisions of Knox remained on paper. The monopoly of the Church in education was firmly established and private tuition at home or education in Catholic countries abroad was expressly prohibited. Parents who sent their children to countries where there was danger of infection from the "leprosy of popery" were ordered to bring them home on pain of excommunication. By an Act of Parliament of 1640, parents who refused obedience to the demands of the Church were deprived of their children, for whose education in the true faith alternative means were provided. Peer and peasant were subjected to the same treatment. Although the monopoly legally existed up to the nineteenth century it was strictly enforced only in the seventeenth century. In the eighteenth century many secessions from the established Church took place and the secessionists started founding their own schools. The Church could not prevent it, as whole presbyteries seceded on many occasions. A real advance towards Knox's ideal was made by the Act of 1696, for "Settling Schools." It ordained that in every parish "there be a school settled and established by advice of the heritors and minister of the parish." Hundreds of parish schools were opened during the first decade, and thus formed the basis of the Scottish national system. The final disruption of the Church occurred in 1843 and ended all pretence of monopoly. About one-third of the clergy with their parishes seceded and formed the Free Church of Scotland, which built up its own parish school system. The various Presbyterian bodies, however, were so territorially intermingled that in practice all schools accepted pupils irrespective of their Church membership and all types of schools gradually grew into one national school system. In higher education all Universities, including the municipal foundation of Edinburgh, were subject to Church supervision. In practice many professors openly propagated unorthodox views and were usually left unmolested. Such Professors of Moral Philosophy at Glasgow as Francis Hutcheson and his successor Adam Smith, by their liberal views influenced many students to free themselves from the rigidity of orthodox Calvinism. The rise of Arianism in England and Northern Ireland is closely connected with the University of Glasgow. In the eighteenth century religious tests were not enforced, but officially they were abolished only in 1853.

Besides England and Scotland Calvinism very strongly influenced the educational traditions of Wales and Northern Ireland. In both countries the Puritans founded Dissenting Academies on the English model and attempted to establish a nation-wide parish school system. The more democratic character of their present school systems and the absence of influential private schools distinguishes Wales and Northern Ireland from England and is undoubtedly the result of the Puritan tradition.

In the Dominions the Puritans contributed considerably to the building up of national systems, but their influence is best seen in the examples of New Zealand and South Africa. In New Zealand the province of Otago was settled by Scottish Presbyterians. When they received the Charter they decided by the terms of purchase to set apart one-eighth of the entire proceeds of the sale of the lands in Otago for "religious and educational purposes," under the control of trustees for the Presbyterian Church of Otago. As soon as the Scots arrived at Otago, they erected a schoolhouse in 1848. Schools were opened in each district "so that every child be taught to read and write" as the public meeting of colonists decided in 1850. The schools were controlled by the Kirk Session. Even when, in 1856, provincial legislation established a Board of Education and enacted a School Ordinance, the schools preserved their strictly Presbyterian character. No one could be appointed a teacher unless he presented a certificate from his minister guaranteeing his fitness to give religious instruction. Any two male parents might impeach the soundness of a teacher's doctrine with the penalty of dismissal without appeal in the event of the charge being sustained. Only in the sixties was the control of the Church weakened, until the schools were gradually secularised and merged into the national system.

The Dutch settlers of Cape Colony brought with them the institutions, the ideas and the customs of seventeenth-century Holland without modification and made them the basis of their cultural tradition. As in Holland the identification of Church and State led to Church control in education in Cape Colony and later in the Boer Republics. The early teachers were servants of the Church and were called "Siekentrooster" (comforter of the sick), and helped the minister and often deputised for him. The local education authority was the Church Court, or "Kerkeraad." After the Great Trek in 1836 the tradition of intimate connection between the Church and the school was transferred to the new Republics. The regulations passed in 1852 gave the control of the schools to the local Kerkeraad. Only members of the Dutch Reformed Church were allowed to teach. At that time two definite parties developed in the two republics, as had happened before in all Calvinist countries. One was more liberal, with a tendency towards the emancipation of education from Church control, and the other an orthodox party, known as the "Doppers." The liberal party found its best exponents in President Burgher and in our own time in General Smuts.

Burgher introduced in 1874 an undenominational school system, but in 1882 the next President, Kruger, the leader of the "Doppers," reversed this decision. One of his main principles was that religious instruction forms an integral part of the curriculum and belongs to the Church. Kruger declared: "School education must be under the guidance of the Church. The Government does not want to establish State schools; they must be Church schools." By his legislation the control was left in the hands of the Church and the Bible and the Catechism remained the crucial subjects. But during the nineties, especially under Mansvelt from Holland, appointed in 1891, the State Department assumed the supervision and control of the schools, paving the way for the present secular system, established since the Union.

In America the chief representatives of Calvinist Puritanism were the Congregationalists and not the Presbyterians. The Congregational Church of New England shaped the early school system which later served as a model for other American Puritan communities. In all the New England colonies, with the exception of Rhode Island, the Congregational Church was established by law at the plantation of the colonies. However there were substantial differences; in Massachusetts and New Haven the identification of the Church and State was understood in its medieval sense as a theocracy, upon which all civil rights depended. The colonies of Plymouth and Connecticut, on the other hand, looked upon the established Church only as a means conducive to religious and social stability, and recognised the claims of other people to civic equality. Rhode Island alone accepted from the start the principle of separation of Church and State. The first colonists of Massachusetts Bay were not Separatists like the Plymouth colonists, but adopted Independency only on arrival in America. The first acts of the people of Salem were the election of a minister and a teacher and the pronouncement of a monopoly in religion. John Cotton, their minister, argued that "theocracy, i.e. God's government, might be established as the best form of government, wherein the people that chose rules are God's people in covenant with Him, that is, members of the Churches" (Congregational). In accordance with this principle, the colonists passed an Act in 1631 admitting to citizenship only members of Congregational Churches, "in good and regular standing." Neither Episcopalians, Presbyterians nor Baptists could be freemen, still less Papists and Quakers. In 1646 the Act against Heresy demanded the banishment of all heretics. The Act of 1697 against "Blasphemy and Atheism" prescribed most cruel punishments for such offences. Papists and Quakers were forbidden even entry into the colony. Four Quakers were executed in 1659 after a return from banishment and many of them were flogged. Not all Congregationalists were so intolerant. The colonists of Plymouth were influenced by their sojourn of ten years in Leyden, where they enjoyed complete freedom. When they settled in America they did not make membership of their Church a condition of citizenship. In 1646, the General Court resolved "that something be done to maintain the liberties of the Churches without intermingling or wronging each other that they may live in peace." A proposition was even put forward for full toleration of religion to all men, without exception of "Turk, Jew, Papist, Socinian or any other." However, it was too advanced even for the tolerant brethren. The founders of Connecticut did not feel quite happy under the Massachusetts theocracy and when, in 1638, they organised a new colony, they accepted the principles of toleration and religious liberty as the basis of the constitution. Citizenship was acquired irrespective of membership of any Church. Rhode Island was an exception among the colonies founded by Congregationalists. Roger Williams, who arrived at Massachusetts Bay in 1631, was elected a minister of Salem, and soon displeased the General Court by his preaching of religious freedom. He fled to Plymouth, where he was made a teacher, but was recalled to Salem in 1633. He continued to preach the separation of Church and State, was tried by the General Court, and banished in 1635. He went to Rhode Island and founded the colony in accordance with his principles of complete freedom of conscience. Pennsylvania was another Puritan colony which adopted the principle of toleration. The Friends, who founded the colony, gave full freedom to all "who shall confess and acknowledge Almighty God to be the Creator, Upholder and Ruler of the World." Although this definition comprised the Papists and the Jews, it definitely excluded the atheists.

Thus the Puritan colonies can be divided into three groups: (i) Massachusetts, New Hampshire and New Haven, which established a theocracy in the medieval sense; (ii) Plymouth and Connecticut, which, adopting the union of Church and State, afforded freedom to dissenters, and (iii) Rhode Island and Pennsylvania, which proclaimed complete freedom of conscience. In these circumstances the development of school systems varied considerably. In the first two groups the educational ideas of the Puritans were backed by the State and introduced as compulsory legislation, whilst in the third group the State left the initiative to local communities. Massachusetts led the way in compulsory legislation. The first Act was passed in 1642 and enjoined that selectmen "shall have the power to take account from time to time of all children, . . . especially of their ability to read and to understand the principles of religion . . . and to impose fines on all who refuse to render such accounts." The famous law of 1647 was still more explicit:

> It being one chief project of that old deluder, Satan, to keep men from the knowledge of the Scripture. . . . It is therefore ordered by this Court . . . that every township within this jurisdiction, after that the Lord has increased them to the number of fifty householders, shall then forthwith appoint one within their town to teach all such children as shall resort to him, to write and read; whose wages shall be paid either by the parents or master of such children, or by the inhabitants in general. . . . And it is further ordered, that where any town shall increase to the number of one hundred families of householders, they shall set up a grammar school, the masters thereof being able to instruct youth so far as they may be fitted for the University: and if any town neglect the performance hereof above one year, then every such town shall pay five pounds per annum to the next such school till they shall perform this order.

The first Education Act of Connecticut, passed in 1650, ordered parents and masters to give their children and apprentices instruction in the "grounds and principles of religion" such "as may enable them perfectly to read the English tongue, and the knowledge of the capital laws, upon penalty of twenty shillings for each neglect therein." Then follows the repetition of the "old deluder" law word for word. That these laws were followed in practice can be seen from many cases of fines imposed on delinquent towns. The majority of New England towns complied with the provisions of the law, and many had schools supported by rates or by land endowment even before 1647. Grammar schools were also founded in almost all the towns subject to law. The schools were free only for poor families; the well-to-do usually paid fees. As mentioned, Rhode Island and Pennsylvania did not enact compulsory legislation, but many towns in these colonies provided for schools by enacting local by-laws. All these schools, whether established by the State in New England or later by Puritan communities in the Middle States, were under the constant and vigilant supervision of the ministers. When the Boston people in 1710 chose five lay inspectors to visit the Latin school, the ministers protested vigorously at the innovation. Institutions for higher learning were also provided from the earliest period. The first and the most famous was Harvard College, Cambridge (Boston), Massachusetts, founded in 1636. The aim was twofold: to advance learning and to perpetuate the ministry. In practice Harvard was under the control of the Congregational Church. In the eighteenth century, Harvard began to develop Unitarian tendencies and the control of the Church was weakened. In 1806 a Unitarian was elected President, and since then Harvard has become undenominational. A second Congregational College was founded at New Haven (Yale) in 1701. This College was strictly denominational and in 1722 religious tests were imposed in which all the tutors had to give satisfaction "of the soundness of their faith in opposition to Arminian and prelatic corruptions or any other dangerous consequences to the purity and peace of our Churches." Since 1792, the State has been represented on the corporation, and Yale College gradually lost its denominational character. The change of attitude was evident in the foundation of the third Congregational College at Dartmouth, New Hampshire, in 1769. The Charter stated "that the College would not exclude persons of any religious denomination whatsoever . . . on account of their speculative sentiments in Religion." Princeton College, founded by Presbyterians in 1746, from the start was open to all denominations. The Dutch Reformed College of Rutgers in New Jersey, 1766, and the Baptist Brown College in Rhode Island, 1764, although controlled by their respective Churches, were open to all from the beginning. Thus in the middle of the eighteenth century Church control began to weaken and the schools and colleges became gradually undenominational. The American Revolution completed this evolution by separating the Church from the State. Although religion was still an integral part of the curriculum, it had lost its exclusive sectarian character. State institutions were founded on a strictly unsectarian basis, and the Churches felt that their denominational interests could no longer be furthered by education in public schools. The public grammar schools entered a period of decay and the compulsory legislation was not enforced. The Churches founded private academies as a substitute, and at the end of the eighteenth century the American system had lost its previous democratic character. The poorer classes continued to attend the public schools, but the wealthier parents sent their sons to expensive private academies. Only gradually was the old democratic structure of the Puritan school system regained in the nineteenth century through the influence of the secular tradition.

In all countries dominated by Calvinism, we have noticed two tendencies among the Puritan Churches. One, the orthodox Calvinist tradition, accepted the general principle of identification of Church and State and endeavoured to realise in practice the idea of theocracy with an intolerant persecution of all dissenters. Calvin himself initiated this policy in Geneva and was followed up by the "Precisians" in Holland, John Knox in Scotland, the Presbyterian Long Parliament in England and the Congregationalists in America. The other, more liberal, drew the logical conclusion from the principles of the Reformation of individual responsibility and defended freedom of conscience for all. Cordier and Chateillon in Switzerland and the Huguenots in France were the pioneers of this tradition. Arminius and Hugo Grotius, in spite of temporary persecution, succeeded in winning Holland for the cause of freedom in religion. The Dissenting Academies in England, with J. Priestley as their greatest man, defended the same principles. And in America Roger Williams established the first province, Rhode Island, on a secular basis. Under the influence of the liberal wing of the Puritans the orthodox party changed their intolerant attitude and abandoned in the eighteenth century the policy of monopoly in education in favour of a national comprehensive system. However, the old tradition of strict Calvinism was not yet dead and was revived in the nineteenth century. Known in America as "fundamentalists" and in South Africa as "Doppers," and being deprived of legislative power, these old-fashioned Calvinists interfered in the curriculum and methods of instruction in the public schools. They protested against the historical and critical interpretation of the Bible and against the theory of evolution, and often caused serious obstruction to the work of the public school authorities. But the overwhelming majority of Puritans of all denominations helped the State to surmount the religious divisions and prejudices inherited from the past. Their own policy from the earliest time was democratic in all countries, and wherever the Puritans went they brought with them the school available to all classes. The principle of universal compulsory education was adopted by Puritan Churches far in advance of their time. In their attitude to higher learning, although they started from a religious-moral and utilitarian point of view, they soon became the pioneers of scientific research and promoters of modern academic subjects. In spite of all their mistakes and temporary aberrations, typical of the periods of history in which they lived and strove, the Puritans were the pioneers and reformers in education and the public school systems of the nineteenth century have grown from the seeds planted by them. The greatest of all educational reformers, John Comenius (Jan Amos Komensky), although not a Calvinist, was a Puritan, and his ideas were accepted in Puritan countries as a basis of this practice.

PART III

SECULAR FACTORS

CHAPTER IX

HUMANISM

Humanism implies both a human and a humane approach to educational problems: human in the sense that human nature and human interests should not be suppressed by religion in favour of an ascetic ideal and a narrow dogmatic interpretation of the world; humane in the sense that the nature of the child and its growing mind should not be suppressed by cruel school discipline and rigid methods of instruction. It was a revolt against the medieval dualism of spirit and body, the latter being "a vessel of evil" to be subdued by severe corporal chastisement. It was a revolt against the monopoly of theology and Church dogma in the theory and practice of medieval life. It was not directed against Christianity; on the contrary, humanism accepted its close connection with the Christian tradition and Christian morality. The universal validity of Christian teaching and its international character was taken by humanists as the foundation of their ideas. In its original setting humanism meant the liberation of reason from the shackles of dogma and a critical study of nature and humanity through the observation of actual facts. The Middle Ages having concentrated on theological questions neglected science, and the scientific achievements of Aristotle, Theophrastus, Pliny or Galen were not surpassed simply because they were known in fragments or in wrong interpretation and could not serve as a basis for further research. To recover that knowledge the humanists insisted on a thorough learning of Latin and Greek so that the original sources could be read. After the birth of modern science and modern philosophy with Bacon and Descartes, this reason for classical studies lost its justification, but the early practice of humanist schools was firmly established and influenced European education for three centuries. Accepted by Protestant reformers and Jesuits alike, this narrow classical interpretation of humanism became as stifling to the progress of secondary and higher education as the medieval orthodoxy before it. "Humaniora" in the broadest sense, including the study of the human body and surrounding

174

nature, were narrowed down to "Humanities" as classical studies. Under these circumstances the grammar schools and Universities still under the official control of the Church lost the true spirit of the Renaissance and became obstacles to rather than promoters of modern science and philosophy. In consequence the true aim of the Renaissance, the liberation of men's minds from Church dogma and the prevalent superstitions, and thus clearing the way for critical scientific inquiry, was represented by learned societies, independent philosophers and private initiative and not by the old Universities. The remarkable movement forward in all fields of human activity, called the Renaissance, was made possible by an exceptional combination of events, which happened in the second half of the fifteenth century. Of all European countries, Italy was best suited for the revival of classical learning and philosophy. Greece was prostrate under the heel of the Turk and could contribute by individual refugees only; Spain had only just been united, after the final victory over the Moors, and concentrated on orthodoxy and national unity. Italy, on the other hand, was politically divided among many rival principalities and republics, which tried to excel each other both in politics and cultural development. No other country afforded such an opportunity for men of talent and new ideas, who could choose the town or court which paid the most and gave the fuller freedom of expression. Italian soil itself was full of classical remains which lay actually on the surface and required only to be picked up. Then three important events followed in rapid succession. Constantinople fell in 1453 and a wave of Greek learned refugees filled the courts of Italy, bringing with them their knowledge and Greek manuscripts. The invention of the printing press by Gutenberg in 1438 made possible a much wider and quicker diffusion of knowledge, and the discovery of America by Columbus in 1482 burst open the narrow confines of the medieval world. Thus the discovery of the ancient world was coupled with the discovery of the new world, and this expansion of the horizon was made available to wide circles through the printed book.

The first Greek refugees arrived in Italy before the actual fall of Constantinople. Gemistos Pletho arrived early in the fifteenth century and revived the study of Plato in Florence, which led to the foundation of the *Academia Platonica* in 1470. He was followed by his pupil Bessarion, Bishop of Nicaea, who settled in Rome and whose activities resulted in the foundation of the

Academia Romana in 1498. Pletho revived Platonic philosophy
with a Neoplatonic interpretation which led him away from
orthodox Christianity. From his point of view God reveals
Himself not only in the Bible and the tradition of the Church,
but perhaps more adequately in nature and natural laws, which
are emanations of God Himself. From which it follows that the
study of nature and the discovery of natural laws are the direct
way to the understanding of the divine purpose in the universe.
Being a Greek and a member of the Orthodox Church and living
in a period when the Inquisition was inactive, Pletho could
openly preach his new universal religion. His followers in the
Platonic Academy of Florence, Italians and Catholics, were not
so fortunate. In the sixteenth century, during the fierce struggle
between the Reformation and the Roman Church, the Inquisition
would not tolerate such heretical theories. Giordano Bruno was
burnt in 1600 for pantheistic opinions. The members of the
Platonic Academy had to pursue their pantheistic speculations in
secret and for that purpose formed secret groups or "lodges" of
"Platonic Christians or Brothers." In these secret circles the
"Brothers" pursued their alchemic experiments in quest of the
"philosophers' stone" or the "panacea," the two clues which
could open the doors to the hidden treasures of nature. Although
the alchemists or "spagyrists" started from wrong premises and
used wrong methods, many of their dreams have found their
realisation in modern scientific discoveries. The Florentine
and Roman Academies were the two early centres of this movement, which resulted a century later in the foundation of similar
societies all over Western Europe. In Italy the most famous
were the Academies of *"Della Porta"* [1] (Naples 1560), *Della Crusca*
(Florence 1582) and *Dei Lincei* (Rome 1603). In Germany the
most lasting and influential was the *Akademie des Palm Baumes*
(Weimar 1616) and in Holland the "old Kamer" of *Eglentier*
(Amsterdam 1519). All these academies pursued the aim of
scientific research and the literary perfection of their national
languages. The discovery of scientific instruments, especially of
the microscope and telescope, the use of logarithms and the
discovery of analytical geometry by Descartes and of the cal-
culus by Newton and Leibnitz changed the haphazard methods
of the alchemists into systematic scientific research. The revival of Neoplatonic philosophy by Pletho developed in Italy
into natural philosophy, the greatest representative of which,

1 *"Societas secretorum naturae"* was the official title.

Giordano Bruno, may be called the first philosopher of modern times.

A definite break with medieval scholasticism was made by the two pioneers of the new philosophy, Francis Bacon and René Descartes. Bacon laid the foundations of the English empirical school by clearly stating for the first time the theory of induction. Bacon's inductive method made all the difference between the experiments of alchemists and the experiments of modern science. The alchemists were full of new ideas, but they lacked a method of research. Although Bacon himself shared many unscientific theories of the alchemists he pointed in the right direction for future research. But his induction was insufficient in itself to promote that remarkable progress of science which we witness in the seventeenth and eighteenth centuries. Modern science is based on mathematics, and analysis and deduction are as necessary for scientific research as is induction. Descartes provided both. By the invention of analytical geometry he found a universal method for all branches of mathematics and by applying analysis and deduction to philosophical problems he freed the mind from dogma and superstitions. His famous sentence: *cogito ergo sum* (I think, therefore I exist) forms the first step of intuitive knowledge, which is beyond any doubt. It is based on personal experience and is made clear by the analysis of common sense free from any dogma. Bacon's empiricism and Descartes's analysis released the accumulated emotional protest against the monopoly of the Church and directed it into scientific channels.

The new criticism based on reasoning did not spare the dogma of the Church and ended by attacking revealed religion in general. Already Bacon deplored the struggle between the rival creeds and pointed out the danger to the State of fanatical distortions of pure religion. He advocated the foundation of a "Solomon's House" as an international clearing-house for scientific research unhampered by any dogma. The next English philosopher, Hobbes, accepted the relative value of religious dogma and advocated State supremacy in religious matters and the subordination of the Church to State needs. Lord Herbert of Cherbury made the next step and professed a new religion based on reasoning or Deism. Locke applied these principles to practical policy and demanded a complete separation of the Church from the State. A natural conclusion of his opinions was the policy of tolerance of all beliefs and of all forms of public worship. His pupil Shaftesbury made the final conclusion and divorced morality from religion; for him morality was innate in human nature and independent of religious revelation. Other pupils of Locke, Toland, Tindal and Collins, quite openly refuted the revelation of Christianity and candidly professed the Deistic philosophy. The impact of these theories on education led to a new evaluation of the aims of education and its methods. The dissemination of the conclusions of the new philosophy and the new discoveries of science was made possible by the activities of many societies and private schools which were free from the traditions of old scholastic institutions. The secret societies which were formed in the early Italian academies came into contact with similarly minded people in other countries and started an international movement for the improvement of learning and the reform of education. Many outstanding philosophers and reformers of all nations took an active part in this movement. The aims were universal brotherhood irrespective of creed or origin and the diffusion of knowledge throughout the human race. Bacon's idea of founding an international centre of scientific research was especially popular in these circles. In the thirties of the seventeenth century the Czech reformer Jan Amos Komensky (John Comenius) became the centre of international interest through his pedagogical works and pansophic ideas. England, France, Holland, Sweden, Poland, Hungary and Germany, and even America, vied with each other to secure his services for the reform of education and the establishment of an international centre of research. At the end of the century, after the death of Comenius, the leadership passed to the famous philosopher G. W. Leibnitz, who initiated the Academies of the eighteenth century. Started as private societies, these institutions developed into national centres of research and received official recognition. The informal "Philosophical or Invisible College" of London and Oxford was incorporated as the Royal Society in 1662; the private scientific academies of Paris became the Académie des Sciences in 1666; the private scientific society in Austria became an Imperial Academy in 1677. This was followed in the eighteenth century by the foundation of national Academies in Germany, Russia and the Scandinavian countries.

The influence of these institutions on the general progress of science and education was enormous, but it was felt more in the field of private initiative than in the Universities, which were still entrenched in Aristotle and Church dogma. The educational aims of these societies were well expressed by the historian of the Royal Society, Bishop T. Spratt, F.R.S., in his *History* in 1667:

> It would be no hindrance to the minds of men if besides those courses of studies which are now followed, there were also trial made of some other more particular ways, to prepare their minds for the world and the business of human life. It is apparent that nothing more suppresses the genius of learners, than the formality and the confinement of the precepts, by which they are instructed. To this purpose I will venture to propose to the consideration of wise men, whether this way of teaching by practice and experiments would not at least be as beneficial as the other by universal rules . . . whether it were not as profitable to apply the eyes, and the hands of children, to see and to touch all the several kinds of sensible things, as to oblige them to learn and to remember the difficult doctrines of general Arts? . . . We load the minds of children with doctrines and precepts to apprehend which they are most unfit, by reason of the weakness of their understandings; whereas they might with more profit be exercised in the consideration of visible and sensible things, of whose impressions they are most capable because of the strength of their memories and the perfection of their senses.

This quotation shows that the reformers demanded both the enlargement of the curriculum with "real" studies and the change of methods to suit the minds of children. The first part of this programme was realised in the eighteenth century in private schools or academies, the second part, the reform of methods of instruction, much later after Pestalozzi and Froebel. Private initiative and individual reformers could introduce new subjects and new methods, but they could not make them available to the masses. To build up a national system the intervention of the State was necessary and the existing Church system had to be secularised. Thus we must distinguish the three tasks which confronted the humanist tradition. The private academies of England are the best example of the new curriculum, the French movement of enlightenment led the way in secularisation and State intervention and the German-speaking reformers introduced the new methods. But all three movements were closely connected and derived their ideas from the same source—the international activities of the seventeenth century and the person of the great educational reformer Comenius.

As already mentioned, the private scientific Academies of the seventeenth century were connected with secret "lodges" of "Platonic Brothers," who were also known as "Rosicrucians." At the end of the century some of them joined the craftsmen's lodges of Freemasonry, and thus combined the medieval organisation of Freemasons with the speculative character of scientific "lodges." When in 1717 Theophilus Desaguliers organised the Grand Lodge of England, its Constitution adopted the tradition of Comenius as its basis. The lodge "Crucis Amicorum" founded by Comenius in the Netherlands later became one of the lodges of Freemasonry. The German "Academie des Palmbaumes" also developed in the eighteenth century into a masonic lodge "Indissolubilis." The Masonry of the eighteenth century inherited the tradition of scientific research and the "diffusion of knowledge" and this particular expression of Comenius is usually repeated in the many schemes of educational reform initiated by Freemasons. In their attitude towards religious creeds the Masons accepted the "Religion in which all men agree," which in fact was the English Deism. The English Constitution was accepted by many Continental groups and thus the Grand Lodge of England became the centre of a very influential international movement in the eighteenth century. In England Freemasonry accepted Locke's principles of tolerance and fostered in general the policy of toleration, which led to undenominational Christianity without antagonising the Protestant Churches. In France, and on the Continent in general, Freemasonry from the start was entangled in a fierce struggle with the Catholic Church and developed a strong anti-clerical secular tendency. But both in England and on the Continent Freemasonry assisted in the emancipation of education from religious dogma and in the introduction of scientific subjects into the school curriculum.

In England the pioneering work was done by private Academies, some of which were connected with masonry. The Dissenting Academies, described in Chapter VIII, were primarily institutions of higher theological learning and only later became centres of scientific research. Private Academies, on the other hand, introduced new subjects in the very beginning of the eighteenth century. We shall mention here two of the earliest Academies of the eighteenth century, which were both connected with Masonry. The first was the Academy in Little Tower Street, founded by a teacher of mathematics, Thomas Watts, in 1715. The curriculum included all branches of mathematics, astronomy, geography, navigation, military science, bookkeeping, and experimental philosophy. The Academy had extensive scientific apparatus and a team of well-known scientists as lecturers. The instruction was imparted by "a new and approved method," which included laboratory experiments in all divisions of physics and empirical work in all branches of applied science. Drawing, music and physical exercise were integral parts of the curriculum. Another Academy of the same character was founded in Soho Square by Martin Clare in 1719. Clare himself was a Fellow of the Royal Society and a Freemason and was well known for his scientific publications. His Academy existed till the nineteenth century and in the second half of the eighteenth century had amongst its pupils many famous men, whose parents preferred it to the great public schools. Although Latin and Greek were also taught, the emphasis was on mathematics, including algebra, trigonometry and astronomy, physics, navigation, geography, architecture, bookkeeping, drawing, music, fencing and physical exercise. Foreign languages were also included. The Academy had a physical laboratory, scientific apparatus and a library available to students. Instruction was based on experiment and examples taken from life. Clare said in his advertisement: "Our principles are built on surest and most rational basis, that of experiment and fact. Since what is by experiment, made the object of our senses, is generally found to leave deeper impressions on the mind, than instruction in any other shape." In the second half of the eighteenth century private academies preparing for business, the Army and the Navy abounded throughout England. They catered for all classes, aristocracy, merchants and artisans, and competed successfully with the classical grammar schools. All these academies were conscious of the rivalry between the old and the new education and in their advertisements never failed to point out the loss of time spent on the formal study of Latin and the advantages of their methods based on experiment. The most ambitious plan was adopted in Bath Academy by J. B. Florian at the very end of the eighteenth century. He had a team of French teachers, who were evidently influenced by the scheme of Condorcet. Florian asserted that "philosophy and the sciences ought to be made the principal study of young persons." He classified all subjects of instruction into three groups: (i) Relation of Man to Nature, (ii) Relation of Man to himself and (iii) Relation of Man to other men. He devised a ten-years' course for the ages seven to seventeen, presuming that boys would enter his academy with a fair knowledge of writing and reading. The subjects included all branches of mathematics, physics, chemistry, astronomy, natural history, applied sciences for the first group; Latin, French, Italian, grammar, logic, rhetoric, poetry, drawing, music and exercise for the second group; and history ancient and modern, politics, economics and biography for the third group. It is most interesting that his wife had a similar academy for girls, with a few necessary modifications.

The influence of these new schools did not penetrate the official classical tradition of the grammar schools for a century, and the latter maintained the narrow interpretation of humanism until the end of the nineteenth century. Even in Germany, where the modern schools (*Realschulen*) had a long and successful career, the classical gymnasia retained their privileges and tradition until the Revolution of 1918. In all European countries the nineteenth century was spent in a fierce struggle between the old classical education, backed by the Churches, and the new scientific education advocated by scientific societies and individual reformers. Inevitably classicism was identified with the Church and science with anti-clericalism.

The anti-clerical character of the new education and the demand for the secularisation of all education were best represented by the French reformers of the eighteenth century. As we have seen, France had her own tradition of liberal ideas in education expressed both by liberal Huguenots and by liberal Catholics—Jansenists. But the Huguenots were expelled and the Jansenists suppressed and the monopoly of the Jesuits was unchallenged by any rival organisation. However, the political situation in the eighteenth century was different. Many of the leading Frenchmen, both the independent philosophers like Montesquieu, and high State officials like La Chalotais, were initiated into English Freemasonry, were influenced by Locke and the English Deists and only waited for an opportunity to attack the Jesuits and Church monopoly. In the middle of the eighteenth century general discontent with the Jesuit colleges was widespread in all Catholic countries. In France all the provincial Parliaments submitted reports, drawn up by official representatives, complaining against the monopoly of the Society and condemning the methods used in Jesuit colleges. They demanded especially the introduction of French as the language of instruction and the teaching of French history and geography. They protested against the moral casuistry and encouragement of bigotry and superstition. In this atmosphere La Chalotais, Solicitor-General of the Parliament of Bretagne, published in 1763 his *Essai d'éducation nationale*, in which he advocated secularisation of education and the foundation of a national system by the

State. Secularisation meant for him both the State control of national education, and the emancipation of the curriculum from Church influence and religious dogma. He advocated the introduction of mathematics, science, history and geography and physics into the curriculum and insisted on the empirical method of instruction. "Nothing to be taught children except facts which are attested by the eyes." "The principles for instructing children should be those by which nature herself instructs them." "It is the State, it is the larger part of the nation, that must be kept principally in view in education . . . and the peasantry . . . ought not to be neglected in a system of instruction." His follower, the president of the Parliament of Paris, Rolland, presented to his colleagues in 1768 a Report on a national system of education. The principle of equality of opportunity was clearly stated by him: "Each one ought to have the opportunity to receive the education which is adapted to his needs." In his report he recommended the centralisation of educational administration by the State and the establishment of State Normal Colleges. Turgot, also a Mason, in his *Mémoires* to the King in 1775, followed the same ideas and suggested a State Council of Public Instruction. The French philosophers in their works advocated similar reforms. Diderot in his *Plan of a University*, written for Catherine II of Russia, Helvetius in his *Treatise on Man*, both of whom were Freemasons, demanded a secular State system of education. Even Rousseau, who is usually regarded as an enemy of the State system, in his *Considerations sur le Gouvernement de Pologne*, definitely advocated a State monopoly of education.

This concentrated attack on the monopoly of the Church did not remain on the shelves of libraries, but resulted in the suppression of the Society of Jesus. The Popes of Rome quite early recognised the danger emanating from internationally organised Freemasonry and issued the first Bull against Freemasonry in 1738, which was repeated by new Bulls in 1740 and 1751. The Bulls were quite candid and denounced the activities of the Masons as the work of Satan. The declaration of war was accepted by the Masons, and when the secular Governments of most European countries were under the control of Masonic ministers they started a concerted action against the Society of Jesus. The first measure was taken in Portugal by the Masonic minister Pombal. He suppressed the Society of Jesus in 1759, with cruelty, and confiscated its property, which was used for the establishing of new secular colleges. Pombal was followed by the

Masonic minister of France, the Duc de Choiseul, who suppressed the Society in France in 1764, and by the Grand Master of Spanish Masonry, Count de Aranda, who as Prime Minister of Spain suppressed the Society in 1767. They were joined by the minister of Parma, Du Tillot, and the Imperial Chancellor of Austria, Prince Kaunitz, both Masons. Under the combined pressure of these ministers the Pope was compelled to issue the Bull of dissolution of the Society of Jesus in 1773. The Pope was even compelled to arrest the General of the Society and to close the famous College of the Gesù in Rome. The estates and colleges of the Jesuits were taken over by secular governments and were used as the financial basis of new State systems. Although in Latin countries the Jesuits returned in 1814 and the post-Napoleonic reaction reintroduced Church monopoly for short periods, the secular tradition already had deep roots and the Church was fighting only a rearguard action. In the Austrian Empire, on the other hand, the reform was final. Kaunitz and his two Masonic advisers, von Sonnenfels and van Swieten, succeeded in achieving the greatest educational reform of the eighteenth century. A new well-organised State school system came into being and the *Toleranzedikt* of 1781 made it undenominational. Thus even before the French Revolution the secularisation of education was realised in most Catholic countries.

The educational ideas of the French Revolution and its practical legislation were influenced both by the preceding secularisation movement in Europe and by the earlier American Revolution. Developed in England in the seventeenth and the beginning of the eighteenth centuries, the theory of secular scientific education was disseminated in France and America through Masonic circles and found its practical application in the secularisation laws of Europe and the legislation of the American Revolution. The French Revolution formed their epilogue and at the same time the prologue of the struggle in the nineteenth century. It is difficult to say, therefore, which of the three countries—England, America or France—contributed most to the development of secularism in the nineteenth century.

The American colonies of the eighteenth century were intimately connected with England and France and actively participated in European movements. Even earlier John Winthrop, the Governor of Connecticut in 1660–76, was a member of the international circle of Comenius and one of the first Fellows of the Royal Society. But the real founder of the secular tradition

in America was Benjamin Franklin. In 1724 he went to London
and met Sir Hans Sloane, the Secretary of the Royal Society,
and other men associated with Masonic clubs. On his return to
Philadelphia in 1726 he founded his club "Junto," an imitation
of Freemasonry. Franklin became a Mason only in 1731. The
aims of the club were to inquire into the problems of Morals,
Politics and Natural Philosophy. In 1743, Franklin founded a
Philosophical Society, which he later merged with his club.
The Society was incorporated in 1780, after the War of Independence, and the Act of Incorporation was written by Thomas
Paine, who was clerk of the General Assembly of Congress at that
time. The Act says: "The experience of ages has shown that
improvements of a public nature are best carried on by Societies
of liberal and ingenious men, uniting their labours, without
regard to nation, sect or party, in one grand pursuit, alike interesting to all, whereby mutual prejudices are worn off, a humane
and phlosophical spirit is cherished and youth are stimulated to
a laudable diligence and emulation in the pursuit of Wisdom."
The Society was instrumental in the publication of several
schemes of secular national systems of education in America and
for many years was the centre of American reformers. Franklin
was also the founder of the first secular Academy in America in
Philadelphia in 1751, which later developed into the University
of Pennsylvania. Franklin's activities were not limited to America.
In his visits to England he took an active part in the scientific
experiments of the Royal Society and was a member of all the
English radical clubs of the seventies. He became a close friend
of all the intellectual leaders of that period and promoted greatly
the growth of secular and Deistic ideas in England. He helped,
among others, the original educational reformer and Deist, David
Williams, whom Franklin nicknamed "The Priest of Nature"
and whose pedagogical works deserve a close study. When
Franklin was appointed the first Ambassador of the United
States in France he became the centre of the scientific and educational activities of French Masonry. Helvetius just before his
death conceived an idea of gathering all the prominent Masons
into one lodge, which would become the centre of the whole
movement of enlightenment. He founded the lodge "Les Neuf
Sœurs" in Paris,[1] 1769, and was its venerable till his death,
when he was followed by Laland. All the élite of the period,

---

[1] The lodge was international and had English, American, Russian and Polish
members.

SECULAR FACTORS

Voltaire, Condorcet, Siéyès, Romme, Camille Desmoulins, Danton, Petion, Brissot, Fourcroy and others were members. The lodge elected Franklin as Venerable Master and on his initiative founded "La Société Apollonienne" with the aim of scientific research and the general diffusion of knowledge. The teaching institution was named "Le Lycée de Paris," where regular lectures were delivered by famous scientists, such as La Harpe, Condorcet, Marmontel, Garat and Fourcroy. In 1802 Fourcroy adopted the name *lycée* for new secondary schools and the institution was renamed "L'Athénée de Paris." Among its later professors were Cuvier, Saint-Hilaire, Benjamin Constant and Auguste Comte. This Paris Lycée or Athénée served as a model for numerous lyceums and athenaeums in all countries, including England and America, established by Masonic groups. Another leader of the American Revolution, Thomas Paine, also a Mason, exercised similar influence in all three countries. English by birth, he took an important part in the American Revolution, was the author of the Declaration of Independence and became famous by publishing *The Rights of Man* and *The Age of Reason*. In England he was recognised as the head of all Deistic and revolutionary clubs and had to flee from England to escape imprisonment. In France he was elected a member of the Convention and helped to edit the declaration of the Rights of Man. Thus he was the author of the two most important public documents of the eighteenth century. Imprisoned by Robespierre, Paine escaped the guillotine on the eve of Robespierre's fall. On his return to America Paine became the leader of the American Deists and founded in New York a "Theistic Church" in 1803. He influenced educational reformers both by his works and by personal contact.

The third American leader who influenced profoundly the subsequent development of education was the third American President, Thomas Jefferson, close friend of Franklin and Paine and also a Mason. Before the War of Independence Jefferson and his older friend the Governor of Virginia, Patrick Henry, were initiators of all the legislation leading to the secularisation and democratisation of the semi-feudal colony of planters. Jefferson took a prominent part in the Revolution and in 1779 succeeded Henry as Governor of Virginia. He submitted his famous "Bill for the more general diffusion of knowledge" which provided for a complete system of secular education publicly maintained and controlled. His chief idea he expressed thus:

"It is the duty of our country's functionaries to provide that every citizen in it should receive an education proportioned to the conditions and pursuits of his life." It is possible that his Bill served as a model for Condorcet's famous Report, as we know that during Jefferson's residence in Paris Condorcet was one of his intimate friends. In his turn Jefferson was influenced by Condorcet's ideas in his later educational activities. On his return to America Jefferson kept contact with French reformers such as Quesney de Beaurepaire, who submitted a plan of an American Academy of Sciences, and Du Pont de Nemours, whose book on *National Education in the U.S.A.* influenced Jefferson's later schemes. It is interesting to note here that Du Pont de Nemours was Secretary of the Educational Commission of Poland in 1766–72, which reformed the Polish school system on democratic lines. The whole movement was international through Masonic connections.

The leaders of all the European countries, including Poland and Russia, and of America, exchanged schemes of educational reform and influenced each other. When the French Revolution broke out, the movement was at its height and the "Neuf Sœurs" lodge in Paris was its intellectual centre. Almost all the schemes of educational reform during the Revolution were written by the members of the lodge: Condorcet, Talleyrand, Romme, Fourcroy, Siéyès, among others. The schemes and measures of the revolutionary period did not introduce any new ideas, but consolidated the movement by actual legislation. The most important was the Report submitted by Condorcet to the Legislative Assembly in 1792. The close connection of democracy with universal education is the foundation of Condorcet's scheme: "A free constitution unaccompanied by universal instruction of the citizens, will come to destruction after a few conflicts, and will degenerate into one of those forms of government which cannot preserve peace among an ignorant and corrupt people." Liberty, Equality and Fraternity were the three principles adopted by French Masonry and later by the French Revolution. On these principles Condorcet builds up his system of national education. The whole conception is permeated with a noble belief in human progress and a pantheistic interpretation of nature. "If the indefinite improvement of our species is a general natural law, man ought no longer to regard himself as a being limited to a transitory and isolated existence . . . but he becomes an active part of the grand whole, and a fellow-labourer in a work that is eternal." Freedom of thought and instruction is another of Condorcet's principles: "Public authority cannot establish a body of doctrine which is to be exclusively taught. No public power ought to have authority to prevent the quest for new truths, or the teaching of theories contrary to its particular policy or to its temporary interests." His system of education is equal for all citizens irrespective of creed or origin and for both sexes. Women should have education identical with men. It should be free from any dogma, religious or political, and must be secular. In his detailed course of studies for different stages of the school system Condorcet emphasises the scientific and mathematical subjects and especially the applied sciences. In this respect it has a strong utilitarian tendency. Condorcet's most important innovation was the *independence of education from the Government*. The whole system should be controlled and administered by a self-governing body of educators and scientists organised in a Société Nationale, based on free elections. His system was not realised in France, where the extreme Jacobins introduced a State monopoly with political indoctrination, but strangely enough it was realised, although imperfectly, in Russia under Alexander I. Condorcet's scheme also was taken as the foundation of the reform of Spanish education introduced by Quintana in 1812. It was reversed, however, by the next reaction. The French Convention led by Robespierre did not adopt Condorcet's ideas of freedom of thought and instruction. During this period municipalities following the Paris Commune prohibited religious instruction in 1793 and tried to supplant it with Republican Catechisms and Jacobin *Evangiles* which were as dogmatic as the Catholic. The rift with the Church was final, and two irreconcilable and opposite French traditions faced each other throughout the nineteenth century. Similar cultural splits into two hostile camps took place in all the Latin countries.

In the Protestant countries, although the struggle between the secularists and scientists and the Churches sometimes assumed a character of open hostility, it never resulted in a split of national cultural traditions into two irreconcilable camps. Whilst in Catholic countries Freemasonry became aggressively anti-Catholic and in the nineteenth century even anti-religious, the Protestant Masons of Teutonic countries retained their Christian beliefs and their connections with the Protestant Churches. Latin Masonry became a political organisation which took an active part as a body in all anti-clerical propaganda and initiated all secularisation laws. The Grand Lodge of England and the related Masonry of Germany and Scandinavia, on the contrary, prohibited its lodges from participating in political and religious controversies and only exerted influence on the outcome of the struggle through individual members and independent societies. In these circumstances the relations between the Protestant Churches and the Masonry of the English tradition were, as a rule, friendly and never flared up in an open conflict. Moreover the reforms of Emperor Joseph II of Austria and Frederick the Great of Prussia had established undenominational State systems of education without an open break with the Churches.

In this milder atmosphere the German-speaking Masons and reformers could concentrate their attention on the reform of the methods of instruction and school discipline. Two names stand out prominently in this respect: Heinrich Pestalozzi and Friedrich Froebel. Both of them were closely connected with the humanist-Masonic circles of their time and in their ideas and practice faithfully interpreted the twin meaning of humanism as human and humane education. They are the true founders of modern methods of education and their influence is widespread over all continents. Pestalozzi, a German-speaking Swiss, was inspired in his youth by the *Contrat Social* of Rousseau and in 1762 joined the group of Swiss radical patriots in founding the "Helvetic Society." The aims of the society were the reform of the aristocratic constitution of Switzerland on democratic lines, the moral regeneration of civic life and the universal education of all citizens. Influenced by *Émile*, published by Rousseau in 1762, the Society encouraged scientific and undenominational education based on the principles of human brotherhood, civic patriotism and religious tolerance. In 1765 the Society started the publication of *Der Erinnerer*, to which Pestalozzi contributed articles. For open criticism of the authorities and radical ideas the paper was suppressed and Pestalozzi was arrested and condemned to pay a fine. His early enthusiasm for radical social and educational reforms never left him and guided all his activities until his death. He greeted the outbreak of the French Revolution with enthusiasm and it was to the revolutionary government of Switzerland that he offered his services as a schoolmaster and thus started his life's work. Pestalozzi's life and work has become a kind of educational legend known to every teacher and need not be repeated here. For Pestalozzi education is based on the laws of nature in two senses: on the study of external nature and on the development of the inner nature of man. The foundation of instruction is therefore *Anschauung*, or intuition based on sense-impressions. The natural objects outside make impressions on our senses and the inner nature of man, his inborn ability, in a spontaneous act of intuition registers these impressions in an ordered manner in space and time. The beginning of all education therefore is closely connected with the development of our senses and the provision of original impressions. Things and not words come first. Experience and experiment are the only way to the understanding of the world. This method combined with the aim of the social and intellectual elevation of the oppressed and disinherited masses of humanity are Pestalozzi's contribution to modern education and are in the direct line of humanist tradition.

His pupil and follower, Froebel, applied these ideas to the period of pre-school education. Froebel was strongly influenced by the philosopher Krause, who represented a school of natural philosophy known as "Panentheism," a variation of the older pantheism. Krause was the leader of German Masonry and his philosophy became a kind of official Masonic creed. His philosophy was especially influential among the Spanish Masons of the second half of the nineteenth century. All Spanish reformers of that period belonged to the school known as "Krausistas" and accepted Krause and Froebel as their prophets. The main idea of Froebel was the interpretation of the growth of the human body and mind as a process of natural unfoldment in accordance with the all-pervading eternal law—which is the divine unity of God and nature. "Education," says Froebel, "consists in leading man, as a thinking intelligent being, growing into self-consciousness, to a pure and unsullied, conscious and free representation of the inner law of Divine Unity, and teaching him ways and means thereto." Applied to early childhood teaching means "leading" the child to self-realisation and not imposing on him the moral or religious ideas of adults. Froebel founded the first "Kindergarten" where he applied his method so successfully that it led to an international Froebel movement and the establishment of pre-school institutions all over the world. Although Froebel used Christian terminology in all his works, he did not escape persecution. The Prussian Ministry of Education prohibited the establishment of Froebelian institutions in 1851 "because Froebelian principles lead youth to atheism." It was a misrepresentation of Froebel's ideas, recognised at last by the

Prussian Ministry, and the prohibition was lifted in 1859. Although Froebel's panentheistic conception of nature was very far from the present scientific theories, he laid the foundation for modern child-study and in some cases discovered by experience new facts of child psychology. By the work of Pestalozzi and Froebel humanism achieved its second aim: it made education not only human but humane. The love of children which permeated their activity and their deep sympathy with human faults and mistakes has become the first condition of any successful teaching practice.

The new attitude of Pestalozzi and Froebel to the growing mind of a child emphasised the qualitative difference. The child's mind is not just the mind of an adult in miniature, but a different mind. Pestalozzi had among his pupils children mentally retarded if not exactly mentally deficient, and his deep sympathy and new approach proved that they could be educated and trained for useful citizenship. His practice shed new light on the whole problem of the education of defective children. The primitive tribes and even our own ancient civilisation had no compassion on defective children and the parents simply disposed of them in the most cruel manner. Christianity brought a marked change of attitude towards these unfortunates, but until the end of the eighteenth century there was no provision for their education. They were allowed to live or rather to run wild and often were an object of ridicule to normal people. Humanism awakened the social conscience and society at last recognised its responsibility. V. Hauy was the pioneer of State institutions for the blind. He founded the National Institution for the Blind in Paris in 1784, which was taken over by the State during the Revolution. Hauy went to Prussia and Russia and initiated the foundation of similar institutions in Berlin in 1806 and St. Petersburg in 1807. Mentally defective children were long considered as uneducable. Pestalozzi drew attention to their educability and in 1857 the first school for feeble-minded children was founded in Paris by Dr. E. Seguin, whose *Treatise on Idiocy* remains a standard work. Since then both physically defective and mentally defective children have been included in the system of national education in most countries.

The struggle of the humanist reformers for a scientific curriculum and secularisation of education continued throughout the nineteenth century in all European countries. Both issues were intimately connected and represented by the same men. But whereas in Latin Catholic countries the main battle was waged on a political plane between the anti-clerical secularists and the Catholic Church, in Protestant countries and in orthodox Russia the struggle was between classicism and modernism or "realism." In the Latin countries the issue is still in the balance, as the Catholic Church has proved to be the most formidable opponent and has shown a remarkable power of resilience. After many crushing defeats at the hands of the secularists the Church has always succeeded in coming back and occupying the positions previously evacuated under the assault of the secularists. The issue of classicism versus "realism" has never attained such prominence in Latin countries as in the Teutonic or Slavonic countries. For the Italians, Spaniards and Frenchmen, Latin is the ancient form of their national languages, is an integral part of their national traditions, and it is doubtful if it will ever be eliminated from the school curriculum. In Italy even now after the defeat of Fascism and the national revolution Latin is a compulsory subject for all elementary school teachers. The situation in Teutonic and Slavonic countries is different. Being Protestant or Orthodox these countries have no reverence for the language of the Catholic Church and for them it is simply a dead foreign language. The insistence of the early humanists on Latin as the language of the contemporary sources of all knowledge has also lost its justification, and in the twentieth century we observe a total elimination of Latin in some Slavonic countries and its gradual disappearance in many Teutonic countries. In Russia the struggle against Latin assumed an acute political significance, as all reactionary circles defended its survival in the curriculum, while all radical and socialist groups invariably demanded its elimination.

In Great Britain the struggle of scientists against the classical tradition was of long standing, but attained its culmination point in the middle of the nineteenth century, especially as a result of the Darwinian theory of evolution. The scientists and secularists of all shades saw in it a powerful weapon against the domination of the Churches in education and the classical tradition. The Churches, on the other hand, at first attacked Darwinism most vigorously and it took a generation before the orthodox clergy accepted the new theory. Even now there are groups of so-called "Fundamentalists" who refute Darwinism as heresy. In this struggle in Great Britain three names stand out: George Combe, Herbert Spencer and Thomas Huxley. Combe began his lectures on phrenology and education in 1830. In 1832 he founded the "Philosophical Association in Edinburgh for the Popularisation of Science." In 1835 he and James Simpson founded the "Edinburgh Society for Diffusing Moral and Economic Knowledge." In 1848 Combe and Simpson opened the Secular School in Edinburgh with an encyclopaedic scientific curriculum. Combe was not a trained scientist and his theories often went astray, but his insistence on "doing" and not "knowing" and on "positive" knowledge as against verbal formalism made a strong appeal to radical circles. His insistence on political education for the masses was especially popular among the new groups of the Labour movement. Much more famous was Herbert Spencer, whose book on *Education* made such an impression on his contemporaries that it is considered a landmark in the history of education. There was nothing new in his book; his ideas are contradictory and can hardly be realised in an actual school, but Spencer's influence on the development of scientific education was profound. Most efficient, however, both in the propagation of scientific education and in actual practice was the third representative of the tradition—Thomas Huxley. His *Essays on Science and Education* have not lost their significance even in our own time. Huxley's campaign was directed against orthodox theology and the domination of education by religious dogma, but not against religion itself. He contended that science was the direct and surest way to understand the divine laws of nature and thus the true basis of religious emotion. He wanted to preserve the Christian moral tradition and even approved of the reading of the Bible in the schools. As a scientist he wanted children to grow up in unity with nature, to have a scientific appreciation of natural laws and to have their minds trained for the free and unfettered examination of facts. As a member of the London School Board he was instrumental in bringing these views into actual school practice, in spite of strong opposition from the Churches. The conflict of Huxley with the Church was the last episode in England in the long history of modern science and secular education, which began with the martyrdom of Giordano Bruno, the official condemnation of the Copernican theory and the humiliation of Galileo. The retaliation came later in the eighteenth century with the dissolution of the Society of Jesus and the open and ruthless persecution of the Church during the French Revolution.

The nineteenth century witnessed many revolutions and

reactionary periods in all the Latin countries during which the triumphant party persecuted its opponents. The last open war was fought in Spain, but it seems that the present peace is only an interlude and not a final solution. So far as we can judge the final solution has been attained in the U.S.S.R., where the Orthodox Church has officially renounced all claims to any intervention in the State policy in education. The U.S.A. is another country where a stable equilibrium has been attained by a division into a public secular system and private denominational schools. The last outstanding representative of the humanist tradition was an American, John Dewey. His life and philosophy are still living influences both in America and in Europe. Several generations of living educators were either directly trained by Dewey or have grown up in the atmosphere of his ideas. Dewey himself gave three names to his philosophy: Pragmatism, Humanism, Experimentalism. His philosophy is pragmatic in subordinating thought to action. It is humanist in locating all values within the stream of human experience. And it is experimental in advocating the supremacy of scientific experimental methods. In his attitude towards any revealed religion Dewey is definitely negative. His philosophy is candidly relativistic and refutes any absolute ideas or truths. "The course and material of experience give support and stay to life and its possibilities provide all the ends and ideals that are to regulate conduct," he says. "The pragmatic theory of intelligence means that the function of mind is to project new and more complex ends—to free experience from routine and from caprice. Not the use of thought to accomplish purpose already given either in the mechanism of the body or in that of the existent state of society, but the use of intelligence to liberate and liberalise action is the pragmatic lesson." That Dewey's philosophy and his practical achievements as school-reformer and University professor have profoundly influenced contemporary education is indisputable, but whether his pragmatic relativism is the last word in the theory of education is very doubtful. The incentive to human thought given by the movement of humanism is not yet exhausted, and we may yet see a new interpretation, not necessarily as relativist as Dewey's.

CHAPTER X

SOCIALISM

Socialism as a term for a social-economic philosophy was used for the first time by Pierre Leroux, who edited the *Globe* as the journal of the Saint-Simonians from 1831 onwards.[1] But the views basic to socialist philosophy are of more ancient origin. As Humanism in its sources is traced back to Plato, so Socialism can also be said to derive its main ideas from him. His two dialogues the *Republic* and the *Laws* for the first time clearly described the socialist economy of the State and its application in the State system of education. The founder of modern socialism, Sir Thomas More, in his *Utopia* was directly influenced by Plato and openly confessed the source of his ideas. The whole school of the early nineteenth-century socialist writers are known as "Utopian," by which their connection with More is generally recognised. When Karl Marx and Friedrich Engels by their *Communist Manifesto* of 1847 founded the "scientific socialism" of today, the term was already in use, and the main works of the Utopian socialists had all been published. Thus we have to start with Plato. He was the first philosopher to recognise that property as the basis of the economic structure of the State inevitably results in the concentration of civil and legal power in the hands of the property-owning class and leads in the end to the division of the people into the owners of the means of production, who do not work, and the workers, who produce but do not own anything. The famous saying about the "two nations" is not an invention of Carlyle or Disraeli, but is as old as Plato. He also declared that when the State is divided economically into two nations with opposite interests, both groups are consolidated into hostile camps, which are in a state of permanent war with each other. We have here the fundamental ideas of socialism about the exploitation of labour by capital and the resulting class war clearly expressed. Plato also recognised that the criminal minority is essentially the result of the existing social order and not solely of the guilt of the individual transgressors of the law. Reform of

[1] Although generally accepted, this fact may be disputed as the followers of R. Owen were organised and known as "Socialists" at the end of the twenties and the term "Socialism" was used in polemics by both the attackers and defenders of Owen in the thirties.

legislation without radical reform of the social-economic structure of the State is only a palliative which ultimately leads to the recurrence of the evil. Plato quite definitely advocated the nationalisation of the means of production (in the *Laws* but not in the *Republic*) as the only way to save the State from the evils of a class war and eventual ruin. In his last work, the *Laws*, Plato says: "First of all the land and the soil and the buildings must be divided amongst all. . . . Each citizen must look upon his allotment as the national property of the State and because his bit of soil is part of his fatherland he has to nurse it better than children care for their mothers." Such a radical change of economic structure can be achieved either in consequence of or side by side with a radical reform of education. This task can only be entrusted to a State with full control of administration and curriculum. The individual citizen must be trained by the State, for the State and in State institutions. All the details of the curriculum have to be decided by State authorities. The necessary division of labour leads to the functional training of citizens, who are selected for future occupations irrespective of their origin, but in accordance with their abilities. Both sexes are treated in the same way without any difference. Plato introduced the principle of State censorship in order to wean the rising generation from the religious superstitions of his time. He also emphasised the necessity of compulsory military training for both sexes. In his last work he even pointed out the principle of compulsory labour training as part of national education. Scientific training, so far as it was represented in his time by the mathematical branches, plays an important rôle in his curriculum. We find in Plato's works all the ideas of the present socialist system of education: State monopoly, scientific training, secularism, actual work, military training and sex equality.

Sir Thomas More in *Utopia* (1515) follows Plato both in the socialist economy of his State and in his educational ideas. Everyone should learn husbandry for two years and afterwards some other craft or profession according to his or her abilities and inclinations. Higher education is available for all, but is obligatory only for those who are "chosen and appointed to learning." The leader of the Digger movement, Gerrard Winstanley, by his description of education in the *Law of Freedom* (1652), can also be described as a socialist reformer. He demands universal and compulsory education. Every child should attend school to learn the laws of the Commonwealth, the arts and the languages.

But there should be no special class of children brought up to book-learning only. "For then through idleness they spend their time to find out policies to advance themselves to be lords and masters over their labouring brethren, which occasions all trouble in the world. Therefore it is necessary and profitable for the Commonwealth that all children be trained to labour and to learning." Science should be made the basis of learning, and knowledge and experiment should replace beliefs and imaginings. Here again we have all the elements of a future socialist educational policy: the negation of differentiation of pupils into future brain and manual workers, the utilitarian basis and a scientific anti-religious tendency. We have pointed out that both Humanism and Socialism derive their main ideas from Plato. But whilst humanists emphasised Plato's idealism and moral t1 aining, socialists laid stress on the economic basis of education. They shared equally the demands for compulsory universal edu. 'ion with a monopoly of the State and they both insisted on scientific training for social and utilitarian purposes.

Most of the Utopian socialists were humanists as well, and More, the author of *Utopia*, was one of the leaders of humanism in England. In the eighteenth century, as we have seen, the humanists concentrated their efforts on the secularisation of education and the introduction of a State-controlled national system. But it would be wrong to assume that the socialist demand for economic equality was entirely absent in the ideas of the French enlightenment. Both Rousseau and Condorcet may be justly called the precursors of nineteenth-century socialism. Rousseau's *Contrat Social* is based on the idea of the "general will" (*volonté générale*) to which the interests of individual citizens should be subordinated. Although Rousseau does not preach economic communism he wished to limit the rights of private property as much as possible. And in his advice to the Corsicans he plainly said: "The State should own everything and everybody should share the common wealth only in accordance with his services." Usually Rousseau is represented as an advocate of extreme individualism in education, because his Émile was educated in isolation strictly guarded from the influence of society and State interference. This overlooks the fact that Rousseau definitely declared that because contemporary society and the State were corrupt he could not entrust them with education. But in his advice to the Poles for a new constitution he clearly stated that education is the main task of the State and that all citizens should be trained in public institutions through civic duties for the purposes of the State, which meant common and equal education for all children. He even advocated patriotic indoctrination controlled by the State. Condorcet also demands common and free schools for all in order "to limit the inequality which results from the difference of property rights and to mix the classes which are economically divided." Otherwise we shall always have "two nations different in education, social habits, character and political opinions." But he did not draw the necessary conclusion of a socialist economy, as a basis of civic equality. The Utopian Socialists of the nineteenth century made the last step in this direction. Pestalozzi just approached the socialist solution but did not clearly define it. He did not recognise "the original legality of the right of property" and demanded equal opportunity for the working class. "The right of every man to an existence suitable for his human nature . . . is above all laws of property and power." But he still advocated a respect for property laws in fear of the anarchy which might follow their abolition. But, as we have seen, Pestalozzi formulated the main principles of socialist education. He insisted on social education through a school community based on manual work. He considered that simple physical and at the same time productive work is the essential foundation of spiritual and cultural development. Even intellectual growth and the training of the reasoning power he connected with manual work. But he was not a socialist in the strict sense of the word, as he did not demand the abolition of private property in the means of production.

The next groups of reformers, Saint-Simon, Robert Owen, Fourier, Cabet and Louis Blanc, were socialists, who advocated practical measures for the introduction of a new social and economic order based on communal ownership of the means of production. Count Claude de Saint-Simon was the oldest of the Utopian socialists and was influenced by D'Alembert in his views. He considered that science should be actively applied to society and economic conditions. The State should be organised on the principles of the communal interests of all the workers, in which each citizen should be rewarded in accordance with his abilities and performed work. The control should be entrusted to scientific experts in the interests of the community. In education the State should control the whole school system as a means of social integration and as a dissemination of common ideas which would bind society together. A central board, composed of scientists and scholars, called the Institute, should be entrusted with the control and supervision of all educational institutions. They should enforce uniformity of instruction for all. The Institute should issue a national catechism of civic and moral duties, which should be taught to all and the knowledge of which should be made a condition of citizenship. The Institute should also formulate general theories for transmission to the rising generation. In religion Saint-Simon would introduce a purified Christianity. He says: "In the New Christianity all morality will be directly derived from this principle: 'Men ought to regard each other as brothers.' All the so-called religions which are professed today are only heresies, that is, they do not tend directly toward the most rapid improvement possible of the welfare of the poorest class, which is the only end of Christianity." But Saint-Simon is against the persecution of dissenters. He says: "The new Christians must develop the same character and follow the same course as the Christians of the primitive Church; they must employ only the forces of their intelligence to have their doctrine adopted. Only by means of persuasion and demonstration ought they to work in the conversion of Catholics and Protestants."

His younger contemporary, Robert Owen, was not a man of noble birth, like Saint-Simon, but the son of a saddler, who received only the rudiments of education. He was essentially a self-made man, who through his own industry and ability became one of the most influential reformers of the nineteenth century. Whereas Saint-Simon arrived at his conclusions through learning and the study of the French philosophers, Owen based his convictions on personal experience and the study of actual conditions of work and school methods. He was an apprentice and worker himself before he became a factory owner and employer of labour. He went to Pestalozzi at Iverdon and in New Lanark he founded his own school, where he tested his new methods. He came to London, met all the leading radical reformers of the day, inspected many factories and was instrumental in the introduction of the first factory laws. In 1816 he started the propagation of the socialist ideas which led to the establishment of workers' co-operative societies. In 1834 his followers affiliated in the Grand National Trades Union, the beginning of the British Labour Movement. He even attempted to realise a socialist community at New Harmony, Connecticut, but it ended in failure, after he had expended £40,000 on it. His views on religion and especially his public denunciation of all sects, in

1817, as fatal obstacles to his plans for the regeneration of mankind, made him an outcast in all respectable circles and greatly hindered the success of his ideas. He was accused of atheism and immorality and was attacked by all the religious bodies. By his later infatuation over spiritualistic séances he even lost the support of his former followers. But his place in the history of socialism and education is assured. His starting-point was the conviction that environment and training can form the character of the future generation. He understood, however, the importance of hereditary traits and stressed that "children may be formed *collectively* into any human character," that is, not so much individuals as societies are the product of environment and training. The individual variations should not be suppressed but inculcated with common civic and moral ideals. He recognised the great importance of the pre-school period and shares with Froebel the honour of being the first practical reformer of infant education. "Instruction of the young," said Owen, "must be, of necessity, the only foundation upon which the superstructure of society can be raised." To implement the re-education of society a national system of schools, centrally controlled, should be established. "Under the guidance of minds competent to its direction, a national system of training and education may be formed, to become the most safe, easy, effectual and economical instrument of government that can be devised." The curriculum and methods of instruction should be based on facts and practical work. "It is of little avail," he said, "to give precept upon precept, except the means shall be also prepared to train children in good practical habits." The pupils should first be taught the knowledge of facts, beginning with those which are most familiar to the young mind, and gradually proceeding to the most useful and necessary to be known. Moral training, physical exercise and military training are integral parts of Owen's curriculum. His attitude towards religion was not negative, as his adversaries proclaimed. He included undenominational Christian instruction as a compulsory subject. He attacked "the imbecility" of dogmatic indoctrination, but not religious education. He wrote in his *Autobiography*: "The priesthood of every denomination . . . should be required to teach . . . the necessity for all to acquire a knowledge of the pure and undefiled spirit of universal love and charity . . . and should cease to torment humanity by their much-worse-than-useless dogmas which no one understands." His religion would consist in "daily undeviating practice in thought, word and action of charity, benevolence, and kindness to every human being." Thus the main features of Owen's socialist education are: a national, secular system, controlled from the centre, with scientific and practical training through work, and physical and military training for defence purposes.

The next Utopian socialist, Cabet, in his *Voyage en Icarie*, follows the lines established by Saint-Simon and Owen. For Cabet "education is the basis and foundation of the whole social and political system," and therefore should be nationally controlled and supervised. It should be universal and uniform in its elementary stage and should include "the elements of all human knowledge." It should be identical for both sexes, with the addition of training in motherhood for girls. Scientific subjects predominate as "study, experiments, science and discovery have so much attraction that they are loved for their own sake." In his curriculum Cabet includes geology, geography, mineralogy, natural history, both botany and zoology, physics, chemistry and astronomy. In a socialist state "all, men and women, without exception, practise a trade, an art or a profession determined by law." Education must provide for the division of labour, and Cabet introduces compulsory specialised vocational training for girls at the age of seventeen years and for boys at eighteen. It must include both theoretical and practical education. The former is given in the schools where the theory and history of each trade or profession is taught. Practical education is provided in workshops, where the apprentice passes through all stages of productive work. The Government through its statistical service knows the exact number of workers needed for each trade or vocation, publishes the needs of each industry and invites the young people to choose; if the number of candidates exceeds vacancies a competitive examination decides the choice. Religion is definitely forbidden as a subject of instruction, but "each citizen admires, thanks, worships and prays to the Divinity, as it may please him, in the interior of his house." Cabet would deprive the priests of all public power and allow them only the function of preachers of morals. As he says: "Justice, fraternity and the consequent love of country and mankind and the submission to the general will are the worship most agreeable to Divinity." The Government must establish a censorship of art and literature from the point of view of morality.

It seems that these representatives of Utopian socialism exhausted all the ideas on education which a socialist policy should follow. The next period of scientific socialism did not add anything new, but connected education more closely with the doctrine of materialism represented by Marx and Engels. Marx was influenced in his philosophy by Hegel's dialectical Process, by Feuerbach's positivism and by French philosophers. His philosophy is called "dialectical materialism," thus combining Hegel's dialectics with the materialistic interpretation of the world. The historical-social evolution of mankind is determined by natural laws, which reflected in individual human minds become the driving forces of all historical change. In their application to human society the natural laws appear as the economic conditions of social life. In the last resort all spiritual phenomena, culture and religion are determined by economic laws and social conditions. Marx does not deny the return influence of culture and religion on the social-economic conditions, but that influence is of secondary character and cannot change the necessary evolution of economic laws. The real bases of the social-economic structure are the technical conditions of production. "The method of production," said Marx, "of material life determines the social, political and spiritual process of life in general." With the change of methods of production all social-political conditions will change by necessity. From these premises he concluded that the industrial revolution which resulted in modern capitalistic methods of production will inevitably lead to the next stage of socialist society based on the nationalisation of the means of production. This social revolution will be effected through the class war between the few capitalists and the proletarian masses and will result in the dictatorship of the proletariat, which is in the vanguard of all human progress. Education in a socialist state must of necessity reflect the new structure of society and the new methods of production. Neither Marx, nor his collaborator Engels, left special works devoted to education, but their leading ideas may be culled from their general works. In 1867 in a resolution of the Geneva Congress of the First International Marx thus outlined his conception of education:

> By education we mean three things: first, mental education; second, physical training as given in schools of gymnastics and military training; and third, technical education which introduces the prospective worker to the general principles of all the processes of production and at the same time gives to children practical information regarding the use of various working tools. The gradual

and progressive march of mental and technical teaching must be in relation with the classification of the young workers. The cost of maintenance of technical schools must in part be covered by the sale of their products.

Marx was opposed to the general prohibition of child labour.

By strictly regulating the worker's time in accordance with his age and by taking other precautionary measures for the purpose of protecting children the early union of productive work with teaching is a mighty instrument for the transformation of the present society. ... The education of the future will combine productive labour with instruction and physical culture, not only as a means for increasing social production, but as the only way of producing fully developed human beings.

The attitude of Marx and Engels towards any religion was hostile. Engels said that "religion is nothing but a fantastic reflection in the human brain of those external powers which dominate their daily existence, a reflection in which the earthly powers take the form of supernatural." Their pupil, the leader of German Social Democracy, A. Bebel, in his book on *Christianity and Socialism*, drew the logical conclusion with no regard for the historical facts. "Religion is only a means to use authority over the masses and still more to strengthen it." "During the last eighteen centuries Christianity has been a religion of hatred, persecution and oppression." "Christianity and Socialism are opposed as fire and water; what is good in Christianity is not Christian but general humanity, and what forms Christianity proper is a cramming of theory and dogma inimical to humanity." "The aim of Social-Democracy in the field of religion is atheism." Bebel's point of view became the official creed of all Marxist Socialists, and if German Social Democracy in 1890 changed its programme and declared its neutrality in religious matters, this was done from purely opportunistic motives to get more votes in elections. The present Marxist Socialists, the Communists, quite frankly declare that atheism is the only point of view compatible with dialectical materialism.

In comparing the Utopian socialists with the Marxists we notice a fundamental difference in their attitude towards morality and religion. Whereas all Utopian socialists set up the moral training of the rising generation as the general aim of education and for that purpose accepted a purified form of Christianity as the basis of such training, the Marxists are openly hostile to any religious-moral training in principle, and it is not an accident that Marx did not include moral training in his conception of education. Engels thus defines the point of view of dialectical materialism: "Morality has always remained class morality; it has served either to justify the domination and to guard the interests of the ruling class, or it has reflected indignation against such domination and has represented the future interests of the oppressed class." From the Marxist point of view "morality is entirely subservient to the interests of the class struggle of the proletariat," as Lenin said.

But the Marxists are not the only socialists in the field. The old Utopian-humanist tradition is still accepted as their guiding principle by many living socialists, and before we pass to the practical application of Marxist socialism in the Soviet Union, we shall mention the views on education expressed by the—let us call them—humanist socialists. The most outstanding representative of idealistic socialist pedagogics is Paul Natorp, the well-known leader of the Marburg philosophical school, the author of many works on Plato and social pedagogics. He accepted the humanist-social tradition of Plato, Comenius, Rousseau, Condorcet and especially Pestalozzi, and in his modern interpretation of their works finds the inspiration for his educational ideals. For him socialism and idealism are not opposed, as for the Marxists, but on the contrary they complete each other and each gives to the other a deeper and more accurate meaning. "Idealism must be social and socialism must become idealistic." The first condition of socialist education for Natorp is the "autonomy of the spirit, which means not only full independence [of the human mind], but a dominating position of it in the whole of social life." Social regeneration means the liberation of all, rulers and ruled, from inner chains of all kinds through the unconditional subordination of all narrow limitations to higher spiritual ideals. The inner co-ordination of mind and work in all productive activity through communal organisation will best promote the growth of the individual and lead everyone to the heights of spiritual freedom in accordance with their abilities. "Education of an individual is conditioned in all important respects by social causes, just as the shaping of the mode of social life is fundamentally determined by the corresponding education of the individual who must participate in that life." Thus the school is a social institution, a social organism and a labour community which educates the individual morally. "The school, however, is a labour community only so far as it places direct

activity and productive work as the centre of its entire curriculum." On the other hand, the school must be a free community
of free individuals, in which each member unfolds his inborn
abilities to their utmost level, thus leading to the differentiation
of functions and at the same time to the integration of all members
into an organic society. The curriculum must include physical
training, agricultural and industrial productive work, civic and
political training, and the humanities, science, art and religion.
Natorp includes religion as an integral part of education, but
for him religion means undenominational, purified and philo-
sophically clarified Christianity. The school community as well
as the economic community, whether a guild or a co-operative
collective, form the foundation stones of the socialist State. The
latter should be rather a confederation of free communities than
a monopolising centralised machine which imprints its stamp on
every activity and every citizen. Only in this way, Natorp con-
siders, is the true realisation of democratic ideals possible: the
government of the people for the people and through the people.
Thus we see here a fundamental difference between the two
varieties of socialism, the dialectical materialism of the Marxists
and the Platonic idealism of the Utopian socialists.

The British Socialists occupy an intermediate position; they
neither accept the totalitarian consequences of Marxist materialism, nor base their aims and policy on Platonic or Kantian
idealism. Their attitude towards educational problems is rather
empirical in the true tradition of Owen and the Fabians. But
as they take into consideration the deep-set English tradition of
tolerance and political freedom as their stepping-stones towards
the realisation of the socialist state, they are inevitably drawn
nearer the idealistic than the Marxist interpretation. As a matter
of fact the British Labour Party is a federation of many groups
with divergent philosophical outlooks, including wholehearted
Marxist materialists, undenominational idealists and believing
Catholics and Calvinists. Under these circumstances the socialist
policy in education must be mainly empirical with tolerance of
opinion as the guiding principle. They accept State monopoly
in education as the only possible foundation for the realisation of
a truly national system of education with equality of opportunity
for each child. But this monopoly extends only to the organisation, administration and financing of education. It does not
include the detailed contents, the methods of instruction or the
inner life of the school community. In their attitude towards

religion they differ in accordance with their philosophical outlooks, but on the whole they would include undenominational Christianity in their curriculum and would like to preserve the positive values of the Christian tradition. So far the policy of the British Labour Party has been determined by the existing empirical situation and the general conceptions of socialism applied to the immediate reforms of education. There is no official declaration of a socialist philosophy of education, as is the case in the Soviet Union. But the trend of socialist opinion in this country can be seen from some publications on education by British socialists. As an example we take Beryl Pring's book on *Education, Capitalist and Socialist*, published in 1937.

> The first necessity in education is fluidity; its golden rule is that the individual child is more important than any consistency in method or curriculum, than any ulterior motive of the teacher or the State. . . . The socialist State should be far more likely to provide these opportunities for individualism, as it is prepared to find and spend the money necessary for such development. . . . Only under a central planning system which can ensure real equality of opportunity can such fluidity and care for the individual be reached. . . . A socialist State should be a democratic State, where the ruled are also the rulers, where the State has no welfare apart from that of its citizens, where the discipline does not appear to be imposed by any power that is impervious to the claims of the individual. . . . Schools and society generally should aim at allowing the maximum of freedom to the individual, including the freedom to learn by his mistakes, that is compatible with the security of other members of the community. . . . The individual at school and in the wider society cannot, however, escape community life, and it is for the socialist to consider what type of social administration is most suitable for school communities. . . . While socialist schools are not concerned with making socialists, education in these schools will have to be socialist. If "propaganda" means any influence of the social system on its members, then propaganda there must be.

The author, therefore, would prohibit any private schools which could inculcate an education contrary to socialist principles and would establish a State monopoly. Therefore "it is impossible to allow the teaching of any orthodoxy in the schools, if the highest possible use is to be made of the powers of logic and intellectual criticism," which means that no denominational instruction can be allowed. "In the socialist schools there will be no teaching of 'truth,' but only the presentation of opinions; the teacher must deny himself the satisfaction of one of the major desires of mankind, the wish to convert." It seems from these quotations that the prohibited orthodoxy includes only religious views, not the fundamental principles of socialism, which must be inculcated by the whole organisation of the school prescribed from the centre. In all other respects, the author accepts all the ideas and practice of the so-called "progressive" education, such as the Dalton Plan, Project method, co-education, productive work, school self-government and so on. We here see clearly the empirical method of combining the monopoly of education and the inculcation of socialist views with the freedom of individual growth and individual methods of instruction. It is a typical English solution which would satisfy neither the German idealistic philosopher, nor the Russian Marxist materialist. But as the English have proved to be masters of empirical solutions based on compromise, it may be realised in this country with success in actual practice. The realisation of socialist ideals in Great Britain, however, will take a long time. Firstly the British socialists are against ruthless revolutionary measures, secondly their parliamentary majority may be temporary, and thirdly the English public school tradition has become part of the national character and its abolition would be met by strong opposition.

We should look for a practical realisation of socialist education in those countries where parliamentary democracy has not been established and where tradition is not so deeply ingrained in the character of the nation. So far there are ten countries where a socialist policy in education has been realised by State legislation: the U.S.S.R., Yugoslavia, Bulgaria, Hungary, Mexico, Czechoslovakia, Poland, Rumania, China and E. Germany. The Scandinavian countries are still in the transition period, although their systems are strongly influenced by socialist ideas. Of the ten countries mentioned the Soviet Union is the most important for the study of socialist legislation and practice. When the Soviet Government was established in Russia in November 1917, the Communist Party had not yet clearly formulated its educational policy and aims. There was no lack of socialist educators in Russia, but most of them were either populist socialists, akin to the English Fabians, or followers of Tolstoy, and their ideas were not closely bound up with the dialectical materialism of Marx. They could sooner be called the followers of the humanist tradition, for whom the development of a free personality in a free community was the final aim of socialist education. The ideas of freedom and individuality were more emphasised than the principles of community and discipline. During the initial period of Soviet government, the Russian Communists, therefore, were strongly influenced by all these progressive reformers, who sided with the new régime in the first wave of enthusiasm. The Communists themselves were carried away by Utopian dreams and expected an immediate realisation of a new social order which would eliminate all class distinctions and all necessity for State compulsion. They saw the anarchist ideal of a free personality, developing its individual abilities and inclinations, without any intervention by the State. Lenin himself in his book *The State and Revolution* declared in 1917 that the functions of the State should be abolished and give place to free and independent collective communities. In this atmosphere the first laws on socialist education were passed. The Education Act of 1918 was preceded by "Basic Principles of the Unified Labour School." Here it was proclaimed that

> The personality shall remain as the highest value in the socialist culture. This personality, however, can develop its inclinations in all possible luxury only in a harmonious society of equals. We do not forget the right of an individual to his own peculiar development. It is not necessary for us to cut short personality, to cheat it, to cast it into iron moulds, because the stability of the socialist community is based not on the uniformity of a barracks, not on artificial drill, not on religious and aesthetic deceptions, but on an actual solidarity of interests.

The conditions of civil war, famine and the general disorganisation of social life, on the one hand, and the closer study of Marx and the application of dialectical materialism to education on the other, very soon changed this initial enthusiasm for absolute freedom. The main principle of Marxist education was expressed by Lenin as early as 1897:

> One cannot imagine the ideal of a future society without a combination of education with the productive labour of the rising generation. Neither instruction and education without productive labour, nor productive labour without instruction and education can be raised to a height demanded by the modern level of technology and scientific knowledge.

Later Lenin said that

> the polytechnic principle does not demand instruction in everything, but demands the knowledge of the foundations of modern industrial processes in general. . . . The problem of the new pedagogics is to connect the teaching activity with the problems of the socialist organisation of society.

Apart from stating such general principles Lenin did not contribute much to the theory and practice of education. Neither did

Stalin. His only important contribution was in the field of national minorities, which indirectly influenced the educational methods of instruction through the medium of native speech. We have discussed this problem in Chapter III. Thus the two builders of the socialist state in Russia did not present to the communist pedagogues a complete philosophy of education. It had to be culled from Marx's writings and the separate pronouncements of Lenin. The ultimate ideals of an anarchist society with no class divisions and no state compulsion could help little in the period of social upheaval caused by socialisation and rapid industrialisation of the national economy. In the period of the dictatorship of the proletariat the principles of the monopoly of the State and totalitarian compulsion are the only means of introducing communism in practice. Or as A. Pinkevich says in his book on *The New Education in the Soviet Republic*: "In the first place the control of education must be in the hands of communists; in the second place communistic ideas must be widely disseminated through the press and children's literature; and finally the whole system of education must be organised in conformity with the communist ideas." Or more plainly: "The aim is," says Pinkevich, "the indoctrination of the youth in the proletarian philosophy." The Education Law of 1923 expressed this aim in Article 32 thus: "The work of the school is based on the detailed theoretical and practical study of the labour activity of men and its organisation. All the work in the school and the whole organisation of school life should promote proletarian class consciousness in the minds of pupils and create knowledge of the solidarity of Labour in its struggle with Capital as well as preparation for useful productive and political activity." It is obvious that such a totalitarian policy must transcend the narrow confines of purely school education and must include political propaganda organised from the centre and embracing the whole nation. That is why the real emphasis of Communist education is placed on activities outside the school hours proper. In 1922 "The Children's Communist Organisation of Young Pioneers in the name of Comrade Lenin" was created as a preparatory stage for the earlier "Young Communist League" (*Komsomol*). In 1925 the younger children were organised in the "Union of Little Octobrists." Thus the whole range of the rising generation was covered by Communist-sponsored organisations. Children up to eleven years entered the Octobrists, from ten to fifteen they belong to the Pioneers, and from fourteen to twenty-three to the

Komsomol. Each young Pioneer before being admitted has to give a pledge in the presence of his comrades and the representatives of the Komsomol and the Party. The pledge runs thus:

> I, a young Pioneer of the U.S.S.R., in the presence of my comrades solemnly promise that (1) I will stand steadfastly for the cause of the working class in its struggle for the liberation of the workers and peasants of the whole world; (2) I will honestly and constantly carry out the precepts of Lenin, the laws and customs of the young Pioneers.

These children's and youth organisations take an active part in all the political and cultural activities of the Communist Party, they participate in all parades and manifestations, and they help by manual work in all drives connected with seasonal work in agriculture or raising production in industry. The close connection of education and productive work is thus not limited to school methods and curriculum, but is carried out beyond the school in the practical participation of children in tasks of national importance. From the social-political point of view the members of these organisations are indoctrinated with dialectical materialism and Communist ideology. Sports, physical and military training are compulsory for all members and form an important part of their activities. They must become "the soldiers of socialism" in every respect and be prepared to fight with modern weapons in their hands for their ideals. Girls receive the same training as boys and in the recent war many of them took part in actual fighting. We shall give a detailed description of the Soviet school system in a separate chapter, and here conclude with the recent definition of Communist education given in 1946 by the president of the Pedagogical Academy in Moscow, A. I. Kairov:

> Communist education is a planned and purposeful social activity, realised by persons specially delegated for it by the State. The contents of this activity include (a) the care and supervision of the development of the rising generation; (b) the arming of it with systematic knowledge, skill and habits necessary for its future practical activities; and (c) the training of it in the necessary emotions, inclinations and interests, habits of behaviour, features of will power and character in accordance with the spirit and principles of Communist morality.

The totalitarian character of Communist education in the U.S.S.R. is thus as absolute as it was in Nazi Germany, but the fundamental difference should be pointed out. The Nazi ideal was based on narrow, unscientific notions of the supremacy, racial and national, of the Germans, and included the subjugation or even extermination of non-German groups. In practice Nazism led to such monstrous perversions of individual and national morality that it aroused the just indignation of the whole world. The Communist ideal, on the other hand, is based on the principles of the brotherhood of all peoples, irrespective of their race, creed, language, nation or sex, and is aimed at the liberation of all oppressed groups from economic exploitation or national and racial subjugation. Behind the formal similarity of Nazi and Communist methods stands the profound opposition of the content of their ideals.

The second country which has introduced socialist education by legislation is Mexico. By the constitution of 1917 the Federal authority of Mexico was empowered to establish a national system of education, which before that date was in the hands of the separate States forming the Federation. The new Federal system from the start was directed towards the enlightenment of the rural Indian peasantry. It was secular, and all religious instruction was prohibited. As we pointed out in Chapter II the system of rural schools was based on the principle of "integral education." The term has been used by socialists since the days of the first International as a description of education in the future socialist state. Peter Kropotkin, the famous Russian anarchist, advocated "integral education" in his *Fields, Factories and Workshops*, where he wrote:

> To the division of society into brain workers and manual workers we oppose the combination of both kinds of activities; and instead of "technical education," which means the maintenance of the present division between brain work and manual work, we advocate the *éducation intégrale*, or complete education, which means the disappearance of that pernicious distinction. Plainly stated, the aims of the school under this system ought to be the following: to give such an education that, on leaving school at the age of eighteen or twenty, each boy and each girl should be endowed with a thorough knowledge of science . . . and at the same time, to give them a general knowledge of what constitutes the bases of technical training, and such a skill in some special trade as would enable each of them to take his or her place in the great world of the manual production of wealth.

This idea applied to the rural agricultural population of Mexico was made the basis of the new system. At the same time it was closely connected with the regeneration of Indian native traditions of social life and craftsmanship. In 1934 President Cardenas proclaimed the introduction of "socialist education" as the development of "integral education," which meant the official recognition of socialist doctrine as the basis of State monopoly in education. As George I. Sanchez said in 1937: "The complete acceptance of indoctrination is the most striking note of present-day Mexican educational philosophy. The schools are organs of propaganda. They are active agents in a plan to change the social and economic order." Education and politics are identified in a socialist reform. The Federal government sends to rural areas so-called "Cultural Missions" which combine the training of rural teachers with adult education of the whole village community. The latter includes agriculture, health, domestic science, citizenship and politics. In many respects the Mexican policy towards the backward Indian tribes is similar to the Soviet policy towards the small national groups within the U.S.S.R. In both cases notable success has been achieved in raising the economic and cultural level of these backward communities.

Besides the U.S.S.R. and Mexico two Balkan Slav States have quite definitely adopted socialist principles as the foundation of their social and educational reconstruction. In September 1944, Bulgaria had a political revolution which overthrew the pro-German nationalist government and established a new régime under the guidance and control of the so-called "Fatherland Front," which is a coalition of five parties, of which the Communist Party was the most influential.[1] The hero of the Reichstag Fire trial and late leader of the Communist International, George Dimitrov, the late Prime Minister, was acknowledged in official publications as the leader of the nation and founder of the "Fatherland Front." In these circumstances the social and educational reconstruction of Bulgaria is strongly influenced by the theory and practice of the U.S.S.R. The socialist principles of education realised in Russia are taken as the foundation of the new Bulgarian system. Article 64 of the Constitution declares: "All citizens have the right to education. Education is secular, imbued with democratic and progressive ideals. All schools are State schools. The right to education is realised through schools and other educational institutions and through a system of scholarships and maintenance grants." Article 11 says: "Labour is recognised as a fundamental social and economic factor.

[1] The elections of 27th October, 1946, resulted in the absolute majority of the Communist Party: 277 Communists, 87 for the remaining four parties of the Fatherland Front and 101 for the three opposition parties. Since then the Communists have eliminated all opposition parties.

Manual and brain work as well as creative and organisational activities are under the protection of the State." Under the guidance of the Communist Party a re-education of the whole nation is being undertaken on political and social lines modelled on Russian experience. Two officially sponsored organisations were created: (a) the "Septembrists" for children from seven to fifteen years and (b) the EMOS (first letters of the Bulgarian equivalent of "United Youth General Union"), into whose hands all the civic, political and physical training of the rising generation is entrusted. EMOS is under the official supervision of the Ministry of Education and has a legal status. The general aim of these two organisations is the fight against Fascism and the brotherhood of all democratic peoples, and especially intimate relations with the Russians and Yugoslavs. A close parallel to the Soviet "Octobrists" and Komsomol is obvious. The State monopoly and secularisation is established by the Constitution, and the whole system is under the centralised control of the Ministry of Education. The aims of education are declared to be the general promotion of the physical and intellectual develop-ment of the rising generation, the weaning of their minds from extreme nationalist and reactionary ideas, the inculcation of the spirit of progress and preparation for creative participation in the economic and cultural life of the country. The socialisation and industrialisation of the national economy is followed by the co-ordination of technical and vocational education with actual production, realised by establishing workshops in the schools with modern industrial methods and by compulsory participation of youth in national drives such as afforestation or "Labour Weeks." In the beginning the official documents avoided the terms "socialist" or "communist," but the spirit and content of the new Bulgarian education are quite clearly following the Soviet example.

Yugoslavia is more explicit in her reorganisation and has openly declared a Communist revolution. Led by an old Com-munist, trained in Russia, Marshal Tito, Yugoslavia has taken the structure and legislation of the U.S.S.R. as the model for her national reconstruction. The unitary constitution of the former kingdom of Yugoslavia has given place to a federal union of six self-governing republics: Serbia, Croatia, Slovenia, Montenegro, Macedonia and Bosnia, and one autonomous republic, Voevodina, within Serbia. All the republics employ their native speech as the basis of their school system, but from the third year all minorities have to study the Federal language, Serbo-Croat.

The non-Slav minorities have schools in their own languages within the common public systems. The secularisation and the State monopoly were introduced by law in 1945. The law also introduced compulsory attendance from seven to fifteen years and a unified school system consisting of three stages: primary school —four years, intermediary school—three years, and secondary school—four years. Communist Pioneers and Youth Unions[1] were established on lines identical with those in the U.S.S.R. The industrialisation of the country and collectivisation of agriculture were accompanied by the development of technical and vocational education based on a combination of school instruction with productive work. Dialectical materialism is accepted as an official creed and is indoctrinated through the activities of the youth organisations controlled by the Communist Party.[2]

Thus all four countries, U.S.S.R., Mexico, Bulgaria and Yugoslavia, have introduced socialist education in its Marxian interpretation. The features common to all are the following: monopoly of the State, secularisation, productive work as an integral part of training, physical and military training, political indoctrination both in and out of school through partisan Youth organisations, and an emphasis on scientific subjects. The freedom of the individual and the idea of tolerance are not accepted for the present period of transition as guiding principles of their policy. The future will show whether with the stabilisation of new socialist States these principles will be gradually incorporated in their educational systems. At present, however, we must acknowledge the fact that, so far, in all socialist States, State monopoly and partisan indoctrination deny the individual the opportunity of forming independent opinions or expressing them freely if he has formed them. On the other hand, the successful solution of the problem of national minorities, the elevation of primitive tribes and their association with European culture and the actual participation of the rising generation in the social and productive activities of their nations are justly hailed by all democratic educationalists as important contributions to educational theory and practice.

In Czechoslovakia, Hungary, Rumania and Poland the reorganisation of education follows the same principles as in Bulgaria and Yugoslavia.

---

[1] U.S.A.O.J.—the first letters of Yugoslav equivalents of "Union of Anti-fascist United Youth of Yugoslavia."

[2] The quarrel of Tito with Cominform did not influence the Communist legislation of Yugoslavia.

CHAPTER XI

NATIONALISM

Nationality as a social factor must be clearly distinguished from the racial, linguistic, religious or civic community. Race is a biological factor, and we pointed out in Chapter II that members of the same race may belong to many nationalities or members of the same nationality may be of different racial origin. A linguistic community is more closely connected with nationality and as a rule members of the same nationality speak the same language. The examples of China or Norway, however, prove that differences in language are not an obstacle in forming a single nationality, as we have seen in Chapter III. Religious communities with few exceptions transcend national differences and become national features only in combination with other factors. Civic communities are based on a definite territory and State legislation, they are nations, but not nationalities. What then is a nationality? It is a psychological group with a common outlook and common tradition based on a myth of common ancestry. Race, language, religion and territory may strengthen the consciousness of nationality, but without that myth of common origin no linguistic or civic group can develop that social phenomenon which we call "nationalism." National feeling then is a state of mind resulting from social environment and education. Nationalism as a movement may be created by propaganda based on intentional misrepresentations of facts.

In the ancient world "nationality" as such was unknown; tribal, linguistic and religious differences were acknowledged, but the civic community of the Roman Empire overshadowed them all. Seneca and Quintilian may be called Spaniards by present-day Spanish writers, but for us they were Romans, and the accident of their birth in the Iberian peninsula does not change the fact. During the Middle Ages, when Latin was a recognised medium of expression in all theological and scientific works, nationalism had no opportunity of developing into a deep sentiment. The clergy and the feudal aristocracy were international, and the peasantry were too ignorant, economically oppressed and separated into small communities to form a basis for a nation-wide consciousness. The birth of national literatures after the Renaissance was the first step in the formation of the modern nations. But consciousness of a common language and traditions is not sufficient to generate that intense sentiment known as nationalism. The interests of a national community must meet with opposition from another national group if a nationalist feeling is to arise. As nationality is a psychological group reflecting a state of mind, it is unimportant whether the opposition of interests is real or imaginary as a result of propaganda. It is sufficient for the group to believe in it to develop a nationalist attitude. But when the national identity of the group is endangered by foreign domination, then nationalism becomes the force of social life overshadowing all other interests. In such colonial empires as those of Great Britain, France or Russia the ruling nationality is too secure in its dominion to become nationalist. The pride in citizenship of a great State takes the place of nationalist feeling. Only during the short periods of national danger did the English, the French and the Russians show signs of a nationalist attitude. Thus the threat of the Napoleonic invasion and recently the threat of the Nazi invasion resulted in the growth of nationalism in England. The same two periods caused nationalist outbursts in Russia. French nationalism was strongest after each of the three German invasions. But when danger is over their nationalism cools down and is relegated to a secondary place in their policy. The Scandinavian countries and the Iberian peninsula have been so well defended by geographical frontiers in the past that they could live their separate lives more or less undisturbed. None of these countries, therefore, could have been the birthplace of modern nationalism.

As a theory and practical policy nationalism was born among the oppressed and dismembered nations. There were five centres of nationalist movements in Europe. Italy, subjugated to foreign dominion in the south and the north and divided into small principalities in the centre for many centuries, was one source. Germany, divided and weakened after the Thirty Years War, and threatened by French imperialism under Napoleon, was the second centre. The Western Slavs—the Czechs and the Poles, deprived of their independence and subjected to forcible Germanisation—supplied the third centre of the nationalist movement. The Southern Slavs, oppressed by both Austria-Hungary and Turkey, were the fourth centre where nationalist fanaticism was reinforced by religious differences. The fifth centre was in Ireland, where the short-sighted policy of the British Government created a nationalist movement similar to the Continental varieties. In the twentieth century the movement of nationalism spread to the countries of the Middle and Far East and with local modifications displays the same features as its European counterpart. Thus in spite of a seeming contradiction in terms nationalism must be considered as an "international" factor, or a factor of general importance equal in its influence to genuine international movements. As a matter of fact in its initial stage nationalism was an international movement.

In its historical development nationalism passed through three distinct phases. During the first half of the nineteenth century nationalism was closely connected with the humanist tradition and defended the right of subjugated nations to an independent existence and indigenous culture. It was expressed in many sporadic revolts and culminated in the abortive revolution of 1848. Defeated by the autocratic régimes of the "Holy Alliance" under the guidance of Metternich and his followers, the oppressed nationalities concentrated on a cultural struggle for survival. The third period started with the Balkan War of 1912 and includes the two World Wars and the intervening period of uneasy peace. It may be said that with the spread of nationalism to non-European nations we are entering the fourth and final phase of the movement. As mentioned, the first period of nationalist movements was permeated with humanist ideals and the demand for the liberation of subjugated nationalities was based on general humanitarian reasons. The extension of the principles of the French Revolution of liberty, equality and fraternity should embrace all national groups as well as the individual citizens of a State. As a rule the first pioneers of nationalism belonged to the international society of Freemasons. Fichte in Germany, Mazzini and Garibaldi in Italy, Adam Czartoryski in Poland, F. Palacky in Bohemia and Ypsilantes in Greece were all Freemasons. Even in Ireland the United Irishmen at the end of the eighteenth century were closely connected with Freemasonry. As such these pioneers could not embrace a narrow and exclusive interpretation of nationalism; nationality for them was only a natural and necessary step in the federation of all nations. Yet in the stress of the national struggle for emancipation in the periods of foreign oppression they had unwittingly sown the seeds of a later exclusive and aggressive brand of nationalism.

The most important and most influential of the prophets of nationalism was the famous German philosopher, J. G. Fichte.

In 1807 after the treaty of Tilsit Germany had lost its political independence and was divided into many vassal states of Napoleonic France. The Rhineland became an extension of France, under a French King and French legislation, Southern Germany was in official alliance with Napoleon and recognised his suzerainty, and Prussia was reduced to half her former size and the Prussian officials had to take an oath of allegiance to Napoleon. French ideas, the French language and French law were supreme, and it seemed that Germany had lost not only her political independence, but her cultural tradition and national identity. In this atmosphere Fichte delivered his *Speeches to the German Nation* (*Die Reden an die deutsche Nation*) in the winter of 1807–8 in the Academy of Science in Berlin. Hardly any other course of public lectures had such a spontaneous and profound influence on the whole nation as Fichte's speeches. They changed the course of German history and served as an inspiration for many generations of German patriots. Based on the idealistic philosophy of Kant and permeated with the humanitarian ideals of the French Enlightenment, Fichte's scheme of new education combined nationalism with socialism within the frame of common humanity. It was not his fault that his ideas were distorted, and, divorced from their idealistic foundation, served as a source for a more modern combination of nationalism and socialism. There is no doubt that had he been alive in 1933 he would have finished his career in a concentration camp; however that did not prevent Goebbels and company from acclaiming Fichte as the first "Nazi" of Germany. Faced with a total collapse of his country Fichte saw the only way of salvation in the moral regeneration of the German nation through a new national system of education embracing all classes and both sexes. "There is no other way out," said he, "but to establish a new system of education, embracing all Germans without exception, not an education of a particular class, but education of the whole nation as such, through which all differences of social classes would be abolished." He believed that the assumption of free will in the pupil was the greatest mistake of previous education. "The new education should deny any free will and should establish strict necessity of its conclusions and train the willpower of the pupils in such a way that any contrary conclusion should become impossible." Taken as it stands and without context this sentence served the Nazis well, but Fichte understood this necessity as a moral training achieved only through the active participation of the pupils, in accordance with the eternal law of the spiritual nature of man. The new education should be organised in school communities "in which every one is subordinated to the community and contributes through work and action to the welfare of all." It should include physical training and work of an industrial and agricultural character. The final aim is the ideal of pure morality based on the independence and autonomy of each individual. This final aim does not belong to the world of experience, but to the world of ideas, which should guide every experience. So far Fichte's scheme has a universal application and is devoid of any nationalist tendency. But the next step of his reasoning led him to assertions of doubtful validity. Although the new system of education is needed by all nations, some particular nation has to set the example and lead the rest towards general moral regeneration. Of all European nations the Germans were, through their geographical position and historical circumstances, the most suitable nation to lead the world in this direction. The Germans were the only original nation in Europe, who remaining in their native land had preserved their original language and culture and thus were able to contribute to humanity original thought and original action. Neither the Latin nations, who were Romanised Celtic and Germanic tribes, and therefore had lost their originality, nor the Slavonic nations, who have not yet evolved any original culture, could assume that leading part in Europe. It is important to note here that Fichte conceived the German leadership only on a moral and cultural plane and not as a political or State domination. Both the Church and the State are for him formal organisations of civic life devoid of original content. He did not insist on the unification of Germany into one State; for him the liberation of Germany was spiritual freedom based on the originality of German language and culture. But he advocated the economic self-sufficiency of German lands as a material basis for their moral regeneration. Few Germans could follow Fichte to the heights of his philosophic conceptions, but every German was ready to accept his assertion of German cultural originality, which was understood as cultural superiority. Unwittingly Fichte started a movement which ended ·in an avalanche. He awakened the national pride of the Germans and his demand for a national system of education for all Germans was quite naturally understood as the unification of all Germans into one State of Greater Germany. Thus the result was the movement of Pan-germanism, with its unavoidable aggressive tendencies.

The next prophet of nationalism, Giuseppe Mazzini, was not an original philosopher as Fichte was, but an ardent political revolutionary and a passionate Italian patriot. Although not a philosopher he was influenced by German idealism and combined the cosmopolitan outlook of Kant with Fichte's nationalism. For him nationality was a necessary stage in the evolution of humanity. "Every nation has its own problem, through the solution of which it adds to the general mission of humanity. This particular mission forms its nationality. Nationality, therefore, is sacred." Or: "it is a divinely appointed instrument for the welfare of mankind," he said in 1834. Democracy and nationality would result in a federation of nations in which "all excuse for war would disappear, and in its place would arise a spirit of brotherhood and peaceful emulation on the road to progress." For Mazzini the interests of different nationalities were not opposed to each other; on the contrary, each nationality should help the other to attain liberty and independence. He started his revolutionary career as a member of the secret society of Carbonarii and in 1831 founded *La Giovine Italia* ("Young Italy"). The aim was the unification and liberation of Italy and the establishment of a democratic republican régime. The means to such liberation were state education combined with armed revolt. In 1834 he founded "Young Europe," an association of all oppressed nationalities, of "men believing in a future of liberty, equality and fraternity for all mankind." Here Italian, German, Polish, Swiss and Hungarian nationalists shared the same ideals and the same adventures. In 1840 he founded a working men's association and published his chief work *On the Duties of Man*. He approached the leaders of the First International, Marx and Bakunin, but their materialism was too distasteful to him and he could not associate with them. A dreamer and an impractical revolutionary, he was too straightforward and honest to achieve the unity of Italy in the atmosphere of intrigues and power politics. But the enthusiasm which he aroused in Italy was used by Cavour for his realistic and successful policy. His idealism underwent the same transformation as Fichte's. His war-cry "nationality is sacred" became the *sacro egoismo* of later Italian nationalists, and separated from his ideal of international brotherhood served Mussolini as an initial step towards Fascism. Nevertheless without Mazzini and his friend and follower Garibaldi, the Italian *Risorgimento* would have been deprived of all its driving force.

The third source of nationalism in Europe was provided by the Slavonic countries. The case of Slav nationalism is different from that of Germany or Italy. German nationalism, even in its Pan-germanic interpretation, was limited to the German-speaking people, and only during the last war did the Nazi leaders attempt to include the Dutch, the Danish and the Norwegian branches of the Germanic family in the ideal of Greater Germany. Italian nationalism never attempted to include other Latin nations in Greater Italy. The Slav nationalities, on the contrary, were always conscious of the affinity of their languages and the close connection of their historical destiny. Attacked from the north-west by the German *Drang nach Osten* (Drive towards the East) and from the south-east by the aggressive Islam of the Turks and Tatars, the Slavs quite naturally saw their only salvation in a common Slav nationalism which transcended their tribal differences and in an ideal of a Pan-Slav federation. Thus Pan-Slavism cannot be considered as narrowly nationalist as the German or Italian movements; it has an international character, especially as the Pan-Slav federation by necessity has to include some non-Slav nationalities. The first step towards a separate Slav cultural tradition was taken by the Slav apostles Cyril and Methodius, who in 855 invented the Slavonic alphabet and translated the Bible into Old Slavonic (actually Old Bulgarian). As is well known, they went to Moravia and converted the Czechs to Christianity, bringing with them the Slavonic Bible and Liturgy. The Russians accepted the alphabet and the Bible at the end of the ninth century. Thus Old Bulgarian or the Church-Slavonic language became the link between the three branches of the Slavs as early as the ninth century. Although the Czechs later adopted the Latin liturgy and joined the Western Church, the memory of the Slavonic origin of their Christianity was revived by the reformation movement of John Huss and Jerome of Prague. Jerome even went to Russia and visited Vitebsk and Pskov in search of Slavonic links in the Russian Orthodox Church. Both reformers were burnt at Constance and the movement was crushed by a Teutonic crusade, but Huss and Jerome became national heroes of the Czech nation. Among the Southern Slavs, the Serbs and Bulgars, the Church-Slavonic language survived all the vicissitudes of the Turkish conquest and Greek supremacy in religious matters. Although both the Western and the Southern Slavs were suppressed, their national cultural development was interrupted by foreign domination and the systematic policy of Germanisation, they preserved their Slavonic identity and looked towards Russia—the only great and independent Slav country—for their liberation. In the seventeenth century these dreams of a Pan-Slavonic federation found clear expression in the works of George Krizhanich (died 1683), a Yugoslav Catholic priest and missionary. He advocated the union of all Slavs in a federation and the adoption of Church-Slavonic as the common language of all Slav Churches. He appealed to the Tsar of Russia to liberate the subjugated Slavs. "You, Tsar, are the only man given to us by God to help the Southern Slavs, Czechs and Poles to understand the depth of their oppression and contemptible existence and enlighten them that they should break the German yoke." Since Krizhanich this hope of Russian intervention and help against the Germans and the Turks has become the national tradition both among the Czechs and the Southern Slavs.

When at the beginning of the nineteenth century the Slavonic nationalities were awakened from long passivity by the revival of the Slav languages and literatures, their nationalism inevitably had a Pan-Slavonic orientation. Even the leader of Polish nationalism, Adam Czartoryski, was for a time the Minister of Foreign Affairs of Alexander I and worked for a Slavonic federation. Only later did he become an inveterate enemy of Russia, dying as an exile in Paris. Russo-Polish relations require a separate volume for adequate treatment and cannot be dealt with here. The fact is that the Poles were the only Slav nation which until recently had abstained from participation in the Pan-Slavonic aspirations of all the Slavs. The Slav revival began among the Czechs. They had a political past full of national events and the tradition of the two Czech leaders Huss and Comenius (Komensky) to build upon. The first of the Czech "Awakeners," as they were called, Abbot Dobrovsky, published in 1809 his *Grammar of the Czech Language* and in 1822 *The Foundations of the Old Slavonic Language*. By these two works Dobrovsky laid the foundations for the literary Czech language and for a common Slavonic philology. The next important contribution was made by Shafarik in his *History of Slav Literature* (1826) and *Slavonic Ethnography* (1842). His rediscovery of the treasures of Slav literature aroused enthusiasm in all Slavonic lands. Shafarik and the Slovak poet Kollar gathered around them Slav enthusiasts from all Slav lands and propagated the idea of Pan-Slav cultural unity. The last of the great "Awakeners," F. Palacky, transferred these ideas to the political field and led the Slav revolt against German domination in 1848. He was chairman of the Pan-Slav Congress of 1848 in Prague. Here he wrote and issued in the name of the Slavs the famous *Appeal to the Peoples of Europe*, in which he defended the right of all Slav nations to an independent national existence. The Slav "Appeal" fell on deaf ears in Europe as the German point of view was more readily accepted in the West. The Pan-German Parliament in Frankfurt definitely claimed the Czech lands as part of Greater Germany on the grounds that the kingdom of Bohemia was an integral part of the medieval "Holy Roman Empire of the German Nation." The Czech leaders refused to participate in the Frank-furt Parliament and demanded the reorganisation of Central Europe in accordance with ethnographic and linguistic frontiers. As is well known, the revolutionary movement of 1848 was sup-pressed because the nationalities could not agree among them-selves and some of them even helped the reactionary governments to subdue their neighbours. Especially deplorable for its conse-quences was the quarrel between the Slavs and the Hungarians. In 1848 both the Slavs and the Hungarians succeeded in their revolts against the Germans. Then the Austrian Government promised the Croats national self-government and the Croats joined the Germans in crushing independent Hungary. The Austrian promises were not fulfilled and the Austrians came to an agreement with the Hungarians, abandoning the Slavs. The Hungarians revenged their defeat by introducing a forcible Magyarisation of the Slavs. Thus the nationalist movement entered the third stage of an embittered cultural struggle between the nationalities themselves. The Germans played the rôle of *tertius gaudens*. In these circumstances each nationality concen-trated its efforts on the education of the rising generation in a narrow nationalist tradition. The ideas of Mazzini and Palacky of a federation of free nations were forgotten and each nationality tried to stake exaggerated claims to frontier territories. In the Balkan peninsula the Russian wars against Turkey secured the liberation of the Balkan countries, but the rival claims of the Serbs, Bulgars, Greeks and Rumanians were not properly adjudi-cated and led to narrow nationalism in all four countries. The Austrians backed by the Germans started their penetration into the Balkans, which ended in the annexation of Bosnia and Herzegovina. By supporting the ambitions of the German king of Bulgaria they succeeded in antagonising the Serbs and the

Bulgars and sowed the seeds of the two World Wars. In spite of the participation of the Western Powers and Italy in both wars, they were primarily wars between the Slavs and the Germans. The Slavs fought for their independence and Slav federation, the Germans fought for Greater Germany and the Germanisation of the Slavs. Both sides, therefore, intensified nationalist tendencies in their education. The extreme and narrow interpretation of national aims was not confined to Italy and Germany alone; it was a more or less general feature. The first World War did not solve the problem of Central and Eastern Europe. Russia was torn asunder by a fierce civil war and was absent from Versailles. A Pan-Slavonic federation was, therefore, out of the question and each Slav nationality received the full status of an independent sovereign State. History repeated itself: divided, the Slavs could not withstand German aggression, their division was again used by the Germans; and this time it was a determined attempt to solve the question by wholesale Germanisation and extermination. But before we deal with National Socialism in Germany, we should turn our attention to Fascism in Italy.

After the war of 1914–18, Italy, nominally a victor, was exhausted by the struggle and disillusioned by the results of the Versailles Treaty. Moreover, she was herself divided, as neither of the two historical traditions was strong enough to lead the nation to unity. The Roman Curia was still unable to reconcile itself to the loss of Rome, and was jealous of the secular State. The secularists, on their part, did not understand that Italy was still Catholic at heart and that the first condition for a united Italy was a reconciliation with the Pope of Rome. The post-war economic crisis added a new source of discontent and resulted in increased Communist activities. The Government was weak and unpopular and could not decide to use force in stemming general disorder amounting almost to a state of civil war. In these circumstances Mussolini organised the new nationalist movement of Fascism. The new creed was a conglomeration of many elements. Nationalism, Syndicalism, Catholicism, the Roman tradition and Socialism all contributed to the new movement, but these heterogeneous points of view were never properly welded together into a distinctly Fascist philosophy of life. Mussolini himself was unable to make a philosophical synthesis and his famous article on the Fascist Doctrine was in fact written by Gentile. Giovanni Gentile, pupil of Croce, was the foremost Hegelian of modern Italy. He accepted Hegel's idea of the

State as a super-personality, as a phase in the realisation of the Absolute Idea or Spirit in history. To this philosophic conception he added Mazzini's nationalism in his own interpretation. He asserted that for Mazzini moral, religious and political values were identical and that this "totalitarianism" of Mazzini was further developed by Fascism. Mazzini's belief in the relative value of each nationality within the frame of humanity was transformed by Gentile into an absolute value of the Italian State, which has a world mission similar to that of the Roman Empire. The historical destiny of the Italian people is to realise this mission through Fascism. Confronted with these absolute values, individual, partisan or class interests are of no consequence. Even the Catholic faith was allotted a subordinate position and was accepted only because it was Roman or Italian. The people are more "catholic" than the Church and the latter must be embodied in the State. "The State's active and dynamic consciousness," said Gentile, "is a system of thought, of ideas, of interests to be satisfied and of morality to be realised. Hence the State is, as it ought to be, a teacher; it maintains and develops schools to promote this morality." When appointed Minister of Public Instruction, in 1923, Gentile tried to reform the school system in accordance with these ideas. As a Fascist Minister he was more explicit in his definitions. "Only those scientists are worthy as teachers who have solved scientific problems quite definitely and clearly. Their solution either agrees or disagrees with the aims of the government, which maintains the schools, furthers education and promotes its own morality for its own ends. If the principles of the scientist are contrary to the principles of the State, their dissemination is dangerous to the State. The State betrays its moral destiny if it does not prohibit them." By making an equation between the Fascist Party and the Government, and between the latter and the State, Gentile arrived at his last conclusion of an absolute "totalitarian" régime, guided and controlled by the "Duce," the leader of Fascism. Mussolini himself in one of his speeches said: "The Government demands that the school should be inspired with the ideals of Fascism . . . it demands that the whole school system in every grade and in every phase of its teaching should educate Italian youth to understand Fascism, to renew themselves in Fascism and to live in the historical atmosphere created by the Fascist Revolution." In the article signed by Mussolini but written by Gentile, Fascism is defined as a moral State, which educates its citizens to fulfil their mission, "it lifts men from the elemental life of a tribe up to the highest expression of power, the *Impero*. Fascism is identical with the will to power and empire; the latter being not only the expression of territorial, military and mercantile might, but of a spiritual and moral strength as well."

To permeate the whole Italian nation with these ideas the school system with the traditional formal instruction was insufficient. Mussolini had a ready example in the Soviet Pioneers and Komsomol. He imitated the whole organisation, substituting Fascist formulas for Communist. In course of time the Youth organisations were unified in 1937 as *Gioventu Italiana del Littorio* (G.I.L.) with the motto "Believe, Obey, Fight." All members had to take the oath of allegiance to the Duce: "In the name of God and Italy I swear that I will carry out the Duce's orders and serve with all my strength and, if need be, with my life the cause of the Fascist Revolution." From six to eight years they were *Figli della Lupa* (Wolf-cubs), from eight to thirteen *Balilla*, from thirteen to seventeen *Avanguardisti*, and from seventeen to twenty-one *Giovani Fascisti*. The girls were similarly organised. Physical and military training and political indoctrination occupied most of their time, but excursions and summer camps included also some cultural subjects. Adult education was centralised and monopolised by the *Opera Naizonale Dopolavoro* (O.N.D.—"Afterwork"), which in fact was a branch of the Fascist Party. After 1933 all teachers and professors had either to be members of the Party or take an oath of allegiance to the Duce. Only eleven University professors refused and were dismissed. All the textbooks were rewritten by Fascist authors and permeated with propaganda. In one respect Fascism had to make concessions. When Gentile reformed the system he retained the secular character of instruction inherited from the Liberal régime. The Church remained outside the school. In 1929, however, Mussolini being more realistic concluded a Concordat with the Roman Curia. Article 36 provided that:

> Italy considers the teaching of Christian doctrine in the form handed down by the Catholic tradition to be the foundation and crown of public education, and therefore agrees that religious instruction should be introduced according to syllabuses agreed between the Holy See and the State. Such instruction should be given by teachers approved by the ecclesiastical authorities. Only text-books approved by ecclesiastical authorities should be adopted.

In the adopted text-books children read: "Religious dogmas are not discussed because they are truths revealed by God. Fascist principles are not discussed because they come from the mind of a genius, Benito Mussolini." Thus both partners were satisfied. In practice the Church gained more ground than it had lost during the whole period of secularised education since the *Risorgimento*. Being the only independent institution in Italy which withstood Fascist penetration it became more popular than before. On the whole the penetration of Fascist ideology in the State school system was not as successful as in the Youth organisations and in adult education. Several Ministers of Education who followed Gentile tried to tighten up the Party control over the school and in the process abandoned many positive features of "Riforma Gentile."

The last attempt was made by Giuseppe Bottai, appointed Minister of Education in 1936. Bottai was the author of the Fascist Charter of Labour of 1927, which formed the foundation of the Fascist Corporate State. According to that Charter the Corporation of Workers had to co-operate with the State in education "for the realisation of the moral aims of the Fascist Corporate State." In 1939 he issued the "School Charter" to implement his ideas of "Fascist-Socialist" education. In addition to insisting on more totalitarian indoctrination in Fascist ideas, Bottai attempted to abolish the traditional division into brain and manual workers in order to provide complete secondary education for the children of poorer families. Bottai put the private schools under more strict supervision, introduced more intensive military training and brought the Fascist Youth organisations into closer contact with the schools. On the whole Bottai's reforms did not much change the situation with the exception of the new measures "in defence of the race." These "racial" laws were enacted in 1938 under the direct influence of Nazi Germany and resulted in the dismissal of all Jewish teachers and professors and the segregation of Jewish pupils. These measures were contrary to Italian tradition and were unpopular, but they were enforced and depleted many institutions of their best professors. Bottai succeeded only in his negative measures; his ideas of a *Scuola Unica* could not be realised owing to war and the subsequent defeat of Fascism. Mussolini had twenty-three years at his disposal to re-educate the Italians in accordance with his ideas, but he completely failed; the Italians conformed externally to new demands, wore uniforms and shouted "il Duce" until they were hoarse, but they were never converted, and after the fall of Mussolini discarded all his ideas together with the Fascist uniforms. In this respect the Italian temperament and their old ability to compromise with the tyrannical laws of their petty princes proved to be their salvation. Outwardly they were Fascists, but they did not believe in it.

The National Socialist revolution in Germany was more successful than Fascism in Italy. Firstly the Nazis were much more ruthless in their policy, and secondly the Germans were accustomed to be led by the Government and as a people take to ideologies more seriously than the Italians. The European revolutionary movements in the wake of the World War of 1914–18 have much in common, not only in their totalitarian character, but in their philosophical background, which historically was connected with the German idealistic school. In Hegelian terms Socialism in Russia presented the thesis, Fascism in Italy the antithesis, and National Socialism in Germany the synthesis. The Marxian conception of the class war, dividing humanity horizontally, was developed in Italy on nationalist lines representing the Italian people as proletarians oppressed by capitalist countries. In Germany, both horizontal and vertical divisions were combined and the German people were represented as oppressed by a bourgeoisie of alien origin. Lenin united all the nationalities of Russia on a class basis; Mussolini united all Italians by appealing to their Roman traditions and nationalism. Hitler united all Germans by combining both ideas in his theory of race, based on the community of "blood" and the connection with "soil." Fichte's passionate nationalism, his belief in a special historical mission of the German people and his ideas of a closed economic community provided the starting-point for the new ideology. The Hegelian conception of the absolute value of the State overriding all individual rights gave the Nazi régime a moral justification for their totalitarian policy. However, these features would not greatly distinguish National Socialism from Fascism if the "racial theory" of Houston Stewart Chamberlain were not added as the crowning and leading idea. We have discussed the racial problem in Chapter II and pointed out the unscientific and unhistorical character of the Nazi racial theory. But to exercise a great educational influence, a theory need not be true or based on strict scientific definitions. It is sufficient if it is believed in by teachers and pupils. And the German people, including their academic circles, swallowed wholesale the racial propaganda of Rosenberg and other leaders of the Nazi Party. It is doubtful whether the leaders themselves believed in all the assertions about the "Master race" represented by the Germans, as they stole hundreds of thousands of children of non-German parents to be re-educated as Germans in approved Nazi families. The elevation of the Nordics as a specially endowed species of humanity ill agreed with the persecution of pure Nordic Norwegians and with the official acceptance of the Dinaric race as one of the basic German races. The official policy of the extermination of the Jews and the Gipsies on racial grounds was accompanied by the extermination of all opponents of the régime irrespective of their racial characteristics. The whole theory was a preposterous hypocritical lie consciously used to create fanatical loyalty in the gullible masses of the German people. And as a means of educational indoctrination it was highly successful. From history and German literature the Nazi leaders selected all the features which fitted into their ideal of the German nation and then presented it to the nation as a proof of German superiority. Every German could share that superiority, but only in so far as he followed that ideal in blind obedience to its living incarnation—Hitler, the "Führer." Nothing but the total subordination of the individual to the national ideal as defined by the Nazi doctrine could lead every German to the pinnacles of power and material well-being. Those German youths who had the necessary racial qualifications and were ready to follow the prescribed path were selected as future leaders and were educated apart from the masses. Thus the Nazi educational system was divided into two school systems: one for the masses, training them to blind obedience, and the other for the leaders, training them to rule and command as faithful paladins of the "Führer." Both systems of education were quite frankly based on political indoctrination. As one of the Nazi educators (Frick) said: "The German school has to form a political man, who in all his deeds and thoughts, through sacrifice and service, is deeply rooted in his people and is inseparably bound with the history and fate of his State" (as interpreted by Hitler). Or in the official language of the *Leitgedanken zur Schulordnung* (1933): "The highest task of the school is the training of youth for service to nation and State in the National-Socialist spirit." Physical and military training as compulsory features of the curriculum were considered the best methods of producing such devoted servants of the Nazi State. As Hitler himself said: "The German youth of the future must be slender and fit, swift as a greyhound, tough as leather and hard as steel from the factories of Krupp." With such a nation, trained for war and politically indoctrinated, Hitler was sure of conquering the world and of establishing German supremacy over the "degenerate" Latin and Slav nations. And if he did not succeed, it was not the fault of Nazi education, but because of the "toughness" and "swiftness" of the "degenerate" opponents, unsuspected by Nazi leaders.

The war of conquest to acquire *Lebensraum* for the Germans was the final goal of the whole system of education. And for that purpose a conscious perversion of facts and of values was systematically undertaken on an unprecedented scale. As one of the prominent Nazis said to Lord Stamp: "I do not mind freedom of thought in the least, provided I can control what facts go into the mind—a logical mind must then draw the 'right' conclusions, the conclusions I want, and its working need not be feared." By this method all school subjects, even mathematics, were "cooked" and in that perverted form presented to the rising generation, all measures being taken to prevent any other information reaching their minds. History and literature suffered most; everything was presented from the "racial" point of view. The "Nordic" Sulla defended the "Nordic" culture from pollution by the hordes of "Mediterranean" and "Oriental" slaves led by the blackbearded Marius in the Roman civil war; the "Nordic" Jesus was persecuted by the Jews; to give only two examples. But the mass perversion of the whole people was not a sufficient safeguard for the "thousand years" rule of the Nazi Party. The partisan élite had to be separated and to receive an additional dose of indoctrination. For this purpose special National Political Institutions were founded (*Napola*) as State boarding schools, which admitted only youths "completely healthy, racially without blemish, with fine character and superior mental ability." These State institutions controlled by the Ministry of Education were open to all German youths who answered the above qualifications. Side by side special partisan schools were founded under the control of the Party (N.S.D.A.P.) and closely connected with the Hitler Youth. In 1937 the Adolf Hitler schools were founded for the members of the Hitler Youth. Admission took place at the age of twelve. Only those boys were admitted who passed all the tests in the Hitler Youth organisation, and who were recommended by the higher officers of the N.S.D.A.P. The Adolf Hitler schools served as a preparatory step for the higher party institutions, called *Ordenburgen* (Castles of the Order). These were boarding institutions for selected married members of the Party, who had completed their education in the Adolf Hitler schools. The whole scheme worked as follows: six years in the Adolf Hitler schools (twelve to eighteen), then the boys enter the Labour Service and the Army. The plan provided for seven years of practical experience in a trade or a profession after discharge from the Army. Then a quarter of the graduates, married men alone, were selected for the highest partisan training in the *Ordenburgen*. These "Castles of the Order" were real old historical castles specially repaired for the purpose and situated in the most beautiful surroundings. The luxury of their equipment surpassed any of the famous English schools. These institutions combined some features of the great public schools of England with the military discipline of the Prussian Military Academies and the political indoctrination of the N.S.D.A.P. One of the Nazi writers (Schnabel) thus describes the training of the leaders: "As in the general schooling in the Hitler Youth, the leadership training is not concerned primarily with transmitting facts and knowledge. The future leader is much more to be directed towards thinking for himself and independent action. He must be politically activated, and must learn to fit every individual happening of the day into a total picture of the world." Military defeat frustrated this long-term Nazi programme on quasi-Platonic lines, but the few hundreds of finished products proved to be very hard nuts to crack.

The Nazi educational system, however, was not limited to schools for the masses and boarding institutions for the élite. Even before the first World War Germany had an original Youth Movement of *Wandervögel* (Wandering Birds), which combined the motives of historical German romanticism, idealistic nationalism and revolutionary protest against the middle-class psychology of their parental homes. As the movement spread the Churches and political parties took alarm and started similar organisations under the tutelage of the Roman Catholic and Lutheran Churches and the Social Democratic Party. After 1918 the Communist Party started its own Youth Movement. When the Nazi Party became a mass movement they followed the example of the older organisations and in 1926 founded the Hitler Youth as an official branch of the N.S.D.A.P. They also had the example of State-organised youth in the Soviet *Kom-*

somol and Fascist *Balilla*. It was, therefore, comparatively easy for them to monopolise the Youth Movement in 1933 and to make it into a most efficient weapon for moulding young minds. Although officially voluntary, membership of the Hitler Youth became with years socially compulsory for every German boy or girl. Every year, on March 15th, all German children of ten years of age had to register with the local branch of Hitler Youth. After a thorough investigation of the "racial" record of his family, the boy was admitted by a ceremony into the organisation. From ten to fourteen he belonged to the Junior Boys, and from fourteen to eighteen to the Hitler Youth proper. The girls at fourteen passed to the "Union of German Girls" (B.D.M.) where they remained till twenty-one, three years longer than the boys in the Hitler Youth. The boys had to join the Labour Service and the Army. The whole organisation was highly centralised on military lines with a "Reichsführer" (Baldur von Schirach) at its head with regional, district and group leaders in strict subordination to their superiors. Although voluntary contributions were collected, the main source of financial support came from the State and the organisation had definite legal rights and duties. It was closely connected with the school system and in fact dominated the latter. The training included political indoctrination, group leadership, sports, camping and military training. School instruction under the old-fashioned teachers was limited to imparting "information," prepared by Nazi experts. All the "spiritual" training, formation of character and physical development passed under the control of the Hitler Youth. In addition the Hitler Youth undertook a nation-wide campaign of vocational training in collaboration with the German Labour Front. Annual National Vocational Competitions were organised in which about a million German youngsters of fourteen to eighteen took part. A "practical examination" was devised for each trade and prizes were distributed to the winners. Besides vocational skill, personality, family record, physical appearance and political activity were taken into account. During the war this vocational as well as military preparedness of the German youth greatly facilitated the "totalitarian" mobilisation of the nation. In the education of girls the same system of indoctrination was established, but the purpose was different. Whilst the boys were directed to develop into fierce fighters for Germany and Nazism, the girls were trained to develop into mothers and wives of Nazi heroes. All their school instruction and training in the

B.D.M. (*Bund der Deutschen Mädel*) was dominated by the repro-
ductive function of women. Hitler thus defined the aim of girls'
education: "Along with the training of boys, the National State
directs the education of girls from the same point of view. Here,
too, the main emphasis must be put on physical training; after
that comes the cultivation of spiritual values, and finally attention
to intellect. The aim of female education must always be the
future mother." As is well known, during the war the repro-
ductive function of unmarried girls was put above old-fashioned
morality and they were encouraged to have children by the SS
soldiers. The success of the Nazi educational system was evident
during the war; the question is whether the results of the indoctrination are of a permanent character or whether total defeat
has cured the Germans of their infatuation. The answer is still
hidden by the chaotic conditions in Germany and will only be
known when the next generation grows up.

Fascism in Italy and Nazism in Germany were only two
extreme forms of a general nationalist tendency noticeable in
many parts of the world. A common characteristic of all nationalist movements is the idealisation of some feature of the past
as the most valuable part of the national tradition. Fascism
attempted to revive the Roman Empire, Nazism to re-create the
racial Nordic character of the Germans, both movements ignoring
the fact that the Roman Empire was not "Italian," and the
original Teutons were not "German." Similarly Irish nationalism concentrated its educational policy on the revival of Irish,
which is a foreign language for the majority, and has small
chance of supplanting English in daily intercourse. The Jewish
movement of Zionism is also reflected into the past and attempts
to rebuild the Jewish state in Palestine in spite of its predominantly Arab character. All these movements lead to national
isolation and antagonism, which was not present in the original
nationalism of the early nineteenth century.

It seems that the Slavs alone have been true to the combination
of national and international ideals, thus escaping the blind
alley of exclusiveness. The post-war developments in all Slavonic
countries show the spirit of national reconciliation prevailing over
long historical feuds. The century-old struggle between the
Russians and the Poles has been finally resolved by the delimita-
tion of their frontier along the ethnic line and the conclusion of
a treaty of alliance and friendship. The feud between the Serbs
and Bulgars has given place to the recognition of respective

rights, but received a setback by the secession of Tito. The new Yugoslav Government has changed the previous nationalist policy to a recognition of each nationality and the establishment of a federation of equal members. The Czechs, who previously erred in their policy towards the Slovaks, have recognised the autonomy of Slovakia and transferred to the U.S.S.R. the predominantly Russian province of Subcarpathian Russia. Even the Rumanians under Slav influence have changed their policy towards the Hungarian minority and have founded in Transylvania a Hungarian school system maintained by the Rumanian State. This similarity of policy and of treatment of the minorities is undoubtedly due to the influence of the Communist Party with its Marxist doctrine and Soviet practice. Whatever our opinion of the Communist doctrine may be, it seems that in the treatment of national problems Communism has found a satisfactory solution and succeeded in subordinating local national patriotism to a wider loyalty of an international character. At present it is only an Eastern European regional confederation, definitely concluded in defence against a possible revival of aggressive German nationalism. It is also tinged with a certain Pan-Slav terminology and a display of Slavonic brotherly feelings, but it is not exclusive, as the Soviet Union includes non-Slav nationalities and the Pan-Slav confederation of necessity will have to include Hungary and Rumania as equal members. President Benesh before his resignation defined the Slav point of view: "The new Slavdom will express two great political ideals: political and social democracy and humanity. They are the true Slavonic programme and true Slavonic policy of the future." Whether he correctly interpreted the future is still a problem.

CHAPTER XII

DEMOCRACY AND EDUCATION

Both World Wars were fought by the Western Powers in the name of democracy and both were won by the democratic side. On these points there is general agreement. When we try, however, to define democracy, we find that the meaning of the term is rather vague and there is no unanimity among those who fought for it. There are two main interpretations which, if not opposed, are contrasted in the present political world situation. The English-speaking countries, and especially America, understand the term to mean a political democracy based on the English tradition of tolerance and constitutional government by popularly elected representatives. The Soviet Union and the Communists in all countries understand by it a social democracy based on a socialist economy and State monopoly. In official pronouncements and constitutional provisions the difference between the two interpretations of democracy is very subtle and during the war permitted the representatives of both views to sign common declarations of aims and methods. The United Nations subscribing to the Atlantic Charter on January 1st, 1942, declared that they have united "to defend life, liberty, independence and religious freedom, and to preserve human rights and justice in their own lands as in other lands." Or as President Roosevelt interpreted it: "The United Nations are fighting to make a world in which tyranny and aggression cannot exist; a world based upon freedom, equality and justice; a world in which all persons regardless of race, colour or creed may live in peace, honour and dignity." The Teheran Declaration signed by Roosevelt, Churchill and Stalin declared as their aim "a world family of democratic nations, whose peoples in heart and mind are dedicated, as are our own people, to the elimination of tyranny and slavery, oppression and intolerance." The freedom of religion, speech, press and assembly were specifically mentioned in the Moscow Declaration of the Four Powers (U.S.A., U.S.S.R., Great Britain and China) after the liberation of Italy, to which was added the right of the people to choose their own form of government. All these declarations followed the well-established tradition based on "natural rights" and the policy of tolerance propounded by John Locke and incorporated in the

American Bill of Rights, the French Declaration of the Rights of Man and many modern constitutions.

The more recent Declaration of the Rights of Man, adopted by *L'Institut de Droit International* in New York in 1929, made a direct allusion to education: "No motive based, directly or indirectly, on distinctions of sex, race, language, or religion empowers States to refuse to any of their nationals private or public rights, especially admission to establishments of public instruction, and the exercise of the different economic activities and of professions and industries." All these declarations may be applied in practice in strict conformity with the letter of the law but contrary to its spirit. The last declaration, for instance, is quite consistent with the most brutal tyranny, provided it oppresses all citizens without any distinction. The problems of economic exploitation and of State monopoly in political and cultural matters are not solved by these declarations. The economic structure of the country may be based on the principle of private property and the law of demand and supply. In such a country political liberties and the policy of tolerance may not safeguard the economic security of the masses of the people and in practice may lead to economic exploitation and inequality of opportunity in education. On the other hand, a socialist economy may lead to the monopoly of the State both in economic and cultural aspects of social life. In the field of education it may result in narrow political indoctrination. It seems that neither political nor social democracy, taken separately, can safeguard the freedom of cultural development and the equality of educational opportunity, which are declared by both to be their goal. The U.S.A. is a political democracy and yet legislation permits racial discrimination in education in the Southern States, prohibits the use of Spanish as the medium of instruction in the Spanish-speaking districts of the South-Western States, and suffers the most unequal distribution of financial burdens in educational administration. The resulting inequality of educational opportunity as between the Negroes and the whites, or between poor and wealthy districts, is well known and is frankly admitted by the Americans themselves. In Great Britain, the classical model of political democracy, the presence of separate expensive systems of preparatory and "public" boarding schools provides an additional opportunity for the wealthy groups and perpetuates the historically conditioned class division.

In the Union of Soviet Socialist Republics we see the other

side of the medal. The Soviet Constitution guarantees to the citizens of the U.S.S.R.: freedom of speech, freedom of religious worship, of the press, of assembly and of street processions. "These rights of citizens are ensured by placing at the disposal of the workers and their organisations printing presses, stocks of paper, public buildings, the streets, means of communication and other material requisites for the exercise of these rights." "The Communist Party represents the leading core of all workers' organisations, both public and State." The Soviet constitution thus formally acknowledges the Communist control of all organisations and in practice all the freedoms can be enjoyed only in so far as they are sponsored by the Communist Party. The socialist economy has abolished the exploitation of man by man and the constitution expressly forbids any racial or national discrimination, but the principle of tolerance is not extended to non-Communist political opinions and activities. In education the equality of opportunity in fact means a universal indoctrination of dialectical materialism.

From these examples it appears that neither the Anglo-Saxon interpretation of democracy as political freedom nor its Soviet interpretation as social equality have resulted in practice in establishing a true equality of educational opportunity for all citizens of their countries. We cannot escape the conclusion that both interpretations of democracy as practised at present are defective. It may be pleaded in both cases that the present period is one of transition and that the true aims of democracy are recognised by both. British democracy has quite definitely started the introduction of a socialist economy and the building up of an all-embracing national system of education, which will ultimately lead to social equality. Soviet democracy during the last years has shown unmistakable signs of lessening the rigid ideological control over the masses and of a more liberal interpretation of the Marxist doctrine. If these tendencies continue there is no fundamental opposition between the two points of view; the difference is only of temporary emphasis, which was conditioned by historical and economic situations in each country. The way to true democracy may start with political freedom or social equality, but it must inevitably lead to the integration of both aspects, neither of which taken separately fulfils its promise. In an earlier work (*The Principles of Educational Policy*) the present writer defined democracy as "a synthesis of individual freedom and social compulsion. . . . The only possible way of social progress is a combination of freedom with compulsion through a democratic legislation. . . . The right of a democratic State to compel its citizens to conform to its laws cannot be challenged, provided all liberties are safeguarded. The question is how far this State interference in the affairs of its citizens can go or where the border line between individual freedom and social compulsion is. If we accept equality of opportunity as the aim of State legislation then we have a touchstone by which to judge any practical measure." Accepting this principle as including economic, social, political and educational equality of opportunity we may arrive at a definition of democracy which covers both the political and social interpretations. But even agreeing on the principle as the basis of our discussion we are confronted with several problems which allow of different solutions from a purely democratic point of view. The most debatable of these are the problems of the relations of the Church and State and religious instruction, the problem of the cultural monopoly of the State, the problem of the differentiation of education and that of the education of women. All these problems are closely related and their solutions should fit into a general system of education, but for the sake of analysis they will be taken separately.

Relations between the Church and the State were poisoned by historical antagonism and mutual persecutions in the past. The solutions arrived at in different democratic countries were largely conditioned by historical circumstances and can hardly be accepted as final and true solutions. It does not necessarily mean that there is only one possible solution compatible with democratic principles, but undoubtedly certain basic conditions should be common to any solution. The practice of many democratic countries knows three main examples of the relations between the State and the Church in education. The most straightforward and perhaps the most logical solution is the monopoly of the State in education. It is adopted in the four socialist countries discussed in Chapter X. The second case of the State secular system existing side by side with the independent Church system is represented by France, America, Australia, New Zealand and South Africa. The third solution of collaboration of the State and the Churches is adopted in Great Britain, the Netherlands, Belgium and the Scandinavian countries. Thus we are faced with three groups of democratic countries each of which would defend its own solution as the most democratic one. We have, therefore, to analyse the whole problem.

State monopoly in education has the advantage of a simple solution. There is no complication of administration connected with the supervision of independent Church schools and no duplication of financial burdens for religious communities. All schools are maintained by the State and local authorities and are subject to the same rules of public supervision and administration. As a democratic State accepts the principle of freedom of religion, religious instruction is permitted on Sundays in the churches or buildings belonging to them. This instruction, however, is in no way connected with the school and must be strictly limited to the dogma and belief of the Church. State schools or institutions for adult education are not precluded by law from adopting an anti-clerical or even an anti-religious attitude in the interpretation of the historical past or of scientific facts. The Soviet Constitution states that "freedom of religious worship and freedom of anti-religious propaganda is recognised for all citizens." There is a notable difference between theset two freedoms. Whereas the atheists are free to "propagate" heir ideas, the religious people are free "to worship" only. The missionary activities of Communist bodies are not only permitted, but officially encouraged and supported, whereas the missionary activities of religious bodies, being regarded as outside the "freedom of worship," are prohibited. In Mexico the socialist State even undertakes the missionary work itself by sending into the country the *misiones culturales*. The State-sponsored and maintained "anti-God" propaganda has been discontinued in the Soviet Union since the adoption of the new Constitution in 1936. After the war a Theological Academy was actually opened in Moscow with the official approval of the State, but the disparity between the two freedoms remains. Dialectical materialism, as the officially recognised doctrine of the U.S.S.R., claims a totalitarian application in all aspects of social or individual life, whether economic, cultural or scientific. Although the Russian Orthodox Church has agreed to limit its activities to strictly religious matters it is officially recognised that belief in orthodox Christian or other religious dogma is incompatible with dialectical materialism and with membership of the Communist Party. As a result the communicant members of the Church are in practice precluded from appointments to higher responsible posts in all branches of State activity. Equality of opportunity in the U.S.S.R. is therefore limited, and there are two groups of citizens, of which only the followers of dialectical materialism enjoy full status in all respects.

The second group of democracies, including France, America and three British Dominions, has accepted the implications of religious freedom in all its aspects and permitted the establishment of independent schools controlled by various Churches. They forbid, however, the diversion of any public funds, whether central or local, to the promotion of any denominational purpose. Thus the independent Church school systems have to be maintained by the voluntary contributions of religious bodies and parents. This solution is attacked from both sides, and both the Churches and the secularists use democratic principles as reasons for their disapproval. The Catholic Church claims the right to public grants for the maintenance of the Catholic schools as the present legislation duplicates the financial burdens of Catholic parents, who are taxed for the public schools and pay the expenses of the Catholic schools. In the opinion of the Catholics this is the denial of equality of opportunity in education. The secularists counter this argument by asserting that the very existence of a separate Church system promotes the segregation of the nation into separate groups and that the denominational secondary schools by charging fees afford an additional opportunity for the wealthy groups and thus perpetuate historical class divisions. In their opinion it results in the inequality of educational opportunity. We shall attempt to resolve this contradiction later.

The third group of democracies, including Great Britain, Eire, Canada, the Netherlands, Belgium and the Scandinavian countries, have come to an agreement with the Churches and have incorporated denominational Church schools into their national systems. In these countries denominational schools are maintained from public funds and are administered by public authorities. The Churches, however, retain spiritual control and influence the appointment of teachers. It seems that the Catholic Church is satisfied with this solution as practised in Holland, Belgium, Scotland and Eire. In England the Catholics have a minor grievance in respect of the subsidies for school buildings, but it is of little importance. The secularists, however, attack this solution as undemocratic. It promotes segregation into groups like the second solution and in addition subsidises from public funds opinions which diverge from national traditions. If every ideological minority has the right to public funds to perpetuate its separate tradition, then Marxists and Fascists can claim public funds for the maintenance of Marxist and Fascist schools. It is futile to limit this privilege to religious bodies only, because modern communism has all the attributes of a religion. The Weimar Constitution in Germany recognised this, and distributed public grants equally to Catholic, Protestant and Marxist schools. It is an extreme and perhaps logical application of the democratic principle of equality of opportunity for all minorities, but it would hardly lead to the building up of a healthy and peaceful democracy. In Germany it resulted in the exact opposite. It may work comparatively well in such old democracies as England and Holland, but will inevitably lead to civil war if applied to countries like Spain or Yugoslavia. Probably there is no universal solution of this problem which would suit all countries.

The democratic principle of equality of opportunity does not mean an equal promotion of all possible ideologies, some of which may endanger the national unity and run contrary to national historical traditions. If the ideological minority, as a proof of their sincerity, is prepared by voluntary contributions to maintain a separate school system the democratic governments should recognise this demand as an actual need and put no obstacles in the way of its realisation, provided that it is satisfied that the movement conforms with the national constitution and that the right of proper supervision is secured. To subsidise or even to permit certain minority ideologies, openly or covertly hostile to democracy, would be suicidal, as the cases of Spain and Slovakia have proved. In countries like England or Holland where the Catholic minority sincerely accept democracy as the form of government, public maintenance of separatist schools does not constitute a danger to national unity and may be the best solution under the circumstances. The difficulties of administration and of consolidation of small schools into larger units will remain, but perhaps it is a necessary price to pay for internal peace and the absence of a genuine grievance. However we may admire the logical simplicity of the monopolistic solution, it certainly is contrary to the fundamental principles of democracy of tolerance and freedom of opinion. The practice of the U.S.S.R., Mexico and the new socialist States in the Balkans may be justified as temporary measures during the period of revolution and transition, but can hardly be accepted as the guiding principle of a democratic State. In this respect the American and French legislations with all their shortcomings are more in accord with democratic principles.

A similar although not identical problem is presented by the

principle of freedom of political opinions. No post-war democracy accepts this principle in its unlimited meaning. Fascists
are banned everywhere, their organisations dissolved, their press
suppressed and their meetings prohibited. Even England with her
traditional freedom of speech would hardly tolerate the re-
appearance of Fascist orators in Hyde Park on Sundays. In
America the restrictions embrace both the Fascists and the
Communists and civil servants are being dismissed for Communist affiliations. In France the former collaborators are hunted
down and imprisoned. In the U.S.S.R. and neighbouring
Eastern European countries the heresy hunt is as strong as ever.
The harsh realities of the post-war period have restricted the old
liberal interpretation of political freedom in all countries as a
necessary safeguard against the revival of Nazism. There is
general agreement that democracy has the right to ensure its own
preservation against the assaults of anti-democratic doctrine.
What is debatable is the right of the State to indoctrinate the
rising generation with some particular ideology. Democracy is
by no means static, its essence is in dynamic growth and the
opportunity for criticism, reform and change should not be
frustrated by the early conditioning of youthful minds. The
adherents of free education, following Rousseau and Tolstoy,
even challenge the right of the parents and teachers to influence
the free mental and moral development of children. This meaning
of "freedom of growth" would soon lead us away from reality.
The idea of "negative education" advocated by Rousseau was
refuted a long time ago by educational philosophers. Democratic
education must be "positive" and train for citizenship and
independence. Our assertion, however, does not solve the problem but only postulates it. What is understood by "positive
democratic education" again depends upon the definition of
democracy.

In socialist countries like the U.S.S.R. democracy means a
socialist economy and ideology and "positive democratic education" clearly means training in dialectical materialism and
socialism. In capitalist countries like the U.S.A. democracy
means economic and political freedom, and "positive education"
is equivalent to training in American traditions definitely anti-
socialist. In Great Britain neither the socialist nor the capitalist
point of view is incorporated in civic training and each teacher
is free to develop his own arguments. The British practice gives
more opportunity for forming independent opinions based on a

critical examination of opposite views and the available information. In the U.S.S.R. the dogmatic exposition of Marxism with
constant appeals to Soviet loyalty and the authoritative pronouncements of Lenin and Stalin conditions the mind of the
pupil so thoroughly that he is psychologically incapable of
criticising any official statement. In the U.S.A. the insistence on
the "American way of life" and the definition of Communism
and Socialism as "un-American foreign imported doctrines"
hinders the pupil from making an impartial examination of the
opposed points of view. Because democracy is dynamic it has to
keep the way open to the possible improvement of social and
political conditions through reform and change based on un-
trammelled criticism of the *status quo*. The only limitation of the
freedom of opinion which a democracy can impose should be
confined to the prohibition of doctrines advocating a violent
change or an armed revolt against the government. Constitutional
criticism, however destructive, should be refuted by the force of
argument and positive legislation. Positive democratic education,
therefore, should train the new citizens by methods of argument
and free discussion rather than by dogmatic indoctrination. It
does not mean that the democratic State is strictly neutral
towards various ideologies; on the contrary, the democratic
constitution of the country should be taught in all schools as the
law to be obeyed and respected by all, including those who
demand a change. Any change should be brought about by
persuasion and the constitutional expression of the popular
demand, which must be made possible by democratic training
in the schools.

The principle of freedom of opinion is still more important in
the domain of higher learning, in Universities and scientific
institutions. The aims of higher education include three different,
but related, tasks: (*a*) the further development of science, (*b*) the
preparation for the learned professions and the Civil Service,
and (*c*) the dissemination of knowledge among the public in
general. Promotion of scientific research cannot be ordered and
supervised by the Government. The latter can only postulate
the problems and afford material facilities; it cannot provide
regulations for attaining results favourable to its opinions. There
can be no possible compromise on this point. Either the scientists
will seek the truth according to their lights irrespective of the
ideology of the Government or they will fulfil the orders of the
Government irrespective of their conception of the truth. In this

respect the policy of the English-speaking countries approaches the democratic ideal more than the policy of the U.S.S.R. or even France. The independence of professors and research workers in the U.S.S.R. is limited by the absence of University self-government and the insistence on dialectical materialism as a condition of appointment to University posts. In France both the administrative and the teaching posts in the Universities are filled by appointment by the Minister of Public Instruction. Although this may lead to a certain pressure and political selection, in practice the French Government has to reckon with academic opinion and very seldom exercises its arbitrary powers. The English and American point of view was well expressed in the Report of American Professors issued in 1915: "It is highly needful in the interests of society at large, that what purport to be the conclusions of men trained for and dedicated to the quest for truth shall in fact be the conclusions of such men, and not echoes of the opinions of the lay public or of the authorities who endow or manage Universities." The existence in a democracy of an overwhelming and concentrated public opinion may also constitute a serious obstacle to the real liberty of a research worker. "An inviolable refuge from such tyranny should be found in the University. It should be an intellectual experimental station, where new ideas may germinate and where their fruit, though still distasteful to the community as a whole, may be allowed to ripen until finally perchance it may become a part of the accepted intellectual food of the Nation or of the world." Only under such conditions can the first task of scientific research be successfully fulfilled.

In the task of training Civil Servants and members of the learned professions, who in a socialist State are *ipso facto* Civil Servants, the influence of the State and its political Government is quite legitimate. The Government may issue regulations and state its requirements and even supervise the examinations for various branches of the Civil Service. Here the professors have to adapt their courses to the actual legislation and their freedom is limited by the written constitution and regulations of various Ministries. The practice again varies. In the U.S.A. the Federal Government does not maintain any institutions of higher learning and the Universities are either State or independent institutions. The Federal Civil Service is recruited by the personal selection of the President or his Secretaries of State. In Great Britain the Government has instituted special Civil Service examinations supervised by Government officials. Recruitment to the teaching profession is entrusted to Universities and Training Colleges under the supervision of the Ministry of Education. In practice the Universities are fully independent in their internal arrangements and the lecturers are free to express their own point of view. In France the influence of the Government is much more rigid and political selection is not excluded. In the U.S.S.R. adherence to dialectical materialism, if not necessarily membership of the Communist Party, is a condition of appointment to any responsible post.

The dissemination of knowledge and the publication of the results of scientific research should be free from restrictions in a democratic State. Yet it is difficult to distinguish scientific theories from political opinions. Certain political theories, like Fascism or Nazism, may be legitimately prohibited, as they are based on distortion of facts and conscious falsehoods. But in many branches of science, history and sociological studies, the known facts permit different interpretations and the experts are seldom agreed on all points. The prohibition of publication of scientific opinions unfavourable to the official point of view would hardly promote the training of the masses for democracy and self-government. Such prohibition is only justified in periods of national danger or in subjects related to national defence, and it was practised in all democratic countries during the war. When the danger of war is finally eliminated by the successful organisation of the United Nations all reasons for such restrictions will undoubtedly disappear.

The next problem of democratic education which is still debatable is the establishment of a highway of education available to all. The question is whether the national school system should present a uniform structure similar to one broad highway or a differentiated system similar to many parallel roads which lead to various ends. In practice this apparent opposition is narrowed down to the question of the age at which the differentiation should begin. There is general agreement that the functional division of work of the adult population demands a certain differentiation of curricula in the school system. A unitary curriculum for all groups of school population could hardly be defended on democratic principles. The differentiation of abilities and inclinations is an established fact and no general ideas of equality can change it. Once again it must be pointed out that equality of opportunity does not mean uniformity. The groups of physically, mentally and temperamentally handicapped children are in all countries segregated into special schools, and thus the problem of differentiation is limited to normal children only. Historically the movement for a democratic school system started as a protest against the differentiation of education according to social distinctions. The old class system took into consideration the diversity of functions in the adult society and in a way was adapted to the needs of various social groups. The main defect of that system was the assumption that every child was preordained by accident of birth to a particular kind of education suitable to his social position. Such an assumption tended to perpetuate class divisions and hindered national unity. The democratic protest quite naturally demanded the abolition of class privileges in education and the establishment of a uniform school system for all groups of the population leading to the University. In the beginning of the nineteenth century the great variety of psychological abilities had not yet been fully realised, while the differentiation of economic and political functions was not so far advanced as at present. The reformers understood the democratic system as a single way towards a University open to all. The first comprehensive democratic system devised by John Knox in the sixteenth century, as we have seen, provided for a unitary ladder of parish schools, grammar schools and Universities open to all groups. In the seventeenth century Comenius divided the whole school system in accordance with four periods of growth: infancy, childhood, boyhood, and youth, into four grades of six years each. "For infancy the mother's knee (modern Kindergarten), for childhood the vernacular school (modern primary school), for boyhood the Latin school, and for youth the University and travel." Thus both Knox and Comenius advocated a single road leading to the University. The scheme of Condorcet for the first time introduced a differentiation in the third grade, age thirteen to eighteen. Here in his *Instituts* he differentiated the curricula into four departments: (1) mathematics and science, (2) philosophical, political and historical studies, (3) applied sciences, and (4) the grammar school. However, all his four departments were largely academic, leading to different faculties of the University, and in fact devised for various professional groups of the ruling class. The majority of the population were not provided for even by his differentiated scheme. When in the middle of the nineteenth century the Americans started building up their democratic system they followed the same lines. To the eight grades of the elementary school they added the four grades of the High School which was not differentiated, usually had a classical bias, and was in fact a preparatory step to the University. At the end of the century they attempted to differentiate the curriculum by introducing four parallel courses: (*a*) ancient classics, (*b*) modern classics, (*c*) science, and (*d*) English history. In fact all four courses were still a preparatory step for the University in spite of differentiation. This interpretation of a democratic system dominated by the idea of University education for all is still visible in many countries even now. In practice this traditional secondary education leading to the learned professions was offered to all young people, most of whom were unsuitable for it, became in consequence a "wastage" and thus lost their social status of equality. A considerable part even of those boys and, later, girls who, prompted by relatives and ambition, eventually reached University lecture rooms had to violate their inborn inclinations and adjust their minds to an academic atmosphere and logical discipline in which only intellectual types can thrive. In practice, therefore, this system proved to be the opposite of equality of opportunity. It was adjusted to a small minority, about 5 per cent, and in another way repeated the defects of the old class system. The development of differential psychology, the study of defectives and the enormous "wastage" in the old grammar schools convinced the democratic reformers that the problem of differentiation must be tackled radically from a new point of view. The monopoly of social prestige and social privilege attached to the grammar school and University had to be abolished and the equality of all social functions to be recognised before a real advance towards a democratic equality of opportunity in education could be attained.

The Americans started the reform of their traditional system before the first World War, but the actual progress in reorganisation was made between the two wars and is not yet completed for the country as a whole. The reform affected both the organisation of grades and the curriculum. The too prolonged elementary instruction, eight years, resulted in loss of time by pupils, who were "marking time" in the last two grades. To avoid it the last two grades of the elementary school were combined with the first grade of the old High School into an intermediate Junior High School. Compulsory attendance was raised by a year to include the new step. The purpose of the new intermediate school is to give complete elementary education to all children of compulsory age and also to differentiate them according to their abilities and inclinations. The third year has selective subjects which give the pupil an opportunity to find a more or less suitable career. The next step—the Senior High School—with three grades has lost its character of a preparatory school for the University. The Federal Government in 1917 granted large sums for vocational education and by this induced the States to include vocational subjects in the curricula of their High Schools. Thus the social prestige of High School education was extended to all walks of life. The Senior High School developed seven different curricula: (a) Cultural, (b) Technical, (c) Agricultural, (d) Manual Arts, (e) Commercial, (f) Home Arts, and (g) Vocational. Only the first is a preparatory step for the University. The American practice, however, with its system of credits instead of matriculation examinations tended to disregard the difference between the cultural branch and other branches of the Senior High School and in consequence lowered the general standard of College entrants. To remedy this defect many Universities have established a two years' Junior College to complete the academic preparation of High School graduates. Thus the Americans have recognised that democracy does not mean lowering the standard of academic education to make it available for everybody. The democratic solution is rather in the direction of raising the social status of manual work than in an attempt to impart an identical education to all. The English Education Act, 1944, quite definitely accepted this interpretation of democracy by raising the social status of modern and technical schools to that of the grammar schools without lowering the academic standard of the latter. We shall discuss the English reform in detail in the next chapter. Recent reforms in the British Dominions and the Scandinavian countries as well as in France, Belgium and Holland all follow the same lines of establishing an intermediate stage after four or five primary grades and differentiating post-primary education according to abilities and functions. The whole trend of these reforms is to raise the social status of the non-academic branches of secondary education while preserving the high standard of the old academic curriculum in those branches which lead to the University. The practice of the U.S.S.R. after a long period of experiments has arrived at a similar solution. At first the Soviet government interpreted democracy in a purely egalitarian sense and opened the doors of the University to all comers after a short period of coaching. The resulting lowering of general culture among the new intelligentsia compelled the Soviet authorities to revise their policy. The entrance requirements to the higher institutions were substantially raised and complete secondary education was considered necessary as a basis for academic training. Thus the old conception of democratic education as a single road for all young people has given way to differentiation in accordance with abilities combined with the equalisation of the social status of all branches of secondary education.

The last problem of democratic education to which lively discussions in many countries are still devoted is the problem of women's education. The main question is whether girls should receive an identical education with boys or have a differentiated curriculum. It is often mixed up with the question of co-education or separate education. As a matter of fact the two questions are not identical and present two different aspects of women's education. There are girls' schools with a curriculum identical with boys' schools, and there are co-educational schools with differentiation for the girls. Historically two countries, England and Russia, were pioneers of women's education. It was in these countries that the first modern secondary schools for girls were established and it was England and Russia which founded the first University Colleges for Women. In England at the end of the eighteenth century several private academies for girls included in their curriculum ancient and modern foreign languages, all branches of mathematics and natural science, history and geography, as well as the conventional "accomplishments." The methods were similar to those used in private academies for boys and were in advance of the antiquated practice of the great public schools. These efforts of pioneering women like Mrs. Bryant or Mrs. Florian did not lead to the general expansion of secondary education for women, but proved decidedly that girls can master and profit from the study of both the humanities and science not less than boys. The next advance was made in the middle of the nineteenth century with the foundation of the Queen's College in 1848, Bedford College in 1849, North London Collegiate School in 1850 and Cheltenham Ladies' College in 1853. From the very start the leaders of these new institutions were divided as to the contents and organisation of female education. Miss Buss of the North London Collegiate School and Miss Davies, the foundress of Girton College, Cambridge, favoured an education identical with that of boys. Miss Beale, the Principal of Cheltenham, and Miss Clough, foundress of Newnham College, on the other hand favoured the evolution of girls' education on lines of its own. The subsequent development followed both lines, and at present girls have ample opportunities either to choose a secondary school indistinguishable from a boys' school or to enter a separate girls' school with a bias suitable for their sex. As usual English educationists are reluctant to accept some uniform and rigid solution and allow each school to solve the problem according to local conditions and opinions. Perhaps the English practice is most in conformity with democratic principles, as neither identical education for both sexes, nor the separate and differentiated education of girls is contrary to the principle of equality of opportunities. The important point is that education for girls should not be inferior to that of boys in quantity or in quality. That condition is fully realised in England and girls enter Universities and professions without any restrictions connected with their sex. The problem of co-education versus separate education in practice is limited only to the secondary stage, as both primary and higher education are in fact co-educational. The English practice again does not accept a single solution and recognises both types as equally justified and equally successful. There are certainly convinced adherents of one or the other way of secondary education, but no English educationist would advocate the compulsory introduction of co-education or its prohibition. In this respect the English do not wish to follow the American example of universal co-education and prefer the freedom of local option.

In Russia the first State system of education established by Catherine II at the end of the eighteenth century was co-educational and secondary schools were open to both sexes. Side by side with the general system Catherine founded separate secondary schools for girls with a differentiated curriculum. Her practice of co-education was discontinued in the nineteenth century, and the secondary schools for girls were inferior to those of boys both in curriculum and in privileges. The Russian intelligentsia, however, both men and women, have accepted the principle of identical education for both sexes since the eighteenth century and the whole movement of women's education in Russia was directed to that end. In 1869 the first University courses for women were founded in St. Petersburg, which were soon followed by courses in other large cities. In order to raise the standard of girls' secondary education some girls' gymnasia introduced Latin into the curriculum, and in many towns special preparatory courses were opened with the full curriculum of boys' gymnasia. This tendency towards equalisation of the sexes found its final expression after the Revolution of 1905, since when women have been admitted to State Universities on the same conditions as men. New co-educational secondary schools were founded by the Government, but up to the Revolution of 1917 they did not develop much, as all old schools remained separate. When the Soviet Government started its educational reform the ground was already prepared and there was no opposition to its policy of identical education for both sexes. A certain opposition was shown to the compulsory introduction of co-education in all secondary schools. Many teachers were specially opposed to the Soviet method of mixing the two sexes of all ages without any preliminary transition period. However, after the initial difficulties were overcome the co-educational system was accepted by all as a matter of course and worked successfully up to the end of the recent war. Women were accepted in all walks of life on equal terms with men. They worked underground in the mines, they served in the mercantile marine and were even accepted in the armed forces during the war and fought both in the ranks and as commissioned officers. In spite of this general policy of identical treatment of both sexes certain difficulties presented the Soviet Government with the necessity of reconsidering the whole problem of co-education. The total character of World War II showed clearly the advantage of the military training of the whole male population before actually joining the armed forces. By this method Germany was able to put into the field a larger army than countries which had to spend at least nine months on initial training. The Soviet Union considered it necessary to introduce universal military training for boys of secondary school age. This inevitably resulted in the differentiation of curriculum between the sexes. On the other hand the loss of thirty million citizens killed in actual fighting or in mass executions by the Germans made a serious gap in the population. And the destruction of homes both in towns and in the country demanded the concentration of effort on home building. Women were urgently needed as home makers and mothers of the new generation, and training for these purposes also required a differentiation of curricula in secondary schools. Soviet psychologists and educationists have recently published articles justifying separate education of the sexes on psychological and pedagogical grounds, but it is doubtful whether the Soviet Government would ever have embarked on such a reversal of its previous practice save for the tragic consequences of the war. During the last years all secondary schools in towns and urban districts have been reorganised into separate boys' and girls' schools with differentiation of curriculum. In the rural districts owing to administrative difficulties secondary schools remain co-educational. The Soviet reform was thus not a clear-cut decision in favour of separate education of the sexes as the only way compatible with democracy. It was rather the result of temporary social conditions which have changed again after the war.

The practice of other democratic countries does not point to a single solution of this problem. In the U.S.A. and in Scandinavia all public schools are as a rule co-educational, but there are many independent schools and colleges for boys or girls respectively. The American system allows a wide selection of subjects and boys and girls can easily adjust their curriculum to the demands of their future careers. In France and the Netherlands, on the contrary, separate education of the sexes is the rule in secondary schools and co-education is unpopular. The influence of the Catholic tradition, very strong in these countries, is evidently the cause of the opposition to co-education. It is interesting to compare the facilities for girls' education in Protestant and Catholic countries. In England, Scotland, the British Dominions, the U.S.A. and Scandinavia both sexes have equal opportunities of secondary education and a high percentage of girls continue their education in the Universities. In France, Belgium, the Netherlands, and Catholic Quebec, not to speak of Latin Catholic countries, secondary education of girls lags far behind that of boys both in number of institutions and in quality. The most striking example is provided by the province of Quebec in Canada. Whereas under the Protestant system 25 per cent of boys and girls of appropriate ages attend secondary schools, under the Catholic system only 17 per cent of boys and 6 per cent of girls have that opportunity. The difference between the sexes is most marked.

The conclusion which can be drawn from this discussion of the theory and practice of many countries is that democracy is not necessarily closely bound to some rigid and uniform solution of these problems. Democracy certainly should be interpreted both from the political and social aspects, but equality of opportunity should mean much more than egalitarian uniformity. If the fundamental rights of the individual citizen, both from the political and economic point of view, are safeguarded by the Constitution, the various ways of building up a democratic educational system should be free to follow different national traditions and adapt themselves to the local conditions of each country.

PART IV

EDUCATION IN FOUR DEMOCRACIES

CHAPTER XIII

THE EDUCATIONAL SYSTEM OF ENGLAND

England is undergoing a radical change in her economic and social structure. Under the combined impact of changed internal and international relations and the theoretical principles of socialism the old England of economic and social individualism is gradually passing away. The country, traditionally based on social stratification and unhampered economic competition, was drawn into a totalitarian war in which her physical and spiritual survival was at stake. The war effort unconditionally demanded the subordination of all group and class interests to one supreme cause—the survival of the nation. The traditional liberties of the individual were curtailed, the whole national economy was directed and controlled by the State, and England, in spite of deep resentment, more and more resembled her totalitarian enemy. It was questionable whether a complete return to pre-war conditions after the defeat of the enemy was possible. With the loss of foreign investments and foreign trade the economic balance was disturbed and the upper groups lost their economic privileges. The war has intensified the old demand of the industrial population for social and economic adjustment and the stage was set for the subsequent socialist legislation. However, England has not followed the Russian example of violent revolutionary upheaval; the radical change is being introduced gradually under the traditional form of parliamentary legislation with the preservation of the old historical structure of the State. Once again England has proved to the world her exceptional ability to incorporate new and radical ideas in the old inherited system without uprooting it. In education as in other fields of national life a similar process is going on, gradually changing the whole school system, preserving the outward traditional features, but substituting a new social content.

The beginning of the new era in English education must be connected with the Hadow Report of 1926, which quite definitely posed the question of a common national system of education. The gradual reorganisation of the old elementary education had

almost been completed before the war, and the next step was
pointed out by the Spens Report of 1938. The Education Act of
1944 was a logical and statutory conclusion of the whole previous
movement. In earlier chapters we have followed the historical
growth of the English system. Side by side with her adherence
to tradition England always produced the pioneers of radical
thought and led Europe on the way to reform. It is sufficient to
mention Wycliffe, Winstanley, Cromwell, Bellers, Locke, Newton,
the Deists, Desaguliers, Priestley, Lancaster, Owen, Darwin and
Spencer to see that almost every movement of educational reform
was connected with broader social or religious ideas and had its
origin in England. Radicalism and reform were thus as much a
part of English tradition as conservatism and the aristocratic
outlook. The present reform therefore is English both in its
radicalism and in its compromise with the past.

The educational practice of England as it was temporarily
crystallised after the Act of 1902 consisted of three separate school
systems. The so-called elementary school system, compulsory
between the ages of five and fourteen and free, provided the
masses with elementary education which ended in a blind alley
at fourteen. For able and persevering adolescents there was an
outlet in the evening classes, but it was cumbered with so many
obstacles that only a small percentage of the masses was able to
take advantage of it. For the wealthy groups who could pay fees
and for a small selected group of elementary school children a
secondary school system was available which led to the School
Certificate and clerical occupations. Again something like a
selected 5 per cent of an age group could proceed to Universities.
For the upper classes there was an independent system of Preparatory and Public schools, very expensive, which led usually to the
two ancient Universities of Oxford and Cambridge. The overlap
between the three school systems was insignificant, and we may
say that English education faithfully reflected the social stratification of the population. Up to the age of twelve years 93 per cent
of the age group attended the Elementary school and 7 per cent
was in Preparatory schools, Private schools or in rare cases had
tutors at home. From twelve onwards up to fourteen, 81 per cent
continued their education in the Elementary and Higher Elementary schools. Twelve per cent of Elementary school boys and
girls, those who could pay fees, and others after a competitive
examination, were transferred to the Secondary school system,
to which 3 per cent from Preparatory schools also passed. About

2 per cent entered the independent "Public" schools and 2 per cent remained in Private schools or at home. The overlap between the elementary and secondary systems thus equalled 12 per cent of an age group, between secondary and private systems 3 per cent, and between the elementary and "Public" school systems there was no overlap at all. In absolute figures it meant that out of an age group of 580,000 boys and girls, 540,000 were in Public Elementary schools and 40,000 in the private system. At the age of twelve, 68,000 ex-elementary pupils were transferred to Secondary schools where they were joined by 18,000 pupils from Preparatory and Private schools. Nine thousand proceeded from the Preparatory schools to independent "Public" schools and 13,000 remained at home and in Private schools. Out of the 68,000 ex-elementary pupils in Secondary schools only 2,000 proceeded to the Universities; of the 18,000 ex-preparatory-school pupils in Secondary schools, 1,200 proceeded to the Universities, and out of 9,000 in independent "Public" schools as many as 6,000. These figures are approximate, but they clearly show the class character of the old English system.

The old Board of Education had no jurisdiction over the private and independent "Public" schools, but the Elementary and grant-aided Secondary schools could be reformed on the lines of *l'école unique*.[1] The reform entailed not only curricular and organisational adjustments but also administrative and financial changes of great importance. Both the Hadow and the Spens Reports recommended reforms in administration and finance, but the opposition of local authorities and vested interests delayed the reform. The English system of administration is neither a centralisation on the French model nor a decentralisation as practised in the U.S.A. It is a "partnership" between central and local authorities, which, while avoiding the defects of undue regimentation in curricula, text-books and control of the teachers from the centre, gives the Ministry (before 1944 the Board) of Education adequate authority for planning the reorganisation of the school system on a national basis. Local traditions and interests always had, and still have, full scope for development through genuine self-government by local education authorities. But there were defects which obstructed the even progress of reorganisation. Many local authorities had before 1944 (and have even now) awkward boundaries with enclaves

[1] See Chapter XV on France.

under the control of other authorities. Some areas were too small, both in population and resources, to maintain a well-co-ordinated system of schools. This was especially true in the case of the whole group of the Part III Authorities, so called because they were listed originally in Part III of the Act of 1902. Of the total number of 316 Local Education Authorities in England and Wales, 62 were County Councils, one the London County Council, 83 County Boroughs and 170 Part III Authorities (146 Boroughs and 24 Urban Districts). County Councils and County Boroughs had jurisdiction over both Elementary and Secondary schools in their areas, whereas Part III Authorities had jurisdiction over the Elementary schools only. This division created dual control over the same area in all non-County Boroughs and Urban Districts and made co-ordinated planning impossible. Before the reorganisation of Elementary schools on Hadow lines the division was more or less clear-cut, but after 1926, when Central Schools, both selective and non-selective, were established all over the country, the historical distinction between elementary and secondary education had lost all its validity. Central schools, collecting pupils of eleven-plus from the Elementary schools of the area, provided a definitely post-primary curriculum in many cases undistinguishable from that of some Secondary schools. But being officially classified under the "Elementary Schools Code" they remained within the jurisdiction of the Part III Authorities, while the Secondary schools of the same area were under the County Councils. This inevitably resulted in many cases in rivalry between the two authorities and lack of co-ordination in building up a post-primary school system. This defect in administration was accentuated by a different financial policy of the Board of Education as to elementary and secondary education. We discussed this problem in Chapter IV, and here only mention again that, while in the field of elementary education the policy of the Board promoted the equalisation of opportunities, in that of secondary education it still further accentuated the difference between the poorer and wealthier areas. The Education Act, 1944, remedied these defects by abolishing Part III Authorities and including their areas within the jurisdiction of County Councils and by extending the equalising financial policy to the old Secondary schools as well.[1] Although the reform reduced the number of

---

[1] Before the 1939 war the central and local authorities shared the costs of education equally, in 1947 the Ministry's share increased to 65 per cent.

L.E.A.s from 316 to 146, it has not eliminated all small areas. Among the historical counties such small areas as the Scilly Isles, the Isle of Wight, Huntingdon, the Soke of Peterborough and Rutland have an insufficient number of children and adolescents for a comprehensive, post-primary education to be organised. Nor did the Act of 1944 rectify the boundaries between the counties and county boroughs, which in many cases are obsolete and do not correspond to the distribution of population. But this reform is connected with the general measures on local self-government and could not be dealt with in an Education Act. Another innovation of the Act concerns the central authority on Education. The historical Board of Education "supervised" the L.E.A.s, but the new Ministry of Education "controls and directs" them for the "effective execution of the national policy." Under the new law the Minister has the power to compel the L.E.A. or even take independent action himself to secure the proper organisation of schools in order to ensure equality of opportunity for all children. This is a new tendency in English education which definitely changes the balance of power in favour of the Ministry.

A second problem of administration and finance was connected with the so-called "Dual System" of control. In the chapters on religious traditions we have seen that both Protestant and Catholic Churches started building schools in England before the State initiated its policy of grants. Thus the Churches have acquired historical and legal rights of control of their denominational schools. The Act of 1870 initiated an undenominational system publicly maintained but recognised the right of the Churches to State support in the maintenance of denominational schools. It was an acknowledged compromise to avoid the "religious difficulty" which was the main obstacle to the progress of popular education. All the subsequent Acts recognised the "Dual System" as a permanent solution and the question was not again raised until the Hadow reorganisation of elementary education brought it into the forefront of educational controversy. The denominational schools, known until 1944 as non-provided schools, were originally founded by churches in their own buildings. When the State undertook their maintenance on the same conditions as that of the publicly provided schools, the buildings remained the property of the churches, and they had to maintain and repair them from voluntary contributions. It is obvious that the "provided schools," coming into existence later, have larger and more modern buildings and having the public purse in support, introduce necessary alterations more willingly than the "non-provided" schools. Most of the latter are small schools in the rural communities often in old-fashioned buildings unsuitable for the reorganisation demanded by the Hadow Report. The Board of Education kept a register—the "Black List"—of those schools which needed replacement and the figures for 1942 clearly show the different quality of buildings of the two groups. The "provided" schools had about 16,000 departments of which only 212 were on the "Black List"; the Church of England Schools had about 10,000 departments of which 399 were on the "List," and Catholic and other schools had about 2,200 departments of which 342 were on the "List." When the Hadow reorganisation demanded the establishment of Central schools or Senior departments the majority of "non-provided" schools were unable to collect enough voluntary contributions for the purpose. During the ten years 1926–36 the denominational schools were the main obstacle to an even progress of reorganisation and a special Education Act was passed in 1936 by which the L.E.A.s were empowered to make grants to the denominational bodies for reorganisation up to three-quarters of the total sum. The Act did not help much; some L.E.A.s refused to make these grants and some denominational schools refused to co-operate. It was obvious that the reorganisation would be delayed in many areas unless a new measure agreed to by both parties were passed. The 1944 Act passed into law a new compromise greatly mitigating the organisational defects of the "Dual System." Under the Act the two groups of schools were renamed Council Schools and Voluntary Schools. Those voluntary schools which can find half the cost necessary for reorganisation receive the other half from public funds and remain under voluntary denominational control. Those schools which are unable to provide half the cost pass under the control of the L.E.A., which will finance the reorganisation. Those voluntary schools which carried out reorganisation previously under the 1936 Act remain under denominational control. The first group of denominational schools is known as Aided Voluntary Schools, the second as Controlled Schools, and the third as Local Agreement Schools.

The 1944 Act also introduced a change in relation to religious instruction, which was the traditional stumbling block in the history of the "Dual System." Since the establishment of publicly provided schools in 1870, the famous Cowper-Temple clause (cl. 14) has prohibited religious instruction "distinctive of any particular religious denomination" in these schools. In the non-provided schools, on the contrary, dogmatic denominational instruction was part of the curriculum. Bible reading, however, was usually included in the provided schools, with the exemption of pupils whose parents objected to it. After 1926 many Anglican and Free Church bodies concluded agreements with the L.E.A.s for the introduction in all schools of an "Agreed Syllabus" in religious instruction on undenominational lines approved by all Protestant Churches and local authorities. This brought the difference between the Anglican and undenominational schools to a minimum, and many Anglican schools were transferred to local authorities. Thus the problem of the "Dual System" would have been solved in time without any conflict, but for the Catholics. The Catholic Church cannot agree to any undenominational religious instruction and refuses to take part in any reorganisation involving the surrender of their denominational teaching. The emphasis of the "Dual System" is now, therefore, between Catholic and non-Catholic schools. The 1944 Act satisfied all Protestant Churches (with the exception of Anglo-Catholics, who in fact are not Protestants) by making the "Agreed Syllabus" a compulsory subject in all Council schools, and the transfer of Anglican schools to the control of the L.E.A. will be accelerated. The Catholics, on the other hand, have apprehensions that those of their schools which, by inability to pay half the cost of reorganisation, will have to pass under the control of the L.E.A., may lose their Catholic atmosphere and therefore are not entirely satisfied with the compromise of 1944. Thus the religious "difficulty" still remains and the compromise bears a temporary character.

Apart from administrative problems solved more or less satisfactorily, the 1944 Act had to deal with two other urgent problems in order to create a national system common to all. First there was the regrading of schools to integrate the "elementary" or primary system with the secondary grant-aided system, and secondly there was the question of independent schools. The first question was solved by the Act, at any rate theoretically; the second question is still awaiting its solution. The Hadow Report of 1926 advocated the substitution for the historical "vertical" division of schools, based on social and economic distinctions, of a "horizontal" division, based on age irrespective of the future vocations of children. The break of eleven plus was selected partly on historical grounds and partly for psychological reasons. As mentioned this reorganisation was carried out before the war in 80 per cent of public elementary schools. But whilst the two separate "Codes," one for "Elementary" and another for "Secondary" schools, continued to exist side by side, the two systems remained apart as before. The buildings, the status and salaries of teachers and the grants to the new Central schools were administered under the old "Code for Elementary Schools," and thus the purpose of social equality for all post-primary schools was not achieved. The Labour movement demanded "Secondary education for all" and considered the Central schools a cheap substitute for the genuine article. The original intention of the Hadow Report to create a new kind of post-primary schools suitable for non-academic vocations was frustrated by the rivalry of L.E.A.s, mentioned above, in consequence of which many Central schools simply tried to imitate older Secondary schools in spite of the disadvantages of the "Elementary Code." The situation was entirely unsatisfactory and demanded revision. The new Spens Report of 1938 tried to solve this difficulty by advocating a clear-cut division into primary and secondary education in which all schools for the ages eleven plus should be classified as secondary. The Report recommended the differentiation of post-primary education into three branches: (a) the traditional academic, given in the Grammar schools, (b) the technical, to be given in the Technical High schools, and (c) a more practical, to be given in the Modern schools. All three kinds of schools should be known as Secondary schools and in every respect enjoy the same status. The Spens Report also recommended the raising of the compulsory school age to fifteen and the introduction of part-time attendance for all adolescents up to eighteen years. All these recommendations have been carried out in the 1944 Act, and the present English system is divided horizontally at the age of eleven plus. Thus at present 93 per cent of children five to eleven plus years (7 per cent are outside the national system) attend Primary schools, either Council or Voluntary, maintained by public authorities. At the age of eleven plus they pass a qualifying and competitive examination for entrance into Grammar and Technical High schools. All the remaining children pass automatically into the Modern schools. The Grammar schools cater for the academically inclined and provide a curriculum of general education which may have a classical, a modern or a scientific bias. They provide complete secondary education up to the age of eighteen, although many pupils leave at sixteen. Those who remain in the upper forms are prepared for the Universities. As mistakes of classification of pupils at eleven plus are inevitable, the first two years of the Grammar schools and Technical High schools are identical in their curriculum, and transfer from one to the other must thus be facilitated. At the age of thirteen plus an internal test and cumulative report of the teachers decides whether the particular pupil is in the right kind of school. To eliminate the influence of financial considerations all Secondary schools aided by public authorities should be made free, but at present only Council schools are free; the Voluntary Secondary schools are free only to a certain percentage of the pupils (from twenty-five to thirty) coming from Primary schools. Those pupils who come from Preparatory and Private schools and attend Voluntary Secondary schools usually pay fees after having passed a qualifying examination. Thus even within the national system there is a small (about 3 per cent of an age group) minority of children who have an additional opportunity of secondary education of an academic type. We shall deal with this question of social privilege in connection with the "Public" schools. We notice that the English new system has the same idea of psychological differentiation and the period of "observation" as in the American Junior High School or the French period of "observation." [1] But there is a fundamental difference; in the American and French plans all children of eleven plus pass into the same school and are directed to different streams after three years (America) or four years (France) in a common intermediate school. In England they pass into three different streams at eleven plus, and although theoretically they can be transferred to another stream at thirteen plus, in practice it will be very difficult, especially in the case of transfer from the Modern school to the two other types. To facilitate such transfers some L.E.A.s submitted plans of multilateral and comprehensive schools. The multilateral school retains the identity of the three streams, grammar, technical and modern, but housing them together in the same large building under a single administration and providing common facilities for sport and social activities is intended to make interchange between the streams natural and easy. The comprehensive school, on the other hand, intends to provide a common core for all children with selective subjects and gradual differentiation. Both types would require the establishment of

[1] See chapters on America and France.

large schools on the model of the American city-school type with
more than 1,000 pupils. The advantages and defects of such
gigantic schools are a matter of lively discussion among English
educationists. The Grammar school teachers are generally
against such organisation of secondary education, and it seems
that in many places these large schools will include only the
technical and modern streams. Whether such a limited application of multilateral or comprehensive organisation will attain the
purpose of social equality is doubtful. The Grammar schools will
retain their social prestige and the parents will continue to strain
their finances to send their children to Preparatory schools with a
view to securing a place in a Grammar school. Large L.E.A.s
like the London County Council have the ability and necessary
school population for such school-giants, but for smaller authorities
it will entail the provision of boarding facilities of hostels for
pupils drawn from a large area. It seems that the grading reform
of the 1944 Act is not final and will need revision after a period of
experimenting on various lines. It is clear that there will be no
uniformity of solution as in France, and that England will follow
her tradition of local variation according to geographical and
economic circumstances and local opinion. The whole problem
is complicated by the existence of independent schools and a
cross-classification of "Public" and grant-aided Secondary schools.

The "Public" schools are a stumbling-block for all foreign
students of English education. In their opinion the term is a
misnomer, as the schools are in fact "private." However, both
historically and legally these schools are "public" as they were
founded with the purpose of promoting public education, were
subject to special Acts of Parliament and were governed by public
bodies established under the original foundations. In England,
at any rate, "private school" means a "proprietary school" run
on the principles of private ownership and profit. The confusion
arose only when the State and local authorities started a system
maintained out of public taxes and rates and the term "public"
was limited in its use. Perhaps to avoid misunderstanding it is
better to call these schools "independent," although with the
present tendency of legislation this is becoming a misnomer also.
But whether "public" or "independent," these schools are an
important part of English education and supplied in the pre-war
period the majority of University students. In the eighteenth
century the nine leading Grammar schools formed a separate
group and became known as the "Public" schools and later as

the "Great Public schools." They were in the sequence of their foundation—Winchester (1387), Eton (1441), St. Paul's (1510), Shrewsbury (1552), Westminster (1560), Merchant Taylors' (1561), Rugby (1567), Harrow (1571), and Charterhouse (1611). Seven are boarding schools and two—St. Paul's and Merchant Taylors'—day schools. Although originally only the larger and better endowed schools among the many Grammar schools, the "nine" through the patronage of the aristocracy became in the eighteenth century the nurseries of the ruling class. Of all the men of the eighteenth century included in the *Dictionary of National Biography* who could be classified as the intellectual élite, 22 per cent were educated in the nine "Public" schools. This pre-eminence of their contribution was not the result of a better organised curriculum and instruction or of better moral training; on the contrary some smaller Grammar schools and many private academies were decidedly better in both respects. But the patronage of the titled aristocracy and the social prestige connected with it raised these schools in the popular opinion above the rest as the best training ground for the ruling class. In the nineteenth century after the reforms of Arnold these schools established the "Public school tradition," an original English contribution to educational practice, and in a way deserved their eminent position on their merits. In the forties new Anglican Schools (Cheltenham, Marlborough, Rossall, Lancing) were founded on the same lines and joined the small group of "Public" schools. Some Nonconformist schools and Catholic colleges, transferred to England from abroad, also remodelled their organisation on "Public" school lines in the middle of the last century. With the similar foundations of the second half of the nineteenth century they formed a group of about sixty, the independent "Public" schools of today. The common feature of these schools is their intimate connection with some denomination; most of them are Anglican, some are Catholic, Presbyterian, Congregationalist, Methodist or Society of Friends. Religious instruction and corporate religious service are an integral part of the curriculum. All of them are represented on the Headmasters' Conference. Here we must note that about eighty schools represented on the Conference have accepted grants from the Ministry of Education and thus cannot be properly classed with the independent Public schools. Some of the independent schools have been inspected by H.M. Inspectors for many years, and before 1944 the majority of the independent Public schools applied for inspection and were included in the official List of Efficient Schools. Since 1944 all independent schools, whether public or private, are subject to the Ministry's inspection and the previous confusion of various classifications has partly disappeared. Side by side with the boys' Public schools a similar group of girls' independent schools grew up during the second half of the nineteenth century, but they are not represented on the Headmasters' Conference and are called "Public" schools only by courtesy. The rôle of independent schools throughout the nineteenth century and even in the twentieth century was similar to the rôle of the nine Great Public schools in the eighteenth century. They supplied almost two-thirds of all University entrants and their alumni form the intellectual élite of the country. The author has selected from the *Authors' Who's Who* 2,500 names of the intellectual élite,[1] of whom 490 were educated in the nine Great Public schools and 843 in fifty-one other "Public" boys' schools, which means that "Public" schools supplied about 49 per cent [2] of all living British authors in any branch of academic study, art and literature. The schools play a rôle in the national life out of all proportion to their numbers. There are many reasons for this. They are undoubtedly very efficient, but so are hundreds of other Grammar schools. They receive the ablest boys of the nation, but so do many of the grant-aided schools. Additional reasons are: attendance at Preparatory schools, the financial resources of their families, and more cultured homes, with additional facilities for intellectual growth. "Public" schools accept boys at the age of thirteen years after an examination. Primary school boys pass into Secondary schools at eleven plus. The two systems do not fit, and with individual exceptions, with which we will deal later, primary school boys cannot be transferred to "Public" schools. A special system of Preparatory schools had to be established to train the boys for the entrance examination to "Public schools." These schools are proprietary schools and very expensive, but they include Latin, French and mathematics in their curriculum and can prepare even boys of average ability for the examination, although they are often poorly equipped and follow old-fashioned methods. But their pupils have two more years of coaching than primary school boys, especially in Latin and French. Not more than 2 per cent of an age group attend these schools, but they

[1] If we deduct Scots and Irishmen, the percentage for *English* authors would be about 66 per cent.
[2] See "Independent Schools and the Liberal Professions" in the *Year Book of Education*, 1950.

represent wealthy families. The same financial selection works in the "Public" schools; they are boarding institutions and in addition to high fees for tuition require fees for boarding. The combined course of Preparatory and "Public" schools comprises ten years or more and the total cost runs into four figures. There are scholarships awarded to winners of a very stiff competitive examination, but they do not cover all expenses and are available to a minority of pupils. Thus only a wealthy family can send a boy to a "Public" school and keep him there till the age of eighteen years. The majority of pupils of grant-aided schools leave the school at the age of sixteen and cannot qualify for higher education. The result is, as mentioned before, that two-thirds of University entrants come from "Public" schools, or similar independent schools. The 1944 Act did not interfere with the independent schools except by imposing compulsory inspection, which as a matter of fact was almost general on a voluntary basis. The Universities, being independent, were not included in the purview of the Act and thus the situation remains as it was. On a secondary level it is not very important that about 2 per cent of an age group enjoy a privileged training; whatever the reform, wealthy parents will always have the advantage of private tutors or of sending their boys abroad. But on the University level the "Public" school boys have an enormous privilege which entirely upsets the principle of equality of opportunity. The Government, even the socialist Government, is reluctant to interfere with the independence of the "Public" schools, fully recognising their traditional cultural value. But during the war a committee was appointed to study the possible association of the independent schools with the national system. The result was the Fleming Report, which recommended the influx of ex-primary-school boys into the "Public" schools to the amount of 25 per cent of all pupils. The State and the local authorities would undertake to reimburse the "Public" schools for the loss of income. The scheme has been accepted by some "Public" schools on a voluntary basis, but it is too early to predict its further development. Until this problem is satisfactorily solved no reform of the national system will be able to realise that equality of educational opportunity which was the aim of the Education Act of 1944.

Another important aspect of the Act was the attention paid to technical education. In Chapter IV we have given a short account of the development of technical and vocational education in England. Up to the twentieth century this education was available in part-time Evening Institutes and Polytechnics which were mainly centred in London and to a great extent catered for clerical occupations. The first full-time technical schools were the creation of the twentieth century. In 1901 the first of the Day Trade Schools was opened in London. In 1913 the Board of Education issued regulations for this category of vocational schools, known since then as Junior Technical schools. Later Junior Commercial schools (recognised in 1925), and Junior Departments of Schools of Art (recognised in 1916) were added to this group of full-time schools. They accepted boys and girls at the age of thirteen after a qualifying examination. They were attended almost exclusively by ex-elementary-school pupils. The courses lasted three or four years and fitted the boys and girls for various branches of industry and commerce and were often recognised as a definite period of apprenticeship. The development of these schools was slow, and just before the war not more than 2 per cent of an age group attended them. Most of the technical and vocational education is still imparted in the Evening Institutes or Colleges, although a certain development of full-time senior courses took place in the twentieth century. The 1944 Act, by creating Technical High schools, has made technical education a regular feature of the national system equivalent in status and importance to general secondary education. As already stated, the pupils pass into these schools at the age of eleven plus, but the first two years have a common course with the Grammar schools, and the specialised vocational education starts only at thirteen years as was the case in the Junior Technical schools before the reform. Side by side with the full-time Technical High school with compulsory attendance from eleven to fifteen, the 1944 Act envisaged a radical reform of part-time vocational education. Attendance at part-time institutions is voluntary, as the attempt of the Fisher Act of 1918 to introduce compulsory Continuation schools for ages fourteen to eighteen failed completely, except at Rugby, where the school remained in being after the suspension of the Act. The 1944 Act again introduced compulsory part-time education for ages fifteen to eighteen, which, however, was suspended. During the interval the L.E.A.s have the duty to extend their part-time institutions to cover the whole population of those age groups which is outside full-time Secondary schools. For the rural areas special County Colleges will be founded, combining general culture with occupational activities. We must here note that agricultural education was neglected by the central and local authorities throughout the nineteenth century, and only after the First World War did the Ministry of Agriculture elaborate a plan for a national system. As it was, in 1937 only about 6 per cent of age groups sixteen to twenty-one occupied in farming attended full-time or part-time courses in agriculture. With the establishment of County Colleges based on compulsory attendance a new opportunity will be open for the farming youth.

As we have said, University education was not included in the reform of 1944. The war and the interruption of the studies of thousands of mobilised students considerably influenced the situation in the Universities. University education in England is represented by two kinds of higher institutions. The two ancient Universities of Oxford and Cambridge, and Durham (nineteenth century) are federations of residential Colleges, and their students, with few exceptions, are boarded in colleges, where they receive tuition in addition to University lectures. The thirty-eight Oxford and Cambridge Colleges are mostly old foundations with large incomes and do not receive State grants. They are very expensive, and their total expenditure amounted to two million pounds before the war. The students' fees for tuition and boarding contributed more than £800,000, or an average of about £150 per student a year. Adding University fees, sport and extras, the total cost of education at Oxford and Cambridge amounts to £250 a year. A three years' course means £750, which only wealthy families could afford. There are hundreds of scholarships for poor able scholars, who pass a competitive examination of higher standard than ordinary matriculation. These "poor" scholars, however, in most cases are not sons of manual workers, but of middle-class families, which had sufficient means to send their boys to "Public" schools, but could not afford the additional £750 at Oxford or Cambridge. There are a few State scholarships for pupils of the State-aided schools, but their number is insignificant among the 10,000 students of the two Universities. The war has radically changed the situation. The returned ex-soldiers were accepted on a priority clause and were aided by the State. The number of ordinary State scholarships was also increased.[1] Whether this practice will continue in future with the passing of the veterans of the war is uncertain, but it

[1] The latest figures show that about 70 per cent of all students in England are aided by the State or local and private grants. The social composition of the students also greatly changed after the war, and at present about 40 per cent are children of agricultural and industrial workers.

will involve granting subsidies to the Colleges, which until now were quite independent of the State.

The University of London and all the new Universities, on the contrary, are day institutions and not so expensive. Their students in a majority of cases come from the grant-aided Secondary schools and include many ex-elementary-school pupils (about 25 per cent). Again the post-war regulations of priority for ex-soldiers have made these Universities still more democratic. Although the standards of London and other Universities are not lower than those of Oxford and Cambridge, the prestige of the two ancient Universities in social life, Civil Service and business circles is much higher. Women are accepted by all Universities on equal terms with men; in London they form about a quarter of the total number of students, in Oxford and Cambridge only about 10 per cent (because there are fewer Colleges for women). All English Universities have the traditional six Faculties: Theology, Art, Science, Law, Medicine and Engineering. But each University has some additional Faculty or School of Study. The usual course for the first degree of Bachelor takes three years, and for the second degree of Master an additional two years.[1]

Higher technical education forms an integral part of University studies, although some branches of engineering often have a semi-independent separate school. The question of higher technical education was the subject of a special Commission during the war. The so-called Percy Report of 1945 recommended notable changes in the existing organisation. The Report recorded the inadequate co-ordination of technical education with the needs of industry and with the new technique of production. To remedy this deficiency the Report recommended the creation of Regional Advisory Councils for the co-ordination of the higher technical education provided in the Universities and Technical Colleges with industry. The Report even recommended the setting up of a National Council of Technology.[2] It is rather a novel idea for England, but it shows clearly the trend towards centralisation noticeable in other fields.

The reforms introduced by the 1944 Act need a great expansion of teaching personnel. The raising of the compulsory age to fifteen, the reduction in the size of classes and the universal establishment of Modern schools call for at least 70,000 additional

---

[1] At Oxford and Cambridge no additional examination for the latter is required, except fees.
[2] This recommendation was accepted by the Government in 1947.

teachers. The war resulted in a shortage, judging even by old requirements. The existing Training Colleges and University Departments were unable to deal with such an increased demand. The McNair Report of 1944 recommended a closer association of Universities with the Training Colleges. But there was no unanimity, and while half the Committee recommended the organisation of Training Colleges round their regional Universities as Schools of Education under University control, the other half was against it. At present all the Universities except that of Oxford, have accepted the suggestion and organised their regional Training Colleges into Institutes of Education. The co-ordination of the training of teachers for Primary and for Secondary schools into a single national system is long overdue. The English teaching profession was divided into two groups by training, social status and salary scales. The teachers for the old Elementary schools were trained in two-year Colleges after acquiring a complete secondary education. The teachers for Secondary schools were trained in a one-year Teachers' Diploma course at University Departments after graduating from the faculties of Arts or Science. The teachers of independent "Public" schools were as a rule Honours graduates of Oxford and Cambridge, who in most cases did not enter for a Teachers' Diploma course. The difference between the three groups of teachers was not only in training and academic qualifications; they were recruited from different social classes and had no strong feeling of professional unity. It was characteristic of the English social stratification that teachers were divided even in their professional associations. The headmasters of the 160 "Public" and similar schools have their own aristocratic Headmasters' Conference; the headmasters of Secondary schools, the Headmasters' Association; the Assistant Masters, the Assistant Masters' Association; the last two are duplicated by women teachers' associations. The teachers of schools under the "Elementary Code" were united in the National Union of Teachers. Since 1944 these divisions are obsolete, but unless the Training Colleges are a part of the Universities, social barriers will persist. The war again forced the development. After the passing of the 1944 Act it was evident that the existing Training Colleges and University Departments were unable to cope with the situation. The Ministry of Education resolved to start a bold experiment. New Emergency Training Colleges were created with a shortened course of a year instead of the regular two years. Another innovation was the admission of men and women without the matriculation certificate, but with experience and qualifications of a different kind. The reform of 1944 will require an annual intake of 15,000 teachers. The total number of matriculated pupils is less than 25,000 boys and girls for the whole country. As a considerable proportion of them are needed in other liberal professions it was clear that teachers would have to be recruited from outside the limited number of matriculated pupils. The Ministry decided to accept any candidate up to thirty years old, who had some kind of post-primary education and a certain experience in practical life or the armed forces. In 1947 forty-eight Emergency Colleges were opened, 2,000 new teachers have been trained and 20,000 are in training. About 15,000 ex-service men and women were on the waiting list to be admitted to the course.[1] This influx of men and women from all walks of life with non-academic practical experience has considerably changed the somewhat narrow professional outlook of the body of teachers and will break down the social barriers between the teachers and the outside world. Fears that the new teachers will lower the standards of the profession are greatly exaggerated, as mature adults with experience of life can achieve in a year of intensive training as much as young boys and girls, direct from secondary schools, in two years.

Adult education and the out-of-school activities of youth were both started in England by voluntary agencies at the end of the nineteenth and in the first decade of the present century. The Board of Education began to aid the University Tutorial Classes in 1907 and in 1921 an Adult Education Committee was established to co-ordinate on a national plan all voluntary agencies in this field. Since then grants have been available for all voluntary and L.E.A. organisations which established classes in accordance with the Board of Education Regulations of 1924. The Youth Movement was entirely voluntary and independent and was represented by many organisations of which two are of world-wide renown—the Boy Scouts and the Young Men's (and Women's) Christian Association. In 1939 the Government set up a Youth Advisory Council which at present under the direction of the Ministry co-ordinates the activities of the L.E.A.s and

---

[1] In August 1947 out of 100,000 applicants 40,000 were accepted and were on the waiting list. The annual output was estimated at 11,000 new teachers from emergency colleges alone. At present some of the emergency colleges are transformed into permanent two years institutions, whilst others were closed.

voluntary bodies and distributes the grants. During the war all three branches of the armed forces (Army, Navy and Air Force) developed pre-service organisations of youth, now integrated permanently with other branches of the Youth Service. Although the pre-service organisations are a preparatory ground for compulsory military service, their importance lies more in the general training of character and preparation for civic duties in a free democracy.

Thus we see that England has definitely broken with inherited social prejudices in all fields of education and entered a new period of radical reforms.[1] However, all the valuable features of the old traditions whether religious, social or educational, are carefully preserved and integrated in the ideal of a free and tolerant democracy based on equality of opportunity for all. Henceforward the new three A's (age, ability and aptitude) will determine the education and future vocation of a child, instead of the old three R's (reading, writing and reckoning) which for centuries were considered as ample education for the masses.

---

[1] The intention of the 1944 Act of providing Secondary Education for all resulted in a controversy about the establishment of Comprehensive Schools. Some of the L.E.A. are in favour, whilst others are against (see table, p. 70). There is a movement for the abolition of the qualifying tests at 11 plus and prolonging common education for all till 15. Two counties have adopted this course but the majority of L.E.A. still retain the division into three streams at 11 plus.

CHAPTER XIV

THE EDUCATIONAL SYSTEM OF THE U.S.A.

Of the four countries discussed in this part the U.S.A. alone is an essentially new country. England, France and Russia can trace back their past for more than a thousand years and in spite of changes introduced by revolutions and radical reforms in these countries their national characters and historical traditions remained the basic influence in their development. America, on the contrary, is still in the making; her past is so short that, from the European point of view, it is part of her present and as such cannot yet play the rôle of stabilising force as in Europe. Indeed in the American estimate the past is ballast in its original sense of a "worthless load" and they often pride themselves on its absence. In such conditions America looks forward and believes that tomorrow is always better than today. This outlook was influenced by the circumstances of the first settlements, by the constantly moving frontier and by the masses of immigrants who passionately wanted to forget their past. The first settlers fled from the persecutions of central governments in Europe because they represented a deviation from accepted traditions, and thus they brought over with them a distrust of the established order and a negative attitude towards the past. The pioneering conditions of the moving frontier in the West dominated by the law of the survival of the fittest promoted independence, initiative and also a certain restlessness and contempt for the written law. The millions of immigrants escaping from the economic misery of Europe were inspired by the tales of unlimited opportunities in America and a burning desire to get rich in the shortest possible time. All these causes added to and consolidated the main fact of American history, her revolt against Europe and the birth of a new and independent nation. The American philosophy of life and her educational system unavoidably reflected the conditions of American growth and tended towards pragmatism and relativism. John Dewey is the representative American philosopher and her leading educational pioneer. His pragmatism and experimentalism gave full expression to the frontier spirit of America and in their turn profoundly influenced the theory and practice of contemporary American education. The deviation

273

from Europe, therefore, is marked, but nevertheless America is closely bound up with European history and culture. All her peculiar features represent minority movements of Europe rejected at home. We have seen in the historical chapters that the two fundamental factors which shaped American tradition—Puritanism and Humanism—were widespread European movements, born and grown to stature in Europe; and although rejected in some parts of Europe they left deep traces even in those countries which are officially traditionalist—Catholic, or authoritarian—Marxist. In so far as America shares this heritage she is a part of the European cultural community and more particularly of Western Europe.

From the first days of independence the constitution of the U.S.A. excluded education from the purview of the Federal authority. The fear of Federal encroachment on the autonomy of the States was especially strong in the South and among religious communities in all States. Each State was left to build its own educational system, and although many States have included in their constitutions the provision of education, in fact they relegated the obligation to the local authorities. Local administration in education is a historical tradition in America established by the first settlers. Isolated small communities, surrounded by hostile Nature and fierce native Indians, clung to their village as the centre and origin of all legislative and cultural measures. Homogeneous in social status and religious beliefs, identifying their local church with their communal representation in a miniature theocratic State, these settlements quite naturally administered and maintained their school. In the later period of frontier life the local unit of administration was best suited to the needs of the pioneers. With the increase of population and consolidation of the States into well ordered large legal communities an adjustment to new conditions was necessary. But all attempts of various States at centralisation of educational administration were met by the strong opposition of local Boards, which valued their right of appointment of teachers suitable to their beliefs and prejudices. The Churches, both Catholic and Puritan, supported local independence as a safeguard against the secularising encroachment of the State. Thus, in spite of a complete change of social and economic conditions, the local unit of school administration survived until now as the typical feature of America.

There are three main systems of local control of education.

The oldest and the most popular is the District system. These school districts are irregular in shape, of various sizes, often most inconveniently delimited from neighbouring districts for reasons having nothing to do with the efficiency of administration. As a rule they administer a one-teacher, one-room school for the children of all ages of the few families who form the district. This system with the increasingly unequal distribution of wealth leads to great inequalities in schools, teachers and equipment and to an unwise location of schools. In the present transition period of progressive reforms the district system is the main obstacle to an even advance of American education. The figures for one of the most progressive States—the State of New York—for 1937 show clearly the extent to which the district system is still predominant in the rural areas. The urban school system of the State consisted of 156 districts, which employed 1,061 school officers and 60,598 teachers for 1,620,274 pupils. The rural school system consisted of 7,756 districts (5,985 one-school districts) which employed 17,822 school officers and 21,059 teachers for 378,365 pupils. Only 631 districts of the total number maintained high schools. Of the one-school districts, 2,075 units had fewer than ten children and 2,804 units from ten to twenty children of all ages. The difference in every respect between a palatial multi-lateral school of New York with more than a thousand pupils and a dilapidated wooden hut with an unqualified young girl as a teacher and five to ten boys and girls of all ages as pupils is so enormous that even the classification of these schools as institutions of the same kind is ridiculous. Professor F. H. Swift, of California University, thus described the results of this system: "Generations of local support and local domination of public schools finds the richest nation on the earth denying multitudes of her children any educational opportunity whatsoever, and herding thousands upon thousands of others in dismal and unsanitary hovels, under the tutelage of wretchedly underpaid and proportionately ignorant, untrained, and negative teachers."[1] The other two forms of local administration—the township system of the Middle West and the county system of the South and Pacific coast—combining the administration of many schools under the control of a local Board of Education, are much more efficient and as a rule have larger and better equipped schools. Nevertheless in the absence of equalising control and financial aid from the State the differences between townships or counties

---

[1] *Twenty-five Years of American Education.*

are great. Of the forty-eight States only one—the State of Delaware—has established the State system of administration with direct control and financial support of all public schools within the State. In spite of this example, which undoubtedly resulted in better organisation and distribution of educational opportunities in Delaware, the remaining forty-seven States are still unable to surmount the conservative and obstinate opposition of their local units to the State control of education. The same story is repeated in relation to Federal control and support of education, only in this case the opposition comes from the States themselves. Especially strong is the opposition in the South, where the whites fear Federal intervention in support of Negro education, which in their opinion will upset the balanced economy of the agricultural South and undermine the historical predominance of the whites. We have discussed the Negro problem in Chapter II and need not resume it here. However, the industrialisation of America with the necessity for technical education, entirely neglected by State systems, and the years of depression inevitably led to intervention by the Federal Government, which is constantly growing and sooner or later will result in a considerable measure of Federal control.

In spite of the American Constitution, which safeguards the rights of the States in education, the intervention of the Federal Government is of long standing. The first action taken by the Federal Government in support of education was the famous Ordinance of 1785 by which lot No. 16 of every township on Federal lands was reserved for the maintenance of public schools within that township.[1] When the Federal territories were carved up into the new States, each State had therefore a land revenue for education. The total amount of Federal land grants equalled 94,000,000 acres. In addition to these direct grants the States used for purposes of education Federal grants of salt and swamp lands which amounted to another 77,000,000 acres. The sale of these lands provided the States with large funds for educational purposes, which were subject to Federal legislation. In practice Federal supervision was inefficient and large parts of these funds were squandered by the States and were lost for education. Nevertheless many land-grant colleges have been founded in most of the States since 1862, when the Morrill Act donated Federal lands for the establishment of schools for agricultural

---

[1] A township is an area of 36 square miles divided into 36 squares or lots, each a square mile in area.

and mechanical training. The attempt at establishing a Federal Department of Education in 1867 was frustrated by the opposition of the States, and the Bureau of Education created in that year had the very limited functions of collecting statistical data and publishing reports. Even that activity was possible only through the voluntary collaboration of the States. A new departure was made in 1917 when by the Smith-Hughes Act a Federal Board of Vocational Education was established and large sums were appropriated by the Federal Government for the promotion of vocational education throughout the country. The new Board, in contrast to the older Bureau (now Office), had powers of supervision and control. The Federal Board had to co-operate with the States in the administration of the Act, to examine plans submitted by the States, and through annual inspection to supervise the proper expenditure of Federal subventions. We must mention that the Bureau (Office) of Education had under its direct control the Indian schools, the District of Columbia and the territory of Alaska. The intervention of the Federal Government became a fact, but it was on such a small scale (about 1·5 per cent of total national expenditure on education) that it could not influence the existing inequalities. There were many attempts in the inter-war period at establishing efficient Federal control, but every time these were frustrated by the opposition of the States and religious bodies. The most bitter opposition came from the Catholic Church, which considered "such measures as both un-American and un-Christian," and earnestly urged all Catholics to oppose these "destructive educational schemes, thus erecting an impregnable barrier against this sinister menace to religion and constitutional menace to family and nation." [1] Faced with such powerful influences the Federal Government could not introduce straightforward legislation. The Advisory Committee of Education, appointed by President Roosevelt, reported in 1938 and concluded that the Federal Government ought to take prompt and appropriate action to relieve the unsatisfactory state of education, but that the administration of the schools should be explicitly reserved to State and local agencies. With such limitations the Federal Government started new educational projects as a part of the New Deal policy. The National Youth Administration and Civilian Conservation Corps took care of unemployed youth on a national scale and provided them with vocational training organised in the Con-

[1] *Louisiana Federation of Catholic Societies.*

servation Corps or helped them to continue their education in the colleges. The war still further increased the intervention of the Federal authorities. The Office of Education assumed general direction and guidance of all education connected with the war. By the Act of 1940 the Office of Education was authorised to provide "short intensive courses of college grade, designed to meet the shortage of engineers in activities essential to national defence." Thus the E.D.T. or Engineering Defence Training programme came into being, which played such an important rôle during the war. The $65,000,000 which was distributed among the States as regular subventions of the Federal Government grew through the adoption of many emergency measures to about $250,000,000 in 1945. But even this enormous growth of Federal aid hardly affected the fundamental deficiencies of American educational finances. The major source of school support is still the local unit and all the Federal grants amount only to about 3 per cent of expenditure on education. The inequalities in every respect are as great as ever, and while some pupils attend schools spending $6,000 a year per classroom unit, others are in schools spending a total sum of $100 per unit. As we pointed out before, equality of educational opportunity can only be realised on a national basis when all the three factors— need, ability and effort—of a sound financial policy are considered. The Report of the Regents Inquiry of New York State of 1938 quite definitely advocated this policy.

The American school system is still in a period of transition. Although the majority of schools have been reformed and re-graded according to the new plan of six-three-three years, the minority continue to follow the old plan of eight-four years. There is no Federal legislation on compulsory attendance; each of the forty-eight States has its own law, which results in great variation in age limits. The majority of States start compulsory attendance at the age of seven years, some at six and others at eight. Again the majority of the States require attendance to continue to the age of sixteen years, some to fourteen and others to eighteen. As a rule we may say that in most States nine years of school attendance are required, which usually embrace the six elementary grades and three Junior High school grades. Attendance at Nursery schools and Kindergartens is voluntary, and these institutions are provided only in large cities. Nursery schools for very young children of two to four years have been developed quite recently under the influence of the English practice. A great impetus to their growth was given by the Lanham Act of 1940, which as one of the emergency measures allotted Federal subventions for the care of young children. About 1,500 Nursery schools with 52,000 children were opened in consequence. Kindergartens, on the contrary, have an old tradition dating back to Froebel, and are attended by about 700,000 children of three to six years. As mentioned, attendance is voluntary, and few families in the cities take advantage of these schools (about 8 per cent of respective ages).[1] Mass attendance begins at six or seven years. The elementary school of America is the historical common school and is attended by all groups of the population, irrespective of creed, origin or wealth. This statement is true for the great majority, but there are important exceptions. In the Southern States the public elementary schools for whites and Negroes are separate. In all States Roman Catholic children as a rule attend private schools and the percentage in private schools for the U.S.A. is as high as 11 per cent. Many Americans are not aware of the fact that in England only 7 per cent of ages six to fourteen are in private schools and that the English primary school is more national in that sense than the American common school. In Russia there are no private schools whatsoever, and in France about 20 per cent of elementary-school children attend private schools. The enforcement of compulsory attendance is not so strict as in England or even France. In England only a fraction of 1 per cent of the compulsory ages remains outside the school. In the U.S.A. the census of 1940 showed about 2,000,000 American children of six to fifteen years outside any school. This means that about 10 per cent of young Americans do not receive even adequate elementary schooling. The same census showed that 10,000,000 American adults have received so little education that they were virtually illiterate. We should, however, mention that a great proportion of these children and adults are Negroes and that the problem of illiteracy is closely connected with racial discrimination in the Southern States. The unreformed Elementary school has eight grades, the reformed only six; the two groups are almost equal in numbers of pupils. These facts once more prove that such generalisations as democratic education in America in contrast to aristocratic education in England need revision.

We have pointed out previously that the American Common

---

[1] In England ages three to four, 7 per cent; four to five, 23 per cent; and five to six, 90 per cent are in school, or 40 per cent for three ages combined.

school is secular and that the elimination of religious instruction from the public system compelled the Catholics to build up their own independent system. Again the variation among the States is great. Whilst some States include Bible reading as a compulsory school subject, other States prohibit even reading of the Bible without comment. As a result a considerable proportion of adult Americans have never read the Bible. On the other hand patriotic instruction and ceremonies are a general feature, and American children are more conscious and more proud of their nationality than the English. In many cases the insistence on the "American way of life" and "un-American" political theories tends to political indoctrination.

In Chapter XII we have described the reasons which led to the reform of the American High school by introducing an intermediate stage of the Junior High school. The progress of the reform is not even throughout the States. In the more progressive North and West the majority of the High schools are already reformed and the movement has been recently accelerated. In the more backward South, especially among the Negroes, the old four-years High school is still the rule. As was pointed out before the functions of the old four-years High school and the new Junior–Senior High school with six grades are different. The old type was meant to be a preparatory school for College and University and is still mainly academic in curriculum, whilst the new type is a comprehensive school for all groups of adolescents. As the compulsory ages overlap the first two grades of the High school all pupils of the eighth elementary grade proceed to the High school grade, but finding the curriculum unsuitable a large proportion leave the school after a year or two of attendance. With the Junior–Senior type the situation is much better. All pupils attend the Junior High school, and those who pass into the Senior High school usually remain until graduation. With the gradual reform of education in the backward areas and the raising of the compulsory age to eighteen years, the Senior High school will be attended by all adolescents in America. Secondary education for all is the ideal accepted in all four countries discussed in this part of the book, but which of them will attain it first is difficult to predict. America started first along the way and was well in advance of the three European countries, but it seems that all three, England, France and Russia, are overtaking the U.S.A. and may attain the goal first. The neglected state of Negro education and the extreme decentralisation of administration keep America back and prevent further progress after the initial rapid advance. Being a comprehensive school for all adolescents the new Junior–Senior High school has to adapt its curriculum to the abilities and inclinations of its pupils. Neither entrance nor final examinations with set standards and subjects can be connected with such an aim. In the Junior school which serves as a stage of psychological differentiation a common core of subjects (English, mathematics, and history and civics) is taken by all pupils; all other subjects are selective, and the range of selection is very wide. Passing without examination into the Senior High school, the pupil is entirely free in his choice. As many as 250 or more different subjects are offered in larger schools and the pupil can make his own combination of them. In most schools the subjects are grouped into systematic courses which are usually divided into: classical, foreign languages, scientific, mathematics, history–social science, technical, commercial, manual arts, household arts, agriculture, fine arts and music. All courses and subjects are equivalent and the same amount of credits is required for High school graduation, whether they were collected by the study of Latin or history or by practical work in the laundry or kitchen. In most schools there is no compulsion to continuous study of any selected subject and the pupil may drop it after having collected the credit for one year's study. The results of this system are not satisfactory, and many American educationists advocate the necessity of compulsory courses. Introduced under the slogan of "child-centred education" with the intention of giving equal opportunity to socially and intellectually handicapped children, the system, it seems, defeats its own ends. Educated and wealthy parents insist on their children selecting academic courses, preparing for the University, whilst less educated and poorer parents insist on vocational subjects in order to cash the results of the training as soon as possible. Thus although all children go to the same school the social differentiation is as marked as ever.

Social mobility is not so great as it was in the pioneering days of the moving frontier, and the privileged groups retain their position in spite of the common school. It is facilitated for them by the presence of private expensive schools, which provide a more suitable preparation for an academic career. About 7 per cent of all secondary pupils attend private schools, which resemble the European secondary schools more than the comprehensive American High school. Many of the private academies are boarding schools on the lines of the old Anglican Public schools of England. Although the terms "public school boy" and "public school tie" are unknown in America and cannot be applied to American private schools, yet the latter play a rôle in American social life not dissimilar to that of "Public schools" in England. Side by side with private secondary schools connected with some religious denomination there are large private schools attached to University Education Departments in independent Universities. Often serving as an experimental laboratory for intending teachers, they are usually among the best-equipped and very expensive. They are attended by children of University teachers and officials. Thus America also possesses schools for the élite, whose graduates have unwritten social privileges. Another factor tending to social differentiation in educational opportunities in America is the absence of scholarships or maintenance grants. All the States provide free secondary and higher education open to all without any restriction, but they do not consider it their duty to aid poor parents or poor scholars financially. As mentioned many able adolescents select vocational subjects in High schools because they have to earn their living immediately after attaining the age of sixteen years. Often the kind of secondary education received even in free High schools does not depend on ability or inclination, but on the financial circumstances of the parents. In this respect England, France and Russia with their systems of State bursaries and maintenance grants are more democratic than the U.S.A.

Technical education in America is of recent growth as a nation-wide movement. Although a few technical schools have existed since the middle of the nineteenth century, the need for technically trained personnel was not realised until the twentieth century, when the increased rate of industrialisation drew attention to it. We have compared the close connection of industrialisation and technical education in England and Russia in Chapter IV. America occupies an intermediate position between the two. During the nineteenth century the U.S.A. on the whole followed the English policy of non-intervention and the development of technical education was haphazard and lagged behind the rate of industrialisation; in the twentieth century, on the other hand, a certain planning became evident in the policy both of the individual States and of the Federal Government. Up to 1860 industries grew very slowly in the U.S.A. and played a minor part in the national economy of the country. From 1860 to 1890 we notice a marked rise in the absolute and relative figures of industrial development, and in the twentieth century it assumed almost a revolutionary tempo. The first impetus to American Technical education was given by the international exhibitions of the seventies, where the Moscow Technical School drew general attention to its exhibits. The so-called "Russian system" was accepted in America, and consisted of set exercises in joinery, turning, forging and other essential manual skills. Many manual training schools were opened both by private initiative and public authorities. In the eighties and nineties several Technical Institutes were founded in addition to half a dozen University Departments and as many Land-grant Colleges established under the Morrill Act of 1862. At the same period private individuals started establishing Commercial and Business Colleges, which at the end of the nineteenth century ran into hundreds with more than 100,000 students. These institutions, however, were of comparatively low standard and did not form a part of the public system of education. In the twentieth century States and municipalities started making public provision for technical education. In 1901 Chicago included the training of apprentices in its system and in 1903 Illinois passed a law making the training of apprentices compulsory. In 1901 Wisconsin provided by an Act free agricultural and household economy schools in every county. Still up to the passing of the Smith-Hughes Act in 1917 there was no national plan and technical education developed unevenly and sporadically. During the first World War a Commission appointed by the Federal Government reported that: (a) there is pressing need of vocational education, (b) the problem of vocational education is too extensive to be worked out except by a national agency, (c) the States are too poor to attempt a solution of the problem, (d) the mobility of the population and of labour demands the application of Federal resources, and (e) the training of teachers of vocational subjects is expensive and teachers are migratory. All these reasons demanded a centralisation of effort and national planning. As a result the Smith-Hughes Act of 1917 was passed. As mentioned, a Federal Board of Vocational Education was established with powers of supervision and control. The Federal grants were divided into three parts: (a) for agricultural education, (b) for trade, household economics and industrial education, and (c) for training teachers of vocational subjects. Beginning with $1,800,000 in 1917–18, the grants increased to their maximum in 1925, since when they have amounted annually to $3,000,000 for agricultural education, $3,000,000 for trade and industrial education, $1,000,000 for teachers' training and $200,000 for investigation. In 1918, 1,741 schools with 164,186 students were aided by Federal grants and in 1921 3,859 with 305,224 students. By 1928, stimulated by Federal aid, thirty-one States introduced compulsory part-time attendance for ages fourteen to sixteen or eighteen for vocational training. In 1934 vocational schools and classes enrolled as many as 1,100,000 students. In spite of this quantitative growth many American educationists were dissatisfied with the situation. All these adolescents were taking vocational courses in the comprehensive High schools under the system of credits and often did not follow any plan or method in selecting their subjects. The war with its enormous need for trained technicians made manifest the deficiencies of this system. Officer candidates in technical fields had no adequate knowledge of mathematics and on the whole there was an acute shortage of the technicians needed for a mechanised modern army. In 1940 Congress appropriated $15,000,000 for vocational training in occupations essential for national defence. Additional appropriations between 1940 and 1945 increased the total amount to $327,000,000 for trade and industrial training and $63,000,000 for agricultural training. It is estimated that during these five years about 11,500,000 young persons took advantage of these courses. We have mentioned the establishment of EDT in 1940 which after the declaration of war became ESMWT—Engineering, Science and Management War Training—under the control of the Office of Education. These courses were provided in colleges and Universities to aid in the efficient planning, production and research necessary in the industrial expansion. More than 1,000,000 students of both sexes were trained there. The war measures filled the gaps both in the quantity and quality of technical education and as in Russia made further rapid advance in industrialisation possible.

Higher education in the U.S.A. is organised quite differently from Europe. European Universities and Higher Technical Institutes are as a rule State institutions, or, as in England, State-aided, deriving most of their revenues from State grants. In consequence higher education in Europe is not expensive and the poorer students receive State scholarships or remission of fees. In the U.S.A. there are two different systems of higher education: State Universities and Colleges, State-maintained and free institutions, and independent Universities and Colleges maintained by various Churches or private foundations, charging rather high fees. All nine institutions of the colonial period are independent foundation Universities and include the most famous names: Harvard (1635), William and Mary (1692), Yale (1701), Princeton (1746), Columbia (1754), Pennsylvania (1755),[1] Brown (1764), Rutgers (1766) and Dartmouth (1769). If we add to this group the later foundation Universities— Cornell (1865), Johns Hopkins (1867), Leland Stanford (1891), and many not so well-known names, we at once realise that the largest and best institutions of higher learning in America are independent and private foundations. As an illustration of these Universities we give the figures for Columbia University during 1940–1. The number of resident students in the winter and spring sessions equalled 16,943; the number of professors and assistant professors 982; total academic staff 3,487. Income from endowments, $5,300,000; income from students' fees, etc., $3,800,000; gifts for current expenses, $700,000. It is noticeable that students' fees form a substantial item in the budget and can be paid by wealthy families only. All these great Universities are surrounded by residential Halls and Fraternity Houses for students where the latter receive full board for moderate charges. With very few exceptions students or their families have to provide the means, and it is an accepted practice for students to work during the vacations to pay for part of the costs. Entrance examinations are comparatively high, and only students from private secondary schools or those who took the academic stream in High schools are able to pass. The degrees of these Universities are highly prized in the U.S.A., and on the whole are equivalent to English degrees. Side by side with these few privileged Universities there are hundreds of Universities and Colleges connected with various Churches. Thus the Catholics control about 200 Colleges of various standards and five complete Universities. The Protestant Churches control more than 200 Colleges and small Universities and the University of Chicago (Baptists). These institutions are much smaller, not so expensive and their standards vary. Many students receive scholarships from their denominational foundations. About 200 Colleges of this group are theological institutions of their respective Churches. The third group of higher institutions are the State Universities and Higher Technical Institutes. All States, with the exception of Connecticut, Massachusetts,

---

[1] Was taken over by the State.

New Jersey, New York and Rhode Island, have State Universities (Pennsylvania University is partly an endowed institution). All State Universities are free and as a rule accept High school graduates without an examination. As a result the State Universities had to adopt the same attitude of "child-centred curriculum" which so much changed the character of the High school. They had to add to traditional academic disciplines courses of study covering every possible vocation. Even the Foundation Universities were compelled to make some concessions in the same direction. Columbia, for instance, in addition to the traditional faculties of Arts, Science, Law, Medicine, Theology and Engineering, has the following faculties: Architecture, Business, Journalism, Library Service, Dental and Oral Surgery, Pharmacy, Political Science. These new faculties, however, could be accepted even in England and can be organised in a true academic spirit. That can hardly be asserted of the courses on dressmaking, hairdressing, laundry-work or salesmanship. They simply do not belong to the University, unless the idea of a University is radically changed. But State Universities, being subordinated to State legislatures, have to cater for all vocational groups, and in spite of academic resistance had to create all kinds of academic certificates and degrees to cover every vocation. That is why the possession of an American degree does not necessarily lead to a profession. University graduates can be found working on the farm, in the mine, in a laundry or in a hairdressing saloon. From the popular American point of view that is the true interpretation of democracy; from the academic European point of view it is a degradation of University studies.

Many American educationists criticised this lowering of academic standards and started a movement of Junior Colleges. The latter are special American institutions absent in other countries. They have a two-years' course and are often attached to High schools or State Universities. After the first World War many private separate Junior Colleges were founded by various denominations. Their purpose is to complete the secondary education of the High school by offering a systematic course in the Arts and Sciences. In comparison with European standards they would be equivalent to the sixth form in England or *Classe de Philosophie* in France. There is a tendency to make the Junior College a preparatory stage for academic study in traditional University faculties. After the war the return of demobilised soldiers to Colleges and Universities swelled the enrolment to

2,000,000 students, of whom 800,000 were ex-soldiers. To aid the veterans Congress has passed an Act by which every qualified veteran receives $500 a year for tuition and $65 a month ($90 if married) for maintenance from Federal funds. Thus the policy of State scholarships was initiated as a special war measure, but evidently will become a permanent feature. A special Commission on Higher Education was appointed by President Truman in 1946 to "re-examine our system of higher education in terms of its objectives, methods and facilities; and in the light of the social rôle it has to play." The report of Harvard University on "General Education in a Free Community" in 1945 shows clearly the trend towards a sounder organisation of academic studies.

The supply and training of teachers is the most acute of all American educational problems. The forty-eight States have different systems of training, certification, methods of appointment and salary scales. Normal schools are maintained by all States; in addition there are many private institutions generally connected with the various Churches. The usual course is of two years after graduation from a High school. About 150 Normal schools are universally recognised as efficient and their certificates of graduation are accepted throughout the country by State Boards of Education. Each State in addition recognises some local Normal schools, which would not be recognised in other States. Teachers of High school grades must have a Bachelor's degree in Arts or Science, following at least four years' study in a College or University; in addition they have to produce a certificate of professional studies in an Education Department. Again nation-wide recognition is afforded only to about thirty Universities, including all the famous foundation Universities and Colleges and the largest State Universities. In addition each State recognises some local institutions including its own State University. Thus inter-State migration is possible only to graduates of the few best Universities. However, this requirement of recognised qualifications is only theoretical. In practice many local Boards appoint any suitable person who agrees to teach in a one-room school for an inadequate salary.

We mentioned previously the great inequality in conditions of service and remuneration. Teachers in District rural schools seldom possess adequate qualifications and experience; as soon as they acquire them after a year or two in the village school they leave it for a better post. Only well-qualified teachers in large city systems remain in the profession for life; the rest consider teaching as a temporary stopgap whilst looking for something better. The war emphasised that tendency by offering many well-paid war jobs. Since 1942 out of 1,200,000 teachers of the U.S.A. 350,000 have left the profession for other work. By necessity local Boards had to appoint uncertificated teachers in thousands. Whilst before the war only 2,300 teaching posts were filled with teachers holding emergency certificates, at present no less than 110,000 teachers possess no standard qualification. There is no remedy for this state of affairs except a nation-wide certification and salary scale. The social status of teachers is low, and in many localities they are treated by members of the Boards worse than domestic servants and are dismissed on the least provocation. On the other hand teachers of High schools in a city like New York enjoy salaries and status equal to those of other academic professions. The whole problem is closely connected with the outdated decentralisation of administration, discussed above.

Adult Education in the U.S.A. dates back to 1826, when the first Lyceum was founded in Massachusetts. It was a voluntary association of farmers and mechanics "for the purpose of self-culture, community instruction and mutual discussion of common public interests." Hundreds of lyceums were opened all over the country during the nineteenth century, but lately they have become commercialised and have partially lost their educational cultural influence. In 1885 the Chautauqua Institution was started in New York as a summer school for two months, followed by similar courses in other places, but most of these institutions also became commercialised later. University Extension was started in 1906 and now is a regular feature of most Universities. A special problem of adult education is the Americanisation of masses of immigrants, who could not speak English and often were illiterate. Since the discontinuance of mass immigration from Europe this form of adult education is gradually disappearing in the North, but is still a problem in the South in view of the large number of illiterate Negroes. During the war out of 17,000,000 men called up 2,000,000 were rejected on educational grounds as they were unable to read orders, signboards and regulations. The armed forces undertook an all-embracing programme of adult training and millions of enlisted men profited by their military service.

The account of American education would not be complete

without mentioning the great philanthropic foundations which influenced education throughout the world. The most famous are the following: (a) the Peabody Education Fund (1867), (b) John F. Slater Fund (1882), (c) the Carnegie Institution (1902) for the promotion of research and higher education, (d) the General Education Board (1903) established by John Rockefeller, (e) the Carnegie Foundation (1905), (f) the Phelps-Stokes Fund (1911), (g) the Rockefeller Foundation (1913), international, (h) the Carnegie Endowment for International Peace (1907), international. These foundations made available millions of dollars for all kinds of educational and scientific activities in all parts of the world.

In conclusion we may say that American leaders are conscious of the defects of their educational system and are endeavouring to realise in practice the full meaning of that "equality of educational opportunity" which was so often proclaimed before in gross contradiction to facts. Even the most difficult and controversial problem of Negro education and racial equality occupies the attention of Federal and State authorities with a view to doing justice to this handicapped section of the American population. The war has brought to the surface many hidden deficiencies and once they have become the focus of public discussion their reform is inevitable.

CHAPTER XV

THE EDUCATIONAL SYSTEM OF FRANCE

As we have seen in the historical chapters, France since the eighteenth century has been culturally divided into the traditional Catholic part and the revolutionary secularist part. The cultural schism was reinforced by the industrialisation of the country in the nineteenth century and the growth of the urban proletarian population. On the whole the agricultural countryside remained faithful to the old Catholic tradition and in politics as well as in education is more conservative, whilst the mining and industrial centres accepted the radical anti-clerical tradition of the French Revolution and in the twentieth century *en masse* joined the ranks of the Socialist and more recently the Communist parties. However, throughout the whole period of their historical opposition both antagonists were essentially French and were proudly conscious of their common heritage and common nationality. Whether Jesuit or Jansenist, Huguenot or Jacobin of the past or Catholic and Communist of the present, all French intellectuals shared the traditions of Descartes and Bossuet, Voltaire and Condorcet and the glory of the Grand Monarchy, the Great Revolution and the Napoleonic era. The same grandeur of conception, the same logical method of application and the same passionate love of France make these two traditions, so often bitterly opposed, twin daughters of the same mother. Descartes was educated in the Jesuit Collège de la Flèche, Molière and Voltaire, Camille Desmoulins and Robespierre were all graduates of the Jesuit Collège Louis-le-Grand, and by their example prove that the transfer from one tradition to another was possible because they were both French. In our own time we have examples of Socialist leaders educated in a Jesuit College and Archbishops educated in the secular *École Normale Supérieure*. When the principal of a Jesuit College was asked how he could be so friendly with his former pupil Paul Boncour, who became a Socialist and secularist, the Jesuit Father answered: "But he is one of the most distinguished anti-clericals who graduated from our institution."

In our study of French education we should constantly bear in mind that there are two French systems, one controlled by the State and independent of the Church and the other controlled by the Church and independent of the State. Both systems are highly centralised, have a similar structure and follow similar methods. In a word they are both French. After more than a century of embittered struggle a certain solution was found in the secularisation laws of 1882 and 1904 by which the public system was secularised and the Catholic system became voluntary and independent. However, the attempt of the State to break the control of the Church over the voluntary schools by prohibiting their maintenance by religious Orders did not bring the desired result. Catholic schools were reopened by individual teachers and groups of parents, but in fact they remained under the strict control of the Church. Although the Church could not reconcile itself with this division of control in education and denounced the public system as godless and immoral, there seemed to be no visible possibility of changing the balance in her favour. The State system became a national tradition, four-fifths of the compulsory age groups attended secular schools, and even in the field of secondary education the Catholic institutions were losing ground after the introduction of free education in the State *Lycées* and *Collèges* in 1936.

The reform of the whole system according to the idea of the *école unique* which was started before the war would have inevitably led to the increase of State control and secularisation. But the war and the defeat of France in 1940 have radically changed the situation in favour of the Catholic tradition. After the armistice Marshal Pétain became a virtual dictator of France under the German protectorate. From 1934 Marshal Pétain openly sided with the Catholic party and strongly condemned the public secular system of education. He deplored the industrialisation of France with the subsequent spread of Socialist and Communist doctrines and wanted the country to return to agriculture and the old traditional ways of life. It suited Hitler's plans for the new Europe and the Germans supported Pétain's policy with military and police measures. Pétain attempted to reverse the course of French history and to place the whole school system under the control of the Catholic Church. He introduced religious instruction as a compulsory subject into all public schools, appointed school chaplains and paid their salaries from public funds. The voluntary Catholic schools received grants from the State and thus the historical dualism was mitigated in favour of the Church.[1] It was an open violation of the French constitution and aroused strong opposition among teachers and parents. In spite of that the Catholic penetration of the public system became a fact which had to be considered by the new Government. The resistance movement was a coalition of all patriotic Frenchmen, including Catholics, Socialists and Communists. After the liberation the three parties formed a coalition Government which shelved the problem of religious instruction and made grants to Catholic schools in order to preserve the unity of the Resistance so important during the initial period of reconstruction. The Catholics naturally want to preserve the advantages they won under Pétain, whilst the secularists demand a return to the secularisation laws of the Third Republic. Although the Government officially proclaimed the re-establishment of the secular public school system the measures of the Vichy régime were in practice continued. The Catholic schools still receive the grants assigned to them by Pétain and religious instruction is still imparted in public schools by chaplains appointed by Pétain. But although the chaplains have the right of entry their salaries were suspended and religious instruction has to be given out of school hours on Thursdays, as was the general practice even under the secular law. The situation is admittedly a temporary compromise and the French parties are sharply divided on the way in which the old dualism should be resolved. The Socialists and especially the Communists favour a State monopoly with prohibition of denominational schools under Church control, whilst the Catholics want to integrate the voluntary Catholic schools within the State system with general acceptance of religious instruction and Church influence. It seems that neither of these radical solutions can be realised in the present situation and that the return to the old dualism of Catholic and secular systems is the only compromise possible without splitting France into an open civil war. With this main problem of French education yet unsolved France has returned to her old system of centralised administration and resumed the reforms interrupted by war.

In administration the public or State system of education in France can be taken as a classical example of centralisation. Its origin dates back to the laws of 1802 and 1808 by which Napoleon created the "Université de France" (*Imperiale* in his time).

---

[1] The percentage of pupils in Catholic Primary Schools rose from 16·5 in 1939–40 to 19·7 in 1941–2, and later even higher.

Napoleon quite consciously imitated the centralised organisation of the Society of Jesus. "I want," said Napoleon, "to create a corporation, not Jesuits, who had their sovereign in Rome, but Jesuits who would have no other ambition except to be useful, no other interest except public welfare. My aim in establishing an educational corporation [*corps enseignant*] is to be able to direct political and moral opinion." For this purpose old Universities with their tradition of independence were dissolved and a single *Université Impériale* (*de France*) embracing the whole school system was created, under the centralised control of the *Grand Maître de l'Université*, appointed by Napoleon. The whole country was divided into *Académies* with uniform administration subordinated to the central office in Paris. The subsequent reform of administration only changed the territorial distribution of *Académies* and abolished the *Grand Maître*, whose place was taken by the Minister of Public Instruction, or more recently of National Education, but the main features and the spirit of the Napoleonic organisation survived through all the revolutions and counter-revolutions of France.

As in the Napoleonic system, at the head of each *Académie* (sixteen in France and one in Algiers) stands its Rector, appointed by the President of the Republic and directly responsible to the Minister. The Rector has almost absolute powers within his *Académie* and directs the whole system from the *École Maternelle* to the University, including the supervision of private schools. Under his control are the Inspectors of the Academy, one for each *Département*. For primary schools, each district has a Primary Inspector subordinated to the Inspector of the Academy. For preschool institutions there are special sub-inspectors, usually women. For the purpose of general supervision of instruction from the centre, special Inspectors of National Education are appointed, who supervise the whole country in their respective subjects. By this organisation a complete unification of administration, school curricula and even methods of instruction is achieved. The local authorities as a rule have no participation in administration whatever. The municipality of Paris as an exception has a certain influence in the field of vocational education and by allotting additional sums from municipal rates has the best system of *Cours Complémentaires* in the country.

In the twentieth century the traditional rigidity of centralised administration was mitigated to some extent by the regionalist movement and the results of modern psychological research. In the last decade of the nineteenth century the old historical provinces of France with linguistic differences showed a revival of interest in their local languages and provincial antiquities. It was not a political movement with separatist tendencies; the Bretons, the Corsicans, the Basques and the Provençals were as patriotic citizens of France as the majority; but they insisted on the reform of administration on a regional basis with the introduction of local dialects as the medium of instruction in primary schools. However, in 1926, the Minister, De Monzie, quite definitely rejected the petition of Provençal delegates to permit the use of dialects and insisted on the French language as the basis of the unity of French culture. No concession in this matter could be contemplated, but the use of local antiquities and local songs in dialects was permitted and has lately become more popular with the introduction of new methods of instruction around a centre of interest.

Before the last war a marked regional difference was tolerated in Alsace-Lorraine, which rejoined France in 1918. The German language was used during the first two years of primary instruction and denominational schools, both Catholic and Protestant, were maintained from public funds. The attempt of M. Blum, whilst Minister of Education, to enforce the secularisation laws in Alsace met with such strong opposition that it was abandoned. During the war Alsace-Lorraine was incorporated in the German Reich and all traces of French culture and tradition were ruthlessly extirpated. The liberation of the two provinces resulted in a strong reaction against everything German and the Alsatians themselves want to be treated on equal terms with the rest of France. The question of secularisation having become a national issue has lost its local importance, and the future solution will evidently be sought on a national basis for the whole of France. The influence of psychological research and the introduction of child-centred methods of instruction mitigated the rigidity of centralisation from another direction and at present teachers and inspectors enjoy much more freedom of initiative and of local variation than ever before. Yet the tradition of central control and guidance is so strong that even now it is the Ministry which decides in what schools the deviation from the general uniformity should be allowed.

In educational finance the French system does not present such strict centralisation as in administration. In the field of secondary, technical and higher education the State is responsible for most of the expenditure and only a small proportion of funds is derived from local or private sources or fees. In the primary schools and *Cours Complémentaires* local authorities, on the contrary, participate to the amount of 30 per cent or more. The communes and municipalities are responsible for the cost of erecting or purchasing school buildings, the purchase of sites, the heating and lighting of classrooms; they pay in addition for the lodging of teachers. They also furnish school equipment and materials of instruction. Any innovation or any additional service such as medical inspection or vocational guidance introduced by a particular commune must be paid for from local rates. In Paris, for instance, better services in every respect are defrayed by the municipality. The *Départements* are obliged to maintain Normal school buildings, to pay additional salaries for their Primary Inspectors, to supply residences to the Directors of Normal schools and Academy Inspectors and to grant subsidies to vocational education. Salaries of the teachers in all grades are paid by the State and all personnel are civil servants. Although the French system of finance guarantees a certain minimum standard for all local authorities it does not preclude variations of equipment and organisation, and wealthier communes and municipalities have as a rule better services. This variation, however, is limited to primary schools and additional services; secondary education has the same equipment and status throughout the whole of France.

Of course these financial provisions did not embrace the Catholic schools. The Catholic primary schools were free as the law prohibited charging fees, but in fact Catholic parents contributed to their maintenance by voluntary efforts. Catholic secondary schools charged fees and boarding expenses, and since the State secondary schools were free after 1936, they were the preserve of the wealthy groups. Pétain by reintroducing fees in the State *Lycées* and *Collèges* and granting subsidies to Catholic secondary schools tried to equalise the conditions in the two groups and thus to check the transfer of pupils from expensive Catholic schools to gratuitous State schools. After the liberation free secondary education in State schools was resumed and the social differentiation between the two groups of schools will grow more and more marked with the unavoidable growth of costs and fees in the Catholic schools.

The educational system of France is undergoing a radical reform, and we have to describe both the pre-war and the new organisation to understand the difficulties and problems of the present period of transition. In this description we have to limit ourselves to the public State system, as the Catholic system on the whole duplicates the public system, but detailed information is not available. If we disregard the temporary setback under the Vichy régime, the old class system has been gradually approaching the *école unique* since 1928, and at present the State system is being rapidly reformed along the new lines. The old system presented two separate ways for the two social groups of the population. For the majority of the agricultural and industrial occupations, including manual workers and the lower clerical and commercial groups, the free school system, consisting of the *École Maternelle, École Primaire, École Primaire Supérieure* and *Cours Complémentaires* provided the only avenue in education which led directly to occupational activity in agriculture, industry or commerce. For the privileged economic groups the fee-paying system opened a wider choice. It consisted of Kindergartens and Preparatory classes attached to State *Lycées* and municipal *Collèges, Lycées* and *Collèges* proper and institutions of higher study, including the University and the so-called *Grandes Écoles*. Transfer from the first system to the second was extremely difficult from the organisational point of view, even disregarding the financial implications. Classical tradition and formal discipline dominated the curriculum of *Lycées* and *Collèges* up to 1925, when a modern side was added. Almost up to the last war the selection of pupils was mainly decided by the ability to pay fees, and only during the last years with the abolition of fees and the closing of the preparatory classes were the pupils of the *Lycées* selected for their scholastic ability. By tradition the aim of French secondary education was to impart that *culture générale* which so distinguishes French intellectuals. But the attainment of logical clarity of thought and style demanded human sacrifice, and only about one-third of the secondary pupils who entered used to pass the final examination of the *Baccalauréat*, without counting those who were lost on the way. Secondary education was centred around the ideal of an intellectual élite which paradoxically was selected on the ground of financial ability! After 1930 the situation was much better, but still the pupils were sacrificed for the ideal. The majority of secondary-school pupils were "wastage," or as the French say *déclassés*; they could not join the *élite* and they were not prepared for commercial or industrial occupations. The same methods of intellectual selection were continued in the Universities and the

Grandes Écoles. The result was a brilliant minority of successful graduates and a large number of *déclassés*.

Psychological investigations during the last years before the war made it quite clear even to the confirmed adherents of the old tradition that a radical reform of secondary education was imperative. On the other hand the increasing industrialisation of France and the introduction of new methods of production both in industry and agriculture demanded the training of large classes of technicians, which the old system failed to do. In 1936 the Ministry started an experiment in fifty French towns involving about 200 classes. All children of twelve years who passed the elementary school certificate examination were admitted into the so-called "orientation classes" where the curriculum was divided into three branches with a common core. In addition one branch had Latin and no modern language, another a modern language without Latin and the third no foreign languages at all and a practical-technical bias. After a short period of observation the children were directed to one of the branches for a year and then were transferred to another branch if necessary, and if the parents consented. There was no compulsion in transfer, but parents were advised on the suitability of their choice. The results of the experiment were very successful, but the war and the Vichy Government terminated it for the time being. However, preparations for the reform were continued both in Algiers after its liberation by the Free French Government and in France by the members of the Resistance. They worked on similar lines, and when France was liberated in August 1944, both groups of reformers were united in a *Commission d'études*, with M. Paul Langevin as president, and MM. Henri Piéron and Henri Wallon as vice-presidents. All three were distinguished professors of the *Collège de France*, Langevin an outstanding humanist and Piéron and Wallon well-known psychologists. Politically they belonged to the Left, and Langevin was even a member of the Communist Party. A national institute of scientific research was founded within the Ministry of Education, and the *Conseil Supérieur de l'Instruction Publique* was reorganised to secure the representation of various teachers' unions and professional bodies. The new organisations started work immediately, and in 1945 presented a plan of reform which radically changed the old French tradition of intellectual training for *culture générale*. The reformers recognised the danger of the formalism and social division of the old system which led to a premature senility of the French spirit and the disunity of social classes. As M. Jean Bayet, Director General of National Education, said in September 1945, the results of this formalism show

> the signs of senility, and a lassitude of spirit among the children. For France it is very grave, as this tendency changes the character of *l'esprit Français*, results in categorisation, specialisation of faculties, a Cartesian division and finally a divorce from life. We have arrived at the redoubtable formalism of the *Grandes Écoles* on the one side and an insufficiency of technical education on the other. And that is the reason, not political considerations, why I am annoyed with our Governments which let people believe that mechanical occupations are inferior and allowed French parents to think that the *Baccalauréat* was the ideal and that it is possible to live outside actual life without applying the spirit to matter.

This criticism pointed out two lines of approach in the new plan. First, change of methods, the introduction of child-centred instruction based on living individuals and using active methods in conformity with the results of psychological research. Secondly, the introduction of manual work and technical subjects as an equivalent variation of the old academic curriculum based on classical languages. In French circumstances this change amounts to a real revolution in education, and it was so defined by French leaders themselves. The reform was launched in practice with the establishment of 190 new classes of the first year of secondary education in ninety towns and communes of France in September 1945. These so-called *Les Sixièmes Nouvelles* worked the whole year on new lines and their success was so marked that the initial resistance of many teachers and parents gave way to general enthusiasm. In September 1946, the original 190 classes continued as *Les Cinquièmes Nouvelles*, whilst 260 new classes started as *Sixièmes*. The reform, however, met with strong opposition on the part of the majority of secondary school masters and the Catholics. After reaching its peak in 1951 with 800 *Classes Nouvelles*, the reform was suspended by the Ministry and only five *Lycées Pilotes* were allowed to continue the experiment. In spite of the suspension of the general reform, the experience of the *Classes Nouvelles* influenced all secondary schools and changed their old-fashioned methods. At the same time, the raising of the status of the old *Écoles Primaires Supérieures* to that of *Collèges Modernes* without Latin, changed the whole structure of the French secondary education. The reform of the secondary stage is only the most important part of the plan, which envisages the regrading of the whole system from the *École Maternelle* up to and including the Universities and the *Grandes Écoles*. We give here a diagram of the Plan of the reform as it was published by Roger Gal, the secretary of the Commission Langevin, in his publication *La Réforme de l'Enseignement* (1946).

PLAN OF THE REFORM OF NATIONAL EDUCATION ACCORDING TO THE PROJECT OF THE LANGEVIN COMMISSION, 1946

	Ages		Adult Education
Higher grades	23 22	3rd cycle	Grandes Écoles d'Application, Research and Agrégation.
	21 20	2nd cycle	Licences—Instituts: technical, scientific, literary —pedology, medicine, law.
	19 18	1st cycle	Pre-university course. Preparatory studies (literature, sciences, medicine, arts) Technical Schools. Normal Schools.
Secondary grades	17 16 15	Sections	2nd cycle—Determination Practical and vocational— apprenticeship — industry, agriculture, commerce Theoretical—technical, classical, modern, artistic.
	14 13 12	13–15	1st cycle—Orientation Options — manual work, Latin, Greek, modern language, science
	11	11–13	Observation
Primary grades	10 9 8 7	École Primaire	9–11 Middle course 7–9 Elementary course
	6 5 4		École Maternelle

The first three years of a child's life are spent as a rule in the family, but with the increasing employment of women in industrial occupations a certain number of crèches should be established in industrial centres as part of the system of national education.

Examinations as they are known at present should disappear according to the plan; they are still used during the period of transition, but with certain modifications. The old *Certificat d'études primaires* has been divided into two sections, the first taken at the age of eleven years qualifies for admission to the secondary stage, the second part is taken at the age of fourteen by those who did not pass to secondary education. With the progress of the reform all children will pass to the secondary stage at eleven and the old *Certificat* will lose its significance. At the age of fifteen plus those pupils who do not continue their secondary education still take the examination for the *Brevet élémentaire*, which is the old examination of the Higher Elementary schools. At the end of their studies in a *Lycée* or *Collège* the pupils take the formidable examination for the *Baccalauréat*. After completing the six forms of secondary education they take the first part of the *Baccalauréat*, which entitles them to pass to the terminal class, which is either the *classe de philosophie* or the *classe de mathématiques*. Then they take, usually at the age of eighteen to nineteen, the second part of the *Baccalauréat*, which entitles them to enter the Universities. For entrance to the *Grandes Écoles* they have to pass an additional competitive examination which requires special preparation. In 1946 a technical *Baccalauréat* was added which was selected by 2,200 candidates and which broke the centuries-old monopoly of classical studies as the only avenue to higher education. The plan of the reform envisages a substitution for the *Baccalauréat* of a *Diplome de fin d'études du second degré* for all theoretical branches (technical, classical, modern and artistic) which will lead to the first cycle of higher education. Thus the severe intellectual grinding known in France as *bachotage* which warped so many promising young lives will pass for ever, to the great relief of future generations.

The pre-school institutions of France have a long history and were the most modern part of the system. They were started in the thirties of the nineteenth century under the name of *Salles d'Asile*. The State started subsidising them in 1837 and their numbers rapidly increased. In 1836 there were only 24 *Salles d'Asile*, in 1837, 262; and in 1883, 5,830 with 679,085 children.

In 1881 they were renamed *Écoles Maternelles*, and since then they have become an integral part of the public system. Historically there were two kinds of pre-school institutions. The *Écoles Maternelles* proper were independent institutions under the supervision of special inspectors. The *Classes Enfantines* were kindergartens attached to primary schools or preparatory classes of *Lycées* and *Collèges*. Kindergartens attached to secondary schools were closed, together with preparatory classes, even before the war and the kindergartens of the primary schools are giving way to *Écoles Maternelles* proper. The plan proposes to make their provision universal (at present about 60 per cent of children three to six attend these institutions) and to raise the age to seven years so that they will be included within the legislation for compulsory attendance. The methods and the equipment in the latest *Écoles Maternelles* could rival the best modern institutions in other countries.

The old *École Primaire* served two quite different purposes. For the great majority of its pupils it was the only preparation for adult life and citizenship. Of necessity it had to include a minimum of general education and civic training and attempted to impart a well-rounded education by the age of fourteen. After the reforms of the inter-war period the *École Primaire* also served as a preparatory step for secondary education, but only a small minority of pupils could pass to the secondary stage. The minority thus had to be trained for the qualifying examination at the age of twelve, whilst the majority had to continue for another two years in the senior division. The two purposes were difficult to combine in the same course and the primary schools suffered from the lack of unity in the curriculum and the inadequacy of methods of instruction which could not pursue two aims at once. The new reform does away with this duality of purposes and makes the primary school a universal stage of training in the tools of knowledge for all children. At eleven plus they all pass to the first cycle of observation. The old *École Primaire Supérieure* and *Cours Complémentaires* even before the war were housed in the same buildings with the *Collèges* and in fact became parts of secondary education. Now they will disappear as separate institutions and are being incorporated in the first cycle of the secondary stage.

The *Lycées* and *Collèges* will remain as theoretical sections of the second cycle of secondary education but their internal structure will be changed. First the lower four forms will become the general cycle of orientation and will include all children irrespective of their abilities or social origin. The three upper forms will lose their strictly academic character and will have four sections: classical, modern, technical and artistic. The last two are new additions. The *Lycées* are perhaps the most French of all French institutions. They date back to Napoleonic legislation when the Emperor dissolved the Republican Central schools with their technical bias and created the classical secondary schools under the title of *Lycées*. Since then they have tenaciously preserved their original atmosphere in spite of all the political changes in the nineteenth century. The *Lycées* are national institutions entirely maintained from State funds. The later secondary schools, the *Collèges*, on the contrary were established by municipalities on the lines of the *Lycées*, but did not enjoy the same status. They are maintained by the municipalities with a State subsidy. Teachers' salaries are paid by the State. The teachers of the *Lycées* are more experienced and better qualified than those of the *Collèges*. In the *Lycées* they are either *agrégés* or *titulaires*, whereas in the *Collèges* they are either *licenciés* or *délégués*, young graduates serving their apprenticeship. The best teachers are transferred to the *Lycées* after serving the probationary period in the *Collèges*. In contrast to *Lycées*, which have identical status and curriculum, the *Collèges* have local variations and often introduce some novel features which are lacking in the *Lycées*. Since 1881 secondary schools for girls have been renamed and gradually remodelled on the lines of *Lycées* and *Collèges* and their numbers have grown steadily, but even now there are only about 200 girls' schools of these types to 360 boys' schools. In small towns not possessing separate *Collèges* for girls, the latter are accepted in boys' *Collèges*, but as a rule France does not favour co-education. Since the abolition of fees and the closure of preparatory classes the historical difference between the *Lycées* and *Collèges* has been gradually disappearing and with the realisation of the new plan will disappear altogether. The horizontal division of secondary education into the four years' first cycle and three years' second cycle will change the structure of the old *Lycées* and *Collèges* very radically. As the first cycle will become universal and compulsory with the raising of the age to fifteen years (present limits of compulsory attendance are from six to fourteen years), thousands of new classes will have to be opened which will have no second cycle and in consequence the old organisation of *Lycées* and *Collèges* could be retained only in the upper three forms. But even here the introduction of new

sections and selective subjects will change the traditional atmosphere. The *Lycées* and *Collèges* as typical French creations in
educational practice have fulfilled their historical function and
have to give way to new secondary schools more in accordance
with modern democracy and the increasing need for technical
training.

Technical and vocational education is the most recent branch
of the French system. The Central schools instituted in 1794
under the influence of Condorcet introduced drawing and
scientific subjects with a technical bias and did pioneering work
for ten years. But in 1804 Napoleon closed them and created
the classical *Lycées* instead. France lost her chance of leading
Europe in technical education at the secondary stage. There were
a few higher institutions of the first rank, but technical education
for the intermediate class of technicians, foremen and managers
was quite inadequate for modern needs. Just before the world
war of 1914–18 France possessed only six schools of arts and
trades (*Écoles d'Arts et Métiers*), six intermediate vocational
schools and eighty-six lower vocational schools educating a total
of about 15,000 boys and girls. It was only in 1919 that the
Astier Law was passed which gave a charter to technical education. In a few years France was covered by vocational and
technical schools, both full-time and part-time, on the model of
the German *Berufschulen*. During the last years before the war
technical post-primary education won its place alongside academic *Lycées* and *Collèges* and in many towns vocational and
academic courses were organised on parallel lines in the same
school buildings. According to the new plan this integration of
technical and academic education will become a general feature
of the French secondary system. In the first cycle of orientation
from eleven years up to the end of compulsory attendance at
fifteen, manual work and pre-vocational training will be of a
more general kind, helping the pupil to find his trade or to choose
a branch of the theoretical curriculum. In the second cycle of
determination from fifteen to eighteen years the adolescent either
enters a practical training for apprenticeship in agriculture,
industry or commerce, or a theoretical branch which includes a
technical section side by side with a classical, modern or artistic.
After eighteen years the graduates of theoretical sections enter
higher institutions—Technical Schools proper and Higher Technical Institutes. Thus within a generation France has radically
changed her attitude towards technical education from previous

neglect to a full recognition of equivalence with traditional secondary education. The institution in 1946 of the technical *Baccalauréat* put a final legal stamp to this change.

Higher education is also affected by the plan of the Langevin Commission. The old medieval Universities of France with their corporate life and academic self-government were dissolved by the French Revolution, and Napoleon created a single *Université Impériale* for the whole country with a highly centralised control. In Paris and the larger provincial towns separate faculties were established as special higher institutions and the old *universitas* either in the sense of a community of masters and scholars or in the sense of a unity of all branches of academic learning did not exist in France for a century. Only in 1896 were the separate faculties again united into a university with limited self-government. The unity and independence of scientific research was thus restored, but the Rectors of the Universities, being at the same time Rectors of the *Académies*, are still appointed by the Minister of Education and not elected by the professors. The professors themselves are also appointed by the Minister on the recommendation of the faculties. All French Universities have the four traditional faculties of letters, sciences, law and medicine and the University of Strasbourg, as an exception, has also a faculty of divinity. All technical and applied branches of studies are supplied in separate institutions known as the *Grandes Écoles*, which as a rule are controlled by their respective Ministries. Thus the Ministry of the Navy controls *l'École du Génie Maritime, l'École Navale* and *l'École de la Marine marchande*; the War Office *l'École Polytechnique, de Saint Cyr, de Saumur*, etc.; the Ministry of Colonies *l'École Coloniale*; the Ministry of Agriculture the *Institut Agronomique*; the Ministry of Education controls only one school of this group, *l'École Normale Supérieure*. The entrance examinations to all these institutions are highly competitive and require as a rule an additional year of preparation after the *Baccalauréat*. The *Grandes Écoles* are unique in the world because of the high standards of their selected students and of their professors. They provide France with her brilliant élite of administrators, experts and intellectual leaders. In this respect the rôle of the *École Normale Supérieure* is especially important. In spite of its name it is not a school of higher pedagogical studies; it is a nursery of that *culture générale* and *esprit Français* of which Frenchmen are so proud. When the author visited the library of this famous school in 1947 he saw thousands of volumes of Greek and Latin authors, thousands of volumes on literature, history, mathematics and sciences, and noticed only one volume on education, which incidentally was in English and dealt with English secondary education! Nevertheless the graduates of this school form the élite of the teaching profession and supply the country with many national leaders in all branches of thought and action.

The severe intellectual grinding and the long period of preparation required by the French Universities for entrance result in social selection of students from wealthy and cultured homes. Of 100,466 students in July 1948, 18 per cent were sons and daughters of members of the learned professions, 16 per cent of commercial and industrial families, 27 per cent of civil servants, 10 per cent of business clerks and salesmen, and only 1.5 per cent of industrial workers and 5 per cent of farmers. Of the four countries, France, England, America and Russia, France is the least democratic in her student body. The French leaders are conscious of this fact, and the new plan endeavours not only to reform the structure of higher education, but also to make it available to wider circles of the population. The reform of secondary education and the *Baccalauréat* will provide the Universities with new groups of students coming from social classes debarred until now from higher education.

The new plan divides higher education into three stages: the first cycle (eighteen to twenty) of preparatory studies for learned professions and of technical and normal schools training teachers and technicians of intermediate grades. The second cycle (twenty to twenty-two) is constituted of faculties preparing for the *licences* (first degrees) in arts, sciences, medicine, law and technology. The third cycle includes the *Grandes Écoles d'Application*, preparation for *Agrégation* and research work. Thus the *Grandes Écoles* will form the third stage of higher education and will accept only students possessing the *licence*. *Agrégation*, which until now was a special State examination for University graduates, will be included in the University course as a third cycle. The graduates of the third cycle will receive Diplomas of the *Grandes Écoles* and special Diploma of higher studies or research.

In this connection it is interesting to note that France already possesses an old institution of research, the *Collège de France*, which occupies a unique position. It is a State institution, controlled and maintained by the Ministry of Education. All professors are appointed by the Minister from the ranks of the most eminent representatives of all academic disciplines. Once appointed, however, the professor is entirely free to carry out any project of research in any subject he chooses. He has no obligation to deliver lectures or to publish the results of his research, but in fact they usually do both. Their public lectures are of such a high standard that all the intellectual élite of Paris attends them. There are no examinations or certificates connected with these lectures, they are free and public. The prestige and reputation of the professors and their associates are so high that whenever the Government wants expert advice they turn to the *Collège de France*. Although it is side by side with the Sorbonne and has intimate connections with it, the *Collège* is quite independent of the University of Paris. This combination of centralised control with absolute freedom of research has no parallel in other countries.

The old system of teachers' training in France was sharply divided into two watertight compartments which reflected the division into the old elementary and secondary education. The primary-school teachers were trained in *Écoles Normales* which as a rule accepted pupils of *l'École Primaire Supérieure* who passed the examination for the *Brevet élémentaire*, approximately at the age of sixteen years. After three years' training both theoretical and practical they received the *Brevet supérieure*, qualifying them for a temporary appointment as teachers of primary schools. After a probationary period they are appointed to permanent posts. The teachers for secondary schools received a much longer and quite different training. All secondary teachers have to pass the *Baccalauréat* and study for the *licence* in the Universities. Having received the *licence d'enseignement* at a University the *licencié* could be appointed to a *Collège* as a teacher in his subject. For an appointment to a permanent post at a *Lycée* further study and the additional qualification of *Agrégation* was necessary. It was a severe competitive State examination in contrast to the University degree—*licence*. Only a very limited number were allowed by the State to receive *Agrégation*, in relation to the number of vacancies in the *Lycées* or in administration. The two groups of teachers —primary and secondary—formed two distinct classes both socially and intellectually, and any interchange between them was quite impossible. With the introduction of the *École unique* it became necessary to have a single teaching profession based on common training and traditions. For this purpose the Langevin Commission proposed to attach the normal schools to the Universities as a part of the first cycle with the entrance requirements equivalent to *Baccalauréat*. Secondary-school teachers as before would proceed to the second cycle for the *licence* and the selected group to the third cycle for *Agrégation*. In this way all teachers will have University education and the transfer from one group to another will be facilitated.

Since the liberation a Department of popular Education and Youth Movement has been created in the Ministry of National Education, whose task is to establish in all the great cities cultural centres for the popularisation of culture among adults and to create cultural institutes and youth centres to be at the disposal of all youth movements. Under the Vichy Government departments of Youth and Sports (*Commissariats à la Jeunesse* and *aux Sports*) were under the Ministry of Foreign Affairs and promoted pre-military and nationalist training of youth. On the whole the attempt of Vichy to capture French Youth was unsuccessful, as only about 7 per cent of young Frenchmen joined these organisations, controlled by Fascist and Catholic agencies. Since the liberation, on the contrary, the youth movement has grown very rapidly and is sponsored both by Catholics and Socialists and Communists.

France is looking quite definitely towards the future and establishing a social and educational equality of opportunity. But in contrast to America and Russia, Frenchmen want to preserve the high quality of their education based on humanist tradition. Neither the American pragmatism nor the Russian Marxism has a chance to supplant the tradition of *culture générale*, common both to the Catholics and secularists. In this respect France can be compared with England in introducing radical reforms without discarding the values of her historical heritage.

CHAPTER XVI

THE EDUCATIONAL SYSTEM OF THE U.S.S.R.

The present Union of Socialist Soviet Republics is a federation of fifteen [1] constituent national republics, including besides the three branches of the Russian people many nationalities or various origins, backgrounds and traditions. Nevertheless all territories of the U.S.S.R., with the sole exception of Subcarpathian Russia (Ukraine), were at one or another time a part of historical Russia or later of the Russian Empire. And if the identification of the U.S.S.R. with Russia in a strict sense of definition is not now correct, the present international federation in its structure, both political and economic, has grown out of the former Russian Empire. Again, the U.S.S.R. is the historical cradle of many ancient cultures, different in language and religious tradition, but the Russian language and Russian cultural tradition were dominant in the past and are dominant at present. The U.S.S.R. was moulded and fashioned by Russians (both Russian-born and Russified non-Russians) on a Russian background. And if other nationalities now fully participate as equal members, they can do so by accepting the common tradition of the Russian past. The Soviet educational system shares these characteristics. Imparted in as many as 180 languages, drawing its contents from the various national cultures, in its form and organisation the Soviet school system is Russian in direct historical descent from pre-revolutionary Russia. Even the Marxian ideology, permeating both the multi-national content and the Russian form, is adapted to Russian conditions and is a Russian variation of the original doctrine of Marx. This fundamental fact of identity between historical Russia and the present international Marxist Soviet Union should be borne in mind in order to understand the theory and practice of Soviet education. We have pointed out before the utilitarian and secular tradition of Russian education since Peter the Great, the democratic tendency of the Russian intelligentsia and local authorities and the egalitarian attitude towards women. These features are as much a part of the Russian past as some reactionary Tsars who attempted to divert the Russian education into the narrow channels of Russification, autocratic government and dogmatic Orthodox creed.

[1] The Fino-Karelian S.S.R. was recently again incorporated in the R.S.F.S.R.

The original Russian State system of education was founded by Catherine II, in 1783. It was free, secular, co-educational and common to all groups of the population including the serfs. Alexander I in 1802 reorganised the schools under the direct influence of the famous scheme of Condorcet. The system consisted of primary, intermediate and secondary schools, each stage following the previous one. All schools were free and common to all groups. After the completion of secondary education they were free to proceed to the Universities. For poor students many State scholarships were established. It was the first democratic *école unique* in Europe, but unfortunately for Russia Nicholas I in 1829 reshaped the whole system on class lines and prohibited secondary education for the serfs and lower orders. In the sixties Alexander II made several attempts to reintroduce the *école unique*, but unsuccessfully. After the revolution of 1905 the State Duma passed several laws leading to the establishing of a democratic common school. The Soviet Government accepted the ideals of the radical Russian intelligentsia and in 1918 established a democratic *école unique*, co-educational and secular and free in all stages.

In administration Tsarist Russia was highly centralised and the local authorities, the municipalities since Catherine II and the county authorities or *Zemstvo* since Alexander II, had a very limited form of self-government. Secondary and higher education was always under the direct control of the Ministry of Public Instruction and only in the field of elementary and adult education was there a certain scope for local initiative and independence of the centre. The non-Russian territories were treated in the same way as the Russian provinces and the national minorities, although not persecuted, had no legal status as separate nationalities. In Chapter III we described the policy of the Soviet Government as regards the non-Russian nationalities from the linguistic point of view, and mentioned that each of the sixteen constituent Republics and many autonomous Republics have school-systems in their own native languages. This linguistic differentiation was accompanied by administrative decentralisation. Up to 1933 there was no Union or Federal organ for educational administration and each Republic had an independent Commissariat of Education. In 1933 "The Federal Committee of Higher Technical Education" was established which started the movement towards centralisation and Federal control. During the war all Commissariats were renamed Ministries and a new Ministry of Higher Education was created as the Union Federal organ. All higher institutions throughout the U.S.S.R. are maintained and controlled at present by this Ministry. All technical and vocational schools of secondary level are maintained by respective Ministries of the constituent Republics, but as regards methods and organisation are subordinated to the Federal Ministry. The lower technical and vocational schools are subordinated to the Federal Ministry of Labour Reserves, created after the war. Thus only the institutions of general education, pre-school, primary, secondary and adult, are administered by the Ministries of Education of the sixteen Republics, independently of Federal control. But the centralised administration of higher and vocational education and the unifying influence of the Federal Communist Party resulted in a uniform structure of the school system throughout the U.S.S.R. in spite of the sixteen independent Ministries of Education. Within each constituent Republic the pre-school institutions and the primary and secondary schools are directly administered by provincial and autonomous regional Departments of Education under the supervision of the Republican Ministry. Adult Education in each Republic is directly administered by the Ministry of Education. Thus a certain combination of centralisation with devolution of powers is achieved and all public authorities, local, Republican and Federal, share in control and maintenance of educational institutions.

On the eve of the Revolution of 1917 the Russian school system was in process of transition. The class system established by Nicholas I in 1829 was still unreformed and consisted of two separate ways, one for the masses, the other for the intelligentsia. The Elementary school both urban and rural had a four years' course for the ages eight to twelve. The Higher Elementary school, in towns only, had also a four years' course for the ages twelve to sixteen. From these schools the boys could enter the Teachers' Institutes or Technical Secondary schools. For the intelligentsia there were two kinds of Secondary schools—the Gymnasia and the Real schools. The entrance age was nine after a qualifying examination. The Gymnasia had eight forms (with the Preparatory form nine) and the Real school seven forms (or eight). The graduates of the classical Gymnasia at the age of eighteen, having received their matriculation, were free to enter the Universities. The graduates at the Real schools could either enter the Higher Technical Institutes after a competitive examination or the Universities after passing an examination in Latin, which was absent in their curriculum. There was a possibility of transfer from the Elementary to the Secondary system, but with a loss of two years. Thus from the Elementary school at the age of twelve boys could enter the first form of Secondary schools (for ten-year-olds) or from the Higher Elementary school boys (age sixteen) could enter the fourth form of the Real school (age fourteen), but in practice it did not work. The State Duma wanted to raise the standard of the two stages of the elementary system to that of the first six forms of the secondary system and make the three upper forms of Secondary schools into a third stage of a common school. The war and Revolution delayed the reform until 1918, when the Soviet Government established the Unified Labour school of two steps: the first, five years, and the second, four years. In 1923 the grades were changed into the School of the First Grade with four years and the School of the Second Grade with five years. The latter was divided into the First Cycle—three years, and Second Cycle—two years.

Actual practice, however, did not follow the Act of 1923. In the rural districts the School of the First Grade (four years) was in fact the old Elementary school. In urban districts the First Grade with the First Cycle of the Second Grade formed the "Seven-years' school" or the incomplete Secondary school, whilst the two grades joined together formed the "Nine-years' school" or the complete Secondary school. With a later addition of one year to the Secondary school the Soviet system has crystallised into three kinds of general schools: four years—Primary school—in all rural areas; seven years—incomplete Secondary school—in all urban and industrial districts and in half the rural areas, and the ten years—complete Secondary school—in all larger towns and industrial centres. Compulsory attendance was introduced in 1930 for the ages eight to twelve in rural areas and eight to fifteen in all industrial and urban districts. After the war compulsory attendance was extended to the age group seven to eight and at present the whole course of general education comprises eleven years—seven to eighteen, and not ten as before. The ages three to seven are catered for by an extensive system of kindergartens which exist not only in towns but on all collective farms in the country. Attendance at kindergartens is voluntary, but in 1954, 1,746,800 children of three to seven years attended about 30,096 kindergartens in the U.S.S.R. The number of pupils of both sexes in the four primary grades amounted to

13,579,000 in 1956. In the three intermediate grades the number of pupils in 1956 grew to 9,268,000 and in the three upper grades (8–10) to 5,253,000. The comparatively small number of pupils in the primary grades is the result of war. Compulsory attendance 7–15 is enforced throughout the U.S.S.R. and about 60 per cent of an age group pass into the upper three grades. This is, so far as the general schools are concerned, without the system of vocational education.

The pre-school system as State-sponsored and controlled is entirely the creation of the Soviet Government. Before the revolution of 1917 only a few private kindergartens (about 250) existed in the larger cities for the infants of the intelligentsia. The Soviet Government made the kindergarten a mass institution for two reasons. First the importance of early childhood for moral and civic training was generally recognised comparatively recently, and secondly the increasing participation of women in industrial occupations demanded their release from domestic duties. As the new Regulations of 1944 say: "The Kindergarten is a State institution for the Soviet civic education of children between the ages of three and seven, pursuing the aim of ensuring their all-round development and education. At the same time the Kindergarten facilitates the participation of women in the work of the State and industry, in cultural and social-political life." In addition to general training of character and mental abilities the Soviet kindergarten teaches children clean and orderly habits in their work and handling of their toys and tools. It promotes team work against the individualistic tendencies of young children and instils the love of their Soviet homeland and its leaders, especially Stalin and Lenin. Great importance is attached to singing and musical exercises and gradual training for work.

The primary school has a four years' course and since 1944–5 with the lowering of the compulsory age to seven the primary stage ends at eleven plus instead of the twelve plus of the Russian traditional Elementary school. This brings the Soviet practice into line with the break of eleven plus in England and France. In rural areas, as stated, the Primary school is still an independent institution, but in industrial and urban centres it is part of the seven-years' incomplete Secondary school or of the ten- (or recently eleven-) years' complete Secondary school. The organisation and curriculum in the first four years are identical whether in separate Primary schools or Primary departments of Secondary schools, so that the transfer from a rural Primary school to the fifth form of Secondary schools is made on the same condition of passing the final examination in Russian (oral and written) and Arithmetic (oral and written). The curriculum is similar to that in Western Europe with special attention to the study of languages. The international structure of the U.S.S.R. requires proficiency in two or even three languages for the majority of Soviet citizens. Only the Russian children in purely Russian provinces of the R.S.F.S.R. are unilingual; the Russian children resident in other constituent or autonomous Republics have to learn the language of the Republic in which they reside. The non-Russian children throughout the Union have to learn Russian in the Primary school. For the Ukrainians and the White Russians it is comparatively easy, but for the Turkish-speaking children it is difficult and requires a greater effort. Certain minority groups have to learn even three languages; for example the Jews of the Ukrainian Republic have to learn Yiddish, Ukrainian and Russian; the Armenians in Georgia have to learn Armenian, Russian and Georgian. In spite of these difficulties proficiency in Russian among the non-Russians is very high and gives them the opportunity of working throughout the territory of the U.S.S.R.

The incomplete Secondary school (seven years) is not yet universal in all parts of the Union, but gradually it will become the basic school, compulsory in the rural areas as well. Even now the peasantry demands its universal distribution and as mentioned above about 60 per cent of an age group pass into the fifth form. The curriculum, in addition to such subjects as history, geography and natural science started in the Primary school, includes algebra, geometry, constitution of the U.S.S.R., physics, chemistry and one foreign language (either English, French or German). In rural areas the curriculum is the same but all subjects have an agricultural bias. After the completion of the course the pupils pass an internal examination for a final certificate of an incomplete Secondary school. The certificate entitles them to pass into the eighth form of a complete Secondary school or into the Technical High schools after a qualifying examination.

During the last years complete secondary schools were opened in many rural areas and attendance in the upper grades rose to about 60 per cent of an age group. In theory any pupil of the incomplete Secondary school with a leaving certificate can enter the eighth form, but in practice the pupils of the lower forms of complete Secondary schools have an advantage. Their families reside in the city, they continue their studies in the same school without changing their surroundings, their school-fellows and their masters. The pupils of incomplete Secondary schools in small provincial towns or rural areas in order to continue their secondary education have to change their residence and their schools. It is also connected with boarding expenses should the pupil have no relatives in the larger city. In actual practice therefore the upper forms of Secondary schools cater for their own pupils, accepting very few additional provincial scholars from outside. The curriculum of the first seven forms is identical with that of the incomplete Secondary school, but the buildings, equipment and qualifications of the teachers are considerably better in large city Secondary schools than in smaller provincial incomplete schools. It is inevitable even in Soviet circumstances that pupils of these city schools come from more cultured homes and have additional facilities for continued education than the sons of the collective farm workers. In addition to subjects taught in the lower seven forms the upper forms include trigonometry, astronomy, and pay special attention to physics and chemistry. In teaching mathematics much importance is attached to its application in technology and agriculture. Natural science includes the theory of Darwinism in the ninth form.

In 1944 internal matriculation examinations were introduced in all complete Secondary schools. Graduates who received excellent marks and were awarded gold or silver medals are accepted in all Higher Institutions without any additional examination; other graduates have to pass a qualifying examination of the respective Institution. Since 1944 co-education has been discontinued in complete Secondary schools and in 1947 separate education of the sexes was introduced in about 400 larger cities of the U.S.S.R. This resulted in a certain differentiation of the curriculum with greater emphasis on military training in boys' schools than was possible in the co-educational incomplete Secondary schools in smaller towns. This reform was the result of war destruction and the necessity of military training of boys. With the reconstruction of normal conditions co-education was reintroduced in 1954 all over the U.S.S.R. In the past the upper forms of secondary schools charged fees, which in addition to other reasons stated above made the upper three forms a privileged group. With the recent abolition of fees and gradual foundation of ten-years schools in rural areas secondary education has become available to the rural population as well.

To counteract the inevitable social differentiation among entrants to the Higher Institutions the Soviet Government created special Secondary schools for adults. It is for the second time during the Soviet régime that promotion of students from the working class became necessary. In 1918 in order to create a new intelligentsia more closely connected with the proletariat the Soviet government initiated the so-called "Workers' Faculties" where adult workers received an intensive and short course of secondary education and were later drafted into the Universities. For many years this policy was continued and in consequence the social composition of the members of academic professions was considerably changed in favour of proletarian and peasant groups. In the thirties after the introduction of compulsory attendance and a regular intake of proletarian students from the general Secondary schools the Workers' Faculties were discontinued as a special feature of social policy. During the war thousands of young workers interrupted their secondary education by devoting their whole time to the war effort. The Soviet Government issued a decree in 1943 creating a new kind of Secondary school for young workers between fourteen and twenty-five years. In 1944 similar schools were established for young peasants. These are evening institutions giving workers and peasants, actually occupied in productive work, a second chance of general secondary education and entrance into the Universities. The curriculum is equivalent to that of regular Secondary schools although the number of hours of study is shortened by one-third. Tuition is free and the pupils receive extra rations and longer leave of absence from work during examinations. In 1956 as many as 1,350,000 young workers and peasants attended these evening Secondary schools. The results of examinations were highly satisfactory, and thousands of young workers and peasants entered the Universities and Higher Institutes through this emergency organisation. A special kind of Secondary schools were founded during the war for the sons of the soldiers and officers of the Red Army and Navy and Partisans and orphans of the war. They are called Suvorov and Nakhimov Schools in honour of the famous Field-Marshal Suvorov and Admiral Nakhimov. They accept boys with a Primary School Certificate at the age of eleven plus and provide a course of seven years equivalent to the complete Secondary schools. They are boarding institutions and the pupils are maintained by the State. In many ways they are similar to the old Tsarist Cadet Corps, with the same uniform, the same military discipline and the same *esprit de corps*. They are intended as a recruiting ground for officers of the Army and Navy. Military training received special attention in general schools as well. Before the war military and physical training occupied only 6 per cent of the total school time; since then the decrees of 1942 increased the percentage to 11 per cent, which means four hours a week on the average throughout the whole school life. During summer vacation the three upper forms of Secondary schools attend military camp for a fortnight. The syllabus of mathematics and physics includes the application of these subjects to military practice.

The general system of education includes special schools for handicapped children and orphanages. The special schools for blind, deaf and dumb, and mentally defective children follow the curriculum of general schools with the addition of vocational training. Special faculties of Defectology in Pedagogical Institutes train teachers for these schools. The orphanages or Children's Homes are State institutions combining boarding with education. During the war the number of orphans increased enormously. Special measures were taken by the Government to provide for them. In 1944 there were about 400,000 orphans in Children's Homes in the R.S.F.S.R. alone. The Homes are of two kinds: for the ages three to seven with kindergarten methods and atmosphere, and for seven to sixteen, which are in fact boarding schools of incomplete secondary grade. Those who pass the qualifying examinations continue their education as State scholars in the upper forms of Secondary schools and in the Universities.

We have already alluded to the extra-curricular activities of school children in connection with the organisations of Pioneers and Komsomol. But even children who do not belong to these organisations take an active part in many circles organised by school outside the time-table. These circles may be divided into four groups: (1) educational, or literary, historical, mathematical, scientific circles, (2) artistic or dramatic, musical, chorus, painting circles, (3) vocational and technical circles, and (4) physical culture and military circles. The participation is voluntary and children join the circle or circles at their own choice. Special Children's Libraries and Pioneer Houses provide facilities in addition to the local school.

Vocational and technical education in view of its economic

importance and close connection with the industrialisation of the U.S.S.R. is directly controlled and administered by Federal organs of the Union. The system of vocational and technical schools may be divided into three groups: (1) post-primary Vocational schools, (2) Technical High schools, and (3) Higher Technical Institutions. Before 1940 the post-primary Vocational schools were administered by Republican organs and each of the sixteen constituent Republics planned its schools according to its limited needs. There was no co-ordination on a Federal basis. The tremendous growth of industrialisation and the connections of various branches of production transcending Republican boundaries necessitated a dovetailing of republican systems into one Federal plan. To achieve this purpose a Federal Administration of Labour Reserves was created in 1940 because "the Union is confronted with the task of ensuring organised training of new workers from among urban and collective farm youth, and the formation of the necessary labour reserves for industry." The Administration was changed in 1946 into the Federal Ministry of Labour Reserves and was entrusted with the organisation and administration of Vocational schools throughout the Union. Three kinds of post-primary Vocational schools were organised from old factory and transport schools. The first two groups, the new vocational and railway schools, accept adolescents of both sexes at the age fourteen to fifteen who possess the leaving certificate of the Primary school. The course varies from two to three years in accordance with the branch of industry. All pupils of these schools receive full maintenance from the State and boarding is provided for pupils from outside areas. The course is not narrowly vocational, as one-quarter of the time-table is devoted to general subjects. The school day consists of seven hours of which two are devoted to general and theoretical subjects and five to practical training in workshops or in the factories. After the completion of the course the young qualified workers are placed in actual jobs by the Ministry, which regulates the numbers of pupils in each speciality with the requirements of corresponding branches of industry and transport. The third kind of vocational schools—the factory and plant schools—are for boys and girls of sixteen to seventeen years who as a rule have completed Primary school and were employed in actual production. The course is much shorter—from six months to a year. The curriculum includes practical training and about 100 hours of the theory of the respective trade. During the last years about

1,250,000 were attending these vocational schools. The pupils are mostly from rural areas (85 per cent) who were trained for a transfer to urban and industrial centres.

The Technical High schools or "Technicums" included before the war purely technical schools and Medical, Pedagogical, Musical and Artistic schools of secondary level. They train specialists of secondary qualifications for all branches of industry and transport and agriculture. The Medical schools train medical attendant personnel and the Pedagogical schools train teachers for Primary schools. The old name "Technicum" which embraced all these schools is now replaced by "Specialised Secondary Education" and the term "Technical High Schools" is only reserved for purely technical branches. Just before the war about a million students attended these schools of which 28 per cent were in Medical schools, 27 per cent in Pedagogical schools and 18 per cent in Technical schools. All citizens of both sexes between the ages of fifteen and thirty who have completed the first seven years of secondary education are accepted after passing an entrance examination. The course includes four years' general, special theoretical and practical training. The graduates pass a State examination and receive diplomas. They may continue their special training in the higher institutions, but whereas the graduates who matriculated from a complete Secondary school can choose any faculty without restriction, the graduates of specialised Secondary schools may enter the respective faculty only or have to pass the matriculation examination if they want to change their speciality. The curriculum of specialised schools includes general subjects such as literature, mathematics, science, physics and chemistry, in addition to special subjects and practical training. As stated they are maintained by Republican Ministries but controlled by the Federal Ministry.

Higher education has grown enormously during the Soviet period, as the figures in Chapter IV have shown. The number of higher institutions in 1939 was 750 with 619,857 students, and the Soviet educationists claim that these figures exceed the combined totals for all twenty-two countries of Europe plus Japan. During the war the numbers naturally decreased considerably and in 1942 fell to 460 institutions with 227,445 students, but in 1946 they rose again to 792 institutions with 653,000 students.[1]

The policy of the Soviet Government towards higher education has undergone many changes during the thirty years of Soviet

[1] In 1956 the total number of students in the U.S.S.R. rose to 1,867,900.

rule. At first misguided by the principle of free higher education for everybody, the Soviet authorities abolished matriculation examinations in 1918 and opened the doors of the Universities to all. After a year of experiment it was clear that the new students could not profit by University lectures without systematic secondary education. To restore the balance of social injustice towards the workers and peasants special Workers' Faculties were founded in 1919, and adult workers actually employed in production were sent to these institutions for three to four years to study the subjects of regular Secondary schools. Side by side with the training of adult workers regulations were issued giving priority to young candidates of proletarian and peasant origin. These measures considerably changed the social composition of the students in favour of the proletarian youth, but at the same time lowered the cultural standard of the new students and in consequence the standard of academic learning. The necessity of rapid industrialisation concentrated the attention of the Government on technical institutes to the detriment of the old Universities. In 1922 the Ukrainian Government even dissolved the Universities into separate special institutes, thus emphasising the applied character of studies. The Moscow Government followed suit in 1930, and for three years the U.S.S.R. had no Universities at all, higher education being imparted exclusively in Technical and Special Institutes. During these years higher education was adapted to "purposive goals" of national economy and needs of industrialisation. The results were not encouraging and the decree of September 1932 stated:

> The actual realisation of previous resolutions led to perversions in practice, which were expressed mainly in one-sided attention to a quantitative growth of institutions and of the number of students, and to an inadequate attention to quality, as well as to an excessive division into specialities. As a result the graduates of Technical Institutes have the qualifications of a technician and not of an engineer. . . . It is necessary to give the specialists a broad basis of general scientific and general technical education.

The subsequent reorganisation of higher education in 1933 led to the restoration of the old Universities and old academic degrees of Candidate, Master and Doctor. In 1934 matriculation examinations were restored, and although the workers and peasants still enjoyed priority, they had to pass matriculation examinations on equal terms with the graduates of Secondary schools. However, all these measures to raise the cultural level of students could not take effect immediately, and the new Federal Committee established in 1933 pointed out in February 1934:

> The existing level of general culture of our students, although in political respects much higher than in capitalistic countries, is characterised by many essential defects (for example in the knowledge of historical facts, understanding of literature and fine arts, general literacy). . . . It is necessary that every student should be a truly cultured man—a proletarian intellectual.

For this purpose every Higher Technical Institute was ordered to establish special courses in general science and humanities to raise the cultural level of future specialists. The cumulative effect of all these measures bore fruit, and whereas the first generation of Soviet specialists were largely ignorant on all subjects except their own branch of applied science, the new generation of the later thirties could rival the old Russian intelligentsia or the Western European professional classes.

With the restoration of the old Universities the higher institutions of the U.S.S.R. are divided at present into two groups. The first are the Universities. They include the old Universities of Moscow, Leningrad, Kazan, Saratov, Perm, Rostov-on-Don, Tomsk, Vladivostok, in the R.S.F.S.R., Kiev, Odessa, Kharkov, Lvov in the Ukrainian S.S.R., Tartu in Estonia, Vilna in Lithuania and Riga in Latvia, which were inherited by the Soviet Government from previous régimes. The Soviet Government has created new Universities in all constituent Republics (White Russia, Georgia, Armenia, Azerbaidzhan, Uzbekistan, Tadzhikistan) and also the four newest Universities in Uzhgorod (1945), Kishinev (1946), Turkmenistan (1950) and Kirghizstan (1951). The total number of Universities is now thirty-four. Fourteen of them are in the capitals of the fourteen constituent Republics and are the cultural centres of each nationality, promoting the study of national history, literature and art. The usual faculties common to all Universities are: Physics and Mathematics, Philology (language and literature), History, Geography, Biology and Chemistry. Some Universities also have faculties of Philosophy, Law, Oriental Studies and Geology. Medicine, Law and Economics as a rule are taught in special independent Institutes. Theology is not included in University studies, but there is a Theological Orthodox Academy in Moscow under the control of the Moscow Patriarch and the supervision of the Ministry of Orthodox Affairs. The second group are the Higher Institutes. They include Engineering, Agriculture, Medical, Educational,

Economic and other Institutes and are also organised into faculties. Thus the Leningrad Polytechnic Institute has the following faculties: Metallurgy, Mechanics, Electromechanics, Power Engineering and Machine-building, Hydraulic Engineering and Engineering with Economics. Medical Institutes usually have three faculties: Practical Medicine, Sanitary Science and Pediatrics. Some are one-faculty institutions, as the Institutes of Navigation, Agriculture or Forestry. The majority of the Institutes are devoted to the training of Secondary-school teachers. In 1946 there were 320 Pedagogical Institutes, 154 Technological Institutes, 99 Agricultural, Forestry and Veterinary Institutes, 74 Medical Institutes, 38 Institutes of Economics and Law, 55 Art Institutes, 15 Physical Culture Institutes and 6 others. In administration there is a slight difference between the Universities and Institutes. The Universities are headed by a Rector appointed by the Ministry, who is the Chairman of the Senate, consisting of Deans of Faculties, professors—heads of departments, the Librarian and some representatives of public organisations connected with the University. The Institutes are headed by a Director, who presides at the Scientific Council, composed of Professors. In the larger Polytechnic Institutes with many faculties the administration resembles that of the Universities. The Deans are elected by the Professors of the faculty and confirmed by the Ministry. All Professors appointed to a chair must possess a Doctor's degree, assistant professors a Master's degree. There is only one degree of Doctor of Science for all faculties, which is awarded for original research in any academic discipline to candidates who possess the degree of Master of Science in the corresponding branch of knowledge. The degrees are awarded by the Senates of individual Universities, the appointments to chairs are made by the Ministry, which is thus limited in its choice. About 5 per cent of the professors and 20 per cent of assistant professors are women. Students are enrolled after passing an entrance examination. Only those who received gold and silver medals from complete Secondary schools are exempted. All other candidates, whether from general or specialised Secondary schools, have to pass an examination in Russian and literature. Most of the higher institutions also require an examination in a foreign language. In addition the candidates have to take two or three subjects relating to the branch of learning in the particular institution. The students pay fees, but the majority are aided. Outstanding students receive State scholarships.

Students coming from distant areas are provided with hostels and canteens. If the students fail in their examinations they lose these privileges. The curriculum of the specialised higher institutes may be divided into three parts: (1) Social-political studies, (2) General education and (3) Specialised subjects. The first two groups occupy one-third of the time-table to give a sound basis of general education to future specialists. Students graduating with distinction remain for a three years' course of postgraduate research in preparation for an academic career and receive State scholarships for the purpose. After passing the postgraduate examination they are appointed as lecturers in the higher institutions. Extra-mural activities are an integral part of the work of all higher institutions and professors and lecturers participate in public lectures and tours outside University towns, lecturing both to adult audiences and school children.

Adult education is sponsored by many organisations in addition to regular state agencies. Trade-unions, co-operatives, collective farms, and the Communist Party all have a widespread net of clubs and homes where regular courses of lectures are delivered to their members.

Libraries and museums were especially developed by the Soviet Government and each constituent Republic has its national library and its regional museum. Mass libraries are available in most rural communities, and at present there are 148,000 mass libraries with a total of 591,000,000 volumes. In Russia and the Ukraine great libraries existed even before the Revolution of 1917, but in the remaining constituent Republics the non-Russian nationalities possessed none, and the millions of volumes in all the languages of the Union are the result of the special care of the Government directed to the preservation and development of the national cultures of all the nationalities.

The training of teachers in Tsarist Russia was organised on three different levels: in Teachers' Seminaries for Primary schools, in Teachers' Institutes for Higher Elementary schools and in the Universities for Secondary schools. The Primary-school teachers were mostly recruited from the peasantry and seldom had secondary education as a basis of professional training. The teachers of Higher Elementary schools were also mostly of peasant origin, but they had eight years' general education (four elementary and four higher elementary grades) and four years of professional training in the Institutes. In exceptional cases some of them continued their education at the Universities. All teachers were trained in Russian and taught through the medium of Russian, even if they were members of national minorities. The Soviet reform of the whole educational system, especially the foundation of schools in the native tongues of all the minorities, put a tremendous strain on the available supply of teachers. If the Russians and Ukrainians possessed a trained cadre of teachers for all stages of the educational system, the remaining nationalities had just a few isolated individuals who could teach in their native languages. In 1915 the Russian Empire had 231,000 teachers, almost exclusively Russian-speaking. In 1941 the U.S.S.R. had 1,222,805 teachers of whom only about 55 per cent were Great Russians, teaching through the medium of Russian; the rest were nationals of other constituent Republics teaching through the medium of their native languages. These new cadres are entirely the result of the Soviet training system. On the whole the old division of teachers' training was accepted by the Soviet Government. The old Teachers' Seminaries were developed into Teachers' Institutes which became the training ground for primary and intermediate schools. At present the completion of seven years' schools is required from the entrants into the Pedagogical Technicums (old Teachers' Institutes) or, as they are now called, Pedagogical Secondary schools. The course lasts four years. The teachers of Secondary schools are trained in special Pedagogical Institutes (usually three years) or in University Faculties (four years). Candidates possessing a matriculation certificate have to pass an entrance examination.

This theoretical division of teachers according to qualifications could not be realised in practice. Before the war the training of necessary cadres always lagged behind the rapid growth of schools and numbers of pupils. A certain stabilisation of qualifications was achieved in the last years before the war, but the casualties of the war upset all plans. Of the 1,223,000 teachers of 1941 only 774,795 were available for teaching work in 1943-4. Of course since then many thousands returned from prisoners' camps in Germany and were demobilised from the Army, but nevertheless the shortage of teachers is very acute and many thousands of emergency teachers had to be appointed.

To appreciate objectively the achievements of the Soviet Government in the field of education we should remember that in 1918 Russia was disorganised and half-devastated after the war of 1914-18. During the three years of civil war, famine and epidemics the economic and cultural level fell still lower. The real reconstruction in all respects was started only in 1925. In 1926 the percentage of literacy throughout the U.S.S.R. (over nine years of age) was 51 per cent and in Central Asia among the rural Moslem communities only 3 per cent. In 1939, just before the war, the percentage of literacy for the whole Union was 81·2 per cent, and at present the fight against illiteracy is successfully completed, even in the Central Asiatic Republics. Side by side with this quantitative growth the improvement in quality of education was noticeable from 1934. The war of 1941–5 interrupted this unprecedented educational expansion, but the latest reports show that in 1947 the wounds of the war were being gradually healed and the U.S.S.R. has resumed with the same revolutionary tempo both the economic reconstruction and the cultural regeneration of all the millions inhabiting the sixteen constituent Republics.

In Chapters X and XII we have dealt with the totalitarian Marxist ideology of the Soviet Government and have pointed out the more liberal tendencies of the post-war period. We can but hope that the establishment of normal conditions of economic and cultural life will gradually lead to the actual realisation of the three democratic principles of equality, liberty and fraternity.

CONCLUSION

The four great countries specially discussed in this part were not selected for the wealth of their economic resources or the expansion of their colonial empires or even because they came out victorious from a deathly grapple with the enemies of progress and democracy. However important the material basis of human culture be it cannot produce anything of permanent value without spiritual ideals to give life and meaning to it. These four countries both in the past and in the present were leaders of humanity in building up a new democratic society and supplied the ideas which later became the property of all nations and all races. England had her Revolution before the others and in the name of Liberty established a balance between tradition and change. America and France had their Revolutions in the following century in the name of Equality and for ever destroyed the remnants of feudal privileges. Russia after a period of another century followed suit in the name of Fraternity with the most potent Revolution of all. The tremors of that spiritual earthquake are still felt throughout the world, and the awakening of the coloured races is the direct result.

The application of these three ideas in education should be studied in those four countries which gave birth to them and the comparison of the four attempts at solving the problem of democratic society is the most instructive part of comparative education. Greco-Roman civilisation, Christianity and modern science are the common bases from which the four Revolutions started. In that respect all four countries are European. Their religious traditions, their humanist and socialist ideals are European, and whatever modifications are produced by geography and the material resources of America or Asia, the human element which shapes the destiny of these four countries was born and bred in Europe and belongs to the same civilisation.

In education all four countries are passing through the period of transition. All four are attempting to adjust the inherited traditions to the ideals of democracy and the changing economic structure of society. The same problems agitate the minds of educational reformers in England and France, in America and Russia. The same old sources of European educational theory are studied anew—Plato and Comenius, Rousseau and Pestalozzi, Owen and Marx, to name only a few, have acquired new significance and a new interpretation. The realisation of the principle of equality of educational opportunity is accepted by all four countries as an immediate goal and all reforms, and mistakes, are the result of impatient striving for that ideal. The *école unique* in all four variations is the European solution quite clearly foreseen by Comenius and Condorcet. The adjustment of education to the new economic order and especially to new methods of production is another problem common to all four countries, which led to a rapid growth of technical education and a temporary eclipse of the humanist tradition. But that grand ideal of *culture générale*, which England and France have never abandoned, is coming back triumphant both in America and Russia, after being subordinated to immediate and utilitarian purposes. Thus the unity of European culture has proved to be stronger than the mineral wealth or mass production of either America or the Soviet Union.

SELECTED BIBLIOGRAPHY IN ENGLISH
AND FRENCH

The following short list is intended only as a guide for further reading. Students who wish to pursue their studies in other languages as well may find additional bibliography in I. L. Kandel's monograph (No. 24) and the present author's two books (Nos. 11 and 12). Abundant material on comparative education can be found in (a) *The Year Book of Education*, 1932–40 and 1948, (b) *Educational Year Book of Columbia University* (edited by I. L. Kandel), 1924–44, (c) the publications of the International Bureau of Education in Geneva, mostly in French, and (d) the publications of UNESCO in English and French.

1. ADAMSON, J. W., *Pioneers of Modern Education*. London, 1905.
2. ARCHER, R., *Secondary Education in the Nineteenth Century*. Cambridge, 1921.
3. BIESHEUVEL, S., *African Intelligence*. Cape, 1943.
4. COMPAYRÉ, G., *The History of Pedagogy*. London, 1900.
5. COULON, M., *Jeunesse à la Dérive*, in three parts. Mons, 1945–7.
6. DENT, H. C., *Education in Transition*. London, 1944.
7. DURKHEIM, E., *L'Évolution pedagogique en France*, 2 vols. Paris, 1938–41.
8. EDWARDS, N., and RICHEY, H. G., *The School in the American Social Order*. New York, 1947.
9. GAL, R., *La réforme de l'enseignement*. Paris, 1947.
10. GRIFFITH, O. M., *Religion and Learning. A Study of English Presbyterian Thought*. London, 1935.
11. HANS, N., *The Principles of Educational Policy*, 2nd edition. London, 1933.
12. HANS, N., "Educational Traditions in the English-speaking Countries." Reprint from *The Year Book of Education*, 1938.
13. HANS, N., *History of Russian Educational Policy*. London, 1931.
14. HANS, N., *New Trends in Education in the 18th Century*. London, 1951.
15. HANS, N., and HESSEN, S., *Educational Policy in Soviet Russia*. London, 1930.

16. HUXLEY, J., HADDON, A. C., CARR-SAUNDERS, A. M., *We Europeans.*
London, 1935.
17. JARMAN, T. L., *Landmarks in the History of Education.* London,
1951.
18. JOHNSON, W., *Russia's Educational Heritage.* Pittsburg, U.S.A.,
1950.
19. JUDGES, A. V., editor, *Pioneers of English Education.* London,
1952.
20. KANDEL, I. L., *Studies in Comparative Education.* Boston, 1933.
21. KANDEL, I. L., *History of Secondary Education.* Boston, 1930.
22. KANDEL, I. L., translator, *French Elementary Schools.* New
York, 1927.
23. KANDEL, I. L., *The Reform of Secondary Education in France.*
New York, 1924.
24. KANDEL, I. L., "Comparative Education," *Review of Educational Research.* Washington, October 1936.
25. KANDEL, I. L., editor, *Twenty-five Years of American Education.*
New York, 1924.
26. MCLACHLAN, M., *English Education under Test Acts.* London,
1931.
27. MALHERBE, E., *Bilingualism in South Africa.* Cape, 1940.
28. MATHEW, D., *Catholicism in England.* London, 1936.
29. MONROE, P., *The Founding of the American Public School System.*
New York, 1940.
30. MOSSO, G., *Education in Utopias.* New York, 1927.
31. MYRDAL, G., *An American Dilemma: The Negro Problem and
Modern Democracy,* 2 vols. London, 1944.
32. O'LEARY, H. O., *Education with a Tradition.* London, 1936.
33. PINKEVICH, A., *The New Education in the Soviet Republics.* New
York, 1929.
34. PRING, B., *Education, Capitalist and Socialist.* London, 1937.
35. SWIFT, F. H., *Federal and State Policies in Public School Finance in
the United States.* Boston, 1931.
36. UNESCO, *Fundamental Education.* 1947.
37. UNESCO, *World Handbook of Educational Organization and
Statistics.* Paris, 1951.
38. VOSSLER, K., *The Spirit of Language in Civilisation.* London, 1932.
39. WARR, C. L., *The Presbyterian Tradition.* Edinburgh, 1933.
40. WEILL, G., *Histoire de l'idée laïque en France au XIXe siècle.*
Paris, 1925.
41. WOODWARD, W. H., *Studies in Education during the Age of Renaissance,* 1400–1600. Cambridge, 1906.

ARTICLES IN *THE YEAR BOOK OF EDUCATION*

HANS, N., Comparative Study of European Education, 1936.
HANS, N., Comparative Study of Education in Latin America, 1937.
HANS, N., Comparative Study of Education in Islamic Countries, 1937.
HANS, N., Regional Provision of Post-primary Education in England, 1939.
HANS, N., Administrative Problems in England and Four Dominions, 1940.
HANS, N., Independent Schools and Liberal Professions, 1950.
HANS, N., The Status of Women Teachers in Europe, 1953.
HANS, N., The Dissolution of the Society of Jesus and its Financial Consequences, 1956.
HANS, N., The Philosophy of Enlightenment and Basedow's-Philanthropin, 1957.
HANS, N., Military Education, 1958.
HANS, N., Higher Technical Institutions, 1959.
Year Book, 1949, articles on Nationalism, Linguistic and racial problems and on Socio-economic conditions.
Year Book, 1950, articles on social origin and selection of students.
Year Book, 1951, Religious Traditions and Morals in Education.
Year Book, 1952, The Reform in Education since 1945. Especially articles on England, France, America and U.S.S.R.
Year Book, 1953, The Social Position and Status of Teachers.
Year Book, 1954, The Underdeveloped Countries.

For post-war developments in all countries, especially England, France, America and Russia, see *Year Book*, 1948, articles by A. C. F. Beales, R. Gal, I. L. Kandel and E. N. Medynsky.

Also articles by N. HANS:

'Definition and Methods of Comparative Education' in the International Education Review, Salzburg, 1951.
'English Pioneers of Comparative Education' in the British Journal of Educational Studies, London, 1952.
'Recent Trends in Soviet Education' in the Annals of the American Academy of Social Science, Philadelphia, 1949.
The latest volume of Unesco on *Education in the Modern World*, 1955, gives the most recent data for all countries.

INDEX

PERSONAL NAMES

Topical Index